Surveillance, Architecture and Control

Susan Flynn • Antonia Mackay
Editors

Surveillance, Architecture and Control

Discourses on Spatial Culture

palgrave
macmillan

Editors
Susan Flynn
School of Media
London College of Communication
University of the Arts London
London, UK

Antonia Mackay
Oxford Brookes University
Oxford, UK

ISBN 978-3-030-00370-8 ISBN 978-3-030-00371-5 (eBook)
https://doi.org/10.1007/978-3-030-00371-5

Library of Congress Control Number: 2018960936

Cover illustration: Brian Jackson / Alamy Stock Photo
Cover Design: Akihiro Nakayama

This Palgrave Macmillan imprint is published by the registered company Springer Nature Switzerland AG
The registered company address is: Gewerbestrasse 11, 6330 Cham, Switzerland

Contents

Notes on Contributors

Lorraine Bowman Grieve is Lecturer in Psychology at Waterford Institute of Technology (WIT), Ireland. She holds an MSc in Forensic Psychology and a PhD in Applied Psychology. Prior to joining WIT in 2013, she worked at Leeds Trinity University College and University of Lincoln, United Kingdom. She is primarily interested in the application of social and forensic psychology to understanding behaviour and phenomenon related to crime, criminality and terrorism. She has researched terrorist use of the internet for over ten years, in particular the content and function of discourses supportive of terrorism and the potential of alternative discourses in counter-terrorism efforts. She is interested in online interaction and engagement and in understanding the form and function of extreme ideology online. She is open to discussing research possibilities at both masters and PhD levels.

Susan Flynn is Senior Lecturer in Media Communications at the University of the Arts, London. Specialising in visual culture, media equality, film studies and the links between the cultural and the digital sphere, her work is featured in a number of international journals and collections. She is co-editor of *Spaces of Surveillance: States and Selves* (2017) and *Surveillance, Race, Culture* (2018).

Joel Hawkes is Lecturer in English Literature at the University of Victoria, British Columbia. He is particularly interested in the practices and performances that create the physical and literary spaces we inhabit. Though primarily a modernist, his work is cross-period and interdisciplinary. Recent publications include "The Theatre of the Self: Repetitious and

Reflective Practices of Person and Place," in *Joss Whedon's "Dollhouse": Confounding Purpose, Confusing Identity* (2014), "The Title of Virginia Woolf's Between the Acts" in *Virginia Woolf Miscellany* (2016) and "Rituals of Madness in the Practices of Place" in the *Journal of Medical Humanities* 37.1 (2016). Forthcoming papers include "Primitive Modern Dogmas of Place: Mary Butts and Christopher Wood in Paris and Cornwall," in *Beyond Given Knowledge: Investigation, Quest and Exploration in Modernism and the Avant-Gardes*, and "Bodies Out of Place in the 21st Century City: *Sherlock, Luther, River* and the Urban Gothic of London's Overdetermined Streets," in *Revenant*.

Stacy M. Jameson is a Lecturer in Film/Media at the University of Rhode Island and Film Studies at Connecticut College. She holds a PhD in Cultural Studies from the University of California, Davis, United States, and has completed an Andrew W. Mellon Postdoctoral Fellowship at the Jackman Humanities Institute at the University of Toronto. She is co-author of the book *Strip Cultures: Finding America in Las Vegas* (2015), for which she wrote an article relevant to this current project titled "Gaming the Senses" that considers how the nonvisual senses are branded and galvanised throughout the city spaces and function to orient us as viewers and consumers. Her work engages a wide range of related questions about food, embodiment and the senses in American film, television and mass culture.

Brian Jarvis is Senior Lecturer in American Studies at the Loughborough University. He is the author of *Postmodern Cartographies: The Geographical Imagination in Contemporary American Culture* (1998), *Cruel and Unusual: Punishment and U.S. Culture* (2003) and co-author of *The Contemporary American Novel in Context* (2011) as well as a number of essays on American fiction and film.

Alexandra Macht is Lecturer in Sociology at Oxford Brookes University. As an early career researcher, her work bridges the sociology of emotions, critical studies of men and masculinities with family and personal relationships, from an intersectional feminist perspective. She holds an ESRC-funded PhD in Sociology from the University of Edinburgh focused on cultural conceptions of love among Scottish and Romanian fathers, exploring the themes of masculine identity, intimate power and capitalism in relation to emotions. She is the co-editor of the annual publication of *The International Network of Leave Policies and*

Research alongside Peter Moss, Sonja Blum and Alison Koslowski. Her additional membership affiliations include the European Sociological Association, The British Sociological Association and The BSA Sociology of Emotions Study Group. Macht uses the Twitter handle (@Alexandra_Macht) to promote personal or academic material.

Antonia Mackay is an associate lecturer at Oxford Brookes University and a postgraduate research assistant for a British Academy/Leverhulme-funded project. She has taught on a wide range of undergraduate and postgraduate modules including American Theatre, American Vistas, Critical Theory, Robots, Cyborgs and Digital Worlds, Contemporary Literature and Twentieth Century Literature. She has published articles on space, technology and identity, and is co-editor of *Spaces of Surveillance: States and Selves* (2017) and *Surveillance, Race, Culture* (2018). She is also co-editor of a collection on HBO's *Westworld*, editor for the *Irish Journal of American Studies* and author of a monograph on urban and suburban spaces in postwar America. In 2014 and 2016, she won the Nigel Messenger Teaching Award at Oxford Brookes.

Jaclyn Meloche is a part-time professor at the Department of Visual Arts, University of Ottawa. Meloche is an interdisciplinary artist-scholar whose contributions to performance studies, feminist art historical criticism and contemporary material culture are informed by the research question: how are [nonhuman] materials such as lines, taste, the environment and smell vis-à-vis the body co-produced, and subsequently co-produce each other to perform in a studio arts practice? She holds a Bachelor of Fine Arts from the University of Ottawa, a Master of Arts in Canadian Art History from Carleton University, a Master of Fine Arts from the School of Visual Arts and a PhD in Humanities (Fine Arts) from Concordia University.

Subarna Mondal is an assistant professor at Thakur Government College, West Bengal, India. She is a research scholar at Jadavpur University and her research interest includes the Gothic tales of late Victorian age, the Gothic on screen and the films of Alfred Hitchcock.

Jennifer O'Mahoney is Lecturer in Psychology at the Waterford Institute of Technology. O'Mahoney lectures in psychology and crime, abnormal psychology and advanced social psychology. Her research interests focus on forensics and victimology, where she has a particular interest in the psychological sequelae of sexual violence.

Alan Reeve is Reader in Planning and Urban Design at Oxford Brookes University. Reeve has a background in both English literature—with a BA from Leeds University, which he took in the late 1970s, and then taught—and architecture and urban design—in which he has another first degree, a masters and a PhD. He has run the masters programme in urban design for a number of years, and has taught for 25 years in this field. He has published book chapters as well as peer-reviewed journal articles and undertaken research in urban theory, urban management, regeneration and in topics related to place and identity.

Luke Reid is a PhD candidate at Université de Montréal. His dissertation, *The Architectural Uncanny and Uncanny Architecture in American Gothic*, uses architectural theory to reconsider the gothic house as inflected by issues of gender, sexuality, race and indigeneity, contending that specific modes of historical suffering have specific poetics of space. He teaches at Dawson College in Montréal.

Kwasu D. Tembo is an independent scholar. He holds a PhD from the Department of Language, Literatures and Cultures, University of Edinburgh. His research interests include—but are not limited to—comics studies, literary theory and criticism, philosophy, particularly the so-called prophets of extremity—Nietzsche, Heidegger, Foucault and Derrida. He has published on Christopher Nolan's The Prestige, in *The Cinema of Christopher Nolan: Imagining the Impossible*, ed. Jacqueline Furby and Stuart Joy (2015).

Lucy Thornett is Lecturer in Spatial Design at the University of Arts, London. She is co-convenor of the Theatre and Performance Research Association's Scenography Working Group, and an associate editor for Blue Pages, the *Journal for the Society of British Theatre Designers.* She is also a founding member of London College of Communication's Space and Place Research Hub.

Alison Torn is Senior Lecturer in Psychology at the Leeds Trinity University. Torn spent nine years working as a psychiatric nurse, specialising in the field of drug and alcohol addiction, and HIV and AIDS. Following this she began a career in research, working on diverse qualitative projects: for example, exploring the emotion work of nurses, identifying problematic drug use in younger people and evaluating city wide health initiatives in Bradford, with a focus on community-led initiatives. Her PhD looked at the relationship between people's understandings of their "madness," and how this related to identity, social positioning and recovery. Her research is focused on the history of mental health and narratives of early education.

Graydon Wetzler is an independent scholar. Wetzler holds a PhD in Performance Studies from the New York University. His dissertation, *Performance in Security*, examined the ways that contemporary security practices and technologies differentially modalise notions of an "act." He has contributed to several social activist initiatives including the Hemispheric Institute of Performance and Politics (NYU) and the Center for Critical Analysis of Social Difference (Columbia University). He also served as a research assistant for Jordan Crandall in preproduction phases of the multimedia installation, *HOMEFRONT*—an exploration of emerging surveillant technology projected through a cinematic lexicon. All of this work develops from his longer creative practice rooted in experimental filmmaking.

Nathaniel Zetter is a PhD candidate in English at the University of Cambridge, where his thesis explores the conceptual exchanges between warfare and sport in twentieth-century culture. His writing on technology and cultural politics has appeared in *Studies in Control Societies* and *Critical Quarterly*.

List of Figures

List of Tables

CHAPTER 1

Introduction

Susan Flynn and Antonia Mackay

Contemporary culture is fascinated by surveillance systems. From the culture industries' appropriation of surveillant narratives to the internal world of personal experience, surveillance captures our imagination and impinges on our collective psyche in a myriad of ways. Our lived environment, too, is implicated in the iterations of surveillance and control which have come to be associated with modern life. The buildings in which we exist not only serve material functions but also embody society, culture, and the social dynamics with which we organise our lives. The built environment speaks to us in ways which are often subliminal, buttressing notions of power, control, and organisation which underscore our communal existence. Buildings may be part of a shared heritage, vital repositories of history, monuments to past societies, or to the current zeitgeist. Architecture is thus a player in the social landscape, in rituals, collective beliefs, and practices. Through a range of diverse academic approaches, this collection seeks to unpack some of the ambiguities of and connections between architecture and discourses of power and control.

S. Flynn (✉)
School of Media, London College of Communication, University of the Arts London, London, UK
e-mail: s.flynn@lcc.arts.ac.uk

A. Mackay
Oxford Brookes University, Oxford, UK
e-mail: antoniamackay@brookes.ac.uk

S. Flynn, A. Mackay (eds.), *Surveillance, Architecture and Control*,
https://doi.org/10.1007/978-3-030-00371-5_1

Extending the dialogues contained in our previous collections—*Spaces of Surveillance: States and Selves* (2017) and *Surveillance, Race, Culture* (2018)—this collection of chapters engages with a wide range of disciplines including architecture, geography, urban planning, performance, film, art, photography, and literature in order to examine the surveilling multiplicities present not only in our cultural psyche but also in the *literal* space housing our bodies. The analysis contained in *Surveillance, Architecture and Control* therefore seeks to articulate the manner in which both culture and cultural spaces have been implicit in watching, viewing, and knowing our identity, ultimately examining the ways in which space is increasingly complicit in the definition of "watched" and "watcher". As this collection makes clear, surveillance is not only found in the lens of the camera and within a technological artefact but can also emerge from *within* the very spaces housing bodies—from urban, to suburban, domestic to institutional—spaces actively enforce the watchful gaze of surveillance.

* * *

In 2016, HBO launched *Westworld*—a show written and created by Jonathan Nolan and Lisa Joy which explored the inherent desires of the human race through the vehicle of a theme park "hosted" by androids. Nolan, in collaboration with his brother Christopher Nolan, had previously written the screenplays for *Memento* (2000), *The Dark Knight* (2008), and *Interstellar* (2014), marking his most recent venture as one with anticipated twists, turns, and fragmented chronology. Whilst scholars and fan theorists have been quick to assert their philosophical and sociological readings of the show in academia (*Philosophy and Westworld* (2018)) and online, few have considered the role of surveillance in shaping both android and human narratives. As Troy Patterson's article in *The New Yorker* (2018) makes clear, Westworld is not simply a space where visitors are entertained, but also a space which entertains multiple levels of surveillance. Consider the duty of Robert Ford (played by Anthony Hopkins) who controls his androids and their respective "roles" via the vast network system at Westworld's headquarters. It is this network which divides the "real" bodies from the "unreal" (humans and android) and further enables a division between the hyperreal space of Westworld's theme park and the real world of human technological invention. The headquarters of Westworld, housed in Delos' ever expansive structure is further a space where Ford, described by Patterson as "the architect of the theme park", can control his game. Lest we forget, this is a built structure—albeit one which is entirely man-made—a structure whose sole purpose is to observe and collect information on those it watches in the hope of "developing [android] consciousness [which] would evolve into a race representing an improvement on humanity". When read according to surveillance studies, *Westworld* is less concerned with the creation of androids and the entertainment of its human guests, and far more interested in watching and collecting data on both "races".

Another example can be found in Hulu's *The Handmaid's Tale* (2016), which similarly features a surveilling frame within which bodies are watched. For Offred (Elisabeth Moss), Gilead plays a fundamental role in the controlling of her body (quite literally) and that of the many other handmaids forced into subservience. Through Gilead's network of spies and informers, the allocation of female identity (as handmaid, Martha, Econowife, Aunt, Wife) is determined not only by attire but also by their position in the domestic environment. The role of Martha, for instance, is attached to an apron, domestic duties and living quarters within (but not part of) the grand houses of the commanders and their wives. Aunts are identified not only by their brown uniform and cattle prod but also by their residence at the Rachel and Leah Centre (or the Red Centre). Offred's own position, as a handmaid, determines her domestic position in the attic belonging to Commander Fred and Serena Joy, thereby marking her body not only as one which is watched but also fundamentally oppressed by spatial location. Reading *The Handmaid's Tale* as a narrative on the malignant effects of surveillance, renders not only "the eyes" as Gilead's overseers but also the built space of Gilead itself. As a surveillant system, Gilead enforces control by threatening to see all in spite of our bodily markings, offering a physical space (not lens, nor single embodied overseer) as all-powerful; or in Megan Garber's words, "here is the panopticon, distributed across a constructed nation" (*The Atlantic* 2017).

Both of the examples provided above feature architectural frames and the division of spatial boundaries which play a fundamental role in the controlling and domination of individuals within Westworld and Gilead. It is this spatial framing which demonstrates the power of architectural space in maintaining prescribed roles for those inhabiting them, and the manner in which these frames (Westworld's landscape and the territory of Gilead) can create surveilled boundaries for bodies which cannot be transgressed. In these narratives of topographical futures, architecture's capacity as a vehicle for surveillance appears to be both inherent and silent in its power exertion, and for architectural frames it can be both large and yet hidden, both unremarkable and active. These are spaces which observe and are not observed. With the advancement of technology, Bentham's panopticon no longer requires the centralisation of localised sight, but rather can be omnipresent throughout a system of spaces for all "visibility is a trap" (Foucault 1975). Flows of people and of culture between interior and exterior spaces are central to many contemporary narratives. To use McLuhan's (1964) term, "the medium is the message"—structures and spaces play an integral part in fictions of control.

Laura Poitras' 2016 *Project X* similarly attests to the power of architectural surveillance. Charlie Lyne's article in *The Guardian* describes the subject of Poitras' project as a seemingly unremarkable "single building in lower Manhattan" (2016) which is revealed by the film to be an NSA spy. As Lyne writes:

> Despite the building's immense size and prominent location, its windowless façade and proximity to other New York skyscrapers render it inconspicuous in daylight. Under nocturnal observation in Poitras' film however, the faceless brutalist tower transforms into a real-life Death Star, a vast nothingness blotting out the twinkling start and city lights. Visible only by interference, it's a fitting metaphor for our uneasy relationship with the web. (*The Guardian* 2016)

Poitras' film unearths society's blinkered view of the role of architectural surveillance—both "faceless" and a "nothingness" to otherwise be ignored. The supposed innocuous and inoffensive nature of the building is much like our belief in the ever-relentless advancement of technology, prompting a recent tongue-in-cheek article from *The Guardian* entitled "Beware the Smart Toaster" (March, 2018). In such articles, we are encouraged to "say hi to the NSA guy spying on you via your webcam", and to "not let your smart toaster take down the internet" (2018). Whilst the tone of Hern's and Mahdawi's article is whimsical, James Bridle's recent article posits a more cautionary piece of advice, observing:

> Something strange has happened to our way of thinking – and as a result, even stranger things are happening to the world. We have come to believe that everything is computable and can be resolved by the new application of new technologies. But these technologies are not neutral facilitators: they embody our politics and biases, they extend beyond the boundaries of

> nations and legal jurisdictions and increasingly exceed the understanding of even their creators. As a result, we understand less and less about the world as these powerful technologies assume more control over our everyday lives. (*The Guardian* 2018)

Such power over us is clear to see not only in our cultural productions (such as in films and television programming) but also in our unseeing investment in surveillance as a means by which to feel secure—the result, in Bridle's words "can be seen all around us". And this omnipotent aspect of surveillance is something which this collection attests has been shored up not only in our prolific purchasing and consumption of the camera lens but also in the structures that house us. As Laura Poitras' film demonstrates, architectural frames perpetuate the division between visible and invisible, being themselves part of the matrix of observer and observed. In a world of ever-increasing methods of social control, traditional design specialisms have broken down. Architecture, service design, and public art are all affected by and *affect* surveillance practices with profound consequences for the division between private and public space. The ambition of modern architecture to blur the division between inside and outside is surely realised, yet the omnipresence of glass and of "being seen" is no longer about transparency, it is about surveillance. The window is a technology of control.

The unique contribution of *Surveillance, Architecture and Control* is its approach to reading manifestations of surveillance through varying types of space. Whilst recent work in the field of surveillance studies has demonstrated the potential for the gaze to transgress the lens of technology, few have considered the possibility of the surveillant eye which resides within spatial and architectural systems relating to art, literature, film, and the body. The chapters contained in this collection therefore seek to expand the interdisciplinary nature of concerns over the surveillance of the individual into that of architecture, exploring instances of surveillance within and around specific architectural entities, both real and created, in works of fiction, film, photography, performance, and art. Drawing both on Bentham's and Foucault's theoretical frameworks as the initial starting point, this collection examines the role of surveillance from within the humanities, social sciences, technological studies, design, and environmental disciplines. *Surveillance, Architecture and Control* provides a cultural studies approach to depictions of surveillance shored up in physical space and seeks to engender new debates about canonical and new narratives, examining how cultural, geographical, and built space produces power relations via surveillant networks, and thereby illustrating the ongoing fascination with contemporary notions of control and surveillance.

Seeing Architecture from the Outside

Whilst the chapters contained in this collection inevitably stem from the theories of Foucault's work on the panopticon (*Discipline and Punish*), in all the chapters included here, there is a push away from this established reading of architecture. Rather than seeing surveillance as shored up in a panoptic design or centralised point, the chapters of this collection demonstrate the possibility for *all* spaces—whether they be urban in design, domestic homes, or even 4D cinemas—to act as surveillant territories.

Much like Elizabeth Grosz's own research in *Architecture from the Outside* (2001), this collection approaches space and built space, from the outside. As scholars broadly based in cultural studies and the humanities, there is a sense in which we begin this investigation by looking from the outside in, in order to find "the third space in which to interact without hierarchy, a space or position outside both, a space that doesn't yet exist" (Grosz, xv). Indeed, the analysis of physical space and geographical space and its corresponding relationship with surveillance is something scholars have not yet turned their attention to. Given, according to Grosz, that bodies and architectural space are interlinked and immersed in the production of signification for one another, it seems surprising that little research into spatial surveillance of this kind has been conducted. If we take cities for instance, Grosz ascertains "cities have always represented and projected images and fantasies of bodies… in this sense, the city can be seen as a body prosthesis or boundary that enframes, protects, and houses while at the same time taking its own forms and functions from the bodies it constitutes" (Grosz, 49). If a relationship of this sort exists between urban space and bodies, it stands to reason that the surveilling qualities of architecture impact the body not only as object but also as subject. Many of the chapters here investigate such notions—from the way in which urban environments can watch, contain, and maintain behaviour of its citizens, to the psychological impact of metropolitan landscapes.

Homes also feature quite heavily in this collection; only unlike the city, the chapters on the home are characterised by their shared investigation into horror and the uncanny. According to Anthony Vidler, it is the architecture of the home which results in readings of the uncanny, where "[the home] acts, historically, or culturally as representations of estrangement" (1992, 12) and results in "the perpetual interchange between the homely and the unhomely" (57). The home as a site of surveillance then is one which elides notions of interior and exterior, offering itself up as a vehicle for others to pass in and out of its boundaries where "it is impossible to leave the house without being seen by those over whom control is being exerted. Object and subject exchange places. Whether there is actually a person behind the gaze is irrelevant" (Colomina 1992, 82). The home then offers itself as a space which can be read as permanently watching, and far from requiring a centralised overseer; the chapters contained in this collection suggest it is precisely the domestic architecture itself which acts as the perpetrator of the surveilling gaze.

Implicit in these readings is also the relationship between gender and space, as many of these chapters involve some aspect of identity and the body. Some of the architectural spaces discussed in this collection have huge significance as places where discourses of power were enacted. Architecture thus serves as social control and creates its own discourse of "appropriate" behaviour. As Louise Durning and Richard Wrigley attest in *Gender and Architecture* (2000), "architecture structures and defines many of the social spaces in which different gendered identities are rehearsed, performed and made visible as a form of shared private and public spectacle. Architecture and the spaces it creates are continuous; thus, architectural space is not the container of identities, but a constitutive element in them" (2000, 1). If we accept then that architecture is a "constitutive element" in shaping identity, it seems it is timely to question and evaluate the role it plays in marking our bodies as watched. The contemporary moment, rather than requiring the panopticon, clearly already has surveilling structures which surround us at all times, wherever we may be located.

Whilst other academics have addressed the issue of architectural surveillance, such as Joseph Piro's article in *The Journal of American Educational Studies* on "Foucault and the Architecture of Surveillance" (2008) and Richard Jones' "The Architecture of Surveillance" in *Criminal Justice Matters* (2007), the issue of reliance upon Foucault as the key methodological frame persists. *Surveillance, Architecture and Control* is unique precisely because it offers a reading of *all* spaces as forms of surveillance, and not simply those which can be read according to Foucault. Rather, the chapters included in this collection consider such varied examples as homes, cinemas, cities, and public art as complicit in the surveillance of bodies, in ways which negate the need for the panoptic built structure. Furthermore, previous scholars have failed to provide a volume of essays which bridges the cultural effects of such surveillant systems. Rather than attesting to the possibility of being watched by our spatial environment, *Surveillance, Architecture and Control* demonstrates the very real issues already at work within our physical space and cultural products, drawing together instances of architectural frames and the contemporary cultural moment as seen through multiple disciplinary lenses, which recognise the importance and relevance of surveillance as a means to watch, observe, and control peoples. The authors herein have sought to move beyond a traditional Foucauldian reading of architectural spaces to provide a nuanced look at the enactment of power and control through buildings.

Scope of the Collection

The chapters of this collection are collated under four parts: "Urban Landscapes and Spatial Surveillance"; "Domestic Architecture and Houses of Horror"; "International Spaces, Performativity and Identity"; and "Technological Cultures of Surveillance". The content of each part has been grouped according to the types of space analysed, from topographical spaces to spaces created through iterations of the body's movement. In each case, these chapters broadly reject the traditional understanding of the panopticon as a methodological framework for understanding surveillance systems shored up in architecture, but all acknowledge the influence of Bentham and Foucault's work in this area. The departure from such established modes of thought offers extensive and voluminous interpretations of the watching and watched paradigm, developing a vision of Lyon and Bauman's "liquid surveillance" which is capable of dripping into each area of modern life—into art, literature, film, lived spaces, and psychic worlds. What the analyses contained here make clear is that no one *place* of surveillance exists—rather, surveillance is not and cannot be localised, existing instead in the very physicality of our buildings, territories, and the spaces in which we reside, both physical and psychological.

Alan Reeve's chapter "Exercising Control at the Urban Scale: Towards a Theory of Spatial Organisation and Surveillance" (Chap. 2) investigates how urban spaces are implicated in the control and surveillance of users in a culture saturated by the notion of the self as a consuming body or entity. Reeve's chapter not only utilises Lefebvrian thought to reconsider the production of space but also draws on the works of Baudrillard as a model for analysing the three dimensions of social spatialisation. "Exercising Control" contends that contemporary public spaces—specifically those used for leisure (such as shopping malls and high streets)—offer spaces of moral, aesthetic, and cognitive dimensions—both as product and as consumed. With reference to the manner in which control is exercised over the individual, Reeve's chapter considers the individual's sense of identity may be constructed through spatial material. The chapter further discusses the dialogue that exists between constructed technologies of surveillance—CCTV, architectural elements such as windows and their placing in relation to the street, and internalised expectations and the self-censorship of identity and behaviour of consumers induced in a culture of highly aestheticised and depoliticised consumption. In doing so, Reeve's chapter demonstrates the implications of contemporary approaches to designing commodities and privatised public spaces in relation to notions of the "public" and "private".

Continuing in this vein, Kwasu D. Tembo's chapter "Staying Awake in the Psychetecture of the City: Surveillance, Architecture, and Control in *Miracleman* and *Mister X*" (Chap. 3) investigates the city spaces of science fiction. Drawing on the concept of society as "petri-dish" in which space is imbibed with heterotopic qualities, Tembo analyses non-human bodies in line with the advancement of technology and virtual reality. Investigating Neil Gaiman's *Miracleman* and Dean Motter's *Mister X*, this chapter considers the tense relationships between architecture and psychogeographical effects of the city on hierarchies of power. Taking De Certeau's discussion of space in *The Practice of Everyday Life*, Tembo's chapter expands on the previous chapter's urban investigation and explores the mediation between subject and architectural arrangement within which they exist and are reproduced.

Lucy Thornet's chapter "Surveillance and Spatial Performativity in the Scenography of *Tower*" (Chap. 4) similarly positions its investigation within urban diegesis, only unlike the previous chapters, does so with a discussion of a practice-based performance staged in Elephant and Castle. Building on the work of Dorita Hannah and her contention that scenography can critique architecture's power structures (2015), Thornet argues that the scenography in *Tower* exploits the notion of surveillance to go beyond the city as panopticon, rather, intervening into the spatiality of the site to underscore other power dynamics inherent in architecture. It is Thornet's contention that the window is a tool of surveillance, effectively blurring the lines between public and private space in the city so that performativity of public selves can also be seemingly in private spaces.

Within the second part of the collection, Jaclyn Meloche investigates Montreal-based artist Isabelle Hayeur's works in *Model Homes* (2004–2007) in her chapter "Houses, Homes, and the Horrors of a Suburban Identity Politic" (Chap. 5). Hayeur's photographs of new housing developments investigate the manner in which the notion of "home" is understood. Meloche utilises this photographic series to investigate how the architecture of the house informs a person's identity as well as that of the community. With use of Chandra Mohanty's work in *Feminism Without Borders,* Meloche attests to the home's ability to be a space of place, and a space of belonging which can inflect a sense of Othering and performativity onto the body. Engaging with postcolonial feminist discourses, this chapter argues that one's locational identity is rooted with one's cultural belonging, and in doing so, suggests a suburban space which can surveil its inhabitants—through the lens of Hayeur's model homes, the "home" becomes a postmodern portrait capable of constructing the suburban body.

In keeping with Meloche's investigation into the home as a site of spectatorship, Subarna Mondal's chapter "One Grey Wall and One Grey Tower: The Bates World in Alfred Hitchcock's *Psycho*" (Chap. 6) engages with the significance of the architectural arrangement present in the Bates House and the Bates Motel in Hitchcock's infamous film. Referencing the position of occupants as both surveyors and those to be surveyed, this chapter considers the house as a space which is hermetically sealed, forbidding intrusion from the outside, only to reveal mysteries within its walls. For Mondal, this is a dual space where the hotel and the house are strategically positioned for surveying each other (and the bodies within them), so that one menacingly watches whilst the other hesitantly pries. With particular attention granted to Mrs Bates seated at the window of the house, this chapter argues that Hitchcock presents Bates as helplessly inhabiting her own space from which she can be watched.

Antonia Mackay's chapter also takes the horror genre as its motivation, utilising the theories of feminist corporeality (Elizabeth Grosz, Beatriz Colomina) in an investigation into *American Horror's Story's* "Murder House". Mackay's chapter "Architecture and *American Horror Story:* Reading 'Murder House' on Murderous Bodies" (Chap. 7) contends that the effect of season one's haunted house is the creation of identity for those who reside within its frame. Rather than attest to the maintenance of heteronormative roles (as espoused by previous studies), this chapter argues for the home's ability to eradicate the Harmon's old identities and instil new ones by transforming them into ghosts destined to remain within its walls. Identifying the architecture (the literal space of the home) as one which is embodied, the analysis contained here argues for architectural gazing which in turn transforms bodies into maimed, morphed, and manipulated selves.

The final chapter to investigate the site of the home is Luke Reid's "Surveillance, Sousveillance, and the Uncanny Domestic Architecture of *Black Mirror*" (Chap. 8). Reid's chapter addresses the extent to which contemporary screen culture has been increasingly enmeshed with surveillance technologies, and turns his attention to Charlie Brooker's *Black Mirror* where data-mining and "sousveillance" processes are marked by architectural constructions. This chapter argues for the use of such technologies in creating virtual realities by means of "smart" gadgetry, resulting, as Reid argues, in the collapse of public and private spaces. Citing the episode "The Entire History of You", the analysis considers the appearance of modern houses as screens upon which the subject's memories are recorded and projected. Such surveillance of domestic life offers itself up to scrutiny and potential self-destruction. With the use of Deleuzian theory, Reid makes clear that architecture's collision with technology creates an extimate self—or foreign body—one where our virtual selves have lives of their own which can unsettle the conventional.

The third part examines various international "public" spaces, opening with Joel Hawkes' chapter "*The Birds:* Public Art and a Narrative of Surveillance" (Chap. 9) discusses the public art in Vancouver, investigating the Olympic Village of 2010. Now offered as residential properties, Hawkes points to this neutral and now empty design being one of rampant surveillance, where private and public cameras can capture movement precisely because "empty" space encourages easeful movement. Pointing to the invitation to gaze at the Square at its heart, Hawkes analyses *The Birds* structure which resides in a "steel rib", illuminated by LEDs. The chapter makes clear that public art such as this is capable of disrupting empty space, enabling discovery of a sort. However, such discovery is borne out of a narrative of surveillance—one which is threatening. With reference to Sennett, Foucault, and Deleuze, this chapter articulates the pernicious nature of surveillance from within empty and public spaces, where *The Birds* can alert the viewer to the reality of a carefully controlled and monitored space.

Following Hawkes' investigation of public space, Jennifer O'Mahoney, Lorraine Bowman-Grieve, and Alison Torn's chapter "Ireland's Magdalene

Laundries and the Psychological Architecture of Surveillance" (Chap. 10) considers how the physical architecture of Ireland's Magdalene Laundries contributed to the experience of being monitored. Investigating the Magdalene laundry situated in Waterford, Ireland, this chapter reflects on this institutional space as a location of psychological architecture. Recognising these sites as spaces of architectural containment which functioned to remove those who were "troublesome" and surplus to the economy from society, the analysis in this chapter points to a continuous state of surveillance enacted on those contained within its perimeter. Taking a predominately psychological approach, O'Mahoney, Bowman-Grieve, and Torn's chapter frames the Magdalene Laundry as a particular cultural and social phenomenon, and considers how the performativity of gender is framed and manipulated by the constant surveillance of the Religious Orders.

The final chapter within the third part is Alexandra Macht's "Performing the Repentant Lover in the Courtroom: An Analysis of Oscar Pistorius' Recreation of Hegemonic Masculinity" (Chap. 11). Drawing on Jonathan Heaney's work (2013), she considers the omnipresence of power with reference to its deeply social connections and emotions. Her argument focused on the emotion of love utilises a sociological framework by which to question the connection love has to power, and the close proximity of such notions which give way to a plurality of identity formation. Interpreting the trial of Oscar Pistorius, Macht's chapter analyses the courtroom scene on two levels—through Pistorius' interactions with members of the defence and through the eyes of the viewer, witnessing the trial. Recognising the role of the gaze in both instances, Macht considers the reversal of the gendered gaze and othering of the male self, identifying the court room as a space for the portrayal of a power-suffused masculine ideal.

The fourth and final part of this collection considers the role of technology in creating architectural spaces of surveillance. Nathaniel Zetter's chapter entitled "In the Drone-Space: Surveillance, Spatial Processing, and the Videogame as Architectural Problem" (Chap. 12) addresses military surveillance drones as both a topic and technological apparatus within videogames. Zetter's argument focuses on their representation of "military strategy" in the game genre, and that in doing so, renders spatial processing as visible—in a manner not unlike the surveillance drone. Arguing for an observation of the specific mode of processing space through surveillance technologies, his chapter first considers the conversance between major theoretical accounts in surveillance studies and the formal properties of gaming, before employing Agre's "surveillance model" in analysing the role of drones in the construction of spatiality in military strategy games.

In addressing this dynamic as a problem of decentralised architecture, he draws on Peter Galison's account of aerial bombing surveys in order to situate this mode both historically and theoretically.

Stacy Jameson's chapter "Sensurround: 4D Theatre Space and the Pliable Body" (Chap. 13) similarly engages with technological forms of spatial surveillance, considering the internalisation of surveillance through public theatre spaces. Focusing on 4D theatres, Jameson highlights the role of the material space of the theatre and the physical presence of the body as intensified by the kinesis of such framed space. Contrary to tradition of alienation which theorises active spectator via distance between spectator and film, this chapter contends that 4D cinema positions the viewer's body outside the film, whilst generating a docile visceral body which can respond automatically to subtle choreography. Surveillance of this sort, according to Jameson, is not an apparatus of the gaze, but rather a state of immersion with no distinction between inside and outside.

In a further nod to the collapse of divides, Brian Jarvis' chapter "Surveillance and Spectacle inside *The Circle*" (Chap. 14) explores the effects of Foucault's claim that "we are neither in the amphitheatre, nor on the stage, but in the panoptical machine" (1975, 217) on the twenty-first-century body. With the use of Dave Eggers' novel *The Circle* (2013) and consideration of James Ponsoldt's film adaptation (2017), he investigates the machine of The Circle's headquarters in California. Offering a biopolitical reading of the intricate mechanisms of panoptic control at the interface between spaces of work and leisure, public and private spheres, bodies and machines, Jarvis considers the manner in which Foucault's "panoptical machine" can be transformed into architectural spectacle, where consciousness and communication might be merged into one.

The final chapter of this collection is Graydon Wetzler's "Wayfinding *re/dicto*" (Chap. 15) which investigates Alvan Lucier's score *I am sitting in a room* (1969) to consider the ongoing laboratory projects which utilise off the shelf hardware in order to reengineer the poetic imaginaries of surveillance, control, spatial practice, and speculative design. With analysis of Doppler's "vibrometer", Wetzler argues for the exploitation of sensorium which taps into invisible spaces, where "interactive infrastructures" may be constructed. It is this chapter's contention that social interaction between place and people, as well as people and things, is found within the neural architecture which supports episodic memory and spatial navigation. Wetzler concludes that a challenge to Foucault's theories lies in the counter-conduct strategy of neuromorphic architecture.

* * *

The collection of essays which makes up this volume and represents our third collection on the theme of the culture of surveillance aims to articulate the manner in which the built environment and architecture have been complicit in watching and overseeing bodies, unveiling a multitude of "silent" surveilling systems at work within our spatial environment. Bridging interdisciplinary gaps between urban planning, geography, film, television, literature, and cultural studies, this collection demonstrates an interconnectedness within the spatial reading of surveillance, where all areas of academic endeavour are touched by a matrix of watched and watching.

Surveillance, Architecture and Control seeks to engender discussion to expose the problematic nature of surveillance culture which is inscribed in architectural frames and through the built environment. Employing a wide range of approaches, the aim of this volume is to foster and expand investigation into surveillance culture within the current climate of increased urban renovation and gentrification in the West, as well as to point to the global implications of such research. Put simply, we hope to imbue our readers with an awareness of our persistent position as viewed/viewee, in ways which might make us reconsider our (autonomous) humanity.

Bibliography

Bridle, J. (2018, June 15). Rise of the Machines: Has Technology Evolved Beyond our Control. *The Guardian.*

Colomina, B. (1992). *Sexuality and Space.* Princeton: Princeton University Press.

Deleuze, G. (1980). *A Thousand Plateaus.* London: Athlone Press.

Durning, L., & Wrigley, R. (2000). *Gender and Architecture.* London: Wiley.

Flynn, S., & Mackay, A. (2017). *Spaces of Surveillance: States and Selves.* London: Palgrave Macmillan.

Flynn, S., & Mackay, A. (2018). *Surveillance, Race, Culture.* London: Palgrave Macmillan.

Foucault, M. (1975). *Discipline and Punish.* London: Penguin.

Garber, M. (2017, May 1). The Handmaid's Tale Treats Guilt as an Epidemic. *The Atlantic.*

Grosz, E. (2001). *Architecture from the Outside.* Cambridge: MIT Press.

Hern, A., & Mahdawi, A. (2018, March 28). Beware the Smart Toaster: 18 Tips for Surviving the Surveillance Age. *The Guardian.*

Jones, R. (2007). The Architecture of Surveillance. *Criminal Justice Matters, 68*(1), 33.

Lyne, C. (2016, November 26). Project X: Laura Poitras Homes in on the Dark Side of the Internet. *The Guardian*.

McLuhan, M. (1964). *Understanding Media: The Extensions of Man*. New York: McGraw Hill.

Patterson, T. (2018, April 19). How Westworld Denies our Humanity, One Pitiless Puzzle at a Time. *The New Yorker*.

Piro, J. (2008). Foucault and the Architecture of the Surveillance. *The Journal of American Educational Studies, 44*(1), 30.

Vidler, A. (1992). *The Architectural Uncanny: Essays in the Modern Unhomely*. Cambridge: MIT Press.

PART I

Urban Landscapes and Spatial Surveillance

CHAPTER 2

Exercising Control at the Urban Scale: Towards a Theory of Spatial Organisation and Surveillance

Alan Reeve

The city is, and always has been, constituted as a contest over space – over its production, representation and regulation; over who is authorised to be in it, and who is kept out; over what constitutes an unpolluted space and what constitutes a transgression of space.
Coleman, R. *(2007, 240)*

Introduction

The above quotation taken from a text in the fields of sociology and criminology on the nature of surveillance in the contemporary city reminds us that the control of urban space has a long history and is even perhaps a necessary condition of a phenomenon in which power is always exercised and exercised unequally. The purpose of this chapter is to explore the forms that surveillance as a dimension of control takes in the contemporary and emerging urban settings. In order to do this, we start with an

A. Reeve (✉)
Oxford Brookes University, Oxford, UK
e-mail: arreeve@brookes.ac.uk

S. Flynn, A. Mackay (eds.), *Surveillance, Architecture and Control*,
https://doi.org/10.1007/978-3-030-00371-5_2

analysis of what has been termed 'social spatialisation' (Shields 1992): the particular regulatory, aesthetic, and material strategies by which control and the subversion of control are exercised; and how the meaning and directedness of such control—through various forms of surveillance—is predicated on notions of space as instrumental and, particularly in the case of city centres, commodified as a space for individuated and life-style consumption. The chapter is also concerned with articulating how surveillance operates not only *from the outside,* and as an apparently natural response to contemporary narratives of safety, conformity, and moral propriety but also from *the inside* with how individuals reflexively self-monitor in response to imposed clues and signals from increasingly aestheticised public environments such as theme parks, through shopping malls to the managed High Street. Finally, the chapter discusses how emerging technologies embodied in the mobile phone both extend the possibilities of a controlling and externalised surveillance and at the same time offer the opportunity for the individual to appropriate space and its narrative meaning in a paradoxical privileging of the very private in the context of the public realm.

The chapter covers a range of themes, starting with the question of how notions of the public and the private are central to understanding what surveillance is. Building on this, it sets out a theory social spatialisation and provides a model of the relationship between the three dimensions of public space—material or formal, regulatory or managerial, and aesthetic or felt. This section places the concept of surveillance/the gaze in its broader theoretical setting related to notions of propriety, safety, image, and identity, and in terms of the political economy of the city.

The chapter then briefly examines how control is exercised in different public settings, from the passive and incidental to the increasingly remote and digital, and briefly how different narratives have been constructed to rationalise and justify these. In particular, the focus is on how space is socially organised through a range of tangible and intangible devices of control as a form of social spatialisation.

The third section focuses on the idea of the entrepreneurial city (Harvey 1990; Coleman 2007) and the use of surveillance technologies along with other management and aesthetic strategies intended to create a new type of public realm—of the depoliticised and atomised consumer as against the civic and the collective—focused on the notion of the panopticon of leisure and consumption.

The final section discusses notions of appropriation and transgression of public space, and the subversion of surveillance by turning the technology on itself—effectively the digitisation of the nineteenth-century *flaneur* as celebrated by Walter Benjamin in the Arcades Project. This section speculates on the relationship between notions of the individual as gazed upon by the other—both as individual and present, and also as remote and 'managerial', or present by their absence; and of the individual as observer or voyeur.

The Public and the Private

Before examining how surveillance as one dimension of control is exercised in the built environment, it is useful to think about two apparently complementary concepts—the public and the private—in so far as they relate to urban space, and its design and management. The reason for this is that the idea of surveillance, at first sight, only has meaning in the context of the notion of the public realm or the public domain—that is, of place (spatial or non-spatial) as being open to more than the individual. As the seminal literature on surveillance (Lyon 1994; Coleman 2007) indicates, the electronic observation of real space in real time is only one dimension of a much larger phenomenon which is concerned with the collection and analysis, for whatever ends, of digital information about individuals as they engage with other individuals. What is important here is that technologies of surveillance which collect and interpret digital data and 'footprints', whilst they refer to specific geographically locatable acts, exist in a sense outside of time and place, in a virtual public space. Moreover, digital data is essentially private in the sense that it is accessed and used by individuals, arguably, in the private virtual 'space' of the electronic device—phones, computers, tablets, and so on—which provides its interface. The surveillance of the spatial public realm, on the other hand, exists in specific geographical locations and, for the most part, in real time. In this sense, it is helpful to distinguish between public space, as a site of surveillance, and private space—essentially the domestic space of the home—where even today most people would regard surveillance by 'outsiders' as unjustifiably intrusive or voyeuristic. Whilst the technology for remotely monitoring behaviour in domestic spaces, or spaces of privacy outside the home, undoubtedly exists (and there is anecdotal evidence of the use of cameras on mobile phones and other devises to observe users without their consent ref), this discussion is concerned with public physical space as properly distinct from the space of the private functioning of the individual.

The Meaning of Public Space

At its simplest, physical public space is space which is given over to public use. That is, within any city it is represented by those spaces, such as streets, squares, plazas, market places, theatres, malls, and railway stations, which are social to the extent that they can be occupied or used by more than the solitary individual and which exist outside of the spaces of work or domestic reproduction. As Henri Lefebvre (1991), amongst others (Mumford 1987; Morris 1979), has suggested, public space is an inevitable dimension of the urban. So, for example, his discussion of space within the Roman society provides a clear definition from the perspective of a spatial dichotomy between the private and the public,

> (public space) is the space of social relationships (as against) private areas (spaces for contemplation and retreat). (Lefebvre 1991, 153)

This is the sense in which public space is often treated by physical designers, as if it were a homogenised product where distinctions can only be made between different kinds of public spaces, according to their pragmatic and cultural functions, de-situated from their ethical and political context: streets as routes, markets as places of commercial exchange, theatres as spaces for performance, or theme parks as places of escape. The design literature approaches the problem of public space as a product precisely from the view that its cultural and functional performance can be measured and designed for (see Whyte 1980; Cooper Marcus and Francis 1998; Carmona et al. 2010).

However, Lefebvre also argues that the meaning of the public as against the private realm has shifted, historically, with changes in the mode of production, and within the present mode of production, in which the definition of what is public and private, and what belongs under each realm depends on who owns what and how it fits within a system of production and social reproduction, used to maintain hegemonic interests. This hegemony can be seen to be exercised through various means of control—including the deployment of technologies of surveillance—whether by the state, or by state sanctioned, but essentially non-civic interests such as those of capital, in this context. Ownership precedes rights of use and is overlaid by class- and gender-specific expectations of power. In Victorian society (Daunton 1983; Jackson 1990), for example, the private sphere was the home, the space of the family and of social and sexual reproduction, with its own rigid power structure. A society dominated by the male 'breadwinner', with social roles and property rights organised along the 'natural' divisions of gender. The public space, the unassigned space of the street at least, was the responsibility of the state as owner in terms of control and organisation. Rights of use and powers to proscribe public behaviour were based on the claims of the state as owner of the space and these were given particular form by the class in control of capital, law making and ownership of the space. Its dominant (class) interests were the preservation of social order, the maintenance of standards of conduct in which the proletariat, for example, were regarded as a permanent threat in the form of the crowd or mob (Golby and Purdue 1984).

Jackson (1990) has claimed that this separation between private and public was lived in the imagination of the dominant group in society to the extent that the public domain became a demonised territory and represented a potential threat to the sanctity of the home,

> The street was symbolically opposed to the home, a profane versus a sacred world....A clear association was assumed between the private virtues of family life in the home and the public dangers of the street. (Jackson 1990, 100)

As we shall see, the sense of the street as a threat to the moral sanctity of the home may have decreased—not least because the home is no longer a space so completely closed off from the world of the street as it was in the nineteenth century—but this has been replaced by a different sense of the threat represented by the street as a place of economic immorality or anarchy which needs to be disciplined (see Coleman 2007), in part by the use of technologies of surveillance.

Daunton (1983) also argued that the street as a public place was a space with no particular purpose or prescription except, on the face of it, as a route or passageway. It therefore came to represent a threat because it was indiscriminately available to any class of individual for anything. This is a key point in our argument: the street in Victorian England stands as a type of public space towards which the state had, at best, an ambivalent attitude: protecting rights of use, but limiting or controlling uses, according to a particular social and moral conception of public order and efficiency. It is no accident that the Victorian period saw a proliferation of bye-laws regulating the use of public spaces, including the street and the new public parks. Little has changed, arguably, since the Victorian period in terms of the presumption that whilst the state has some rights to control, regulate, and legislate over behaviours out of the public gaze (i.e. the home), it has an absolute right to observe behaviours in public space. Indeed, over the last 20 years in the UK, there has been a further proliferation of laws to control and demonise forms of behaviour in public spaces in the UK—to which we will return. The key point here is that the distinction between the public and the private is central to assumptions about what spaces can and ought to be surveilled, and to how these are then justified or legitimated by agencies who have the resources and the desire to exercise such surveillance in its various guises.

It is also significant that with respect to what have been termed 'third places', as they have been called (Oldenburg 1989), surveillance technologies have become commonplace. Third places are public spaces assigned to specific semi-public functions, in which codes of conduct, customs, and practices were historically prescribed by 'in-house' rules as well as social norms particular to those spaces. Such spaces would include theatres and concert halls, pubs, and buses, and even hospitals and schools. These 'third places' are actually quite complex in the sense that they may also be seen as spaces for private, or at least personal, projects. But what is interesting today is that few people would object to the presence of closed circuit television (CCTV) cameras in such settings, as though being observed anywhere except the home has become normal and even expected—particularly in the UK.

In contemporary culture, from the later part of the last century, it has been argued that the distinction between the private and public is being transformed, if it has not already been entirely lost (Harvey 1990; Bauman 1992, 1994; Jackson 1990; Shields 1992; Giddens 1990, 1992). The home remains the private space for accommodating the interests of the nuclear family and of social reproduction, as well as a space for the retreat of the individual from the collective project and gaze. But the public sphere, as the space of public duty and responsibility, of collective and community identification, and as a territory for the expression of the community interest, has been argued to be under threat (see, for example, Heller and Feher 1988; Bauman 1992, 1994). The question is whether this threat is because of the privatisation of space or the privatisation of interests, or both.

The physical nature, the apparent social space of the city of the 2010s is not, arguably, much different to what it was in the nineteenth century. It may still be physically categorised under the headings already alluded to: the domestic space of the family, or of social reproduction, the public domain of the street as a pathway, the nodes or dedicated spaces within the urban fabric, such as squares and plazas which are capable of being appropriated for collective ends, and the 'third places', of entertainment, worship or refreshment. (The family, of course, is different today to that of the nineteenth century in the sense of having contracted to two parents and 2.5 children, or the (contradiction of?) the one-parent family. But the point still holds, that the family, whatever its actual makeup in terms of numbers or extension, can be conceptualised in terms of the social unit of parent(s) and children.) There is also a relatively new type of public space, the mall, the internalised common space for personal consumption in which surveillance takes on a particularly intensive policing, managerial, and even aesthetic function.

Social Spatialisation

Having briefly sketched in the nature of the complexity of the two concepts of the public and the private, we can now begin to think about the place that surveillance as a concept has within the broad field of social spatialisation—which is, the theory of the relationship between or interdependence of space—here urban space—and the social. That is, the chapter is interested in how surveillance operates through the design, management, and, indeed, use of social space, and the question of how these different strategies of surveillance may operate differently in public and private settings. Our argument, in addition to this, is that the new technologies of surveillance—elided as they are becoming with social media more generally—mean that some of the historically significant distinctions between the public and the private domains of the individual are becoming fuzzy, if not entirely meaningless.

The term has been used to relate social practices with spatial organisation (Shields 1991, 1992; Jackson 1990). It understands the meaning of all social space as socially constructed, both from the social situation of a particular place (its historical associations, and the control over its uses and values ascribed to it by competing interests) and objective material relations (in particular, access to the means by which spaces are manufactured and managerially organised). This construction is an active and dynamic process. There are discrete spatial practices within design, management, and promotion, which can be analysed in terms of their relationship to the issue of spatial control. In essence, the term 'social spatialisation' has been used

> to designate the ongoing social construction of the spatial at the level of the social imaginary (collective mythologies, presuppositions) as well as interventions in the landscape (for instance the built environment). (Shields 1991, 31)

In terms of understanding the place of surveillance in the physical public realm, on the basis of this concept, we can begin to grasp that the use of different devices or spatial strategies of control—including the technological such as CCTV and the architectural such as the placing of windows to provide eyes on the street—are only one part of a larger whole. This larger construction of the urban is made up of a number of components, both tangible and intangible, which create or impose identity on place. These components include designed elements—such as street furniture and building facades—as well as discursive elements—narratives of place either deliberately constructed through place promotion campaigns to attract, say, tourists or visitors, or manufactured in a more ad hoc fashion in press articles, usually focusing on the negative aspects of identity such as crime or anti-social behaviour. Strategies and instruments of control and surveillance represent one of the means by which a normative sense of place is created or sustained, in conjunction with other both physical (design) and non-physical (advertising and place promotion, management, and policing) tactics of place making.

Surveillance as Spatial Practice

Social spatialisation is not limited to explaining the existence of social meanings and how these are reflexively modified over time. It can also be used as a way to understand the material and technical practices used in the manufacture of real spaces, alongside the tendency of such practices to be complicit in the creation and enforcing of a particular hegemonic identity—bound up in notions of what is acceptable and appropriate in relation to behaviour and individual performance, or identity.

The term 'spatial practices' derives originally from Lefebvre's (1991) philosophical analysis of the production of space. According to this view, space in its material form (as both built environments and existing landscapes), as well as in how it is represented in maps and discourse and in what it is imagined to be for (utopian and other visions of the future), comes into being as a social fact through distinct technical, intellectual, artistic, and other practices of individuals, institutions, and other agencies. Every social space can be understood in terms of the particular spatial practices which have brought it into being and which maintain its meanings and availability for particular ends. Lefebvre's contention is that space is a product of particular interests—generally class interests—and its design, along with its management in the broadest sense, and its appropriation in use are conditioned by these particular hegemonic interests. Again, surveillance can be regarded under this view as an aspect of this exercise of hegemonic interest, and one which is, as we shall see, foregrounded or hidden in particular narratives of the city: for instance, in the promotion of the idea of city centres as safe from crime or social disorder, or terror.

Developing the concept of spatial practice and how surveillance as a practice in itself can be understood today, it is helpful to analyse it in terms of what the sociologist Zygmunt Bauman (1994) implied as distinct 'fields of experience' and how these are addressed in the manufacture and control of public space.

> social space is...far from simple and needs...unpacking. In particular it ought to be seen as a complex interaction of three interwoven yet distinct processes – those of cognitive, aesthetic and moral 'spacings' – and their respective products...If the cognitive space is constructed intellectually, by acquisition and distribution of knowledge, aesthetic space is plotted affectively, by the attention guided by curiosity and the search for experiential intensity, while moral space is 'constructed' through an uneven distribution of felt/assumed responsibility. (Bauman 1994, 145–6)

What Bauman is suggesting is that social or public space is experienced in terms of three things: its cognitive possibilities (what we believe or think it is for, functionally), its moral possibilities (how we ought to act in it, particularly in relation to others), and its affective possibilities (how we experience it as a site of pleasure or discomfort). What I want to argue is that these three modes of experience are provided for in the design and management of public space, consciously or not, in order to reinforce or instantiate particular hegemonic interest. In neo-liberal settings, these interests are generally commercial and focus on the individual as a consumer whose behaviours must conform to the interests of the neo-liberal economic system, be predictable, but also feel as though they are voluntary and undirected—all within a context that feels both safe and comfortable/fun. Different public-space settings demonstrate this hegemonic tendency or reality in different degrees—that is, some public spaces are more controlling and surveilled than others—from the domestic or residential street at one end of the spectrum to the mall or theme park at the other. It goes without saying that the more physically or discursively controlled access to a particular part of a city is, the less it needs to be surveilled and controlled through CCTV and other such methods. Indeed, highly aestheticised places of leisure (of play or shopping) exhibit the co-ordination of design and management strategies at perhaps their greatest intensity, and for the reasons suggested again by Bauman in his trenchant analysis:

> If reality is oozy, ubiquitous, straggly, spattered all over the place, play is securely protected behind its spatial and temporal walls...play has its place... as well marked, by stage frame, fence, guarded entrance. (Bauman 1994, 173)

Here cognitive distinctions and moral responsibilities can be suspended. However, this may only happen in a situation in which cognitive spacing has already occurred so that the aesthetic experience can take place free from the threat of the intrusion of the unwanted other, 'Only in the well administered and policed space can the aesthetic enjoyment of the city take off' (Bauman 1994, 169).

Likewise, moral claims are anathema to aesthetic experience, and the aesthetic experience can only be enjoyed in a space free from the pressing presence of, say, 'real' suffering or poverty. The best aesthetic spaces in this sense are the liminal, bounded, separated off (temporally or spatially) and which have their own artificial game rules or codes which inform users how to play in an 'as if world'.

Bauman cites the Arcades and streets of Baron Hausmann's Paris in the second part of the nineteenth century as a type of the space of play for the late nineteenth-century French bourgeoisie, the game played to its fullest by the *flaneur* (see below). However, the street as the broader territory of the *flaneur* is now too dangerous, too cognitively indiscriminate, to allow the play it once guaranteed. That play—the safety of the aesthetic experience—has retreated to the well-surveilled and guarded spaces, such as the mall. But that play has in turn been transformed by the very nature of the mall as an over-specifying space. (This term refers to the tendency of spaces such as the mall to be designed, managed, and controlled in such a way as to powerfully imply certain requirements in the way that individuals ought to regard themselves: as players acting out a script which they have not written).

The other characteristic of the aesthetic which is of interest is its contemporary ambiguity. Spaces such as malls appear, on the one hand, to be places of the liberation of experience in which outer reality is held at bay or apparently suspended and, on the other, are surveilled and *produced* spaces with 'real' intentions. At once an apparent space of freedom, they can be read as spaces in which freedom is curtailed by being directed towards particular and instrumental goals which are not voluntarily scripted or invented by the spectator in any authentic sense.

The three fields of experience designated by Bauman, the cognitive, moral, and aesthetic, can be turned around for the purposes of understanding surveillance as a dimension of public space, by examining how these are addressed in the design and operation of such space. That is, it is possible to categorise techniques of management, design, promotion, and so on under the three headings: *form, image,* and *rules. Image* involves both aesthetic and cognitive spacing and has to do with the 'look' of a place as well as its discursive status and its manufactured affective associations. In practice, image is produced through strategies such as advertising and place promotion, as well as through retrofitting or redressing public space to make it more aesthetically attractive, or the appearance of being well maintained. Likewise, *rules* have to do with moral and cognitive spacing, controlling through both explicit and informal codes how space may and may not be used, and how individuals may relate to each other in them—what is permissible. These would include both criminal and civil law (such as Anti-Social Behaviour Orders in the UK) expressed through the presence of CCTV and signage warning against such things as drinking in public. *Form*, on the other hand, has to do with the material organisation and disposition of parts according to a cognitive strategy, but with moral and aesthetic outcomes. This is illustrated in gated communities, where public space is privatised through physical exclusivity, or shopping malls, which either have doors or a particular aesthetic to signal that the user is moving from the civic space of the street to the commercial space of the shopping centre. Particular techniques of social control, such as the use of CCTV, can be interpreted as having a complex function: enforcing rules, contributing to an image and having formal characteristics, as well as moral, cognitive, and aesthetic implications. Figure 2.1 illustrates how these categories are interrelated.

Each of these strategies (rules, image, and form), in practice, affects and is affected by each of the others; the dominant quality of any public place will depend directly on the degree to which and by whom these strategies are deliberately ***articulated together*** to add up to a particular environment. The ontology of a place which is the product of a unified intention in its image, form, and rule strategies is arguably quite different to that where a number of intentions exercised at different times have had an influence over each of these qualities. Arguably, in a highly surveilled society, these three strategies are strongly unified. This is particularly so today where both the public and private spheres are increasingly dominated and saturated by a form of aestheticisation, and the triumph of the commodity, as a consequence of the neo-liberal tendency to privilege the values of the market over those of the citizen.

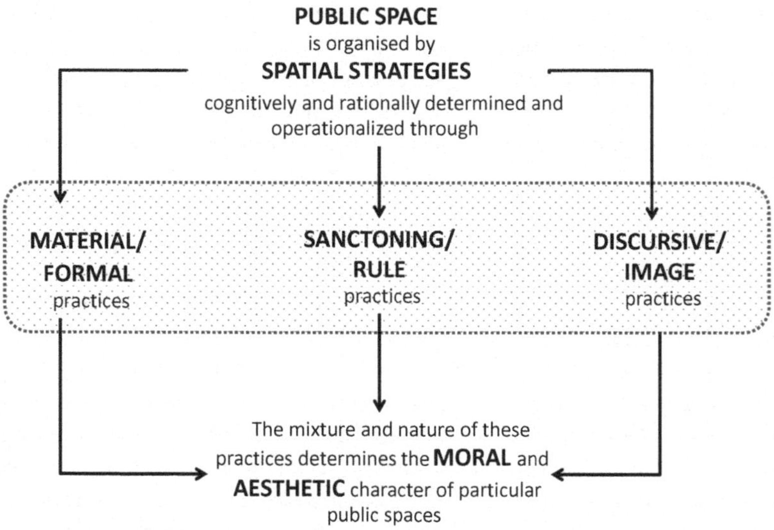

Fig. 2.1 Diagram of spatial practices and public space

'Single Minded' and 'Open Minded' Social Space

We have already touched on the idea that some types of public spaces are more controlling—and more co-ordinated in terms of their formal, aesthetic, and managerial characteristics—than others. It is worth expanding on this a little, since it has a direct bearing on the question of both where and in what ways forms of surveillance operate.

In the 1980s, Michael Walzer (1986) proposed a distinction between what he called 'single minded' and 'open minded' space:

> Zoned business and residential areas are single minded, as is the modern dormitory suburb. The central city (as it once was) and also the 'quarter', the neighbourhood with its own shops and small factories constitute 'open minded' space. (Walzer 1986, 471)

Essentially 'open minded' space is, in theory, social space that is available and accessible for more than one purpose and to more than one interest. It is also space which is capable of being experienced for more than one end by its users. It is pluralistic both in its appeal and function. It is space which is reflexive or responsive over time, capable of being imaginatively and functionally appropriated for different ends. Walzer clearly associates it with the space of the 'traditional city'.

'Single minded' space, on the other hand, is space dedicated to particular ends, and intended to be used, in its contemporary context, for the satisfaction of private goals. He implies at least that it is coming to replace 'open minded' space,

> Designed by planners or entrepreneurs who have only one thing in mind, and used by similarly single-minded citizens….
>
> The reiteration of single mindedness at one public site after another (is) something societies should avoid. (Walzer 1986, 470)

He claims that we not only use these spaces differently because of the single function that they house, but we also feel differently in them. We recognise an intention towards us that the space contains in its design, management, and in the type of individual it attempts exclusively to attract. He also suggests that this 'single mindedness' is a general cultural characteristic of modern day life, in which time is increasingly spent in spaces either physically separate and private, such as the car, or instrumentally separate and given over to personal ends (see Table 2.1 for a summary of spaces dichotomised as 'open minded' and 'single minded' by Walzer).

Table 2.1 'Open minded' and 'single minded' spaces (after Walzer 1986)

'Single minded' space	*'Open minded' space*
Zoned business district	Quarter/neighbourhood
Dormitory suburb	The street
The highway	Forum
Government centre	Square
Medical centre	Courtyard
Green belt	City park/playground
Housing project	Urban block
Urban mall	Cafe/pub
Fast food restaurant	Urban hotel
Motel	Long-distance train
Airplane	Theatre
Cinema	Urban fair ground
Exhibition centre	Row of shops
Department store	University campus

Helpful as Walzer's distinction is, we need to make an important caveat thrown up by thinking about surveillance as an aspect of the contemporary public realm. The first is that, as the work of Rustin (1986) and Vidler (1978) imply, 'open minded' space can be historically located as the chaotic space of the *petite bourgeoisie*, the space of the nineteenth-century public street or square. That is, it is in part a romantic ideal which no longer effectively pertains, precisely because of the technological possibilities of remote and ubiquitous surveillance, alongside the neo-liberal turn represented by both the commodification of even mixed-use streets combined with the rise of the solipsistic and aesthetic project of the individual.

Despite these qualifications, one measure of the success of an urban space must be how pluralistic it is, how constraining and in whose interests it is managed and designed.

Forms and Associated Narratives of Surveillance and Control: From Eyes on the Street to the Panopticon

Surveillance as an aspect of the urban, as we have seen, is a highly complex phenomenon, in that it can be exercised in different ways—formally and informally—and for different purposes, from state control to individual safety and even pleasure. In order to unpack the nature of this complexity and to better understand how surveillance operates as a dimension of public space, this section briefly highlights the key narratives which have either critiqued or been used to justify surveillance within public space over the last few decades, and attempts to link these with a broader political perspective in relation to notions of individual agency as against hegemonic control. The following analysis suggests first that surveillance is a strategy that has to be understood in relation to other methods, tactics or tropes of control (discursive, managerial, and formal) and is co-opted to reinforce the power of these other aspects of place; second, that the function of surveillance as a 'protective' mode of the urban can be understood in relation to the dominant interests within a place—from the domestic, suburban street to the High Street and the shopping mall.

A helpful starting point for this analysis is the work of Gold and Revill (2000), who have attempted to list the common features of 'safer cities' as they called them (Table 2.2). It is worth highlighting that the features that they identified range from the physical, such as walls, the regulatory, such as signage, the managerial, such as street ambassadors, the technological, such as CCTV, and the 'natural' (what they refer to as the 'animated'), such as the presence of people. Different narratives of the city, as we shall see, justify or explain, and even celebrate the use of these various components of public space depending on their underlying ideological perspective, and their alignment or otherwise with the dominant narrative of the city—for instance, currently that of neo-liberalism, anti-terror, and entrepreneurialism.

Having set out an at least provisional set of spatial strategies through which control is exercised in public space, we can now turn to different perspectives and narratives of public space, and of how such surveillance should operate and to what ends. Essentially there are two largely opposed positions in the debates about how cities should be surveilled—on the one hand, the liberal view that takes the urban as a place of community and neighbourliness; on the other, the instrumental view that public space is part of a neo-liberal political economy where its economic security and performance is paramount. I want to argue that these opposing positions are apparent in those strategies of surveillance argued for and deployed in practice. For the sake of simplicity, and drawing on Gold and Revill's analysis, I have termed these the *animated city* and the *panopticon city*.

Table 2.2 Urban design approaches to safer city centres

Safer city approach	*Common features*
Fortress	Walls
	Barriers
	Gates
	Physical segregation
	Privatisation of territory
	Exclusion
Panoptic	Control of public space
	Privatisation of space
	Explicit police presence
	Presence of security guards
	CCTV systems
	Covert surveillance systems
	Erosion of civil liberties
	Exclusion
	The 'police state'
Regulatory	Management of public space
	Explicit rules and regulations
	Temporal regulations
	Spatial regulations
	CCTV
	The 'policed state'
	Ambassadors/city centre reps
Animated	People presence
	People generators
	Activities
	Welcoming ambience
	Accessibility
	Inclusion
	24-hour/evening economy strategies

From Gold and Revill (2000, 193)

The Animated City

The underlying presumption in the view that streets and other public spaces are genuinely public if they are animated—that is, well used by a variety of individuals for multi-valent ends—is that the public realm is the civic realm, a democratic place that is pluralistic and open minded. This is an essentially romantic ideal that has its origins in the Greek Agora and the Roman Forum.

One text, above all, that has been deeply influential in promoting the idea that public space is safe and even humane if it allows for 'eyes on the street'—that is, natural surveillance—is *The Death and Life of Great American Cities*, by Jane Jacobs, first published in the early 1960s. Jane Jacobs was a journalist and urban activist whose views on the quality of urban spaces, and the need for design to enable and encourage diversity of use and users, arose from her personal experience of living in a mixed neighbourhood in Boston in the 1950s and early 1960s. Her writing powerfully conveys her sense of the humanity of city streets characterised by mixed use—combining residential apartments above independent shops, bars, and cafes, in high-density neighbourhoods. Her seminal book is highly anecdotal, as here where she describes the response of her neighbours to an attempted abduction of a young child:

> As I watched from the second-floor window, making up my mind how to intervene if it seemed advisable, I saw it was not going to be necessary. From the butcher beneath the tenement had emerged the woman who, with her husband runs the shop; she was standing within earshot of the man, her arms folded, a look of determination on her face. Joe Cornacccchia, who with his sons-in –law keeps the delicatessen, emerged about the same moment and stood solidly to the other side. Several heads poked out of the tenement windows above, one was withdrawn quickly and its owner reappeared a moment later in the doorway. Two men from the bar next to the butcher shop came to the doorway and waited. On my side of the street, I saw the locksmith, the fruit man and the laundry proprietor had all come out of their shops and that he scene was being surveyed from a number of windows besides our own. Jane Jacobs (1984, 48)

From this and other personal experiences of living in this particular neighbourhood, she generalised a set of design principles which still dominate the thinking and practice of many urban designers to this day, although often observed more in the breach. The following extract captures part of her thinking:

> There must be eyes upon the street, eyes belonging to those we might call the natural proprietors of the street. The buildings on a street equipped to handle strangers and to ensure the safety of both residents and strangers must be oriented to the street. They cannot turn their backs or blank sides on it and leave it blind. Jane Jacobs (1984, 45)

What she successfully advocated was a response to a narrative of the city as a sociable, self-policing, and largely self-managing setting where civilised neighbourliness would be enabled through a combination of particular elements—doors and windows onto public space, a mixture of different land uses (including housing) to ensure variety and, as far as possible, 24-hour vitality and activity, and connected and permeable route systems to ensure both choice in movement and a pedestrian-friendly layout.

The notion of a naturally surveilled place was taken up by Oscar Newman in his book *Design Guidelines for Creating Defensible Space* (Newman 1973) in relation to residential development. Again, the underlying presumption is that spaces are safe if they are naturally surveilled by users—in this case residents—where strangers can easily be identified and where there is a sufficient sense of community for those residents to feel they own their 'territory'. This principle of self-surveillance and natural policing can be seen to be expressed in quite detailed design terms in the context of domestic environments: for instance, housing design which provides a set-back in the forms of a defined front garden and the use of windows at ground floor, which allow for an unobstructed view of the street (see Fig. 2.2)

In addition, in the UK—following precedents in the US—many residential streets employ Neighbourhood Watch schemes, involving local

Fig. 2.2 Residential street and surveillance from the space of the home

residents, police, local authorities, and other agencies with the intention of making such environments safer through active monitoring of activity and users, and providing mechanisms for reporting unusual or potentially criminal acts.

There is, of course, a double edge to surveillance strategies such as Neighbourhood Watch (Fig. 2.3) that whilst intended to create a sense of neighbourliness and community also reinforce a sense of the otherness of strangers, and invoke notions of the acceptable and unacceptable, which are highly normative.

Much of the design guidance literature (e.g. *Responsive Environments*, Bentley et al. (1985), and the *Urban Design Compendium*; English Partnerships 2000), that has informed the approach taken by urban designers over the last 50 years has adopted both the implicit rules of good public space making in the work of Jacobs and the underlying liberal notion of the city and its streets as civic and social space, which implicitly treats users as ends in themselves as against either instrumentalising or

Fig. 2.3 Surveilling the domestic street – Neighbourhood Watch schemes

'othering' them. On the face of it, it makes no presumptions about who belongs or has rights to the city and who does not.

Other narratives of the city—often to do with place promotion and marketing—ironically draw on images of the animated street and public space, but are underpinned by conceptions of place as exclusive, and as 'performative' (see Coleman 2007), where users are judged in terms of their contribution to the public realm as safe, economically productive and conforming to a limited notion of the aesthetically acceptable and morally appropriate, as we shall see.

The Panoptic City

The so-called *panoptic city* might be seen as the opposite of the *animated city* and it is also worth sketching in the background to this commonly used trope employed in debates about the surveilled city (which Gold and Revill's analysis mentions), and also how it links to the broader notion of the disciplinary society (see also Reeve 1996, 1998; originating in Foucault's seminal text *Discipline and Punish* (1973)).

On the face of it, Foucault's book is simply a historical account of the disciplining and punishment practices of European societies. It examines the legal institution and cultural practices of punishment, incarceration, torture, and surveillance. The fundamental idea of a society as a whole, managed through the exercise of physical constraint, of power of the state or other institutions over the body, extends as a metaphor in Foucault's work, but beyond the actual spaces of imprisonment. In a similar vein to Guy Debord's notion of spectacle (1973), punishment and discipline are seen as ideological and material techniques used to maintain the hegemonic interests of particular dominant classes or groups, at different historical moments. Discipline, Foucault argues, suffuses modern, rational society to such a degree that it has become an internalised value: we discipline ourselves whilst being reminded, through the physical institution of prisons, that discipline is necessary for the healthy functioning of society. What crimes are considered worthy or necessary to punish is an indication of the interests of the dominant groups in any particular society. Attitudes inscribed in punishment, proscribed for particular crimes against property or crimes against the person or state, will vary depending on how these relate to the threat they represent to the dominant interests within a society.

But the exercise of power through discipline and punishment has an important spatial dimension. As Shields has said, 'spatial control is an essential constituent of modern technologies of discipline and power' (Shields 1991, 39). For Foucault, the disciplining mode of nineteenth-century capitalism, for example, in part took spatial forms: in certain building typologies associated with certain social practices—the prison, the clinic, the asylum. Markus (1993) has demonstrated that the internal layout of many nineteenth-century and earlier institutional buildings can be interpreted as 'texts' of social control exercised through spatial dispositions.

One of Foucault's particular interests was, as suggested above, the prison, and particularly the Panopticon designed by Jeremy Bentham in the late eighteenth century. The peculiar characteristic of this spatial arrangement was the organisation of cells off of a central observation tower from which all prisoners could be observed whilst the design of the building ensured that prisoners were not able to see each other. Again, Markus (after Foucault 1973) has subjected this type to a close spatial scrutiny,

> The governor was in a tower at the centre of a cylinder of cells....invisible to the prisoners and to the turnkeys who patrolled an intermediate annular passage, whilst the prisoners, lit from behind, were continuously visible. (Markus 1993, 123)

As Rabinow and Dreyfus (1982) have noted, commenting on Foucault's work,

> Discipline proceeds by the organisation of individuals in space, and it therefore requires a specific enclosure of space. In the hospital, the school, or the military field, we find a reliance on the orderly grid. Once established this grid permits the sure distribution of the individuals to be disciplined and supervised; this procedure facilitates the reduction of dangerous multitudes, or wandering vagabonds, and docile individuals. (Rabinow and Dreyfus 1982, 154)

Arguably, the contemporary 'amusement culture' no longer requires the disciplining power of a rigid organisation and segregation of space, given the ideological power of spectacle. However, this culture has also, ironically, witnessed the evolution of new types of disciplinary space—managed, surveilled, and sometimes, although not always, enclosed. These include spaces like the mall which are arranged to better facilitate the efficient turnover of capital through the selling of banalised leisure.

A third, contemporary, element can be added to this debate. The last few decades, the period of the rise of global and disorganised capital, the era of deregulation, the free market, and the erosion of the welfare state, the era of entrepreneurialism, have seen a profound shift in the social conditions of many late capitalist cities (Castells 1989). Symptomatically, this shift has included increased social discontent, a rise in street crime, a polarisation of incomes and working conditions, an increase in the number of homeless on the streets of many cities, and more begging. This has meant that those spatial strategies associated with the nineteenth-century disciplinarian institutions such as surveillance and spatial management are being revisited, with the aid of new technologies such as digital surveillance.

The Entrepreneurial City

So, perhaps the dominant narrative today which has a powerful influence in decisions about the design, regulation, retrofitting, and management of city spaces is that of the entrepreneurial city. It is here where all the strategies of control cohere and are articulated together to produce public space as the space of neo-liberalism—that is, the space of economically efficient performance, in which the market is allowed to dominate, and in which the state exercises minimal control over the public sphere where it comes up against commercial imperatives. In an important sense, both public and increasingly private space have been colonised by the interests of selling, both of goods and services, directed at the individual. The regulation of this interest on the part of the state is limited to ensuring that the setting for consumption is efficient and safe. However, as we shall see, the countertendency (if it is this) in contemporary liberal societies—to celebrate and protect difference—both operates a constraint on the market and creates further opportunities for market segmentation by appealing to/endorsing aesthetic differences. It is also here that the use of remote electronic surveillance, principally but not exclusively in the form of CCTV, is most evident.

The concept or category of the entrepreneurial city is not a very recent one. David Harvey (1987) sketched out the idea in an article in Antipode in the 1980s, at a time when many cities were having to repurpose themselves following their decline as centres of production, in an increasingly competitive global market. In effect, the making of commodities became replaced by the making or offering of services, and was—and continues to be—associated with places as settings for leisure consumption, and as attractors for foot-loose capital. In this context, cities have had to market themselves through discursive strategies of image making (Ashworth and Voogd 1990; Knox 1993), requiring the product of place to correspond with the projected and metonymised image. In this context, there has been a powerful and ineluctable tendency for cities to develop or create a particular 'look' or aesthetic in order to attract visitors, as well as investors. Coleman (2007) has argued persuasively that this entrepreneurial drive, in which places need to be visually pleasing, can be directly linked to surveillance and other mechanisms of control and exclusion—managerial, and regulatory. Setting the scene, he says that,

> As the latest trope in a reinvigorated pursuit of urban spatial order, camera surveillance in the UK is a normal feature of city development that propagates the idea of 'capable guardian's', and symbolizes the state imaginary with respect to urban order in the UK. (232)

He goes on to suggest that

> The notion of the visually pleasing space is tied to aesthetic considerations concerning the moral probity and appropriateness of behaviour in public space. (234–5)

And finally that

> The visible 'differences' that homeless people, the poor, street traders and youth cultures bring to the city, undermine the hegemonic notions of 'public' spatial utility and function. Indeed, for these groups, it is often merely their visibility alone and not their behaviour that is deemed problematic. (239)

Several decades ago, my own research work (Reeve 1996, 1998; Reeve and Simmonds 2000) demonstrated that there has been a growing convergence between conceptions and expectations of the High Street and that of the shopping mall, which points up Coleman's argument. There is no reason to believe this convergence has ended. The shopping mall, in a sense, has always been a space apart from the everyday and from the fully formed public space of the city—a 'single minded' space, to use Walzer's term. Its techniques of control and surveillance have been well understood, and to a degree accepted because of the difference of such space to the civic space of the street. The use of private security guards, the aestheticisation, even theming, of the interior, along with the use of CCTV to monitor users simply revealed its difference, and normalised it as liminal space which applied these strategies in order to be economically viable, and to deliver a special experience—these are places of spectacle, in which the user becomes a spectator of the 'gift' (Maus 1969), and therefore, again, assumes a different identity to that in the real world of the public street. In this context, CCTV, to use Coleman's term, offered a form of visible guardianship, the paternal eye.

However, it can be evidenced and argued that precisely the same strategies of guardianship, in which consumer identity is privileged over other identities, have found their way onto the street—and have been reinforced through such things as Town Centre Management, Business Improvement Districts (see Reeve 2008), and a raft of legislation from ASBOs (Anti-social Behaviour Orders) to Public Space Protection Orders brought in under the UK's Anti-Social Behaviour, Crime and Policing Act 2014, which effectively criminalise historically normal modes of conduct in public space. As an aside, these strategies also include the use of such designed elements as 20-minute seating, seating so designed that it becomes uncomfortable to sit on after a short while, and impossible to lie down on. I would argue that the increasing monitoring of city streets, along with the licence given under the 2014 Act in UK town and city centres, represents increasingly desperate efforts to maintain the aesthetic mythos of town centres as spaces of safe leisure in a context in which real poverty, homelessness, and the other visible consequences of the failure of the state are becoming more and more evident and intrusive (Figs. 2.4 and 2.5).

What is perhaps particularly alarming for those on the liberal left is the degree to which this situation has become normal: particularly the extensive use of CCTV to surveil public space. In *Ground Control*, Anna Minton (2009) suggested that 'when asked, most people like the idea of CCTV and agree that its introduction would make them feel safer' (168). However, she goes on to say that whilst there is little evidence that it has had any impact on crime figures, its use has resulted in a 'retreat' from 'collective and individual responsibility to self-interest and fear' (169). In other words, the much-celebrated tendency for animated spaces to offer natural surveillance has been eroded by the presence of the technology of surveillance. In addition, the normalisation of CCTV as an aspect of

Fig. 2.4 Seating as a form of control

everyday life is underpinned by the extent of its use—in 2009, 4.2 million cameras in the UK according to Minton, and, by implication, the vested commercial interest in finding reasons to justify its continued use. No one knows how many cameras now operate in public space, but estimates have put the figure at around six million (Fig. 2.6).

As an aside, the logic of economic neo-liberalism in the city also finds expression in the suburban and residential setting, principally in the form of gated communities. These are exclusive enclaves, often heavily CCTV'd, which literally turn their back on the larger public realm, and whose privately owned dwellings attract a premium because of their emphasis on both safety and exclusive community.

Transgressions in the City: Appropriating the Gaze

Having explored surveillance in the contemporary city as an expression of control, social, political, economic, and so forth—and the way in which the various modes of control are articulated together as an expression of the current neo-liberal hegemony—we can now examine surveillance from

Fig. 2.5 Rules of use as a form of spatial control

the complementary or opposite perspective, that of the individual situated in public space.

This is a highly complex theme, which can only be briefly outlined here; but in essence, it incorporates the idea of the user as increasingly private, but one whose choices in terms of identity in particular have become increasingly aestheticised in a culture of over-production of competing signs and signifiers of the self. The individual, as a body situated within urban space (i.e. located historically and geographically), moreover, has

Fig. 2.6 CCTV in public space – Oxford

today not only the possibility of exercising his or her gaze at the other in their immediate and unmediated physical context, they also have the means via digital technology of locating and expressing themselves to others who are physically distant, and thus appropriating new and potentially empowering narratives and identities in the juncture between the real and the virtual. At the same time, the new technology allows the environment to respond at an individual level to the apparent gendered and other identity characteristics of users in real space—for instance, in the responsiveness of advertising screens that change their content according to the dominant characteristics of those present within their space.

The final section thinks through the idea of the counter-hegemonic strategies of individuals as occupiers of the city by drawing on concepts of appropriation, critical making, walking as a narrative, and the *flaneur* as a now technologically empowered focus of experience and identity. The key sources here include Walter Benjamin's *The Arcades Project,* begun in 1927 (1999), Lefebvre's *The Production of Space* (1991), and De Certeau's *The Practice of Every Day Life* (1984).

The Aestheticised Self of Public Space

In order to appreciate the nature of the surveilled and the surveilling self in the contemporary city, it is important to grasp how this self in post-industrial and culture after modernism is different to its predecessors. A number of cultural theorists have identified two recent cultural changes which mark out the present state of public space from the past, in their extreme forms at least: first, the privatisation and aestheticisation of all aspects of social existence, at the level of the individual; second, and connected with the first, a general loss of the meaning of the collective and the community which so powerfully underpinned the political assumptions of the modernist period. This was represented historically by the welfare state (at least in Britain from the late 1940s to the 1990s) and the division of public from private responsibilities, duties, and rights. These values have been displaced by the 'rightsism' of the individual, who has become the apparent arbiter of social values and goods, a situation in which identity politics has displaced the politics of the collective, where the interests of the individual were arguably secondary to those of his or her class, nation, or other constructs. ('Rightsism' refers to what might be termed an informal, moral movement, the main characteristic of which is to define the individual in terms of the rights that they might make claim to within society, thus emphasising the centrality of the individual over the collective, or community.)

With different emphases, a number of social scientists, writing at the beginning of this moment of change (Featherstone 1992; Bauman 1992, 1994; Shields 1991, 1992; Giddens 1991; Harvey 1990), stressed that one of the cultural characteristics of post-modernism is the rise of the individual as a solipsistic, or at best family-centred, project, situated in a culture where there are no longer any objective and external guarantees of value. Under this view, the individual is private in a new sense: not simply a subject occupying a separate social territory in his or her feelings and actions (the home in particular), as distinct from the polis, the (urban) world of collective actions and responsibilities. The individual was now seen as a subjective project, even in the heart of the polis, of the social.

Taking this position in one direction, identity is guaranteed not so much by class or structural social allegiances, but increasingly by reference to unstable taste or life-style categories. In this sense, the individual finds his or her sense of self, in its public dimension, with great difficulty, and often only through its apparent opposition to other taste groups, its aesthetic difference. In an important sense, then, the self as an object of surveillance in the public domain is the subject whose intention is to be surveilled and therefore to be visible on the basis of their predominantly aesthetically expressed characteristics—whether of gender, sexuality, life-style group, race or other visual aspects of being. In a sense, the individual can be seen as *subject to* the identity giving claims of a relatively new and aggressive consumer culture in which 'life-styles' become the anchor for the manufacture of self, both the foundation and arbiter of projects for the individual. The claims of collective responsibility, the sense of the *other* as being there in their own right and demanding some moral recognition because of that are, according to this view, under increasing threat (Bauman 1992, 1994). The argument is that both as a consequence of the techniques of consumer persuasion (seduction according to Baudrillard 1990) through product advertising in particular and as a resource for its continuing manipulation, the self is what it consumes.

The counter-view is that the whole of the public domain of contemporary free market societies is not saturated by consumerism and its attempted effect of instrumentalising the self as a subject of consumption. If this were the case, we would have to cynically accept that the neo-liberal economic project, whose aim is to reduce individuals to politically neutered vectors of consumption, had succeeded. The opposing position is that individuals creatively appropriate the possibilities for self-expression, the expression of identities which are not given by consumer culture (gender based, tribe based, sexuality based, etc.) by re-engineering or repurposing the products of consumer culture to their own ends. Fiske (1989), after Gramsci, refers to this as *excorporation*, a process in which elements of the dominant culture—in this case, free market consumerism—enter the domain of the popular and emerge transformed. This is a form of appropriation not dissimilar to Lefebvre's use of the term, and particularly in his argument regarding *spaces of representation* and *representations of space*. The distinction he makes here is between the imposed identity of urban space which is manufactured by certain political or economic interests—through image, aesthetics, and regulation (representations of space at their most obvious in environments such as shopping malls)—and the created identity of urban space made through the appropriation of users collectively and individually, where the given identity is transgressed or contradicted as a form of spectacle. Along with De Certeau (1984), Lefebvre uses the term 'lived space' to designate that space which is appropriated by individuals and groups for their own ends, as opposed to space which is simply a setting for the instrumentalised expression of manufactured, inauthentic, and alienated identity.

However, Fiske (1989) reminds us that what he calls the 'guerrilla tactics' and the micro-political appropriation or 'critical making' of public space can only achieve occasional, irregular, and often illusory, or compensatory, change: such appropriation affects the situation of place, but rarely the underlying structures of power or economic inequality.

In terms of the notion of surveillance, the discussion of appropriation and excorporation, particularly via the notion of the spectacle, Reeve (1995) reminds us that the city and its public spaces provide a setting or stage set, in some sense, for the performance of individuals either as the cyphers of consumption or as at least partial agents of their own identity, who can be the object of the gaze of others. In addition, it can be argued that acts of appropriation and excorporation provide opportunities for connecting with others who share at least some of the same provisional identities, and in that sense transgress the strangerhood of the urban. Bauman (1984) sees this alienating character of cities—what he calls 'privatism'—as the inevitable product of a historical process integral to urbanisation. In urban cultures where almost every encounter is an encounter with a stranger, we have learned not to recognise others: 'societas' has replaced 'communitas'. This failure to see the other means that we occupy social space as if we were for the most part alone, seeing only the surface of the other and therefore not recognising any moral or ethical responsibility towards the other. I want to argue that, paradoxically, the fact of the urban as a site of surveillance—albeit that of the individual—provides a place for at least a provisional and momentary overcoming of the alienation of the urban.

The Surveilling Self of the City

The previous section presented the idea of the surveilled self as both an object and subject of the city—both controlled through surveillance by CCTV, for example, and controlling via the expression of at least negotiated and temporary identities (often centred on the apparent or visible characteristics of the body) via transgressive appropriation of given stylistic tropes of appearance. This section briefly explores the idea of the individual as an active appropriator of the city, and how the gaze of the individual is a key aspect of this mode of being, enhanced by the new technologies of the mobile phone and other personal technologies of surveillance. The discussion draws on three or four themes relatively well rehearsed in the philosophical and sociological literature of the city—from Walter Benjamin, Lefebvre (again), De Certeau and John Urry (1990, 1995)—which again include the notion of the *flaneur*, the idea of the urban as a setting for 'desire', the idea of the city street as the raw material for the creation of 'scripts' of the self, and the concept of 'gaze' of the outsider—the tourist or visitor. I want to argue that these themes are linked together not only by their common setting—the urban—but also through the view that surveillance for these experiences and acts is a form of mediation in which the world as observed is interpreted or (and sometimes creatively) made through the act of surveillance, in which the facticity of the street is given particular personal, affective or social meaning in real time.

In a sense, De Certeau's essay, and particularly within this the chapter *Walking in the City*, provides the starting point for understanding the potential of the individual as an appropriator of the city at the personal level, and the function of what can be seen or surveilled within this. *Walking in the City* begins with a brief account of a view of Manhattan from the top of the World Trade Centre (ironically, of course, since destroyed by an act of terror broadcast and gazed upon by a global audience), which De Certeau presents as a kind of metaphor for seeing as an act of fiction, or of myth making:

> His elevation transfigures (the spectator) into a voyeur. It puts him at a distance. It transforms the bewitching world by which one was 'possessed' into a text that lies before one's eyes. It allows one to read it, to be a solar eye, looking down like a god. The exaltation of a scopic and gnostic drive: the fiction of knowledge is related to this lust to be a viewpoint and noting more. (92)

He sets this privileged, surveilling—scopic—perspective against the experience of the practice of walking the city, which he takes as an essentially creative-act-like speech:

> The act of walking is to the urban system what the speech act is to language or to the statements uttered. ...it is a process of appropriation of the topographical system on the part of the pedestrian. (97–8)

And,

> If it is true that a spatial order organizes an ensemble of possibilities (e.g. by a place in which one can move) and interdictions (e.g., by a wall that prevents one from going further), then the walker actualizes some of these possibilities. In that way he makes them exist as well as emerge. But he also moves them about and he invents others, since the crossing drifting away, or improvisation of walking privilege, transform or abandon spatial elements. (99)

One reading of De Certeau's argument is that there is an essential difference between the god-like perspective of the spectator—the one who surveils the city from a distance or on high—and that of the individual engaged in the city as a practice, mediated solely by the 'narrative' skills and linguistic (as a metaphor) competencies of the individual pedestrian. Looking or surveilling in this sense is a simple act of pragmatic observation engaged in way-finding and way making. It is a position adopted in more recent approaches to understanding the relationship of the individual to place in non-representational geography (Thrift 2010)—and theories of place as affect (Bohme 1993) in which the individual becomes the focus of sensation, and what they see—the world out there—is mediated only through its 'atmospheric' conditions.

However, it is clear that other conceptions of the individual as appropriator or practitioner of the city acknowledge that that appropriation, and how the individual sees place as having meaning and their own relationship to that meaning, is conditioned by aspects of identity and power which they bring to the experience and seeing of place, and therefore is bound up with their own authentic or inauthentic intentions towards it. To use De Certeau's terms, the individual in space creates a meaningful narrative by imposing or interpreting that space in relation to or by means of their own 'voyeurism', or set of essentially personal, political, and mythic constructs.

Ironically, the *flaneur* gets us somewhat closer to an understanding of this relationship between the city as a setting for personal narrative and self-making. The term was used most evocatively by the nineteenth-century French poet Baudellaire:

> The crowd is his element, as the air is that of birds and water of fishes. His passion and his profession are to become one flesh with the crowd. For the perfect flâneur, for the passionate spectator, it is an immense joy to set up house in the heart of the multitude, amid the ebb and flow of movement, in

> the midst of the fugitive and the infinite. To be away from home and yet to feel oneself everywhere at home; to see the world, to be at the centre of the world, and yet to remain hidden from the world—impartial natures which the tongue can but clumsily define. The spectator is a prince who everywhere rejoices in his incognito. The lover of life makes the whole world his family, just like the lover of the fair sex who builds up his family from all the beautiful women that he has ever found, or that are or are not—to be found; or the lover of pictures who lives in a magical society of dreams painted on canvas. Thus the lover of universal life enters into the crowd as though it were an immense reservoir of electrical energy. Or we might liken him to a mirror as vast as the crowd itself; or to a kaleidoscope gifted with consciousness, responding to each one of its movements and reproducing the multiplicity of life and the flickering grace of all the elements of life. Quoted in Benjamin (1964)

In his essays on Baudellaire, Walter Benjamin, —*The Painter of Modern Life* (1964), and *Charles Baudelaire, A Lyric Poet in the Era of High Capitalism* (1983), saw the *flaneur* as both urban spectator and participant in urban life, whose projects of urban exploration were allowed by his appearance of economic independence, and directed by a desire for a separateness of identity to the crowd, and the intention to demonstrate, by their disguised visibility, a critical disposition towards the anonymity of modern urban life. De Certeau's naïve idealising—that the city can be appropriated as a narrative through the simple act of walking—is perhaps highlighted if we acknowledge that the *flaneur* was always a male figure. As Elizabeth Wilson (1991) in the *Sphinx in the City* provocatively suggests, the female equivalent to the *flaneur* in nineteenth-century Paris was the prostitute—whose visibility was likewise a theatrical one, but whose power or autonomy was constrained entirely by, for the most part, her lack of economic choice, in which her body became a resource for the exploitation—both visually and in other ways—of the male gaze (another form of surveillance).

Lefebvre's work is again helpful in allowing us to think about another dimension of the appropriation of public space through the surveillance by the individual, which is linked to the foregoing discussion: the distinction between needs and desires:

> Specific needs have specific objects. Desire, on the other hand, has no particular object, except a space where it has full play: a beach, a place of festival, the space of the dream. (Lefebvre 1991, 353)

It is at least arguable that urban spaces, precisely because of the aestheticisation necessitated in the recent and current neo-liberal economic and competitive context, are increasingly experienced as 'dream spaces'. This is clearly evident in environments such as the shopping mall—which, as we have seen, are often set apart from the space of the everyday street through a combination of styling, management, function, and image. But it is increasingly evident in the everyday street of the city, with their increasingly aestheticised qualities. In this context, at least for the consumer, if not for those who service that consumption (who, for instance, in Disney World are referred to as 'cast members' in relation to users who are seen as 'guests').

John Urry's seminal text *the Tourist Gaze* (1990) further amplifies the point that users surveil the city intentionally—either as an expression of desire or through expectations already constructed for them on the basis of advertising or place promotion. Urry's argument is that, in essence, users as tourists gaze on the spectacle of place in order to recognise its conformity to the stereotyped or metonymised representations experienced before the reality is encountered. In order to do this—as in Lefebvre's notion of the leisure space set aside from the everyday—certain conditions have to be in place, such as the presence of a guide, the schedule in which elements of the tourist object (the city) are parcelled up in accordance with a structured timetable and so on.

Finally, some consideration has to be given to the way in which the relatively new technologies of surveillance—mobile phones with apps to guide the visitor, mapping, GIS, pop-up informatics, and so on—both mediate what is seen and offer on the face of it, opportunities for a new kind of *flanerie*, voyeurism or flirting, and even sexual assignations in real time, which would previously have required the actual presence of the other.

Remote or digital surveillance is most commonly associated with CCTV, particularly in public settings such as malls, high streets, and even third spaces, as we have seen. However, the use of technology at the personal level, and for private ends within public space, has become common place and indeed ubiquitous. This has implications in terms of how users inhabit space directly—that is, in their physical engagement or disengagement with the street—and also in terms of how they access its virtual or physically un-immediate risks and opportunities. Twenty years ago, the sight of pedestrians—and even drivers and cyclists—on their mobile phones whilst navigating the street would have been highly unusual. There are now cities which are retrofitting streets with slow lanes for mobile phone users.

However, more relevant to this chapter are the modes of use of technology to observe and interface with the city and beyond, via the virtual. Clearly, at a pragmatic level, apps such as Google maps allow individuals to navigate the city, along with downloadable city guides, more conveniently than other media—and place the user in real space. But even this functionality is mediated for the user through adverts for local facilities and amenities—effectively creating an edited or electronically manufactured discursive identity of place. The counter-side to this, of course, is that the phone provides access to other, blogged, readings of the city which users can personalise, or self-create, and share with others to add to or even create new communities of taste.

The new technology can also extend the gaze of the users—so that it becomes possible to surveil the city and beyond, in order, for example, to locate and track other users (e.g. Snapchat). The technology can also be employed, with the right apps or platforms (Tinder is notorious) to seek out others for ends once highly private, and again to create private and exclusive communities of, say, erotic interest in the context of the public domain: again in non-deferred real time. In terms of the opportunities for surveillance—both surveilling and being surveilled—the new(ish) technology is, then, capable of both being transgressive and reinforcing normative spatial practices.

Conclusion

This chapter has attempted to capture some of the key issues and theories around the problematic of surveillance in public space, informed from the perspective of both sociological and political theory, as well as from my own view point as an academic researching and teaching in the field of urban design.

We began with a review of the nature of public space by setting the notion of the public, more generally, against the idea of the private—and by implication the concept of privacy. It sketched out a theory of social spatialisation, in which three aspects of the making of public space—form, image, and regulation—were seen to be articulated together, particularly in spaces increasingly given over to consumption—the entrepreneurial city and its neo-liberal tendencies. In this, I sought to contrast what the seminal literature highlights with respect to two key modes of surveillance, control, and safety—the *animated place*, in which natural surveillance/eyes on the street is taken as the preferred option, and the *panopticon place*, in which surveillance happens remotely and without the consent of the surveilled.

The chapter concluded with a consideration of the user as appropriator of space via their own gaze, and use of space, but also through the emerging technologies of personal surveillance, in which certain aspects of the private are experienced and reproduced in public settings.

Finally, surveillance is an inevitable condition of public space—the question is, to what ends and for what ends is the gaze of the other exercised in such settings, and to what degree are designers, managers, and society more generally complicit when such surveillance is used to restrict liberty and identity as opposed to creating the possibility for authentic self-expression and enjoyment?

Bibliography

Anderson, S. (1986). *On Streets*. Cambridge, MA: MIT Press.

Ashworth, J., & Voogd, H. (1990). *Selling the City*. London: Belhaven Press.

Baudrillard, J. (1990). *Seduction*. Basingstoke: Macmillan Education.

Bauman, R. (1984). *Disclaimers of Performance*. Paper presented at the annual meeting of the American Anthropological Association, Denver, CO.

Bauman, Z. (1992). *Intimations of Post-Modernity*. London: Routledge.

Bauman, Z. (1994). *Post-Modern Ethics*. Oxford: Blackwell.

Benjamin, W. (1964). *Charles Baudelaire, "The Painter of Modern Life"*. New York: Da Capo Press.

Benjamin, W. (1983). *Charles Baudelaire, A Lyric Poet in the Era of High Capitalism*. London: Verso.

Benjamin, W. (1999). *The Arcades Project*. Cambridge: Belknap Press.

Bentley, I., et al. (1985). *Responsive Environments, a Manual for Designers*. London: Architectural Press.

Bohme, G. (1993). Atmosphere as the Fundamental Concept of a New Aesthetics. *Thesis Eleven, 36*, 113–126.

Campbell, C. (1987). *The Romantic Ethic and the Spirit of Modern Consumerism*. London: Blackwell.

Carmona, M., et al. (2010). *Public Places – Urban Spaces*. London: Architectural Press.

Castells, M. (1989). *The Informational City: Information Technology, Economic Restructuring and the Urban Restructuring Process*. Oxford: Blackwell.

Coleman, R. (2007). Chapter 16: Surveillance in the City. In P. S. Hier & G. Greenberg (Eds.), *The Surveillance Studies Reader* (pp. 231–224). Maidenhead: McGraw Hill/Open University Press.

Daunton, M. J. (1983). *House and Home in the Victorian City*. London: Edward Arnold.

de Certeau, M. (1984). *The Practice of Everyday Life*. Berkley: University of California Press.

Debord, G. (1973). *The Society of the Spectacle*. Detroit: Black and Red.
English Partnerships. (2000). *Urban Design Compendium*. London: English Partnerships.
Featherstone, M. (1983). Consumer Culture: An Introduction. *Theory, Culture and Society, 3*, 4–9.
Featherstone, M. (1991). *Consumer Culture and Post-Modernism*. London: Sage.
Featherstone, M. (1992). Post-Modernism and the Aestheticisation of Everyday Life. In J. Fieldman & S. Lash (Eds.), *Modernity and Identity*. Oxford: Blackwell.
Ferguson, H. (1992). Watching the World go Round, Atrium Culture and the Psychology of Shopping. In Shields (Ed.), *Lifestyle Shopping*. London: Routledge.
Financial Times. (1992, June 5). *EuroDisney*, p. 21.
Finkelstein, J. (1991). *The Fashioned Self*. Cambridge: Polity.
Fiske, J. (1989). *Understanding popular Culture*. London: Routledge.
Ford, L. (1994). *Cities and Buildings, Skyscrapers, Skid Rows and Suburbs*. Baltimore: Johns Hopkins.
Foucault, M. (1973). *Discipline and Punish*. London: Pantheon Books.
Foucault, M. (1986). Other Spaces: The Principles of Heterotopia. *Lotus International, 48/49*, 9–17.
Giddens, A. (1990). *The Consequences of Modernity*. Cambridge: Polity Press.
Giddens, A. (1991). *Modernity and Self-Identity: Self and Society in the Late Modern Age*. Stanford, CA: Stanford University Press.
Giddens, A. (1992). *Transformations of Intimacy*. Cambridge: Polity Press.
Goffman, E. (1959). *The Presentation of Self in Everyday Life*. New York: Doubleday.
Golby, J. M., & Purdue, A. W. (1984). *Civilization of the Crowd, Popular Culture in England from 1700–1900*. London: Batsford Academic and Educational.
Gold, R. G., & Revill, G. (2000). *Landscapes of Defence*. Harlow: Prentice Hall.
Harvey, D. (1987). Flexible Accumulation through Urbanization. *Antipode, 19*(3), 260–287.
Harvey, D. (1990). *The Condition of Post-Modernity*. Oxford: Blackwell.
Heller, A., & Feher, F. (1988). *The Postmodern Political Condition*. Cambridge: Polity Press.
Jackson, P. (1990). *Maps of Meaning: An Introduction to Cultural Geography*. London: Routledge.
Jacobs, J. (1984). *The Death and Life of Great American Cities*. Harmondsworth: Peregrine Books.
Jameson, F. (1991). *Post-Modernism, or the Cultural Logic of Late Capitalism*. London: Verso.
Knox, P. (Ed.). (1993). *The Restless Urban Landscape*. New York: Prentice Hall.
Lefebvre, H. (1991). *The Production of Space*. Oxford: Blackwell.

Lyon, D. (1994). *The Electronic Eye: The rise of surveillance society*. Cambridge: Polity Press.
Marcus, C. C., & Francis, C. (Eds.). (1998). *People Places*. New York: Van Nostrand Reinhold.
Markus, T. (1993). *The Power of Buildings*. London: Routledge.
Maus, M. (1969). *The Gift*. London: Cohen and West.
Minton, A. (2009). *Ground Control, Fear and Happiness in the Twenty-First Century City*. London: Penguin Books.
Morris, A. E. J. (1979). *History of Urban Form*. London: George Goodwin.
Mumford, L. (1987). *The City in History*. London: Penguin.
Newman, O. (1973). *Defensible Space*. London: Architectural Press.
Oldenburg, R. (1989). *The Great Good Place*. New York: Paragon House.
Rabinow and Dreyfus. (1982). *Michel Foucault, Beyond Structuralism and Hermeneutics*. Chicago: Chicago University Press.
Reeve, A. R. (1995). *Urban Design and Places of Spectacle*. Unpublished PhD thesis, Oxford Brookes University, Oxford.
Reeve, A. R. (1996). The Private Realm of the Managed Town Centre. *Urban Design International, 1*(1), 61–80.
Reeve, A. R. (1998). The Panopticisation of Shopping. In C. Norris et al. (Eds.), *Surveillance, Closed Circuit Television and Social Control*. Aldershot: Ashgate.
Reeve, A. R. (2008). Town Centre Management, towards a research agenda. In G. Morçöl (Ed.), *Business Improvement Districts: Research, Theories and Controversies*. Boston: MIT Press.
Reeve, A. R., & Simmonds, R. (2000). Hyperreality in the Shire: Bicester Village and the Village of Bicester. *Urban Design International, 5*(2), 141–154.
Rojek, C. (1993). Disney Culture. *Leisure Studies, 12*, 121–135.
Rustin, M. (1986, Fall). The Fall and Rise of Public Space. *Dissent*, pp. 486–494.
Shields, R. (1991). *Places on the Margin: Alternative Geographies of Modernity*. London: Routledge.
Shields, R. (Ed.). (1992). *Lifestyle Shopping: The Subject of Consumption*. London: Routledge.
Thrift, N. (Ed.). (2010). *Taking-Place: Non-representational Theories and Geography*. Farnham: Ashgate.
Urry, J. (1990). *The Tourist Gaze: Leisure and Travel in Contemporary Societies*. London: Sage.
Urry, J. (1995). *Consuming Places*. London: Routledge.
Vidler, A. (1978). The Scenes of the Street. In S. Anderson (Ed.), *On Streets*. Cambridge, MA: MIT Press.
Walzer, M. (1986, Fall). Pleasures and Costs of Urbanity. *Dissent*, pp. 470–475.
Whyte, W. (1980). *The Social Life of Small Urban Spaces*. Washington, DC: Conservation Foundation.
Wilson, E. (1991). *The Sphinx in the City*. London: Virago.

CHAPTER 3

Staying Awake in the Psychetecture of the City: Surveillance, Architecture, and Control in *Miracleman* and *Mister X*

Kwasu D. Tembo

Introduction

The concept of society-as-a-petri dish in which a specific population, group, or topological space with heterotopic qualities, as well as the attendant ideas of surveillance and paranoia within spaces, has been addressed in numerous works of contemporary fiction and science fiction. The petri-dish/brain-in-a-vat scenario can emerge as a direct result of a particular group's agenda (not always human), advanced technology, or in heterotopic spaces such as dreams and virtual reality. The current Occidental zeitgeist's response to the various themes and issues inherent to the praxes of mass surveillance, at both state and local levels, can be described as abject. While being ostensibly repulsed by the notion of further impositions on personal and civil liberties being sanctioned and exacerbated by governmental, religious, and/or cultural institutions and authorities, there exists a concerted interest in the notion of mass surveillance. It persist in

Kwasu D. Tembo is an Independent Scholar.

K. D. Tembo (✉)
Harare, Zimbabwe

S. Flynn, A. Mackay (eds.), *Surveillance, Architecture and Control*,
https://doi.org/10.1007/978-3-030-00371-5_3

our entertainments, most notably in contemporary television, examples of which include, but are not limited to, the following: Lisa Joy and Jonathan Nolan's *Westworld* (2016–present), Bruce Miller's *The Handmaid's Tale* (2017–present), Ramin Bahrani's *Fahrenheit 451* (2018), Charlie Brooker's *Black Mirror* (2011–present), Sam Esmail's *Mr. Robot* (2015–present), and Jonathan Nolan's *Person of Interest* (2011–2016). This phenomenon pervades contemporary Occidental cinema as well. Some particularly good examples include, but are not limited to, *The Truman Show* (1998), *Dark City* (1998), *The Matrix* (1999), *The Thirteenth Floor* (1999), *Existenz* (1999), *Inception* (2010), *Paranoia* (2013), *The Signal* (2014), *The Circle* (2017), *Closed Circuit* (2013), *Captain America: The Winter Soldier* (2014), and *Snowden* (2015).

These examples reveal that though contemporary audiences' reliance on technology and mass media interfacing produces fears of the proliferation of dystopian sociopolitical and sociocultural praxes, we still both have a fascination with and participate in potentially reifying said Orwellian outcomes. The various texts cited above also typically frame this paradoxical relationship between strategies of surveillance and individual, cultural, and national participation therein as architectural arrangements, whereby a network of systems of surveillance form a stack under which all onto-existential and psycho-emotional phenomena can be monitored, controlled, or both. In this sense, being and the architectural spaces within which it occurs are predicated on curated boundaries, limitations, lines of flight, "blind-spots", and spaces of total visibility—all within which architecture itself exerts both ostensible and surreptitious power over the lives of human beings. As a direct result, discourses on contemporary architecture, the dialectic of observer/observed, any seen/being seen dyads, and generic or abstract distinctions between inside and outside must include questions of surveillance and power.

Indeed, there are numerous highly lauded examples of the comic medium's engagement with these aforementioned concerns through its various genres and subgenres. Examples include Alan Moore and David Lloyd's *V for Vendetta* (1988), Alan Moore and Dave Gibbons' *Watchmen* (1986), Frank Miller's *The Dark Knight Returns* (1986), Mark Miller's post-9/11 meditation on personal liberty and State surveillance in *Marvel's Civil War* (2006–2007), Edmond Hamilton et al.'s *Batman* Vol. 1, No. 109 (1957) featuring drone surveillance technology and personal tracking devices, and perhaps most fundamentally Superman and the alien's x-ray vision. There also exist numerous non-superhero-related examples of the medium's exploration of mass surveillance and sociocultural/sociopolitical control, for example, the "paparazzo" of Brian K. Vaughan and Marcos Martin's *The Private Eye* (2013), the open Circuit of Brian K. Vaughan and Fiona Staples' *Saga* (2012–present), and the Agape and Lodovica of Alessandro Barbucci and Barbara Canepa's *Sky Doll* (2000). Notable political editorial comics concerning surveillance, mass media, and social media platforms by artists such as Mike Peters, Mike Luckovich, Matt Wuerker, and Joel Pett are further represented within the medium. There are even non-fictional or semi-fictional comics on the topic, such as Pratap Chatterjee and Khalil's award-winning *Verax: The True History of Whistleblowers, Drone Warfare, and Mass Surveillance – A Graphic Novel* (2017).

While it would appear that the comics medium has a rich tradition of engaging with issues and debates surrounding the praxes of surveillance, less explored therein is the medium's concern with issues and debates surrounding the praxes of surveillance *in conjunction with* their relation to architecture and/or city planning. In terms of the relationships and tensions between the architectural and psycho-geographical effects of the city on hierarchies of power, the seeing contra being seen dyad at the core of surveillance praxes and the onto-existential biopowered influence exerted by the gaze on bodies, agencies, and identities, contemporary comic books do not receive as much scholarly attention as other manifestations of these ideas in other visual media and mediums. Beyond scholarship such as Rebecca Wanzo's "The Superhero: Meditation on Surveillance, Salvation, and Desire" (2009) and my own piece "A Brain in A Vat, An Earth in a Bottle: Paranoiac Horror & the Latent Panopticism of Superman in *Red Son*" (2018), very little academic analyses exist that first centre on the comics medium's exploration of surveillance *and architecture*. With a view to redressing this shortcoming and encouraging further discussion and interdisciplinary scholarship in this area, this chapter will explore the abovementioned tensions that mediate the relationship between subjects and the architectural arrangements within which they exist and are reproduced, citing two examples, namely, Neil Gaiman's *Miracleman* No. 21 (1991), illustrated by Mark Buckingham, and various stories from Dean Motter's *Mister X* (1984–2009) comics, as dialogic case studies. As an analytical framework, this chapter will theorize the relationship between spatial design and surveillance, the spatio-existential illnesses that result from psychetecture as designed by idealistic architects, and modes of their resistance through Michel de Certeau's discussion of strategy and tactics in relation to structures of power in *The Practice of Everyday Life* (1984). In so doing, this chapter aims to demonstrate that the comics medium, with its panels that resemble windows—a technology of surveillance *and* control—is a particularly effective aesthetico-narratological platform through which to discuss the issues and debates surrounding surveillance and architecture.

Encephalograph Skyline: Theorizing the City and Urban Space

There are several ways of theorizing the city and the urban space in relation to psychetecture. I will briefly discuss three such ways. The first refers to the English architect Nicholas Hawksmoor. A noted figure in late seventeenth- and early eighteenth-century English Baroque architecture, Hawksmoor is remembered for not only his prolific output or age of first successes, but the sheer preponderance of his architectural accomplishments. These include St Paul's Cathedral, his contributions to contemporary architect Christopher Wren's City of London churches, Blenheim Palace, and Castle Howard. His work has served as a literary inspiration for noted poets and prosaists such as T. S. Elliot, Iain Sinclair, and Evelyn Waugh. A poem about Hawksmoor, his architecture, and the concept that said architecture expressed an onto-theological and psycho-emotional effect on those it oversaw, housed, or enclosed appears in Sinclair's 1975 collection of poems *Lud Heat* titled "Nicholas Hawsmoor: His Churches". In this piece, Sinclair promulgates the notion that Hawksmoor's singular architectural style could be parsed as a type of "psycho-geographical/psychetectural" template for the onto-theological and psycho-emotional ideologies and praxes of Theistic Satanism. While no ancillary evidence exists to corroborate this theory, it has served as a literary inspiration for contemporary authors operating in diffuse fields. The novelist Peter Ackroyd, for example, refracts Nicholas Hawksmoor into Nicholas Dyer, a consecrated Satanist, in his novel *Hawksmoor* (1985). This idea found its way into the mind of Alan Moore, one of, if not the most lauded, comics authors, whose minor opus *From Hell* (1989) illustrated by Eddie Campbell could be read as an extended meditation on "psycho-geography", here understood as the intra-psychic effects architecture and city planning express on psycho-emotional (and subsequently onto-existential) aspects of the lives and bodies of people living in a city. In Moore's narrative, the premise binding architecture and the occult centres on Jack the Ripper (Sir William Gull, chief physician to Queen Victoria), who employed

Hawksmoor's buildings as both a part of and a means to exacerbate the effects of his Masonic ritual magic, involving the sacrificial murder of women. The notion here is that fictionalized Hawksmoorian psycho-geography affirms that there is an inextricable link between architecture, and how people think, feel, and live. If the architect's skill and intent behind the manufacture of said architectural and broader city-wide arrangements, from churches to libraries, footpaths to harbours, were infused with occultic force, then all those subsequently subject to said space(s) will also be subject to the intent predicating the creation of said space. In terms of the two examples I have chosen, the intent behind architectural and/or spatio-temporal arrangements can lead to psycho-emotional distress, paranoia, and onto-existential subjugation. In *Mister X*, the link between madness and architecture is an accidental bi-product of an ostensibly benevolent architectural design, eschewing the combination of the architectural and the supernatural for a combination of the architectural with the psycho-medical. In *Miracle Man*, the intent behind the text's prison city is precisely to engender such feelings and succeeds in doing so, but is achieved through the design applications and onto-existential omnipotence of god-like superbeings (Sinclair 1975; The Bohemian Blog).

Perhaps the most direct analogue between my conception of psychetecture and more established theorizations of space and architecture can be found in the concept of psycho-geography as elaborated by Guy Debord. For Debord, psycho-geography was a praxis, mindset, and world view that emphasized the exploration of urban environments unbound by the stricture of a determinate relationship between start and end point, beginning and destination. As a result, psycho-geography places a premium on playfulness, and the "art" of "drifting". More technically, Debord defined psycho-geography as "the study of the precise laws and specific effects of the geographical environment, consciously organized or not, on the emotions and behavior of individuals", as well as "a whole toy box full of playful, inventive strategies for exploring cities… just about anything that takes pedestrians off their predictable paths and jolts them into a new awareness of the urban landscape" (Debord 1955). Furthermore, in *Sur le passage de quelques personnes à travers une assez courte unité de temps* (1959), Debord argues that "when freedom is practised in a closed circle, it fades into a dream, becomes a mere image of itself. The ambiance of play is by nature unstable. At any moment, 'ordinary life' may prevail once again. The geographical limitation of play is even more striking than its temporal limitation. Every game takes place within the boundaries of its own spatial domain" (Debord 1959).

The link between architecture and psycho-emotional, let alone onto-existential/physical, control is further elaborated through Debord's quotation of Marx in the film: "people can see nothing around them that is not their own image; everything speaks to them of themselves. Their very landscape is animated. Obstacles were everywhere. And they were all interrelated, maintaining a unified reign of poverty" (Debord 1959). From these definitions, a latent paradox immediately emerges within the very conception of psycho-geography. Liberating on the one hand, "centred" on play, derive, drift, anchorlessness, framlessness, and a bricolage of affective movement. On the other hand, however, psycho-geography can also be used as a soporific anaesthetic within the psychetecture of a somnopolis. The same set of spatial praxes within cities and urban spaces, therefore, can be used to liberate individual subjects and their onto-existential experience of space-time as constructed, reproduced, and reified within the parameters of a city, and more fundamentally its architecture. Simultaneously, the same set of spatial praxes within cities and urban spaces can be used to prohibit, by degree or entirely, this same sense of pscycho-spatial play through architectural design and city planning. In this sense, Debordean psycho-geography can be thought of as a combination of subjective and objective praxes and studies. But the paradoxical nature of the underlying idea of psycho-geography, being liberated through a circuitous and aimless wandering through and limited by a specific urban chronotope, led him to produce what can be considered a more pragmatic "Theory of the Dérive" in 1958. The document serves as a guide or manual with regard to the physical praxis of important psycho-geographic procedures based on the act of dérive or drift. "In a derive", according to Debord,

> one or more persons during a certain period drop their usual motives for movement and action, their relations, their work and leisure activities, and let themselves be drawn by the attractions of the terrain and the encounters they find there… But the dérive includes both this letting go and its necessary contradiction: the domination of psychogeographical variations by the knowledge and calculation of their possibilities. (Debord 1956)

Based on this description, the dérive or drift resembles most closely de Certeau's concept of Tactics, which I shall elaborate upon further below.

Lastly, in both example texts, there is a central tension concerning the character of the city and urban space, namely, the tension between the city/urban space as an incubator of Order contra Chaos, freedom contra control, the known contra the unknown. These psycho-geographical dialectics both manifest and break down in Edward Soja's concept of Thirdspace. Soja, a self-proclaimed urbanist and lauded postmodern political geographer and theorist of urban planning, developed a theory of "Thirdspace" based on the idea of psycho-spatial bricolage, saturation, confluence, and admixture. For Soja, in Thirdspace, be it sequestered within a city or urban space, or taken as the sum total of such spaces, "everything comes together… subjectivity and objectivity, the abstract and the concrete, the real and the imagined, the knowable and the unimaginable, the repetitive and the differential, structure and agency, mind and body, consciousness and the unconscious, the disciplined and the transdisciplinary, everyday life and unending history" (Soja 57). He further elaborates that Thirdspace should be defined "as an-Other way of understanding and acting to change the spatiality of human life, a distinct mode of critical spatial awareness that is appropriate to the new scope and significance being brought about in the rebalanced trialectices of spatiality–historicality–sociality" (Soja 57). In so doing, Soja gestures to other theorizations of the city and urban space, including but not limited to Henri Lefebvre's discussion of spatial trialectics in *The Production of Space* (1974) and Michel Foucault's concept of heterotopia developed in "Of Other Spaces: Utopias and Heterotopias" (1967). In terms of Thirdspace's relation to psychetecture as I use it, the former, being a radically inclusive concept, draws attention to the constant state of onto-existential and psycho-emotional flux cities and urban spaces necessarily produce in their populaces. In Thirdspace, epistemological, ontological, and historically determined dualisms and dialectics break down, always-already pushing towards Otherness and hybridity as opposed to dialectical staticity (Soja 61). That said, included in the mercurial milieu of Thirdspace are simultaneously benevolent and malevolent amalgams of psycho-geographical arrangements wherein there can be no concrete distinction drawn between the architectural and spatial characteristics and theories, and oppressive sociopolitical, socioeconomic, and sociocultural praxes. For example, in Thirdspace, lost are clear demarcations of carcerality and the lived urban space, the city and the prison, or "home" and a trap. This radical sense of hybridity, therefore, can be exploited in the strategy of a devious architect, and equally, incorporated into the tactical praxis of a resisting citizen.

There Is Nothing Beyond the City: Theorizing Psychetecture

The associative link between drawing away the mind, madness, and distraction in each text offers an apt description of the psychetecture of a city. As a working definition, I describe psychetecture as a set of apparatuses and psycho-emotional effects and both physical and ideological processes expressed in the relationship between architecture and the inhabitants of a city. I also refer to a city under psychetectural panopticism as a lebenskäfig or "life-cage". If psychetecture is viewed as an engine of onto-existential control of the subjects of a city, then *distraction* is its fuel. I choose to describe the fundamental operative aspect of psychetecture as distraction because of the word's paradoxical etymology, which bares interesting theoretical fruit. In English, distraction refers to (1) the act of distracting, (2) the state of being distracted, (3) mental distress or derangement, (4) that which distracts, divides the attention, or prevents concentration, as in, the distractions of the city, (5) that which amuses, entertains, or diverts; amusement; entertainment, and (6) division or disorder caused by dissension; tumult (Dictionary.com 2018). Etymologically, the English word distraction-as-the drawing away of the mind stems from the Latin *distractionem* "a pulling apart, separating", a "mental disturbance" and/or "a thing or fact that distracts" (Etymonline.com 2017). As such, psychetecture refers to the psycho-emotional and onto-existential effects a city has on its citizens, which manifest and function through its architecture. As psycho-spatial traps, Motter's Radiant City and Gaiman's city of spies represent systems in crisis. Each text explores "how people actually operate within a social context where things are either falling, or have fallen apart. Architecture always seems to present this impossibly rosy view of the future and seems unable to deal with the possibility of failure, even though all architecture in some way fails [..., the] desire to face up to a future that deals with a system in crisis" is interestingly expressed in each text (Clear 2008).

In essence, psychetecture describes a collection of praxes and apparatuses designed to facilitate and ensure the altering of people's consciousness through architectural design. As such, both the inhabitants of Radiant City/Somnopolis and the city of spies inevitably surrender the possibilities of motility, their freedom of movement, and ultimately their sanity or psycho-emotional equilibrium to an omnipresent architect, one whose designs would circumscribe being within the inescapable parameters of an endless city, one whose endlessness manifests as psychosis, the other as paranoia. In the case of the latter, the difference in scale must be acknowledged because Miracleman has the power and resources, both reified in his body, to not only build city-cages for former spies and other individuals perceived as undesirable, but to explode the panopticism of such psychetecture to encompass the entire planet, turning Earth into an endless city with himself as its architect.

The Key to the City Does Not Open Anything: On Utopia and Dystopia in Comic Book Cities

There are numerous examples of famous illustrated urban spaces throughout the various traditions and publication histories of comic books. Cataloguing a range of these spaces and architectures, from the ruinous, ancient, nostalgic, to the hyper-futuristic, is beyond the remit of this analysis. However, some well-known instances of comic book cities whose psychetectures influence their citizenry include, but are not limited to, the following: Gotham, notably depicted in Frank Miller and David Mazzucchellis' acclaimed *Batman: Year One* (1987), which depicts the city as an exaggerated 1970s and 1980s New York City. Mazzucchelli's Pre-Disney Times Square characterization of the city emphasizes the seemingly inextricable link between corruption and the saturnine atmosphere pervading Bruce Wayne/Batman's city. Gotham is littered with porn shops and theatres, gangs, prostitution, police corruption, mob-politics, suggesting that the post-Gothic architecture contains within it latent Gothic themes of paranoia, the supernatural/Otherworldly and an atmosphere of imminent danger which, in turn, has psycho-emotional and onto-existential effects on its polis as expressed in the violence and psycho-physical disfigurements of both the best and worst of its citizenry; Metropolis, envisioned by artist Alex Ross in texts such as *Kingdom Come* (1996) and *Superman: Peace on Earth* (1998) as a sprawling Deco metropolis whose Helial motifs, smooth curves, and sharp angles are built of chrome, glass, and steel; Daredevil's New York (the Hell's Kitchen district, in particular), portrayed as a Gothem-esque cathedralic city-slum in Frank Miller and Mazzucchellis' *Daredevil: Born Again* (1986); Moebius and Dan O'Bannons' cyberpunk city from *The Long Tomorrow* (1975); Francois Schuiten and Benoit Peeters' unrivalled draftsmanship seen in the city Urbicand from their bandes dessinées series *Les Cites Obscures* (1983) set on a fictional Counter-Earth in which humans live in independent city-states, each of which has developed a distinct civilization characterized by a distinctive architectural style; Tsutomu Nihei's manga *BLAME!* (1998), which features a megastructure simply referred to as The City, an endless vertical space featuring artificially constructed walls, stairways, and caverns, separated into massive "floors" by nearly impenetrable barriers known as "Megastructure". So vast is The City in *BLAME!* that the Moon is integrated into it psychetecture, and the gigantic pseudo-ecumenopolitan sprawl Mega-City One in John Wagner and Carlos Ezquerras' *Judge Dread* (1977) series.

While some of the aforementioned cities appear relatively benign at a cursory glance, what is interesting to note with regard to the theme of the tensions and relationships between cities and surveillance is the heterogeneity of apparatuses, techniques, and teloi brought to bear in the onto-existential control of the citizenry who occupy these cities. For the cities of *Les Cites Obscures*, Mega-City One and Radiant City, their respective narratives centralize the relationship between architecture and sociocultural control. Less apparent to some is the fact that the same principles of biopower reified through the surveillance and policing of city-spaces manifest the same way through the idiosyncratic, supra-legal, and often violent administration of "justice" by the vigilantes, aliens, and mutants of both DC and Marvel Comics, such as Batman, Superman, and Daredevil.

The two examples I discuss are situated in the interstice between these ostensibly dialectical portrayals of comic book cities and their respective relationships and tensions with the praxes of surveillance as a means of sociopolitical and onto-existential control of their respective subjects. Motter's Radiant City appears in Vol. 1, No. 1 of *Mister X* debuting in 1984 under the banner of Vortex Comics (Motter 1984). In the *Mister X* diegesis, the City, built upon an idealistic utopian vision summarized by the bromide "the city of tomorrow", was intended to be a metropolis founded and forged on the principles of aesthetic beauty whose design would both enrich and inspire its denizens. It subsequently falls into nightmarish chaos and disrepair as the series progresses. The reason for this urban decay, which in the narrative also manifests itself psycho-socially, is due to the unforeseen results of its "psychetexture", design elements fundamental to the city's overall design intended to enhance its residents' states of mind. Conversely, the psychetecture of the City ends up driving its inhabitants insane. Instead of incubating a city of thinkers and dreamers, Radiant City becomes a crucible of mental illnesses, manias, and mass psychoses—all of which its citizens suffer, resulting in widespread crime, corruption, and an epidemic of sleeping sicknesses (particularly insomnia) and delusions. As a result, Radiant City comes to be known as Somnopolis. Here Motter draws an essential link between the onto-existential and psycho-emotional experiences of citizens and the city in which they occur, suggesting that architecture is an expression of the *being* of societies as much as physiognomy is the expression of the being of individuals.

In this milieu of paradoxical, sheer Art Deco angles and crooked Caligarian shadows, the titular Mister X emerges. An emaciated, bald, Nosferatean man, who stalks the sprawling Bauhaus-cum-Deco edifices of the City, claiming to have once been one of its original architects, Mister X represents a contemporary extension of a tradition of more established city surveyors, reconnoitring vigilantes, and night detectives he follows such as Spring-heel Jack, Sherlock Holmes, and The Shadow. Motter's protagonist is characterized as unstable as his City, a murderer, a terrorist, a clinically insane man and addict who uses a drug called Insomnalin to avoid ever having to sleep, ostensibly dedicating every waking hour to repairing his broken metropolis. Twenty years following *Mister X*'s debut, Motter rebooted the series with 2009's *Mister X: Condemned*. The narrative is set during a time when Radiant City's architectural principles of mood-soothing psychetecture first disintegrate, then reverse, causing assorted mental and emotional disorders in its inhabitants, ranging from anxiety, insomnia, to dementia. In response, the local government decides to raze the metropolis and build anew a programme of urban demolition enacted by giant robots that kill a respected pseudo-mystical secret sect of architects, leaving 150 of their number ironically dead in a building. In response to the programme, the City's alleged enigmatic designer Mister X returns from exile after having disappeared years earlier with the hope of restoring sanity to the City by endeavouring to recover its original blueprints while also eluding the corrupt government, vicious gangsters, and the police. The text's avant-garde themes and ideas merge to form a narrative with a paradoxical nostalgic predictiveness, whereby Radiant City appears to be simultaneously a city set in a time that has both yet to and already come to pass.

Architecturally speaking, *Mister X* is an amalgam of three main aesthetic sensibilities: the retrofuturism of Art Deco, German Expressionism, and Bauhaus architectural aesthetics. Motter acknowledges as much in a 2008 interview with Emmett Furey for *cbr.com* (CBR 2008). Both the original *Mister X* and its subsequent squeals are both tonally and aesthetically indebted to the noir genre. Motter cites Billy Wilder's *Double Indemnity* (1944), Jules Dassin's *Naked City* (1948) and *Night and the City* (1950), Fritz Lang's *M* (1931) and *Metropolis* (1927), William Wyler's *Dead End* (1937), Jon Huston's *Maltese Falcon* (1941), and Jean-Luc Godard's *Alphaville* (1965) as aesthetico-narratological inspirations, as well as more recent neo-noir such as Ridley Scott's *Blade Runner* (1982), the Coen Brothers' *The Man Who Wasn't There* (2001), and *The Hudsucker Proxy* (1994).

Miracleman No. 21 "Spy Story" is featured in Neil Gaiman's run on comics creator Alan Moore's 1980s retcon of a British 1950s superhero comic originally called *Marvelman* published under Eclipse Comics. The series centres on Michael Moran, a man who works as a reporter and has dreams of life as a superhero. Upon rediscovering a magic word ("Kimota!") which transforms him into the titular superbeing Miracleman, Moran resolves to first become a superhero in the inclement sociopolitical and cultural landscape of Thatcher's Britain during the 1980s. The series' initial narrative centres on the political, moral, economic, cultural, and philosophical circumstances of Moran's existence, the tension in his marriage caused by having two different identities in a single body, and his reunion with childhood acquaintances, Johnny Bates (Kid Miracleman) as well the series antagonist Dr Emil Gargunza, a scientist responsible for Moran and Bates' memory loss. Moran subsequently meets another superbeing amnesiac named Miraclewomen (Avril Lear) after which the main series narrative enters a cosmic dimension. The Miracle Family subsequently ventures into outer space and encounters various alien beings also possessing superpowers. Moore's run concludes in Nos 15 and 16, with Miracleman drifting away from humanity and using at times questionable strategies and the combined efforts of the Miracle Family and other superbeings, to redress the world's sociopolitical, economic, medical, environmental, and cultural problems, thereby establishing an age of miracles and a somewhat unstable utopia on Earth.

Gaiman's run takes the series in a radically different direction. In a series of one-shot vignettes, Gaiman focuses primarily on the lives of normal people attempting to adapt to life in the wake of the omnipotent Miracleman's utopia and his presiding strategies of control and surveillance over the citizens of Earth from his gargantuan megastructure stronghold called Olympus. Some of the narratives form a subplot that directly engages with Miracleman, such as No. 17's "A Prayer and Hope" (1992), which tells the story of a group of pilgrims seeking alms via an audience with the deity. "Spy Story", however, possesses only a minimal connection to the larger narrative established by Moore. Loosely based on the British television series *The Prisoner* (1976) and science fiction author J.G. Ballard's short story "War Fever" from an anthology of short fiction from 1975 to 1989, "Spy Story" focuses on what would happen in Miracleman's utopia if the covert intelligence communities were dismantled. What begins as a straightforward spy thriller is revealed to be, amongst other things, a study of paranoia, surveillance, and panoptic control. In the story, the former-spy protagonist Ruth Browning is a woman who learns that she is experiencing a programme designed around a city of spies intended to rehabilitate her back into so-called normal life. The story concludes with the suggestion that said programme was successful; however, Gaiman includes numerous repetitive aesthetic and narrative motifs, intimating that having discovered the existence of a carceral panopticon designed to keep the former spies it incarcerates docile using elaborate espionage narratives, she is simply reinserted into another broader concentric city-cage. The leitmotif pervading Gaiman's run is a humanistic study of adaptation in the face of monumental sociocultural change following the Miracle Family's superpowered interventions into terrestrial life. Like Motter's protagonist, Gaiman's former spy attempts to employ various clandestine tactics to circumvent the strategy of panoptic surveillance and sociocultural control in psychetecture of the texts' respective cities. While Mister X attempts to intercede in the dystopia that results from his city's psychetecture attempting to manipulate the onto-existential and psycho-emotional experiences of its citizens, Ruth seeks to escape the panoptic psychetecture of the carceral city, the petri-dish city, or city-cage entirely.

Despising for You, This City: Strategic Panopticism and Anarcho-Tactics in the Lebenskafig

In order to describe how psychetecture functions in "Spy Story" and *Mister X*, as well as how both Ruth and Mister X represent what the French theorist Michel de Certeau would describe as strategists and tacticians in *The Practice of Everyday Life* (1984), let me first define these terms. According to de Certeau, strategy is always primarily concerned with the purview of power, describing strategy as

> the calculation (or manipulation) or power relationships that becomes possible as soon as a subject with will and power (a business, an army, a city, a

> scientific institution) can be isolated. It postulates a place that can be delimited as its own and serve as the base from which relations with an exteriority composed of targets or threats (customers or competitors, enemies, the country surrounding the city, objectives and objects of research, etc.) can be managed. As in management, every "strategic" rationalization seeks first of all to distinguish its "own" place, that is, the place of its own power and will, from an "environment". (de Certeau 1988, p. xix)

Strategy is therefore self-segregating, in the same way apparatuses of administration and management are self-segregating, creating a dialectic of inside/outside, abject/valid. The strategist, who could rightly also be called the architect and her/his city a strategy, becomes the subject, while those they oversee, directly or indirectly through the panoptic psychetecture of the lived spaces they design become the objects. Therefore, strategy also describes

> a mastery of places through sight. The division of space makes possible a panoptic practice proceeding from a place whence the eye can transform foreign forces into objects that can be observed and measured, and thus control and "include" them within its scope of vision. To be able to see (far into the distance) is also to be able to predict, to run ahead of time by reading a space. The ability to see gives more control over time, more control over space…[and also more control of those subject to the chronotope controlled by a particular strategy]. (de Certeau 1988, p. 36)

In contrast, de Certeau characterizes tactics as the purview of the non-powerful and, further, as an adaptation to the environment that results from the strategies of the powerful. Tactics describe a

> calculated action determined by the absence of a proper locus. No delimitation of an exteriority, then, provides it with the condition necessary for autonomy. The space of a tactic is the space of the other. Thus it must play on and with a terrain imposed on it and organized by the law of a foreign power. It does not have the means to keep to itself, at a distance, in a position of withdrawal, foresight, and self-collection: it is a maneuver "within the enemy's field of vision," as von Bülow put it, and within enemy territory. It does not, therefore, have the options of planning general strategy and viewing the adversary as a whole within a district, visible, and objectifiable space. It operates in isolated actions, blow by blow. It takes advantage of "opportunities" and depends on them, being without any base where it could stockpile its winnings, build up its own position, and plan raids. What

> it wins it cannot keep. This nowhere gives a tactic mobility, to be sure, but a mobility that must accept the chance offerings of the moment, and seize on the wing the possibilities that offer themselves at any given moment. It must vigilantly make use of the cracks that particular conjunctions open in the surveillance of the proprietary powers. It poaches in them. It creates surprises in them. It can be where it is least expected. It is a guileful ruse. In short, a tactic is an art of the weak. (de Certeau 1988, p. 37)

While the architect-strategist may determine the placement of the streets of a city, its citizens, pedestrians, and drivers may experiment with ways with which to navigate the lived reality of said streets. Both strategies and tactics are therefore concerned with an operational logic.

De Certeau draws attention to the fact that strategy makes two presumptions: control and an inside group not subject to the subjugating effects of city psychetecture. The contradiction here is that while certain edifices and physical features of a city may ostensibly not change, the interpersonal situations that occupy them are inherently prone to flux. If the situation upon which a stratagem is built is always-already changing, then there will always-already be aspects of the strategy that will always-already be obsolete. This is why Mister X and the other architects of Radiant City/Somnopolis failed to anticipate the fact that their original utopian psychetectural strategies would invert into a pathologically somnambulistic dystopia. Similarly, despite the efficacy of the design of the city of spies, some inhabitants like Ruth eventually become aware of the fact that the city itself is a psychetectural strategy of panoptic control. The myopia of strategy is predicated on the dialectic of inside/outside it is built upon; here panopticism blinds itself to anything beyond its own strategy.

In contrast, de Certeau suggests that because tactics are in a constant state of recalibration and mutability based on direct observations of the lived environs of the city, there is no assumption of dialectical rigidity with regard to being in the city. The efficacy of tactics inheres in their adaptability, fluidity, play, drift, creativity, unpredictability, combination, and openness. While strategy presumes staticity, tactics move towards flux and a type of onto-existential agility through awareness of chance opportunities. Tactics view an individual not as a prisoner but as "a locus in which an incoherent (and often contradictory) plurality of such relational determinations interact" (de Certeau 1988, p. xi). In this way, the architect is a strategist; the citizen is a tactician whereby unpredictability undermines the strategy, but empowers tactics or the-art-of-being-in-between. In view of de Certeaus' understanding of strategies and tactics, life for Mister X and Ruth becomes a paranoiac conundrum as a result of the panoptic distraction of the psychetectures of their respective cities. Firstly, from a certain vantage, I acknowledge the strategy of the city of spies to be brilliant in its economy. By engendering paranoia and exploiting its inhabitants' skills for espionage, the populace of the city spy and, by extension control, one another, requiring little to no intervention from external authorities. A city of spies is perhaps the purest expression of the panopticon as well as its principle of observation. In contrast, though the *Mister X* diegesis features flying cars, robots, and instances of Deco-inspired retrofuturistic technology, futurity here is a trap within Radiant City. The City's descent into becoming Somnopolis suggests that within the psychetecture of a somnopolis, dreams, of the future or any kind, are biopower, the psycho-emotional spaces of the subconscious are carceral, and the city itself is little more than a panopticon of sleep. Ultimately, the concepts of Radiant City and Somnopolis, as well as the city of spies, are undifferentiated by the same psychetectural principles and teloi: panopticism, distraction, and carcerality. In each instance, the city doubles not as a fortress, quarantine, or jail, but simultaneously as a literal and figurative sleep state, where being in the lebenskafig is "a life of intermission [...it] is no place to be addicted to another place" (Motter 1984, p. 12).

How do you trap an architect? Give him a broken city to repair. In a story featured in *Mister X: Eviction and Other Stories* (2013) aptly titled "Control", Mister X pursues one Mr Cadwalder Shrodinger, a former traffic controller of Radiant City's condemned aeroport following numerous electrical and traffic malfunctioning in Radiant City. Having no friends, family, or social life, Shrodinger is described as singularly dedicated to order, control, symmetry, choreography, and the efficient management of the City's air traffic. Following his dismissal from his position due to the implementation of the mayor's aggressive renovation initiative, Shrodinger falls into a depression which he overcomes by learning how to manipulate the City's transit grid, using homemade jury-rigged relays and his experiences and somewhat obsessive interest in traffic control to re-route local traffic in the City, effectively turning the City into his own petri dish. Mister X ends up pursuing a lead in the sewers of Radiant City, discovering a "nest of retrofitted conduits, patchwork wiring [...] cables and trunk lines, power and signal wires, bypasses and jump cords [all] far more than the system had ever been designed for" (Motter 2013, pp. 65–7). Mister X is asked how he knows all of this. In response, Motter provides a panel in which Mister X draws up the left sleeve of his shirt and coat to reveal tattoos of indecipherable grids not unlike Michael Scofield's (Wentworth Miller) architectural tattoos in Paul Scheuring's *Prison Break* (2005–2009). It is at this point that Mister X occupies an interesting liminal space between strategy and tactics. As one of the City's original architects, he is representative of de Certeauean strategy. However, as an individual within the City attempting to countermand its dilapidating strategies, he is also representative of de Certeauean tactics. However, in having the blueprints and what one is led to assume to be municipal gridworks of the City *upon* his body means that he not only reifies the strategy of the City through the lived experiences of his body but also embodies tactical attempts at their circumvention *through* the disruption of the normal functioning of said body. The relationship therefore between the City's failing strategy and Mister X's emaciated and addicted physiognomy and, by extension, the moral opprobrious of his actions as a terrorist and murderer pathetically mirror the corruption of Radiant City/Somnopolis and its psycho-emotionally corrosive effects on its citizens.

How do you trap a spy? You give her an unsolvable riddle. This is how Gaiman shows psychetecture to function: it is predicated on paradoxes. "Spy Story" turns the City into a petri dish for spy yarns. Unlike Radiant City/Somnopolis, its chronotope is not governed by the distractedness of somnambulism, but with an opposite type of distraction: a hyperawareness regarding the nature of the surveilled polity and the psychetectural limitations thereupon imposed. The city of spies therefore turns the concept of a city into a conglomeration of distractions predicated on puzzles, traps, logical riddles, an illusion of (dis)order and (chaos)design intended to simultaneously monopolize individual attention and draw the mind away from the panoptic and carceral reasons underlying its unsolvability—all jointly meant to create a psychetectural lebenskafig. At the conclusion of "Spy Story", the director of the City, a former antagonist of Miracleman named Evelyn Cream, speaks to Ruth who has discovered the truth about the City. He reveals that Ruth Browning a.k.a. 1860 a.k.a Casablanca does not exist in that she was *supposedly* born Sandra Walsh. Cream, a former spy himself, gives the following reason for the existence of the City and a theory of its psychetecture:

> my colleagues are engaged in a grand and wonderful task. It is given to them, dear lady, to perfect the human race. To usher in a GOLDEN AGE. They have cured the sick and made the insane WELL. They have

> abolished CRIME and WAR. But at EVERY step they confront new challenges to be overcome. Philosophically and actually. For example: one of the hardest groups of people to rehabilitate are members of the community I was once a part of – commonly known, for reasons that now escape me, as INTELLIGENCE. Spies, miss Walsh. People who voyage forever through a milieu of deceit and double-dealing. To whom treachery is as natural as breathing and for whom lies and subterfuge are the only truths. My colleagues couldn't make any of you happy in the world OUTSIDE. Treachery and betrayal were woven TOO firmly into your lives: they offered you PARADISE, nut you REJECTED it. So we took you out of it. We removed you like a malignant tumour. My COLLEAGUES built the city and all of you – aided by judicious para-reality programming – became its inhabitants and I, back from the dead, was made its official KING. Its NUMBER ONE. (Gaiman 1991, pp. 18–19)

The City as panopticon is designed to lull its citizenry into subjection and docility. Ironically, in "Spy Story", the success of the psychetecture of the City's distractiveness is predicated on its attention to detail. In "Spy Story", the distraction of the spy city's psychetecture is very elaborate so as to provide enough detail to make the reality of the City credible or, at least, credible enough for its subjects to accept it as the chronotope of their lives. It has to be in order to keep a city of spies, individuals of investigative and observational prowess, convinced of and acclimate to the veracity of an illusion. This manifests in Gaiman's use of spy-thriller motifs, a genre known for narratological complexity, Gordian, labyrinthine plots of double and triple agents, uncertain motives, shadow players, and a sense of ever-present danger much in the same way Motter's interpolation of noir tropes does. Miracleman and his acolytes therefore build the City in a way that is believable and palatable to a spy, even at its worst. Like Weir's *Truman Show* (1998), this is a monumental feat of logistics, engineering, architecture, and city planning pertaining not only to the physical aspects of the City but also everyone Ruth encounters therein—fruit vendors, cab drivers, couples on the bus, fish mongers, attendees of a party, a love interest, her superiors, and so on. In the city of spies, every interaction, every step, edifice, experience is psychetecturally coded. The City's psychetecture thereby also necessarily produces an inextricable paranoia wherein those subject to it believe that any and everyone is a potential agent. In such a chronotope, there is no such thing as an "empty gesture". It is an arduous place of exhausting layers of insignificant signification—all designed to be a distraction.

I describe life in Gaiman's lebenskafig as tiresome, but for who? As Ruth's unrelenting paranoia indicates, Gaiman suggests that life in the city of spies is tiresome for those aware of and/or constantly thinking about the City as a life-prison. Keep in mind that unlike Mister X, Ruth has no access to anything resembling Insomnolin, which allows Mister X to be able to unrelentingly observe, monitor, and move within the City as well as bare, just barely, the strain of being constantly aware of the true nature of Somnopolis. As such, the psychetecture of the city of spies manifests in Ruth's circadian rhythms. The very being and lived experiences of her body are simultaneously disrupted and circumscribed by the panoptic distraction of the City itself. She falls asleep and wakes up under the aegis of its psychetecture, a psychetecture that constructs a world of spy versus spy, in which her life is a seemingly endless narrative with "facts", players, and allegiances so Gordian has to become meaningless save for the *fact* of its unresolvability. This is a paradox as the seemingly unresolvable panopticism inherent to the distracting psychetecture of the City is *precisely* what is used to resolve the problem of the spy community in the post-Miracle world. Surveillance, paranoia, and espionage are therefore imprinted or tattooed on the psycho-physical space of the bodies of the inhabitants of the City, but are also animated and (re)circulated through the paranoid and surveilled lives of said bodies. At the foundation of the City is a design, physical and ephemeral, intended to keep Ruth and all the others' minds subject to a particular mode of thinking, moving, and being. By living, or dreaming of living in cities like the city of spies and Radiant City/ Somnopolis, the body reifies its own subjugation. Both Motter and Gaiman explore, in their respective ways, how a city, its onto-existential properties, its buildings, and the people that occupy them double as psycho-emotional parameters and the principles of architecture redound to being expressions of behavioural algorithms, in the last instance.

Bibliography

Clear, N. (2008). *Architectures of the Near Future: An Interview with Nic Clear. Interviewed by Simon Sellars.* Updated 24 December 2008. Available at: http://www.ballardian.com/near-future-nic-clear-interview. Accessed 9 May 2018.

De Certeau, M. (1988). *The Practice of Everyday Life* (trans: Rendall, S.). London: University of California Press.

Debord, G. [1955] 2018. *Introduction to a Critique of Urban Geography – Published in Les Lèvres Nues No. 6 (1955). Situationist International Online.* Available at: https://www.cddc.vt.edu/sionline/si/theory.html. Accessed 6 June 2018.

Debord, G. (1956, November). Theories of the Derive. *Les Lèvres Nues* #9. Reprinted in Internationale Situationniste #2 (December 1958).

Debord, G. (1959). *Memoires*, Edite Par L Internationale Situationniste.

Etymonline.com. (2017). *Online Etymology Dictionary.* Available at: https://www.etymonline.com/word/distraction. Accessed 7 Apr 2018.

Furey, E. (2008). *CCI: X-25 – Motter Talks Mister X.* Available at: https://www.cbr.com/cci-x-25-motter-talks-mister-x/. Accessed 11 Apr 2018.

Gaiman, N., & Buckingham, M. (1991). *Miracleman, 4*(21). California: Eclipse Comics.

Kariger, B, & Daniel. (2018). *Dictionary.com.* Available at: http://www.dictionary.com/browse/distraction. Accessed 11 Apr 2018.

Knabb, K. (2003). *On the Passage of a Few Persons Through a Rather Brief Unity of Time.* Available at: http://www.bopsecrets.org/SI/debord.films/passage.htm. Accessed 6 June 2018.

McDonough, T. (2004). *Guy Debord and the Situationist International: Texts and Documents.* Edited by Tom McDonough. Boston: MIT Press.

Motter, D. (1984). *Mister X, 1*(1). Toronto: Vortex Comics Inc.

Motter, D. (2013). *Mister X: Eviction and Other Stories.* Milwaukee: Dark Horse Comics Inc.

Richter, D. (2015). *An Occult Psychogeography of Hawskmoor's London Churches.* Available at: http://www.thebohemianblog.com/2015/10/an-occult-psychogeography-of-hawksmoors-london-churches.html. Accessed 15 May 2018.

Sinclair, I. (2012). *Lud Heat.* London: Skylight Press.

Sinclair, J. M., & Coulthard, R. M. (1975). *Towards an Analysis of Discourse.* London: Oxford University Press.

Soja, E. (1996). *Thirdspace: Journeys to Los Angeles and Other Real-and-Imagined Places.* London: Blackwell.

CHAPTER 4

Surveillance and Spatial Performativity in the Scenography of *Tower*

Lucy Thornett

Introduction

Two women appear in two windows of a high-rise building. They go about their daily lives: preparing food, dressing, reading, dancing. Unseen by them, a small group of people stand on the street, watching them with binoculars, listening to their movements and conversations with headphones. This was the premise of *Tower*, a site-specific performance I created and presented in Elephant and Castle in London in 2017 (Fig. 4.1). In this chapter, I will discuss this work as a case study for what I argue is a productive collision between surveillance and scenography. Scenography, originally associated with stage design, is now understood as an expanded and autonomous practice concerned with designing and arranging performative space (Brejzek 2011). My claim is that scenography is capable of bringing together discourses of architecture, surveillance and performance. Though there is a growing body of research on how performance as both a theoretical concept and an artistic practice can intervene into surveillance studies, none of this research specifically discusses scenography's role in performance. This is an omission, as scenography's role in

L. Thornett (✉)
University of the Arts London, London, UK
e-mail: l.thornett@lcc.arts.ac.uk

S. Flynn, A. Mackay (eds.), *Surveillance, Architecture and Control*,
https://doi.org/10.1007/978-3-030-00371-5_4

Fig. 4.1 *Tower*. (Photographer: Amy Thornett)

distributing the visual and spatial in performance means it has much to add to discourses of surveillance. Within discourses of scenography, its ability to reframe architecture theoretically and interrogate it in practice has been discussed by many scholars. Scenography's ability to intervene into architecture's performance of power is of particular interest in this chapter. The relationship between watcher and watched is coded as having a particular power dynamic, and as such discourses of surveillance are inherently concerned with interrogations of power relations. It is my contention then that the space in between these two pairings of surveillance and performance on the one hand, and scenography and architecture on the other, is fertile ground for a discussion of how surveillance and architecture relate to one another. I argue that scenography is an ideal lens for intervening through theory and practice into architectures of surveillance due to its ability to reveal architecture's spatial performativity; its ability to subvert hegemonic visualities; its role as a relational strategy that constructs relations between spectator, site and performance; and its ability to produce particular kinds of spectatorship. I build upon the work of other scholars who have argued that surveillance might be utilised subversively as a tool within performance to argue that scenography—through its positioning of spectator, site and performance—might co-opt surveillant strategies in order to playfully subvert the power implications of the gaze and interrogate other power relations within the built environment.

I will outline this argument in several stages. First, I will discuss existing literature on the overlaps between performance and surveillance. I will then introduce current discussions on the connections between scenography and architecture, and the notion of architectural performativity. I will discuss the architectural context of the performance by outlining the specificities of its site and by situating it within a brief discussion of some aspects of the modernist architectural project. Following this, I will present an analysis of the performance, and through a reading of Michel Foucault's conception of Jeremy Bentham's panopticon discuss how the windows acted as tools of surveillance while the urban site itself enacted a panoptic discipline on the audience. I contend that rather than simply critiquing surveillance, *Tower* utilised surveillance—drawing on its associated disciplines and pleasures as well as its ability to make visible—to reveal the broader power structures at work in the built environment of the site. I frame these power structures in terms of Foucault's concept of *biopolitics*. Finally, I discuss scenography's ability to produce countervisualities that resist spaces of surveillance and power, and the role of the spectator in producing the performative event. I hope to show that scenography, as a mode of visual and spatial organisation, is able to arrange spectator, site and performance in relation to one another in ways that are particularly useful for understanding the relationship between architecture and surveillance.

Performance and Surveillance

Much research has focused on the productive interface between surveillance and performance. Here, performance is understood both culturally as a quotidian practice and artistically as an aesthetic practice that can usefully intervene into surveillance society. Hall et al. have pointed out that the notion of performance runs through much surveillance scholarship (2016, p. 153), while others have argued that surveillance, like performance, is itself a cultural practice (Mcgrath 2004; Monahan 2011). This makes performance an ideal paradigm to bring to bear on surveillance. A number of scholars have made a case for the ability of artistic performances to productively interrogate surveillance society (e.g. Hall et al. 2016; Mcgrath 2004, 2012; Monahan 2015; Morrison 2015, 2016) and to, perhaps, even produce "a space of resistance" (Hogue 2016). Performances may not only enact a commentary *on* surveillance; some of the examples discussed by the researchers above work *with* surveillance by employing it radically to produce new agencies and subjectivities (Mcgrath 2004, 2012; Morrison 2016). Elise Morrison has discussed how the similarities between surveillance and theatre allow for a productive interface between the two paradigms (Morrison 2016). Taking surveillance as both a performative act and a mode of representation, Morrison argues that both theatre and surveillance are concerned with "which bodies are put on display" and "practices of watching and being watched, carefully calibrated visibilities and invisibilities, and the power dynamics that attend each of these arrangements" (pp. 37, 38). The crossovers between surveillance studies and performance studies can be put into practice in ways that broaden normative surveillance discourses.

John McGrath contends that surveillance studies' focus on questions of privacy and civil liberties has failed to take account of the complexities of our interactions with surveillance. He argues "that surveillance has proliferated not least because we desire it – we enjoy it, play with it, use it for comfort" (Mcgrath 2004, p. vii); that is, that the pleasures of watching and being watched play a role in the ways in which we come into contact with surveillance. McGrath concedes that concerns around privacy do shape experiences of surveillance; however, he contends that surveillance can also make visible what was previously hidden in ways that might produce a sense of agency for those being watched. As he points out, "for those without controlling public power, the apparent invasion of privacy can sometimes seem welcome" (Mcgrath 2004, p. 58). This is echoed by Flynn and Mackay, who say that surveillance can sometimes provide bodies "with an identity that can be determined as real – I am watched, therefore I am" (2017, p. 3). Utilising surveillance as a practice that might reveal and make visible in subversive ways is key to my discussion of it in this chapter, as particularly crystallised in the notion of countervisuality.

Countervisuality is a useful way of thinking through how performance—and in particular scenography—might utilise surveillance in ways that resist dominant power structures. Visuality is defined by Nicholas Mirzoeff as the visualisation of history: the authority to classify, separate and aestheticise the visible, the "authority to tell us to move on and that exclusive claim to be able to look" (Mirzoeff 2011, p. 474). Countervisuality, then, is a resistant practice that consists of a "performative claim of a right to look where none technically exists" (p. 478). Torin Monahan has discussed how strategies of countervisuality can be employed within artistic performances in order to perform resistance in spaces of surveillance by "[denaturalising] the discriminatory orders imposed by state-corporate apparatuses" (2015, p. 161) and by proposing "alternatives to totalising regimes of state visuality" (p. 172). It is my contention that scenography is particularly suited to producing such countervisualities due to its ability to organise the visual within performance. I will expand upon this point later. For now, I want to note the tacit scenographic nature of much of this literature.

Though none of the theorists working in the crossovers between performance and surveillance specifically reference scenography, I would argue that many of their concerns are decidedly scenographic. McGrath suggests that surveillance could be utilised as a "surprisingly productive perversion of spectacle" (2004, p. 7), while Morrison contends that surveillance can propose new modes of spectatorship. Scenography both produces spectacles and organises spectators in relation to the performance event and its site. Both McGrath and Morrison highlight the inherent spatiality of surveillance performance. Morrison argues that surveillance art is always a spatial practice (2016, p. 20); McGrath proposes the notion of "surveillance space" as a way of thinking about "the lived experience of surveillance and the cultural products that reveal our lives under surveillance to us" (Mcgrath 2004, p. 2). Scenography, as the practice of designing and organising space in performance, is thus particularly apposite for interrogating surveillance—especially in relation to architecture. McGrath uses the term "performative space" (p. 12) to discuss the shift in the atmosphere of a performance space that occurs when surveillance technologies are introduced. Building on the work of Dorita Hannah, I will discuss the performativity of space in relation to scenography. Scenography's ability to heighten architecture's performativity makes it a particularly useful strategy for interrogating and intervening into, and expanding the relationship between, architecture and surveillance.

Scenography and Architecture

Scenography originally denoted stage decoration or spectacle. The term has now expanded to encompass the entirety of the material and sensory aspects of a performance (Aronson 2017). Beyond the theatre, scenography is an interdisciplinary practice that spans performance, visual art and design. Arnold Aronson has discussed this interdisciplinarity, arguing that "by focusing on the organisation of the visual field and spatiality – we can see theatre scenography residing within a much larger framework of art, architecture and social practice" (Aronson 2017, p. xiv). It is scenography's ability to organise visuality and spatiality within site-specific performance that I would like to focus on here. Contemporary expanded scenography often deliberately disrupts the spatial conventions of theatre and its pre-ordained arrangements of spectator, space and performance. A number of scholars have articulated the way scenography operates within sites outside of theatre buildings. In these site-specific performances, the performance space is found rather than designed. What scenography does in this context has been variously described as "deconstructing" (Irwin 2008, p. 44); "editing and curating" (Lotker and Gough 2013, p. 5); "transforming" (Aronson 2017, p. xv); and "framing" (Brooks and Collins 2017, p. 98) *found* spaces. Joslin McKinney and Scott Palmer define scenography as "as a mode of encounter and exchange founded on spatial and material relations between bodies, objects and environments" (McKinney and Palmer 2017, p. 2). They also propose "relationality" as a key concept for understanding how scenography operates (p. 8). In this chapter, I will discuss how scenography—as a mode of encounter that arranges spectators, performers and sites in relation to one another—is well suited for thinking through and, crucially, expanding upon discourses of surveillance, architecture and power.

Like surveillance and performance, the disciplines of scenography and architecture have produced many productive crossovers, with much scholarly attention having been devoted to the overlaps and divergences between these two practices of designing spaces (e.g. Brejzek 2017; Rufford 2015; von Arx 2016). A repeated theme in this existing research is a critique of the binary that understands architecture as dealing with stable and static spaces, and scenography as concerned with ephemeral performances and events. Architect and theorist Bernard Tschumi critiques this misconception of architecture by arguing that "[t]here is no architecture without program, without action, without event" (Tschumi 1996), and that, as such, the notion of the event renders architecture inherently unstable. Building on Tschumi's work, Dorita Hannah posits the concept of event-space as a useful way of understanding how architecture, in fact, performs. In her conception, considering space through the lens of performance "repositions built and imagined space as both embodied experience and evolving time-based event, where the constructed environment itself (whether architecture or scenography) is no longer perceived as a static object but as volatile spatial subject" (Hannah 2011, p. 56). She later expands upon this by linking the performance of architecture to the way in which power is performed as an active force within the built environment (Hannah 2015). Her conception of event-space becomes a way of thinking through how power relations are performed within both architecture and spaces of surveillance.

Though event-space allows us to conceive of how architecture is *always* performing, scenography as a practice is able to intervene into the built environment in ways that bring architecture's quotidian performance into contact with the aestheticised scenographic event—overlaying the site with the relationality of spectator, aesthetic performance, space and the performance of daily life. Hannah argues that through such interventions, scenography is able to directly critique "architecture's role in reinforcing power structures" (2015, p. 126).

It is my contention that scenography—as both a practice and a theoretical framework—is particularly useful for discussions of architecture and surveillance, due to both scenography's ability to interface with architecture and reveal its performativity and scenography's relationship to visuality. I will discuss later how scenography's role as a strategy of organising the visual allows it to produce countervisualities that reveal the ways in which power is performed through the architecture of the site. Before I continue, I want to make one final note on terminology. Though *Tower* did in fact include the presence of human actors *performing*, I refer to it as a work of scenography rather than one of performance. Beyond my own situated practice within scenography, the reason for this is the work's primary focus on spatial performativity rather than narrative performance. The performance of the space itself and the embodied experience of the audience within the site were of primary importance when creating the work, and the presence of the performers used to heighten this spatial performativity. Before expounding on how this took place, I will first trace the architectural context in which the work was sited.

Elephant and Castle: Modernism, Social Housing and Transparency

Elephant and Castle is an area of London located south of the Thames in the Borough of Southwark, not far from Central London. The junction of many major arterial roads leading into Central London, it was devastated by bombing during the Second World War. It was rebuilt in a flurry of optimism at a time when social housing was being constructed on an unprecedented and unrepeated scale throughout the United Kingdom to replace housing that had been destroyed during the war. The architectural typology of the high-rise residential block epitomised this modernist ideal of housing for all, and these towers dominated the skyline at Elephant and Castle until recently. The area is home to a building designed by architect Ernő Goldfinger—one of the key names associated with the modernist tower blocks built in mid-century Britain—as well as Europe's first indoor shopping centre. However, perhaps more famously, it was also home to the Heygate Estate, a residential social housing estate built in the early 1970s, which housed more than three thousand people. Elephant and Castle is an interesting case study for the impact that government housing policy has on the architecture of the city.

The area is currently in the midst of another period of redevelopment. The local authority Southwark Council, in partnership with private developer Lend Lease, is in the process of removing the modernist blocks and, along with them, the social housing provision in the area. The Heygate Estate was demolished in 2014. These buildings are being replaced with new high-rises containing luxury inner-city apartments. Southwark Council's own statement about the need to remove the "monolithic single use structures" (Southwark Council and Mayor of London 2012, p. 23) that dominate the area seems rather odd in light of the equally monolithic structures with which they are being replaced. Another possible motivation for the redevelopment was hinted at by Southwark Council's former Director of Regeneration, who stated that social housing attracts the "wrong sort" of residents (quoted in Wehner 2002). We can see Elephant and Castle as a microcosm for how architecture renders state and corporate power material, and, moreover, the way in which housing certain kinds of bodies in particular locations within the city can be read as an act of categorisation.

Alongside the dream of housing for all, another key modernist architectural ideal is one of transparency. Anthony Vidler states that:

> Modernity has been haunted, as we know very well, by a myth of transparency: transparency of the self to nature, of the self to other, of all selves to society, and all this represented, if not constructed, from Jeremy Bentham to Le Corbusier, by a universal transparency of building materials, spatial penetration, and the ubiquitous flow of air, light, and physical movement. (Vidler 1992, p. 217)

Advanced by proponents such as Le Corbusier and Walter Gropius, the new architecture of transparency meant a rejection of the cosy domesticity of the Victorian era, turning instead to an "honesty of thought and feeling" (Gropius 1935, p. 19). A number of scholars have connected this to surveillance. Nigel Whiteley has traced a genealogy of architectural transparency, pointing out that "something initially associated with honesty rapidly became problematic once the power of the gaze was noticed" (Whiteley 2003, p. 8). Henriette Steiner and Kristin Veel contend that transparent architecture, together with surveillance practices, has reconfigured cultural notions of "the visible and the invisible". In their conception, "changes at the aesthetic and material level take part in much wider cultural processes of cultural re-orientation" (Steiner and Veel 2011, p. 216). Both Whiteley and Scott McQuire discuss the continuation of the architectural project of transparency beyond the modernist era, with both arguing that societal responses are now largely ambivalent. For Whiteley, this is due to the fact that "transparency is so much a part of the urban architectural experience that, for the most part, we are completely unaware of it" (Whiteley 2003, p. 8), with transparency no longer used to reveal but merely as visual spectacle (p. 12). McQuire, on the other hand, argues that though glass architecture has proliferated, its surveillant capacities have been outstripped by electronic media (McQuire 2013, p. 103).

The link between modernist windows and media has also been made by Beatriz Colomina. As a departure from the common pairing of modern architecture with the machine age, Colomina connects the architecture of the modern era with the rise of mass media. In her reading of the buildings of modernist designers Le Corbusier and Adolf Loos, she argues:

> The organising geometry of architecture slips from the perspectival cone of vision, from the humanist eye, to the camera angle. It is precisely in this slippage the modern architecture becomes modern by engaging with the media. (Colomina 1996, p. 335)

Here, windows act as cinematic or photographic frames on exterior or interior space. If the modernist window can be understood as a communication tool, then it follows that, like the camera, it can also become a tool of surveillance. Colomina acknowledges the panoptic nature of windows. For someone inhabiting a lit interior at night, the window constitutes a gaze, whether or not anyone is actually watching (Colomina 1996, p. 482). This notion that transparent architecture acts as a disciplinary and quite straightforwardly panoptic tool of surveillance is echoed by Steiner and Veel. In discussing a study conducted with contemporary inhabitants of a glass-walled building in the Netherlands, they note, "even if no one is looking…the *feeling* of being visible clings to the ways the inhabitants talk about their domestic situation" (Steiner and Veel 2011, p. 223). Conversely, they also point out that the disciplinary codes enacted by glass architecture do not apply only to those within the interiors; passers-by also must avoid committing the transgressive act of looking too obviously or for too long into these supposedly private spaces (p. 226). For Colomina, the window is also a categorisation device—"a viewing mechanism that produces the subject. It precedes and frames its occupant" (Colomina 1996, p. 483). By understanding the window as a representational frame, both a tool of communication and surveillance, we can begin to discuss how it might be utilised subversively by scenography.

If, as Whiteley and McGrath contend, we are now largely immune to the surveillant impact of transparent architecture, making this visible through scenography could allow the power of the built environment to perform in other ways. Surveillance here, as in some of McGrath's and Morrison's examples, is not merely the subject of the artwork but a productive tool for staging, in this case, power relations in and with architecture. In what follows, I will discuss the scenography of *Tower*, and in doing so make a case for scenography's ability to intervene in particular ways into spaces of surveillance.

Tower

Tower was a site-specific practice-research performance that I created in Elephant and Castle in 2017. As described earlier, two performers enacted a series of quotidian actions in two windows of a high-rise tower block (Fig. 4.2). A small audience of approximately 15 people sat on coloured plastic chairs across a busy road, watching the performance with binoculars and listening to the performers' movements and voices through headphones. The premise constituted a literal invitation to the spectators to participate in the surveillance of others. Rather than perform heightened or dramatic actions, the performers engaged in mundane activities such as eating, sleeping and conducting one-sided phone calls whose import was never made clear, almost in real time. These banal performances further blurred the line between fiction and reality within the site. Though aware that they were surveilling actors and not real inhabitants of the building, a number of audience members expressed discomfort or guilt about watching and listening to such private performances. Despite this discomfort,

Fig. 4.2 *Tower* video still. (Videographer: Justin Batchelor)

the work was undoubtedly an appeal to the voyeuristic pleasure of surveillance that McGrath and Morrison refer to. Private dwelling spaces are visible to us, framed by windows, as we move through the public space of the city in our daily lives. However, while disciplinary codes of behaviour usually necessitate taking only furtive glances at these spaces, *Tower* invited the spectators to indulge in the subversive pleasure of gazing for longer. A number of audience members were seen to use their binoculars to explore the surrounding site, peering into the windows and real domestic spaces of surrounding apartment buildings, demonstrating the pleasure available in this invitation.

In Morrison's discussion of surveillance and performance, she presents an analysis of *Contains Violence,* a production by David Rosenberg staged at the Lyric Hammersmith in 2008. The production contains a number of similarities to *Tower,* so Morrison's analysis is useful here for tracing the convergent and divergent ways in which surveillance was staged in the two works. Like *Tower, Contains Violence* equipped audience members with binoculars and headphones that enabled them to see and hear performers who were positioned in a building across the road. Morrison argues that this casts the audience as part of the fictional landscape of the performance, using surveillance tools recognisable from representations in film and television to appeal to their desires around voyeurism. However, she contends that the relationship to this fictional space was rendered unstable by the work's relationship to the everyday. She also argues that in disorienting the visual and aural experience of the performance, the headphones and binoculars defamiliarise "habits of theatre spectatorship, making them re-emerge as new and strange to themselves" (Morrison 2016, p. 55). These readings could also apply to *Tower*. I have argued elsewhere that the headphones and binoculars act as scenographic prostheses that create a sensory disjunction as they mediate the performance space (Thornett 2018). This could be seen, via Morrison, to allow for a productive collision between surveillance and theatre spectatorship that defamiliarises habitual modes of spectating. However, there are also a number of differences between the two performances. In Rosenberg's work, a murder is staged, in contrast to the banal actions of the performers in *Tower*. *Contains Violence* was staged on the roof of a theatre building, grounding the work within a theatrical context and separating it from the everyday performances taking place on the street below. In *Tower*, the refusal to differentiate between the actions of the performers and those of the real inhabitants of the surrounding windows, alongside the immersion of the audience in the urban fabric of the street, further blurred the line between fiction and reality. This allowed for the performance of the everyday to enter into dialogue with the fictional performance, arguably destabilising the power relations of the site. The key difference between the two works was the fact that in *Tower*, the audience were seen to be watching.

Throughout the performance, the pleasure and power of watching were undermined as the spectators grew increasingly aware that they had become a spectacle and were drawing attention from passers-by (Fig. 4.3). The binoculars and glowing LED-lit headphones acted as props or costume elements that heightened the spectators' performance of watching within the site. These surveillance tools, along with the coloured chairs, also marked them as part of a group. The audience were positioned on a small patch of grass in front of a set of traffic lights that functions as a pedestrian crossing for a busy four-lane road (Fig. 4.4). Behind the audience was an underground train station and alongside them a cycleway. The choreography of the site's quotidian performances took place around the spectators while they remained still. They sat in a transitory space which was clearly not designed to be occupied in such a way and performed the act of watching. This constituted a transgression of the disciplinary norms of the site. Though their attention was focused on the windows of the performance, to passers-by who stopped to ask what

Fig. 4.3 *Tower* spectators. (Photographer: Amy Thornett)

Fig. 4.4 *Tower* spectators. (Photographer: Amy Thornett)

they were looking at, these looked like any of the other windows illuminated in the surrounding site. Replicating the positions of watched and watcher in differing relations to one another complicated the expected power binary between these two subject positions as the audience became vulnerable as well. As Morrison has suggested, surveillance performances "might articulate new relationships across surveillant interfaces, imagining the possibility for understanding and collaboration between subject positions that have been traditionally divided between 'given to be seen' and 'given to see'" (Morrison 2016, p. 71). Through a reading of Foucault, I will expand upon the productive interface between scenography and surveillance in *Tower*. In doing so, I hope to show that by staging surveillance within the built environment of the city, the work was also able to bring multiple temporalities of the performance of architectural power into dialogue with one another, thereby troubling conventional readings of architectural surveillance.

Beyond the Panopticon

> At one point, I noticed someone on a passing bus taking a photo. I then wondered about this being uploaded to social media and started thinking about people I don't know commenting and discussing a picture of me and the rest of the audience and how this was essentially what I and the audience were/might be doing with the Tower actors; looking at anonymous silhouettes and trying to apply some sort of narrative or meaning to their actions. (*Tower* audience member)

I have already discussed how the windows are utilised as panoptic tools of surveillance, following Colomina. I have also touched on how the audience themselves subverted the disciplinary boundaries of the site through their performance of watching, troubling a straightforward reading of the power dynamic between watcher and watched, but I would like to briefly expand on this here. Foucault's notion of the panopticon is one in which individuals do not need to exercise power. Rather, the possibility of being watched means we self-discipline, modifying our own behaviour (Foucault 1977). Through a reading of Judith Butler's notion of "performativity" (Butler 1990), Morrison has discussed the ways in which our relationship with surveillance is performative: it is "expressed through repeated, and potentially revised series of behaviours, gestures, clothing choices, and uses of language" (Morrison 2016, p. 18). The ways we perform in public space is then, following Butler, conditioned through the repetition of acceptable behaviours. I previously discussed how these repeated performances operated in the context of the Elephant and Castle site. As a junction of many overlapping thoroughfares, the disciplinary logic of the site is defined and performed through movement. Though the audience inhabited the edge of what is essentially a pedestrian square where people do gather for various reasons, the specific position the spectators occupied—on a patch of grass near the road—is not used as a space for gathering. The presence of the chairs signalled the intention to remain for a period of time, further announcing a stillness performed by the spectators in marked contrast to the quotidian performance of movement going on around them. This undermined the power granted to the audience through their watching, and upended the relationship between spectator and spectacle.

Foucault positions spectacle in opposition to the panopticon (Foucault 1977, p. 216, 217): the role of the theatre is to allow many people to watch a few, whereas the panopticon reverses this by allowing the few to watch the many. Yet he also speaks about the panopticon in quite theatrical terms:

> By the effect of backlighting, one can observe from the tower, standing out precisely against the light, the small captive shadows in the cells of the periphery. They are like so many cages, so many small theatres, in which each actor is alone, perfectly individualized and constantly visible. (p. 200)

Here Foucault begins to speak to the desire and pleasure inherent in the act of watching, something that I have discussed earlier in relation to surveillance. This desire complicates Foucault's contention that surveillance and spectacle are opposed. I would like to propose here that spectacle can be used to productively interrogate and intervene into spaces of surveillance. As I have outlined, contemporary expanded practices of scenography are concerned with disrupting conventional theatrical arrangements of spectators, performance and space. I will later expand upon the ways in which spectacle can be recuperated through scenography, with particular attention to the role of the spectator.

Foucault also discussed discipline in terms of how bodies are categorised, stating "the disciplines characterize, classify, specialize; they distribute along a scale, around a norm, hierarchise individuals in relation to one another and, if necessary, disqualify and invalidate" (Foucault 1977,

p. 223). This discussion of categorisation is prevalent in surveillance studies. Following Colomina, I argue that in *Tower*, the windows and the architectural typologies themselves acted as devices that categorised the bodies within. The tower block of the performance was not actually a residential block but rather an educational building, built in the same mid-century period and style. Through the performance of domesticity, the building was recast as a social housing block. I have already discussed the kinds of value judgements that exist around the residents of such housing, leading to the demolition and rebuilding currently taking place in Elephant and Castle, as shown by statements made by Southwark Council's former director of regeneration. Through this, we can see that architecture and in particular windows that frame occupants already act as classification tools, where, following Foucault, particular kinds of architecture might come to disqualify and invalidate particular kinds of bodies over time. *Tower* quite deliberately utilised and made visible this act of categorisation, in the hope of questioning the assumptions that underlie it.

However, the concept of the panopticon only goes so far in explaining the performance of architectural power within the site. I would like to propose that Foucault's later notion of *biopolitics* is more pertinent to discussions of the way in which a city's architectural landscape is shaped by state and corporate power and how this, in turn, is experienced materially in the bodies of the population. For Foucault, biopolitics describes the way power is exercised over populations—rather than individuals as is the case with discipline (Foucault 2007, p. 11). He specifically links his theory of biopolitics to urban planning and its role in circulating bodies and materials. Sven-Olov Wallenstein argues that architecture became a biopolitical tool with the emergence of modernism, through modernist architecture's materialisation and spatialisation of power (Wallenstein 2012, p. 14). The frame of biopolitics is useful for thinking about the way architecture's performance of power takes place at multiple temporalities simultaneously within Elephant and Castle. Beyond the immediacy of the way discipline codes performances, there is the slower movement of the city's landscape as its architecture is demolished and rebuilt in order to designate which bodies will be housed in which locations. This recalls McGrath's and Morrison's argument that aesthetic practices can intervene *through* surveillance practices in ways that go beyond simple commentaries *on* surveillance. I would like to claim again that scenography, rather than simply performance, can highlight architecture's performativity in spaces of surveillance. McGrath argues that surveillance can be utilised creatively to make visible those without agency (Mcgrath 2004, p. 15, 58). *Tower* does this in ways that reveal the broader biopolitics of the site. Building upon Dorita Hannah's notion that scenography can intervene into architectural power, I would like to add that it can do this in ways that go beyond how architecture controls behaviour by revealing how architecture shapes how and where we live. Foucault said that:

> Power has its principle not so much in a person as in a certain concerted distribution of bodies, surfaces, lights, gazes; in an arrangement whose internal mechanisms produce the relation in which individuals are caught up. (Foucault 1977, p. 202)

Scenography, as a practice that is also concerned with the "distribution of bodies, surfaces, lights, gazes" and in producing relations, is ideally placed to intervene into spatial distributions of power.

Countervisuality and Spectatorship

Finally, I would like to discuss the particular ways in which scenography produces the spectator and how this creates productive interactions with architectural surveillance. I will return here to Mirzoeff's notion of countervisuality. As outlined above, Mirzoeff defines countervisuality as a resistant practice which claims a "right to look", in the face of an authority that says "move on, there's nothing to see here" (Mirzoeff 2011, p. 474). Morrison echoes this in noting the way surveillance art can replace the disciplinary gaze of surveillance with a "mischievous, transformative second glance" (Morrison 2016, p. 19). I link this to scenography specifically through Mirzoeff's definition of countervisuality as a strategy of rearranging "the relations of the visible and the sayable" (p. 474). Scenography, as a practice of arranging the visual, can thus produce resistant countervisualities when staged in relation to surveillance and architecture. In the case of *Tower*, it does so by inviting the spectators to take an extra look at (fictionalised versions of) bodies that are being moved on by changing architectural strategies. This invitation to the spectator sets all of the relations in motion, which necessitates a brief discussion of spectatorship here.

Perhaps the most famous discussion of spectatorship is Jacques Rancière's concept of the *emancipated spectator*. Rancière questions traditional assumptions that equate the gaze of the theatrical spectator with passivity and that place the pairings of "viewing/knowing, appearance/reality, activity/passivity" (Rancière 2009, p. 12) in opposition to one another. In his framing, these false equivalencies and oppositions "define a distribution of the sensible, an *a priori* distribution of the positions and capacities and incapacities attached to these positions" (p. 12). In an echo of Mirzoeff's concept of countervisuality, Rancière argues that spectators can be emancipated from this supposed passivity through an understanding that "viewing is also an action that confirms or transforms this distribution of positions" (p. 13). Though it is not particularly ground-breaking to suggest within the context of surveillance studies that viewing is an act imbued with agency, it is useful to consider what particular modes of spectatorship bring to bear on the theatrical spectacle. For Rancière, the spectator is emancipated by the fact that art is not a direct transmission from artist to audience. Rather, works of art have their own agency:

> There is the distance between artist and spectator, but there is also the distance inherent in the performance itself, in so far as it subsists, as a spectacle, an autonomous thing, between the idea of the artist and the sensation or comprehension of the spectator. (p. 14)

McKinney has built on this idea specifically within the context of scenography. She proposes the model of the "embodied spectator" to articulate how the act of looking at scenography is multi-sensory. In this model, scenography is "a material and spatial environment within which awareness and understanding can be triggered" (McKinney 2018, p. 112). Her conception is different from Rancière's in that it rejects his ultimate dismissal of spectacle as a theatre where audiences are "seduced by images" (Rancière 2009, p. 4). McKinney recuperates the notion of spectacle, arguing that:

> To look at scenography is to apprehend not only illustrations or depictions, but to notice the composition and orchestration of materials and feel the way they work on us at a bodily level. This is a way of knowing and a kind of action. (McKinney 2018, p. 115)

In *Tower*, it was the bodily presence of the spectators that produced the spatial performativity that emerged. The work was initially envisaged as a meditation on public and private space, intimacy and distance, and the way in which architecture might frame private performance. However, by placing the bodies of spectators in a real site with its own attendant realities, quotidian performances and materialities, these simple commentaries were thwarted and the site began to enact its own logic on the scenography and the performance. The precise way in which the site performed came as a surprise, rendering the performance unstable in unexpected ways by setting forth unpredictable relations between watcher and watched, and among spectators, performers and passers-by. The scenography was also deliberately staged in relation to the politics of the regeneration of the site, but done so in the knowledge that the way in which this relation would perform itself would not be entirely controllable.

In acknowledging the subjectivity of spectatorship, I must also acknowledge here that for those audience members unaware of the details of Elephant and Castle's regeneration, the biopolitics of the site would not have revealed themselves in quite the same way. However, to those without this prior knowledge, the presence of cranes and half-completed buildings throughout the site would still have made apparent the fact that this was in a site in a state of flux, potentially allowing the work to take on resonances relating to the biopolitics of development across London or in other locations. In this way, following Rancière, the work performed autonomously, a thing in itself between my intentions, the spectators and the site. However, following McKinney, it also utilised the orchestrated spectacle of the bodies and lights in the windows to produce the embodied spectator. Due to the points of connection between surveillance and spectatorship, and those between embodiment and architecture, scenography thus becomes a bridge between these paradigms and a potent site for understanding the relationship between architecture and surveillance.

Conclusion

Tower demonstrates that scenography is a fruitful lens for examining architecture, surveillance and power. On first reading, the work shows how scenography might comment on modernist architecture's disciplinary urges and reveal something of our ambivalent attitude to transparency and thus privacy in contemporary architecture and by extension contemporary life. While this is certainly a layer present within *Tower*, it perhaps more interestingly utilises surveillance as a strategy to reveal how urban planning is an instrument of *biopolitical* power.

Due to the pervasive nature of surveillance in our daily lives, there is a level of familiarity that we as contemporary subjects have with it. The relationship between watcher and watched is coded by its own disciplinary norms and understandings; we come with presuppositions about the power dynamic this relationship connotes. The way that we enact everyday performances in public space is also conditioned by disciplinary norms. These disciplinary norms and presuppositions make surveillance, as a cultural practice embedded in the built environment, a rich space in which to stage resistance. These practices of resistance can critique surveillance itself, revealing the complexities in how it operates in relation to architecture, and additionally utilise surveillance as a tool that might make visible bodies and power relations that were previously hidden.

Scenography has already been shown to challenge power structures within the built environment. By organising visually and spatially the relationship among performer, spectator and architecture, scenography can intervene productively *with* spaces of surveillance to reveal architecture's performance of power. By bringing scenography to bear on discussions of surveillance and architecture, we open up a space where buildings perform power in different temporalities, and where spectacle and spectator produce one another within a space of encounter.

Bibliography

Aronson, A. (2017). Foreword. In J. McKinney & S. Palmer (Eds.), *Scenography Expanded* (pp. xiii–xxvi). London/New York: Bloomsbury Methuen Drama.

Brejzek, T. (2011). On the Authoring of Space. In T. Brejzek (Ed.), *Expanding Scenography: On the Authoring of Space* (pp. 8–15). Prague: The Arts and Theatre Institute.

Brejzek, T. (2017). Between Symbolic Representation and New Critical Realism: Architecture as Scenography and Scenography as Architecture. In J. McKinney & S. Palmer (Eds.), *Scenography Expanded* (pp. 63–78). London/New York: Bloomsbury Methuen Drama.

Brooks, E., & Collins, J. (2017). Scenography Matters: Performing Romani Identities. In J. McKinney & S. Palmer (Eds.), *Scenography Expanded* (pp. 95–109). London/New York: Bloomsbury Methuen Drama.

Butler, J. (1990). *Gender Trouble*. New York/London: Routledge.

Colomina, B. (1996). *Privacy and Publicity: Modern Architecture as Mass Media*. Cambridge, MA: MIT Press.

Flynn, S., & Mackay, A. (Eds.). (2017). *Spaces of Surveillance: States and Selves*. Basingstoke: Palgrave.

Foucault, M. (1977). *Discipline and Punish: The Birth of the Prison*. Reprint, 1991. ed. London: Penguin.

Foucault, M. (2007). *Security, Territory, Population: Lectures at the College De France 1977–1978*. New York: Picador.

Gropius, W. (1935). *The New Architecture and the Bauhaus*. Reprint, 1956. ed. London: Faber and Faber.

Hall, R., Monahan, T., & Reeves, J. (2016). Editorial: Surveillance and Performance. *Surveillance & Society, 14*, 153–167.

Hannah, D. (2011). Event-Space: Performance Space and Spatial Performativity. In J. Pitches & S. Popat (Eds.), *Performance Perspectives: A Critical Introduction* (pp. 54–62). Basingstoke/New York: Palgrave Macmillan.

Hannah, D. (2015). Constructing Barricades and Creating Borderline Events. *Theatre and Performance Design, 1*, 126–143. https://doi.org/10.1080/23322551.2015.1032501

Hogue, S. (2016). Performing, Translating, Fashioning: Spectatorship in the Surveillant World. *Surveillance & Society, 14*, 168–183.

Irwin, K. (2008). The Ambit of Performativity: How Site Makes Meaning in Site-Specific Performance. In D. Hannah & H. Olav (Eds.), *Performance Design* (pp. 39–55). Copenhagen: Museum Tusculanum Press.

Lotker, S., & Gough, R. (2013). On Scenography: Editorial. *Performance Research, 18*, 3–6. https://doi.org/10.1080/13528165.2013.818306

Mcgrath, J. (2004). *Loving Big Brother: Surveillance Culture and Performance Space*. London/New York: Routledge.

Mcgrath, J. (2012). Performing Surveillance. In K. Ball, K. Haggerty, & D. Lyon (Eds.), *Routledge Handbook of Surveillance Studies* (pp. 83–90). London: Routledge.

McKinney, J. (2018). Seeing Scenography: Scopic Regimes and the Body of the Spectator. In A. Aronson (Ed.), *The Routledge Companion to Scenography*. Abingdon/New York: Routledge.

McKinney, J., & Palmer, S. (2017). Introducing "Expanded" Scenography. In S. Palmer & J. McKinney (Eds.), *Scenography Expanded: An Introduction to Contemporary Performance Design* (pp. 1–20). London/New York: Bloomsbury Methuen Drama.

McQuire, S. (2013). From Glass Architecture to Big Brother: Scenes from a Cultural History of Transparency. *Cultural Studies Review, 9*, 103–123. https://doi.org/10.5130/csr.v9i1.3587

Mirzoeff, N. (2011). The Right to Look. *Critical Inquiry, 37*, 473–496.

Monahan, T. (2011). Surveillance as Cultural Practice. *Sociological Quarterly, 52*, 495–508.

Monahan, T. (2015). The Right to Hide? Anti-Surveillance Camouflage and the Aestheticization of Resistance. *Communication and Critical/Cultural Studies, 12*, 159–178. https://doi.org/10.1080/14791420.2015.1006646

Morrison, E. (2015). Surveillance Society Needs Performance Theory and Arts Practice. *International Journal of Performance Arts and Digital Media, 11*, 125–130. https://doi.org/10.1080/14794713.2015.1084812
Morrison, E. (2016). *Discipline and Desire: Surveillance Technologies in Performance*. Ann Arbor: University of Michigan Press.
Ranciere, J. (2009). *The Emancipated Spectator*. London/New York: Verso.
Rufford, J. (2015). *Theatre and Architecture*. Basingstoke: Palgrave Macmillan.
Southwark Council, Mayor of London. (2012). *Elephant and Castle Supplementary Planning Document and Opportunity Area Planning Framework* Available at: https://www.southwark.gov.uk/planning-and-building-control/planning-policy-and-transport-policy/supplementary-planning-documents-spd/spd-by-area?chapter=6 (Accessed 1st April 2018).
Steiner, H., & Veel, K. (2011). Living Behind Glass Facades: Surveillance Culture and New Architecture. *Surveillance & Society, 9*, 215–232.
Thornett, L. (2018). Prosthetic Scenographies: Scenographic Extension of the Senses and Mediation of the Performance Space in *Tower*. *International Journal of Performance Arts and Digital Media*, 14, 1–16. https://doi.org/10.1080/14794713.2018.1413225
Tschumi, B. (1996). *Architecture and Disjunction*, First MIT Press Paperback Edition. Cambridge, MA: MIT Press.
Vidler, A. (1992). *The Architectural Uncanny*. Cambridge, MA: MIT Press.
von Arx, S. (2016). Unfolding the Public Space: Performing Space or Ephemeral Section of Architecture, PQ 2015. *Theatre and Performance Design, 2*, 82–94. https://doi.org/10.1080/23322551.2016.1183351
Wallenstein, S.-O. (2012). *Biopolitics and the Emergence of Modern Architecture*. Reprint edition. New York/London: Princeton Architectural Press.
Wehner, P. (2002 April 13). Profits Wrangle Proves to be Elephant's Graveyard. *Estates Gazette*, p. 39.
Whiteley, N. (2003). Intensity of Scrutiny and a Good Eyeful: Architecture and Transparency. *Journal of Architectural Education, 56*, 8–16. https://doi.org/10.1162/104648803321672915

PART II

Domestic Architecture and Houses of Horror

CHAPTER 5

Houses, Homes, and the Horrors of a Suburban Identity Politic

Jaclyn Meloche

Introduction

In *Architecture and Suburbia: From English Villa to American Dream House, 1690–2000*, architectural historian John Archer understands that the interior structure and location of a home are both dialogical and political apparatuses that contain a person (or family) as well as frame a body's identity. Not dissimilar to the conventions and principles surrounding society and selfhood established during the Enlightenment more than three centuries ago, he explains that Western values continue to position the self in relation to place. In other words, his argument is that the material world that surrounds the body needs to support both structurally and existentially the needs of the body. According to Archer, the Enlightenment philosophy, while framing a dialogical discourse between the self and society, also informs the ways in which architects, designers, and builders think about their profession: "[t]his laid important groundwork for architects, landscape designers, and eventually planners to provide new terms in which to formulate some material solutions to the existential challenges of Enlightenment selfhood" (Archer 2005, xvii).

J. Meloche (✉)
Art Gallery of Windsor, Windsor, ON, Canada

S. Flynn, A. Mackay (eds.), *Surveillance, Architecture and Control*,
https://doi.org/10.1007/978-3-030-00371-5_5

Drawing from Archer's theory that architecture is in essence performative, I am reminded of the ways in which transnational feminist scholar Chandra Talpade Mohanty understands home, belonging, and community vis-à-vis the gendered body. Similar to Archer, Mohanty argues that the design, layout, and geography of the home inform the conditions of selfhood, and subsequently identity as well as the body's social consciousness inside the home and within the confines of suburbia. By asking how does the architecture of a house (versus a home) inform an identity, and perhaps even a neighborhood's identity, Mohanty flirts with the idea that architecture and place are performative as well as models of social surveillance. Inspired by Hayeur's series of model homes, I ask, does architecture perform the body? Does suburbia perform the body? Moreover, when combined, do architecture and the politics of suburbia perform white middle-class consciousness?

In *Model Homes* (2004–2007), Montreal-based artist Isabelle Hayeur frames the construction and commercialization of suburban housing, suburban ideologies, and quite literally the foundations on which suburbia is built in a manner that blurs the lines between architecture and surveillance. In keeping with urban historians and feminist scholars who understand the built environment as performative, Hayeur's photographs entitled *Jade* (2004), *Nadia* (2004), *Ellen* (2005), *Tiffany* (2005), *Catherine* (2006), and *Cassandra* (2007) translate suburbia into a sprawling system of surveillance through the performativity of architecture. Likened to the artist's camera that documents the social circumstances of the body in real-time, place, and space, the model homes become embodied structures whose architecture and geography serve to manifest the ways in which bodies behave, live, and work in and around the domestic sphere as well as the suburban landscape.

Hayeur's decision to position large picturesque houses against modernist notions of home becomes a strategy for complicating the structures of family, community, and arguably the bourgeoisie. However, through a feminist lens, this body of work also instigates a political debate surrounding the ways in which suburbia functions as a system that controls the behaviors and belief systems inherent within the gendered body. As a result, Hayeur's photographs perform a critique of the complicated subculture that is suburbia and how its architecture, design, and layout embody performativity by imposing preconceived ideas pertaining to class, gender, and race onto the female body.

Depicting skeletons of houses that look anything like a home, each structure in Hayeur's photographs becomes what urban historians Dolores Hayden, Doreen Massey, and Pamela Moss argue is the primary role of feminist geography—to deconstruct the complex entanglements between place, space, and body in order to reframe gendered identity politics in Western urban cultural studies. In her edited collection of essays entitled *Feminist Geography in Practice: Research and Methods*, Moss explains the complexities surrounding what it means to practice feminist geography in contemporary society. In her own words, the latter is both an epistemological and methodological form of research in which "spatializing the constitution of identities, contextualizing meanings of places in relation to gender, and demonstrating how gender as a social construction intersects with other socially constructed categories within particular spatialities" (Moss 2002, 3).

In the context of my research on Isabelle Hayeur's photographs of model homes, the concept that place is performative frames my argument that both architecture and geography are dialogical in their inherent ability to construct selfhood—in particular a woman's identity both inside the home and within suburbia. Deeply embedded within postcolonialism and transnational feminism, Mohanty's theory is that a body's identity is rooted within one's cultural, economic, political, and social experience of belonging. More specifically, that a woman's spatial conditions inform her identity, surveil her social behavior, and subsequently ground her political consciousness. When paralleled with domestic architecture, can the argument that place is performative also apply? If so, then Isabelle Hayeur's model homes become symbols of the ways in which suburban architecture embodies performativity and enacts a model of social surveillance.

The Performativity of Architecture

Michel Foucault, a poststructural pioneer in the fields of power, sexuality, and modern spatial theory, established important economical and philosophical distinctions between the terms *place* and *space* arguing that each is inherently dialogical through the ways in which they establish power relationships between the body and society. In *Discipline and Punish: The Birth of the Prison*, one of the most influential investigations into power and the penal system in the twentieth century, Foucault argues that architectural structures, albeit the prison or the home, influence identity as well as the performance of human behavior. Or rather, as I understand it, that architecture is performative.

When appropriated as a methodology for surveillance, what is most significant in Foucault's writing is the notion that a structure embodies watching power, and thus serves as an apparatus that both watches and ultimately controls the subject of the gaze. Drawing from Jeremy Bentham's design of the Panopticon, Foucault exemplifies the ways in which watching vis-à-vis being watched become performatives that challenge the exchange of power between bodies and structures. In the context of postmodern architecture, Archer suggests that Foucault's appropriation of the Panopticon as an embodied structure for surveillance serves as a prime example of the ways in which new technologies are changing the kinds of lenses being deployed for controlled methods of observation. In his own words, "Foucault's approach focuses on the rise of nineteenth-century technologies such as measurement, classification, forensics, surveillance, recording, and cartography, and delineates the manner in which these could accord any given person an identity as unique as any point in a vast multidimensional matrix" (Archer 2005, 12).

When putting aside the metaphor of "discipline and punish," what remains at the core of Foucault's writing on power is the argument that architecture is agential, and thus has the inherent capability of surveillance. Likened to a vehicle for visibility, the performativity of architecture extends beyond a discourse of the penal system. In fact, Foucault notes that surveillance through architecture occurs in the public realm, the city, and the even the home: "[t]he camp is the diagram of a power that acts by means of general visibility. For a longtime this model of the camp or at least its underlying principle was found in urban development, in the construction of working-class housing estates, hospitals, asylums, prisons, schools: the spatial 'nesting' of hierarchized surveillance" (Foucault 1979, 171–172).

Since the 1970s, a shift in the study of human geography, and subsequently architecture has proposed to shift spatial theory into a relational and social investigation of the body. In this respect, then it is true what Foucault suggests that architecture is not solely intended to contain the body, but that it is a space through which to watch, influence, and perform human behaviors and subsequently social consciousness. "A whole problematic then develops: that of an architecture that is no longer built simply to be seen (as with the ostentation of palaces), or to observe the external space (the geometry of fortresses), but to permit an internal, articulated and detailed control–to render visible those who are inside it; in more general terms, an architecture that would operate to transform individuals: to act on those it shelters, to provide a hold on their conduct, to carry the effects of power right to them, to make it possible to know them, to alter them" (Foucault 1979, 172).

In keeping with Aristotelian and Heideggerian notions that architecture is performative is the idea that space is no longer characterized as a container for the body. According to Aristotle, space is qualified and quantified as an agent, an embodied phenomenon that does onto the body. But what does this say about the architect? Furthermore, who, or what in the field of architecture embodies material and spatial agency? According to Archer, "architects, theorists, and clients soon joined in a process, slow at first, more rapid by the nineteenth and twentieth centuries, that transformed the private dwelling into one of the most effective media for (literally) constructing that individuality" (Archer 2005, 4). Coupled with the notion that architecture is an instrument that has the ability to control and manipulate a thing or person, Hayeur's suburban homes thus become performatives—at least according to John L. Austin's definition of the word.

Historically rooted in linguistics and semiotics, Austin explains that a performative is born out of the inherent activity of a word: "it indicates that the issuing of the utterance is the performing of an action–it is not normally thought of as just saying something" (Austin 1962, 6–7). More specifically, performative depicts a conceptual method of doing that translates into an exchange and activation of agency in time and place. When appropriated as a theoretical framework for the interpretation of architecture through a feminist lens, performativity thus offers a language through which to understand how place, albeit a house or suburbia can influence, inform, and ultimately control an identity politic within society. When coupled with Hayeur's photographs of under construction and uninhabited model homes, Austin's theories on performativity offer a lens through which to complicate the static nature of a house. More than a container for the body, or a family, a house thus becomes a performative that ultimately *does* an identity. And when appropriated as a theoretical model for decoding Hayeur's photographs, performativity offers a critical framework for reconsidering the relationships between *Jade*, *Ellen*, and *Cassandra* and the gendered body in suburbia.

Framing Feminist Architecture

What is feminist architecture? Moreover, how does its discourse inform the performativity of suburban homes in Isabelle Hayeur's body of photographs entitled *Model Homes*? In nineteenth-century feminist writings about architecture, in particular the home, writer, educator, and amateur architect, Catharine Esther Beecher was among the first women to challenge the male-dominated world of domestic architecture. Although an early example of essentialist feminism, she believed that women were to nurture the interior of the home while men were expected to be responsible for the exterior of the home. And while an outdated notion, Beecher argued in the 1830s that domestic work was a woman's *true* responsibility inside the home. Riddled with problems, this statement, however, became the basis for the ways in which she would eventually complicate domestic architecture. In addition to renaming the traditionally gendered spaces inside the home, she redesigned and relocated their whereabouts to better serve the efficiency of women's work. For example, Beecher renamed the parlor the *home room*, the kitchen was changed to the *work room*, and the dining room would become the *family room*.

Arguably her most significant architectural intervention inside the home was the physical relocation of the kitchen from the basement onto the ground floor. Historically, the kitchen was located in the back of the home, or in the basement. The placement of this room in non-centralized locations in the home meant that women had additional physical demands put on their bodies in order to perform their duties. An activist for women's domestic labor rights, Beecher designed in her *Treatise on Domestic Economy* (1841) a preliminary floor plan that would help minimize domestic labor, thus making women's work in the home more painless and more efficient by relocating rooms, such as the kitchen as well as the nursery to the main floor of the home.

According to John Archer, "[m]uch of Beecher's concerns lay in the amount of labor demanded of women householders, a situation made worse by room plans that made concessions to what [Clarence] Cook would call 'social lives' at the expense of increased and inefficient labor" (Archer 2005, 198). In comparison to the patterns and trends that were popular in domestic architecture of the period, Beecher advocated for what Dolores Hayden names a *domestic feminism*: a "vision of domesticity [that] was explicitly gendered: women were to create a peaceful domestic world, removed from the stresses of work in the city, and although women would find themselves excluded from the political and economic arenas of public life, they would receive a reward in heaven for their self-sacrifice" (Hayden 2003, 35). Well before becoming its own critical discourse, Beecher's methods of feminist architectural intervention considered the needs of the gendered body inside the home in addition to the existential entanglements between selfhood and society.

Beecher's analysis of domestic architecture coupled with her contributions to design was grounded in what is today referred to as gender essentialism—a system of beliefs in which gender is considered innate and universal. By placing concrete boundaries between gender roles and the architecture of the home, she constructed assumed identities and stereotypical roles inside the home—roles that arguably continue to frame identity politics within suburban communities in the West: "[n]ineteenth-century authors addressed this spatial separation of influence by referring to the notion of "woman's sphere" or the "domestic sphere" (Archer 2005, 201). Lydia Sigourney did so as early as 1835 in *Letters to Young Ladies*, noting that "the sexes are manifestly intended for different spheres," those of women being what she called "eminently practical" in connection with her discussion of the science of housekeeping. However, it was termed the notion of the woman's sphere incorporated on its surface an understanding of the female as the one who physically maintained the household" (Archer 2005, 200–201).

As early as the eighteenth century, patriarchy remained at the heart of all domestic architectural designs. Spaces such as the nursery and the kitchen were traditionally designated "women's rooms," and not just because they were located in the basement of the home: "[t]he exterior, for example, often served to represent the beliefs and aspirations of the man, while the kitchen and nursery were domains in which the woman was the principal and sometimes sole presence" (Archer 2005, 201). In present day, the stereotype that the kitchen is a gendered space continues to perpetuate identity politics inside the home. And arguably in society at large.

With reference to Foucault's discourse of power vis-à-vis the gendered body, the kitchen becomes a curious space that is not dissimilar to the ways in which he understands as well as frames the architecture of a prison. In keeping with his argument that a prison is designed to observe and essentially control the body through surveillance, the kitchen in its new centrality within the home too becomes a space for watching and being watched. Colloquially known as "the heart of the home," Beecher's relocated kitchen thus replicates the positioning and function of Bentham's watch tower inside the Panopticon—the center tower structure where officers are able to surveil prisoners at all times.

A quintessential example of a gendered space embedded within suburban architecture, the kitchen thus translates into an Austinian performative. And while it is not a specific space of inquiry in Hayeur's photographs of model homes, the kitchen does remain a politically loaded domestic space in the context of suburban architecture. Moreover, when considered within the argument that architecture is performative through its disbursement of (watching) power, the kitchen, like a prison, becomes a political example for the ways in which surveillance can be deployed inside the home as well as within a suburban community. Drawing from Michel Foucault's theory that prisons are controlled structures that monitor the body's social behavior, the kitchen too becomes a controlled space that performs a woman's body inside the home as well as her social status within the confines of suburbia: "architecture [that] is no longer built simply to be seen, or to observe the external space...but to permit an internal, articulated and detailed control – to render visible those who are inside it; in more general terms, an architecture that would operate to transform individuals: to act on those it shelters, to provide a hold on their conduct, to carry the effects of power right to them, to make it possible to know them, to alter them" (Foucault 1979, 173).

According to Pierre Bourdieu, the architectural layout and design of a home historically informed gender roles within the home as well as the ways in which men and women behaved and interacted within the domestic sphere: "relations such as high (in a dais) and low (below stairs), facing and oblique, exposed (a dormitory) and enclosed (a private chamber) all establish social identities through bodily location and orientation" (Archer 2005, 11). Embedded within contemporary spatial theory coupled with poststructural and feminist geography, the gendered body becomes a contentious site for debate because space has been historically, philosophically, and theoretically framed by and *through* its inhabitant(s), its spectators, and according to Michel de Certeau, the identity of the *everyman*—the male body. In fact, although labeled a domestic feminism, even Beecher's understanding of space was quantified through the male body as well as the male gaze.

In her feminism, architect and urban historian Dolores Hayden argues that space, albeit urban or suburban, is shaped by and *through* the experience, behavior, history, and role of the gendered body. Although at first concerned with the aesthetics of place and the idea that architecture informs both the urban and suburban identity, Hayden's analysis understands the body as inherently dialogical: "[p]eople's experiences of the urban landscape intertwine the sense of place and the politics of space. If people's attachments to places are material, social and imaginative, then these are necessary dimensions of new projects to extend public history in the urban landscape, as well as new histories of American cultural landscapes and the buildings within them" (Hayden 1995, 43). In other words, it is impossible to separate (the space of) place from the body's identity.

In *The Power of Place: Urban Landscapes as Public History*, Hayden makes an important distinction between place and space arguing that both terms, although conceptually precarious, perform different relationships with the body, and subsequently identity politics. For example, place serves to situate the body, specifically the female body within a social hierarchy that has historically valorized the body's worth in urban studies: "[i]n the nineteenth century and earlier, place also carried a sense of the right of a person to own a piece of land, or to be a part of a social world, and in this older sense place contains more political history. Phrases like 'knowing one's place' or 'a woman's place' still imply both spatial and political meaning" (Hayden 1995, 16).

In keeping with an Aristotelian inspired understanding that place signifies the practice of localizing historical, philosophical, and political meaning, Hayden explains that place also represents the practice of identity politics writing that "[t]he politics of identity–however they may be defined around gender or race or neighborhood–are an inescapable and important aspect of dealing with the urban built environment, from the perspectives of public history, urban preservation, and urban design" (Hayden 1995, 7).

Parallel to Hayden's complication of the political and gendered hierarchies that continue to shape the urban landscape, Doreen Massey is also working to consider the binaries embedded within feminist geography as the result of the philosophical tensions characterized in debates between place and space. Writing through a Foucauldian lens, she inserts the problematic of identity politics into her inquiry to argue that place, such as suburbia is inherently influenced by gender relations and the subjectivity of the body. A necessary component of feminist geography is to consider the entangled relationships between place and the gendered body. According to Massey, place, like space, informs, and is informed by, the social relations that interact within it: "[t]hinking of places in this way implies that they are not so much bounded areas as open and porous networks of social relations. It implies that their identities are constructed through the specificity of their interaction with other places rather than by counterposition to them" (Massey 1994, 121).

Yet, by blurring these distinctions, Massey is dismantling the political hierarchies that have historically defined them. Rooted within a feminist strategy to complicate the gendered binaries inherent within Western urban cultural studies, she is challenging the politics that define the boundaries of place within space—or rather the kitchen within the suburban home—to reevaluate that ways in which a gendered identity becomes the result of performative architecture within both suburbia and feminist geography. According to Archer, "[b]uilt space is a critical element of the reference system within which knowledge is produced and applied, and the physical forms according to which people establish and discipline their lives are correspondingly instruments for shaping social relations" (Archer 2005, 11).

The gendered dichotomies that are historically inherent within architecture not only serve to perform the body inside the home, but also inform the exterior of the structure—at least according to Isabelle Hayeur. In a direct response to the ways in which the home is spatially classified, in particular that the exterior of the home is male, and the interior of the home is female, Hayeur's *Model Homes* propose to complicate the stereotypical distinctions that have historically defined the architecture and spatial organization of the home. For example, each home in the series is given the title of a traditional female name, such *Jade*, *Nadia*, *Ellen*, *Tiffany*, *Catherine*, and *Cassandra*. By gendering the typically suburban homes located within sprawling, yet isolating landscapes, Hayeur is complicating the traditional methods of gendering the home, and subsequently domestic architecture. By blurring the architectural lines between a home's exterior façade and its (invisible) interior, she is challenging the essentialist feminist associations that historically defined domestic space in the nineteenth century.

By assigning female names to each home, Hayeur both critiques the growing sprawl of suburban communities in Quebec as well as dismantles the gendered stereotypes that historically defined the home. Yet, this so-called feminist intervention is more than an aesthetic complication of gender stereotypes vis-à-vis architecture. The photographs, while they focus on the architecture of the home also question the surrounding suburban landscapes in which the homes are located. Extending beyond a discourse of urban cultural studies, Hayeur's series of model homes too are embedded within a discourse of social feminism. More than studies of suburban architecture, they instigate critical debates about the very nature of suburbia and the ways in which living on the periphery performs selfhood and identity politics in the West.

Resembling inhabited homes occupied by families with cars in the driveways, and holiday decorations that adorn the front yards, *Tiffany*, *Catherine*, *Cassandra* act as stages occupied by the *perfect* family. Characteristic of the typical middle-class family home, these houses contribute to a romanticized idea of the suburban family. Expanding upon Andrew Jackson Downing's contributions to middle-class suburban landscapes and Beecher's definition that describes the perfect domestic life as one that perpetuates gendered hierarchies within the home, Hayeur's *Model Homes* become existential mirages. In their perfect, yet skeletal states, each house translates into a performative that serves to control the gendered body inside the home, and subsequently suburban identity politics in the West.

Suburbia and Surveillance

What is suburbia? Moreover, what are the particulars of the suburban home? Originally referred to as the borderlands, suburbia was born in the mid-1800s by developers who believed that by extending their reach onto the newly established subdivided property, they could promote urban living on the peripheries and create new communities for capital growth. In response to the borderland architecture that was becoming more and more popular in the early 1800s, architects and landscape architects became increasingly interested in designing and building what Dolores Hayden refers to as "picturesque enclaves"—picture-perfect communities with manicured lawns, flawless landscaping, and large beautiful homes that look soulless and unlived in, just like they do in *Model Homes.* Although *Ellen* and *Jade* are literally shells that are under construction, their desolate location offers a brief glimpse into the beginnings of the picturesque enclaves that today are the foundation for suburbia. In "her" post-construction state, *Catherine* looks like a mini castle designed with a small turret, a limestone facade, a surrounding moat, and keeps that decorate the rooftop. In other examples, *Cassandra* and *Tiffany*, although adorned with more subtle castle-like features, flirt in a more direct fashion with Hayden's definition of an enclave. With hints of homes, community, and people in the distance, these homes represent early signs that an enclave is being born.

In the context of urban cultural studies, Hayden explains that "[p]icturesque enclaves were the most important secular manifestations of a wider communitarian movement whose adherents believed that building a model community in a natural setting led to the reform of society" (Hayden 2003, 45). In other words, suburbia translates into a pattern for social reform instigating gradual change in a community—changes that pertain to systems of class, gender, and race as well as the social politics that influence the roles and rights of the body both inside and outside of the home. Moreover, that said community patterns of reform (in the early nineteenth century) perpetuated mythic models of families living in the borderlands.

"If suburban space has sometimes resisted ethnic diversity, it has been even less accommodating to changes in household composition and women's roles. Men of all classes have portrayed the suburban home as a retreat from the cares of their jobs. But since the time of the borderlands, houses have been workplaces for millions on women of all classes and all ages – paid cooks, cleaning women, and nannies, as well as unpaid housewives and mothers" (Hayden 2003, 13). Constructed of the stereotypical white middle-class family consisting of a husband who works in the city, a mother who works inside the home as a homemaker, and children who bus into a nearby school, suburbia was born a space for racial, religious, and class segregation: "[e]thnicity and gender, to mention only the two most obvious other axes, are also deeply implicated in the ways in which we inhabit and experience space and place, and the ways in which we are located in the new relations of time-space compression" (Massey 1994, 164). Through a political lens, suburbia functioned as a model for surveillance serving as an apparatus that controlled gender roles, social ideologies, religious beliefs as well as the overall consciousness of a community.

At the turn of the twentieth century, French sociologist Emile Durkheim questioned the traditional formation and patterning of the borderlands noting that they perpetuated a particular suburban hierarchy, one that embodied the psychology in addition to the economy of the white middle class. Through its function of community segregation and social control over the body, suburbia developed a certain level of power over selfhood by influencing one's identity inside its boundaries. According to John Archer, "[b]y documenting homologies among the physical spaces that a people inhabited, the clans and other apparatuses by which they organized their collective interests, and the cosmic spaces of their belief system, Durkheim analytically examined the instrumentality of built space in the production of consciousness" (Archer 2005, 9). In essence, his argument was that suburbia, albeit its geography, its architecture, and/or its politically charged belief system, informed the basis for Western modern consciousness.

In keeping with the argument that architecture is performative, Durkheim argues that the social conditions of the borderlands serve a performatives within society demonstrating a dialogical power over the body, selfhood, and the overall Western expectations of social roles, both inside and outside of suburbia.

In the discourse of human geography and subsequently poststructural spatial theory, the idea that place performs the body is not revolutionary per se. In his contributions to the study and practice of social productions within the West, French sociologist Henri Lefebvre believes that spatial theory is a more inclusive system of analogy that considers the representation of space, the experience of space, spatial relationships, and lastly, the power of space vis-à-vis the gendered body. Through a Marxist lens, Lefebvre argues that space is a social, economic, and representational site for production noting that "[i]t is reasonable to assume that spatial practice, representations of space and representational spaces contribute in different ways to the production of space according to their qualities and attributes, according to the society or mode of production in question, and according to the historical period" (Lefebvre 1991, 46).

Although writing some 50 years before Lefebvre, Durkheim understood space, in particular the social structures that define space as dialogical. And in the context of *Model Homes*, his argument serves as a methodology through which to shift suburbia from being the economic result of industrialization in an urban landscape into a neoliberal and social experiment that is ultimately performative: "[a]s such, space articulates many of the parameters according to which personal identity is established. Put another way, because built spaces shape what people do and how they live in highly specific ways, they also necessarily shape who those people are" (Archer 2005, 5).

In contemporary popular culture, the subject of suburbia, both as a social system for identity politics and as a model of surveillance, has become a growing topic of critical debate. In addition to challenging the locational boundaries as well as conservative ideologies that frame its landscape, non-urban spaces wedged on the periphery of a city have become metaphors for the performativity of social and political control within a community. Although more problematic is the idea that suburbia, like the Panopticon, functions as a structure that facilitates watching, and subsequently the act of being watched.

In the 2010 song *Sprawl II (Mountains Beyond Mountains)*, written and performed by the Canadian indie rock band Arcade Fire, the lyrics embody just the right amount of neoliberal criticism, fear, and pessimism that comes from growing up in the suburbs. Born in Montreal, but raised in the suburbs of St-Lambert, Quebec, lead singer Régine Chassagne's interpretation of the song's lyrics transport listeners into the complex social and gendered networks that urban geographers are challenging and destabilizing in what they refer to as the borderlands: "a place where prosperous families who disliked urban congestion might set up housekeeping, lured by the scenic charm of living near farmers' fields and woods" (Hayden 2003, 22). In the spirit of an ethnographer, the Montreal-based musician reflects on her childhood experiences of suburbia to understand how its construction and socioeconomic foundations continue to define both the gendered body and the political systems that make up her contemporary society. Referencing Marxist colloquialisms in the lyrics, Chassagne echoes the monotony and sameness that are threaded throughout the majority of suburban communities in North America. Moreover, through a first person narrative and their ubiquitous references to the aesthetics, culture, and topography of suburbia, the band transcends the lines between their personal experience of place and their listeners' own individual interpretations of it to prevent essentializing the social structures and social effects inherent within living in the suburbs.

However, while the individuality of the experience is clear, what translates as a commonality between the lyrics of the song and theories of performativity is the notion that suburban architecture does onto the body. For example, Arcade Fire sings the lyrics "[d]ead shopping malls rise like mountains beyond mountains" (Arcade Fire 2010) as a metaphor for the economic changes that ultimately frame the topography of the suburbs. While predominantly residential, suburban landscapes are not solely made up of large picturesque enclaves as depicted in *Model Homes*, they are also home to miles of commercial and industrial spaces. In addition to mass produced homes that often resemble one another, and similar square foot lots that span miles, suburban communities also contain miles of retail spaces, such as the increasingly popular big-box stores, outdoor outlet malls, and ever-popular Costco's found in almost every borderland around the world. "Describing suburbia as a residential landscape would be wrong, however, because suburbs also contain millions of square feet of commercial and industrial space, and their economic growth outstrips that of older downtowns" (Hayden 2003, 3).

Through a feminist lens, Hayden is critical of suburbia describing it as a falsified sense of community through its social, cultural, and economic lacks: "[t]he residents' hope of unspoiled nature fails because open land vanishes with increased development. Their hope of community is betrayed when tracts of houses, hyped as ideal 'communities,' lack social and economic centers, parks, schools, and necessary infrastructure. Contestation—between residents who wish to enjoy suburbia and developers who seek to profit from it—lies at the heart of suburban history" (Hayden 2003, 9). A model of society founded on patterns of political exclusivity, suburbia thus exemplifies constructed concepts of both community and identity through the ways in which its embodied performativity both frames and surveils the body, in time and place.

Conclusion

In this chapter, the politics of the Panopticon coupled with research in urban cultural studies and feminist geography offers a strategy through which to consider the architecture of suburbia as a form of surveillance. Although historically designed for the purpose of organizing urban settlements within smaller villages, suburbia has become a performative vehicle through which to frame gender and identity politics in the fields of economics, history, geography, and arguably contemporary art.

Organized into three distinct sections, "The Performativity of Architecture," "Framing Feminist Architecture," and "Suburbia and Surveillance," architecture, in particular the architecture of suburban homes found in the confines of the borderlands becomes the subject of critical debate. No longer solely understood as the physical structure that contains the bodies of a family, exemplifies the patterns of Western consciousness, and subsequently defines the gendered roles within the household, the architecture of suburbia translates into a dialogical structure that in essence performs the body as well as perpetuates the ideologies on which its belief system is based upon. To be blunt, suburbia translates into an architectural and systematic network that embodies the power of surveillance.

In the context of Isabelle Hayeur's body of work entitled *Model Homes (2004–2007)*, the Panopticon becomes an architectural metaphor through which to deconstruct the empty and soulless homes that sit idle in sprawling borderland landscapes as well as challenge the gender roles that are perpetuated within the suburbs. More specifically, Hayeur's work stages the stereotypes of suburbia and the ways through which they continue to perform the gendered body inside the home. Through a feminist lens, while *Tiffany*, *Catherine*, and *Cassandra* are strategic reminders of the aesthetics that shape the suburbs, they also shift the preconceived notions that have historically defined the interior of the home as female and the exterior of the home as male. In their various states of construction, *Jade*, *Nadia*, and *Ellen*, in comparison, are early instigators of the ways in which domestic architecture, through a feminist lens, complicates the gendered spaces that make up the home in contemporary art.

In the context of feminist geography, suburbia, although a socioeconomic method for mapping the boundaries of urban and non-urban communities, translates into a political strategy for segregation-turned-surveillance—the surveillance of class, gender, and race. And when considered through Hayeur's *Model Homes*, the architecture of this neighborhood becomes an ideal case study for deconstructing the entangled relationships between non-urban communities, the gendered body, the racial body, and dare I say Marxism in the twenty-first century. Albeit in the writing and research of urban cultural historians, the contributions to contemporary spatial theory by feminist scholars, such as Dolores Hayden, Doreen Massey, and Pamela Moss, or the lyrics to Arcade Fire's anthemic song *Sprawl II (Mountains Beyond Mountains)*, the complicated and politically layered subject of suburbia becomes a powerful system for watching, monitoring, and ultimately controlling the horrors of a suburban identity politics.

In conclusion, whether drawing from the Canadian indie rock band Arcade Fires' politically charged songwriting, Michel Foucault's contributions to discourses of power and sexuality, or Hayden's approach to domestic feminism, this chapter is evidence that the material and philosophical ways in which the performativity of architecture becomes a device used for practicing surveillance challenge the stereotypical identity politics that have been perpetuated inside non-urban homes for centuries. In other words, when architecture is deployed as a feminist strategy for deconstructing the economics of identity politics inside the frame of domesticity, the results parallel Canadian artist Isabelle Hayeur's dark interpretations of suburban architecture.

Bibliography

Arcade Fire, *Sprawl II (Mountains Beyond Mountains)*. (2010). Merge Records (North America), Mercury Records (United Kingdom), #15 on *The Suburbs,* Studio Album.

Archer, J. (2005). *Architecture and Suburbia: From English Villa to American Dream House, 1690–2000.* Minneapolis/London: University of Minnesota Press.

Austin, J. L. (1962). *How to Do Things with Words.* Cambridge, MA: Harvard University Press.

Foucault, M. (1979). *Discipline and Punish: The Birth of the Prison.* New York: Vintage Books, Random House, Inc.

Hayden, D. (1995). *The Power of Place: Urban Landscapes as Public History.* Cambridge, MA: MIT Press.

Hayden, D. (2003). *Building Suburbia: Green Fields and Urban Growth 1820–2000.* New York: Vintage Books.

Lefebvre, H. (1991). *The Production of Space* (trans: Nicholson-Smith, D.). Oxford: Blackwell.

Massey, D. (1994). *Space, Place and Gender.* Minneapolis: University of Minnesota Press.

Moss, P. (Ed.). (2002). *Feminist Geography in Practice: Research and Methods.* Oxford: Blackwell Publishers, Inc.

CHAPTER 6

One Grey Wall and One Grey Tower: The Bates World in Alfred Hitchcock's *Psycho*

Subarna Mondal

Introduction

Alfred Hitchcock throughout *Psycho* (and perhaps throughout his oeuvre) grappled with the problem of how to gain an adroit, precise, and detailed control over domestic space—to make visible those who reside within it. He was looking for an architecture that would prove instrumental in transforming the inhabitants and their relationship with one another, in affecting them, in making them aware of the pervasive effects of power, and in changing them.

Psycho (1960) has been filmed at a crucial stage of American surveillance history. The post-World War II cultural climate was ripe for debates over the relationship between the individual and the state. The extremes of Cold War security and the consequent proliferation of concerns regarding privacy shaped the modern rhetoric of surveillance and the ambivalence inherent in it. The 1950s and 1960s noir films often brought forth in crime narratives this dilemma of preserving or destroying the sanctity of a private precinct. Private space thus became a paradoxical site. *Psycho* (1960) may be seen as a significant product of an age that was grappling

S. Mondal (✉)
P. R. Thakur Government College, West Bengal, India

S. Flynn, A. Mackay (eds.), *Surveillance, Architecture and Control*,
https://doi.org/10.1007/978-3-030-00371-5_6

with the idea of control through surveillance, was interrogating its efficacy, and was pondering over the dilemmas inherent in the clear demarcation of private/public sphere that also formed a major concern of Cold War literature. The primary setting of *Psycho* (1960) may itself be read both as a contrast and an interpermeation of the private/public sphere. While the Bates house is initially emblematic of a zealous demarcation between private and public, the Bates motel is a product of post-war roadside commercial architecture that brings forth the fluidity of the private/public divide.

Analytical Framework

This chapter aims at using home and its architecture as used in Alfred Hitchcock's *Psycho* (1960) to show how the all-pervasive practice of surveillance penetrates the most private of spaces. It attempts to examine the various levels and sources of surveillance—the viewer, the on-screen characters, the filmmaker, and the formal state authority—through a careful rummaging of architecture and the domestic space within. Theoretical underpinning is sought to be provided through surveillance studies as an analytical prop that has been applied in detailed shot and site analysis of the Bates world. In exploring the motifs of horizontal and vertical structures, peepholes, window blinds, empty eye sockets, glass-eyed stuffed birds and the role they play as architectural props to further ideas of surveillance in *Psycho* (1960), it is necessary to situate the dissertation within a theoretical framework that draws upon disciplinary discourses and traces significant trends in surveillance studies.

Foucault: A Layered Discourse of Panopticon and Panopticism Surveillance, according to Michel Foucault, plays a significant role in shaping the architecture of modern institutions. Foucault situates the permeation of private and public sphere in the institutions of the Enlightenment through a thorough account of the corrective tools of modern states and the confessional mode of modern subjectivity. Foucault in *Discipline and Punish* (first published in 1975) takes Bentham's panopticon as a dominant model for a broader social study.

The subjugation of the setting to the logic of the look forms the premise of panopticon. Subjecting the space to a single point of observation, Jeremy Bentham's design of a spherical building with central surveillance unit that would perform the task of controlling individuals was an apt construction that would cater to the demands of all institutions dealing with human regulation. Power in this construct is vested, not in the hands of a particular authority, but in the meticulous plotting and arrangement of light, scrutiny, and architecture. Power is derived from a supposedly constant observation of a perpetually visible subject.

For Foucault, it is the unverifiability of the presence or absence of the observer that ensures obedience and conformity of a subject within a panopticon structure (1991, p. 201). However, Foucault places equal emphasis on the processes and measures that locate individuals in a corrective discourse. Foucault's discussion on "Panopticism" begins with a description of the cautionary steps taken by seventeenth-century state authorities to curb the contagious spread of plague. Surveillance may thus be seen as one of the features of panopticism which has a wider social significance that embraces technologies of control, the categorisation of subjects, and a pervasive impact on individual self-analysis. Punishment, investigation, scrutiny, surveillance, fixed routine, and rigid code of conduct all perform together to construct a regime of institutional control that works as much through self-examination and self-policing of the inmates as through coercion.

Psycho and Hypersurveillance Foucault's analysis of a disciplinary discourse is taken to the next level by a number of surveillance studies in the years that followed. Anthony Giddens in *The Nation-State and Violence* (1985) considers surveillance as a rationalising structure in the composition of modern nation-states. David Lyon, on the other hand, speaks of "surveillance *society*" rather than just a surveillance state in "Surveillance, Power and Everyday Life" (2007). Highly advanced information and communication technologies and data processing programs have in recent years brought about a new phase of hypersurveillance where panopticism prevails without the control mechanism of the panopticon. Roger Clarke terms this invisible web of scrutinising the everyday life of individuals through such advanced technologies as "dataveillance" (1988).

However, the coupling of surveillance with discipline may not always be applicable in the private/public debate. Surveillance is a nuanced concept that is not always limited to discipline. In *Psycho* (1960), Hitchcock explores various facets of surveillance—the observer and the observed, the predator and the victim, the film, the filmmaker, and the audience are seen through various lenses of surveillance: from surveillance of the self to surveillance of the other, from surveillance associated with discipline to surveillance associated with transgression, from the efficacy of surveillance to the futility of surveillance. *Psycho* (1960) becomes a cinematic space that often stages the subversion of control mechanism. Surveillance, in *Psycho* (1960), cannot at times be separated from voyeurism, speculation, and introspection.

Alfred Hitchcock's *Psycho* (1960) shows a world where dataveillance, cyberveillance, and mobiveillance (Lyon 2007) are yet to arrive. Though *Psycho* (1960) is filmed in an overall atmosphere of suspicion and mistrust, a world where CCTV has already been introduced, it nevertheless remains a world where a private investigator has to hop around more than two hundred motels before he reaches his destination; a world where a woman, without the convenience of a GPS, loses her way in blinding rain; a world without digital surveillance or cell phone tracking devices, where the information regarding a fugitive has to be attained through letters, photographs, and motel registers, and yet it is a world where almost every frame has the feel of prying.

The camera here acts as the agent of surveillance as the audience ironically has a foreboding of a presence that is actually absent. Mrs Bates' prying eyes, we presume, pervade the entire narrative. But Mrs Bates is an illusion, the source of an empty gaze. *Psycho* (1960) departs from previous horror films where the monsters are real, like a Dracula or a Frankenstein's Creation; or a monster within, like a Hyde or a Dorian Gray; or non-human like a Godzilla or a Zombie. It is the invisible but potent surveillance of a Mother who does not exist that *Psycho* (1960) exploits: a feature that prefigures the mechanism of hypersurveillance in this digital age—an age where invisible and therefore inescapable surveillance is the order of the day.

Thematically the film pivots around a constant fear of being watched. The numerous windows in front of the Phoenix hotel room, the eyes of the highway patrolman behind reflecting shades, Marion's (Janet Leigh) constant peering into the rear view mirror, the dead birds watching over Marion and Norman (Anthony Perkins), the peephole behind the picture of *Susannah and the Elders* (another drama of being watched and ravaged), the Mother's invisible eyes watching over the motel rooms, and the prison cell with its thousand imaginary eyes, are continuous, unrelieved narratives of relentless surveillance. *Psycho* in 1960 speaks of the all-encompassing influence of surveillance that has seeped into "everyday life, at work, at home, at play, on the move" (Lyon 2003, p. 13).

Visual Trope: The Vertical and the Horizontal

The 1950s America witnessed a post-war boom in photojournalism and a rise in television viewing that prompted the overall gritty look of *Psycho* (1960). Compared to the lush extravagance of *North by Northwest* (1959) and the dreamy melancholy of *Vertigo* (1958), *Psycho* (1960) is bare, drab, and minimal. The grim details and news photography of the grisly killing in Wisconsin (on which the novel *Psycho* (first published in 1959) and in its turn the film *Psycho* (1960) are based) along with Ed Gein's menagerie littered with hacked bodies may have inspired motifs of confinement, claustrophobia, and voyeurism in Hitchcock's film.

From the window blinds through which the camera peers in the Phoenix hotel room to the first shot of Marion supine on bed and Sam standing beside the bed, from the vertical position of the highway patrolman and the horizontal movement of the cars on the highway, the vertical slashing down of rain and the horizontal movement of Marion's car's wipers, to the famous architectural contrast between the vertical mansion and the horizontal motel, one can find instances that metaphorically bring forth the idea of a pervasive presence of invisible entrapment. Being watched is being confined in a way.

The Motel

Chester Liebs in *Main Street to Miracle Mile* (first published in 1985) while tracing the evolution of American roadside architecture from the early 1900s to the 1970s gives us a history of the origin and development of highway motels.

Free makeshift camps of the pre-war years gave way to free municipal motor camps after World War I. The end of 1920s witnessed the rise of private campgrounds and home stays. The 1930s was a time for private cabin camps as the business class discovered that travellers were willing to pay more for permanent structures for private accommodation. These cabins were sparse with minimal facilities and are described by Liebs as "[w]ooden enclosures with screened openings, often without furniture" (1995, p. 174). The term "camp" was gradually replaced by a more sophisticated term "court" that suggests a more decent reserve. The interiors of these motor-courts were more lavish compared to the earlier scant amenities of private cabins. Liebs states: "Real beds, dressers, desks, rugs, lamps, pictures ... helped make cabins feel less like camp and more like a guest's own bedroom" (1995, p. 177).

While the beginning of World War II saw the architectural profession and magazines like *Tourist Court Journal* urging the motel owners to adopt a more modern and sleek motor court interior, the post-war years witnessed a change in architecture of roadside courts that paid closer attention to a Spartan decor. The term "court" was ousted by the word "motel" (a retrenchment of the terms "motorist hostel" and "motor hotel", Liebs 1995, p. 182). By the end of the 1940s, the word "motel", extolled in neon, dotted American wayside to attract the road-weary transients.

Home had become a very dear concept especially after the insecure heady days of the War. Liebs cites *Hotel Management*'s recommendation of furniture and accessories that were required in a "proper" motel room: "Heavy Chenille bed spreads; Percale sheets.- Dresser with large mirror; Writing desk … Two large easy chairs … Large floor lamp, bed lamp … Cross ventilation … Bathrooms have: Tile shower; Plastic shower curtain; Bath mat; Facial tissue in chrome container … Three bars of soap; Four face towels, four bath towels, two wash cloths" (as mentioned in Liebs 1995, p. 183).

The evolution of the motel, in keeping with contemporary commercial architectural prescriptions, suggests that a constant supervision should be carried out so that every article is painstakingly plotted. It is the repetitiveness of one particular way of living that is being dished out. And travellers snuggle back to that mundane routine so that they can be ready for the next day's adventure. The motels try to assert to the road-weary traveller that it is the routine of soft beds, clean sheets, and a hot bath that replenishes us. These spaces regulate us, organise us, and discipline us after the heady ventures of the road. Home is associated with routines, with regulated movements and predictable transformations.

In contrast to a tent, a motel by replicating the space called "home" pre-arranges and somewhat choreographs actions and movements of the guest through a meticulous arrangement of familiar interior and its accessories. In *Psycho* (1960), for instance, the peephole is strategically made on the wall facing the bathroom as that would be a predictable place where a guest would take off her clothes. Or, conversely, by situating the bathroom opposite the wall with the peephole, the motel owner here predetermines the guest's action of stripping in front of the peephole. The architectural arrangement within a motel room manipulates a guest's movements. The architectural costumery pre-organises a guest's actions that they perform within their home and prompts them to act out those same actions under a stranger's roof. Thus, the transformation of roadside dwelling from "camps" to "courts" to "cabins" and finally to "motels" is also a history of a gradual transformation of a backpacker with tins and pots and tents from subjecting his/her body to the vicissitudes of roadside unpredictability, to gradually being lured within the comfortable folds of a pseudo-home at the end of the day. The motel with its carefully plotted architecture pays close attention to a return to routine that would ensure the reconstruction of a predictable body.

Cabin No. 1

The Bates motel in *Psycho* (1960) is exactly the kind of conventional post-war American wayside motel that Leibs speaks of in *Miracle Miles*. The draft of the motel consists of an L-shaped floor plan with a front office, a back parlour, and a series of 12 cabins. The interior is not lavish but is equipped with basic amenities required by a fatigued traveller. Despite the apparent air of privacy, the motel room ironically brings forth the idea of visibility and openness. The room that Marion occupies renders her vulnerable as the room has a peephole on a wall. Door, a pair of windows, a mirror, and a peephole give the room an air of porosity. Even the bathroom is made of "wild walls" that can be removed and rearranged according to the wishes of the filmmaker. Marion within such an open shelter in a roadside motel seems vulnerable.

This vulnerability of Marion becomes more prominent after her death as Norman searches the room to wipe off her material remnants: her clothes, her shoes, her handbag, her money, and her body. It ironically reminds us of hotel rooms being cleaned after the departure of a guest: the careful scrutiny and wiping off of the remnants of a lived-in space of the previous occupant as the room gets sanitised again to receive the imprints of the next occupant. We leave our marks behind in waste bins, in bedspreads, in drawers, in wardrobes, in ashtrays, and in washrooms that are subjected to scrutiny and then erased as they are prepared for fresh marks of the next boarder. Our lived moments are thus witnessed in burnt cigarette butts, dirty towels, empty condom packets, used sanitary napkins, and indents on bed. Waste bins, ashtrays, bed sheets, towels, wash basins, and bath tubs become texts of our sexual, gustatory, and scatological narratives that remain open to investigation and speculation which in turn may prescribe preventive surveillance. It is like revisiting the past with wastes and remnants of lived body/bodies as signs to recreate what has passed before (a recurrent feature in crime fictions).

The Parlour, the Birds, and the Peephole

The architectural arrangement of the Bates motel in Hitchcock's *Psycho* (1960) includes a parlour. The parlour contains two important motifs that are intimately related to surveillance and voyeurism: the stuffed birds and the peephole.

It is the peephole that renders Marion's room vulnerable as it becomes a device that merges the two spaces—the room and the parlour—and disrupts the privacy of space that a motel should ensure. The peephole succeeds in creating a new cinematic space. The composition of the shots that follow are a study in contrast as the darkness of the parlour is juxtaposed with the luminous tiles and light of the bathroom that Marion is about to enter. The peephole sequence is choreographed in the following manner: Norman is framed in a close shot between two birds whose dead eyes watch him intently while he removes the picture of *Susannah and the Elders* to reveal a deep gash beneath, that, in turn, reveals the space in front of Marion's bathroom. Here voyeurism of Norman is coupled with the surveillance of his mother. The eyes of the dead birds replicate Mother's accusingly watchful eyes. But, ironically, it is the surveillance of the dead.

The screenplay reads the parlour as "a room of birds … beautiful, grand, horrible, preying" (quoted by Rebello 1990, p. 69). In *Psycho* (1960), Norman stuffs birds to "fill" his "empty" time. The recreated birds reflect Norman's need to construct passive docile bodies. The parlour scene shows Norman in long shots framed or rather "trapped" amid birds who watch him in a dense dark composition. Norman seems surrounded and captured in this world of recreated corpses as the birds watch him while he watches Marion. It seems that the compliant bodies that Norman has littered throughout the parlour not only remain sites of the creator's desire but also become a source of a life-like gaze.

Surveillance takes vulnerability of the body as its premise. The destruction of a natural body by making it constantly conscious of being scrutinised closely, and the consequent recreation of an indoctrinated body, and its preservation by that same process of continued *imagined* surveillance is how the process of indoctrination functions. These three methods of control find a more pronounced corporeal version in the art of taxidermy.

Taxidermy has been a rich source of study in colonial and gender discourses as it predominantly rests on the power relationship between the predator and the prey. Donna Haraway in *Primate Visions* (1989) looks upon the enterprise of taxidermy as "the commerce of power and knowledge in white and male supremacist monopoly capitalism" (p. 21). Rachel Poliquin in *The Breathless Zoo* (2012) considers how a taxidermied body serves as a signifier of Oriental exoticism (p. 87). Thus, destruction, recreation, restriction, control, and the use and abuse of a body that would serve the interests of those in power find a concrete materialistic presence in the stuffed birds of the Bates motel parlour (*Did He Smile His Work to See*, Mondal 2017).

The Bathroom

Commode, the flushing of a toilet and a girl hacked to death while taking a shower are unprecedented instances in Hollywood filmmaking till 1960. In *Psycho* (1960), it is the architecture of the bathroom that stages the most dramatic moment of the narrative. The bathroom conventionally relates to hygiene and replenishment. But it also has its associations with waste and excrement. In *Psycho* (1960), the bathroom is filmed as dazzlingly white with no hint of a shadow. The horizontal cells of Panopticon too, we may recall, were flooded by light. There too fear of being under surveillance lurks in light. Darkness becomes an integral part of the comfort and reassurance of light in Hitchcock sets (the crop-duster attack in *North by Northwest*, the corpse floating by a glittering Thames in *Frenzy* [1972] the dead body stumbled upon amid rolling Vermont hills in a bright autumnal afternoon in *The Trouble with Harry* [1955]).

In *Psycho* (1960), Hitchcock has to achieve the maximum effect of the shower-murder horror in a mise-en-scene constricted within a minute space where he cannot afford to show either the murderer clearly or the direct nakedness of Marion. He thus resorts to extreme splitting of shots—a tremendously fast-paced montage burst of stabbing and screaming carried out by extreme close-ups and strategic marginal revelation of the victim's anatomy. After the ruthless stabbing, and the abrupt departure of the murderer, Marion is left to die alone. Rem Koolhas, the curator of the 2014 Venice Biennale exhibition on architectural components, describes bathroom as "the fundamental zone of interaction – on the most intimate level – between humans and architecture" (Stamp 2014). Hitchcock here shows the interaction between the polished steel of toilet accessories and the thin stain of blood that meanders towards the drain.

Hitchcock through a series of close shots frames the helpless stark body of Marion amidst inanimate objects that fill the screen. The montage of the shower head, the crushed shower curtain, the cold bathtub, the sterile walls, and the gaping mouth of the drain in a dazzlingly white bathroom blatantly brings forth the reduction of a lively young human being into a wasted body at the mercy of our eager gaze. The filming of the surrounding objects amid which Marion is awkwardly sprawled succeeds in increasing the loneliness of the scene as the viewer remains watching a space where no signs of life remain. It drives home the bitter awareness of our own yearning for appalling sights lightly veiled under a veneer of stunned compassion. For the viewer, voyeurism switches to a surveillance of the self as awareness dawns.

Bates House

The Bates house, situated alongside a highway between Phoenix and California, is one of the casualties of road realignments in the fast-emerging 1950s American landscape. Both the dilapidated Victorian house brooding over the landscape and the motel (apparently a product of urbanization and road culture of contemporary commercial world) are cut off from the mainstream.

Hitchcock describes the architectural style of the Bates mansion as "California Gothic" (*Hitchcock/Truffaut*, 1985, p. 269). Rebello describes the architectural design of the Bates world in the following way: "the former like a skeletal finger pointing skyward, the latter a rangy horizontal – on a hill off 'Laramie' street" (1990, p. 68). Both Stephen Rebello in *The Making of Psycho* (1990) and Steven Jacobs in *The Wrong House* (2013) trace Edward Hopper's 1925 painting *House by the Railroad* as a direct inspiration behind the external structure as well as the basic mood of the house: "from its garret-story, roof-cresting and oculus window, to its cornices and pilasters". Rebello warns, "One might almost expect to glimpse Mrs. Bates silhouetted in the window of the sloping dormer in Hopper's 1925 painting" (1990, p. 69).

The house is an assemblage of several parts of other buildings brought together to create an imposing and yet melancholy-looking mansion: "Clatworthy and Hurley cannibalized several 'stock unit' sections, including a tower from the house used in the James Stewart man-and-his-rabbit comedy *Harvey* (1948), as well as magisterial doors originally from the Crocker House of San Francisco" (Rebello 1990, p. 69). It may be said that the house as an ensemble is in absolute tune with the assembled or recreated body of its occupant, Mrs Bates. Mrs Bates, ironically, apart from being a stuffed corpse who is preserved by her son, is filmed by

Hitchcock as a medley of various bodies and voices. Mrs Bates, though predicted by viewers as Norman while killing Marion and Arbogast, is actually a blend of "a variety of doubles, including a female 'Lilliputian'" on screen—"Her voice is three different people's; one was provided by a man, another by Jeanette Nolan" (Durgnat 2002, p. 14). Thus, the "patchwork" architecture of the house is a reflection of the "patched up" body of the one confined within it.

The viewers, as they enter the house, are greeted with sturdiness and depth. The left of the screen shows a long narrow passage that leads to the dining and the right shows a few steps of the stairway. The heavy carpet with strong motifs seems like a visual barrier that even Norman hesitates to transcend. The architecture here creates a space of layered depth: dense, dark, and solid. And this sense of a barrier is reinforced as Arbogast's attempt at climbing the stairs is thwarted by a fatal blow of Mrs Bates' knife. Hitchcock here surprisingly films the reversal of roles between the investigating authority and the subject of his investigation. Arbogast pays the price of being a private eye prowling into forbidden territory and the stairs here act as his nemesis.

The same sense of approaching doom is re-established as Lila (Vera Miles) approaches the house. The music and the camera movement suggest a kind of entrapment and enclosure. The forward tracking point-of-view shots of Lila coming closer to the house are balanced by the entire structure of the house coming forward to overwhelm her. Jack Sullivan in *Hitchcock's Music* (2006) states: "Everywhere the music suggests enclosure. The grim figures in contrary motion during 'The Hill' draw Lila toward the house we desperately want her to not enter, the violins sliding down as the basses creep up—a brilliant evocation of entrapment" (p. 257).

Lila's entry into Mrs Bates' room is the fourth blatant invasion into one's private space (the first being the Phoenix hotel room, the second being the peephole scene, and the third being the obvious slashing in the shower). Mrs Bates' bedroom reminds us of Walter Benjamin's depiction of a typical Victorian domestic space: "The nineteenth century... conceived the residence as a receptacle for the person and it encased him with all his appurtenances so deeply in the dwelling's interior that one might be reminded of the inside of a compass case where the instrument lies embedded in deep, usually violet, folds of velvet" (Benjamin 2004, p. 220). Benjamin who ekes out cultural significances of the material and spatial compositions consider turn-of-the-century Victorian domestic space as predominantly modern in its efforts to strongly demarcate the line between the private and the public. Penny Sparke in *The Modern Interior* (2008) explains: "Materially, according to Benjamin, the interior held on to the past through 'an abundance of covers and protectors, liners and cases … on which the traces of objects of everyday use are imprinted' [quoted from Benjamin's 'Paris, Capital of the Nineteenth Century', in *Reflections*, 1986, pp. 155–6]. Nowhere was that attempt to capture the past for the present more evident than in the mid-nineteenth century domestic parlour, where layers of textiles covered the walls, the furnishings, the mantelpiece and the windows" (p. 23).

In Mrs Bates' room, we are greeted with a similar sight: Venetian blinds, thick carpet, velvet-covered upholstery, heavy Victorian furnishing, huge gilded mirrors, and a bed dominating the entire room. In sharp contrast to the utilitarian bare-bone feel of the motel room, the packed surface of the house, along with the intimidating stairway, pronounces a sense of temporal and spatial incarceration.

The imprint of Mother's body left on the bed is a potent symbol suggesting the presence of an absence. The room with all its ornamentation somehow leaves us with the perplexing notion of hollowness. Existence and non-existence are locked up in an intricate synergetic relationship in *Psycho* (1960) as the material presence of the body of Mrs Bates on screen indicates her actual absence, and the absence of her body on the bed apprehends her physical presence. Lila is the only outsider who establishes the first direct contact with Mrs Bates through the indent on the bed. However, she fails to recognise that the hollow of the bed is telling her much more than that. This perhaps is a statement on the futility of surveillance. A deserted room has numerous signifiers, but the observer should be equipped enough to decode their signification.

Failure of the Prying Eye

The suspense of *Psycho* (1960) hinges on the identity of Mrs Bates. While trying to conceal the reality of Mother, and yet not deliberately cheating the audience, Hitchcock resorts to the method of brevity. The plot of the film demands two clear on-screen presence of Mrs Bates: the murder scene of Milton Arbogast, and when she is carried forcefully by Norman to the basement. Hitchcock describes the Arbogast murder scene in the following manner: "I used a single shot of Arbogast coming up the stairs, and when he got to the top step, I deliberately placed the camera very high …

in order not to give the impression that I was trying to avoid showing her [Mrs Bates]" (*Hitchcock/Truffaut*, 1985, p. 273 and 276).

Norman's carrying his mother to the fruit cellar had been executed in the following way: "I had a hanging camera follow Perkins up the stairs, and when he went into the room I continued going up without a cut. As the camera got up on top of the door, the camera turned and looked back down the stairs again. Meanwhile, I had an argument take place between the son and his mother to distract the audience ... In this way the camera was above Perkins again as he carried his mother down and the public hadn't noticed a thing" (*Hitchcock/Truffaut,* 1985, pp. 276–277). Such meticulous camera movement and positioning ensure that Mrs Bates is not seen throughout *Psycho* (1960). Spatial architecture created by camera positioning in the likeness of CCTV brings forth the idea that architecture here itself is surveillance par excellence that raids domestic space to document crimes, and yet fails to identify the criminal.

The Basement

The basement is an apt setting for the discovery of Mrs Bates: stark, bare, with an old rickety bunk, a chair where the body is planted, and some old empty wicker baskets littered around. It is dark, cramped, neglected, and looks like a hole where one dumps one's unwanted secrets. It carries memories of all the nineteenth-century basements and attics where aberrant bodies were kept in confinement, from Bertha Mason in *Jane Eyre* (1847) to Catherine in *Wuthering Heights* (1847). Women who refuse to give in are physically confined in the marginal spaces of a dwelling: the basement and the attic. As Lila turns the chair around, confrontation between the investigator and the investigated in this shadowy world of the basement brings about a point in the narrative where surveillance reaches its moment of crisis. When Lila confronts the object of her investigation, silence prevails, pierced a moment later by her own scream. Lila, the object of an imagined surveillance of Mrs Bates, and Mrs Bates, the object of active investigation of Lila, are two women who carry forward Marion's fear of being watched in the film bringing forth the fact that surveillance becomes even more intense in case of an aberrant female body.

Psycho's (1960) overall architectural design produces a tale of hapless women trapped in a world of mustiness and preservatives and it is the architectural arrangements of the sets that bring home the idea of claustrophobic confinement. Voyeurism, entrapment, fragility, and transparency of private space are ironically brought out by architectural details that pay close attention to a simultaneous structuring and blocking of the view: the abundance of dark windows, Venetian blinds, the light from dormer windows, shower curtains, mirrors, wipers blurred by heavy rain, peep holes, and swinging bulbs.

The Motel, the House, and a Body from Which There Is No Escape

Norman's house may be seen as a museum tableau, an extremely subjective idyllic space. But the Bates house is also a dystopic studio. For Norman, it is at once a refuge and a source of horror as it conceals the shock of matricide. Thus, paradoxically the house is a "refuge" from which he wants to "claw" his way out. Seen from this perspective, the motel is transformed into a temporary shelter for a son tormented by the memories of a mother he has killed.

The vertical house and the horizontal motel are not merely juxtaposed visually. The Bates house is a hermetically sealed world, one that forbids the intrusion of any outsider. On the other hand, a motel by definition is a shelter for outsiders. Norman Bates by being a motel owner and a taxidermist has to balance his urge for privacy and a compulsion to interact.

As viewers we are often offered simultaneous and parallel views of the two dwellings: one forbids visitors, the other waits for visitors, one seething with mysteries, the other open to be invaded by strangers. By positioning the demented Mrs Bates on a window frame of the house, Hitchcock presents Mrs Bates as securely inhabiting her own demarcated space. It is only when she comes out to wreak havoc on a space meant for outsiders that we feel the fluidity of the two apparently contradictory spatial boundaries, making it evident that Norman has no place to "claw" out of. It is neither the house nor the motel that has confined him. It is his body that has become a space of his asphyxiation. And it is the construction of such a body that is desired by panopticism: a body that will be its own observer, a body from which there is no escape. Norman by being both the mother and the son is the guard in Bentham's tower as well as the inmate in Bentham's cell. Bates House, like Norman and his mother, is both a brooding watcher that scans the motel below as well as a vulnerable space that cannot escape the invasion of outsiders.

The Private/Public Divide

"Home", by definition a private space, remains a locus of curiosity and a tempting zone of surveillance. Till the seventeenth century, home was associated with outside activities where production and management of the external world could easily penetrate a drawing room or a parlour. From eighteenth century onward, "home" started being related to "privacy". The turn-of-the-century Victorian houses were considered to be "modern" by Benjamin precisely for the fact that they had completely dissociated themselves from the public. By becoming "personal", they ironically became coveted sites of surveillance and prying.

Advertisements, journals, and magazines showcasing "ideal" homes, tours of famous houses, ethnographic studies conducted by sociologists where spaces are studied, commented upon and documented are all instances where the home is opened up for the public eye. Studies that relate self-identity to interior design proliferate highlighting the domestic space as a lived experience, a material composition, and an intangible image. Interiors are signposts that speak of narratives of strict regimentation, of shallow exhibitionism, of futile dreams, and of repositories of lost days. They are studied as a continuous performative setting. And these very significant and indispensable practices of culture studies also help in raising some very crucial questions: How much invasive are we being? Where does academic curiosity end and prying begin on part of both the researcher and the reader? Does this entire effort relate in some significant way to the idea of surveillance? And how reliable can a reflective rebuilding of private domestic spaces and their contents be?

Home as a Crime Site: Its Interpretation and Reconstruction

As part of the pre-release marketing strategy, Hitchcock takes his audience to a guided tour of the Bates world. Hitchcock makes us visit the empty spaces of the house hinting that unspeakable crimes have been committed there. The possibilities that lurk in the architectural composition of the Bates house are thus being used as baits for the audience.

The preview of the Bates architecture that we are invited to watch anticipates a current trend of observation and knowledge-generating practice. Surveillance at present does not merely restrict itself to information gathering or crime prevention, it also lays claim on crime prediction. Unlike Foucault's analysis of power based on the visible/invisible dyad where the peripheral one is always conscious of being watched, Mark Poster contends that advanced data-handling technologies or super-panopticon produces "individuals with dispersed identities, identities of which the individuals might not even be aware" (1995, p. 93). Consumers are constructed by mining information stored on databases derived from an individual's surfing habits and purchase history. Such constructions at times become important aspects of an individual's identity. This is a telling example of the blend of the personal and the public that helps at times to track criminals and even detect potential criminals.

Hitchcock's pre-release strategy of granting us a crime site tour seems a rudimentary and yet a prophetic strategy that can help us to identify and undertake pre-emptive surveillance of other such "crime-prone" settings. The architectural organisation of the Mother's room (set on a lonely stretch of raised land, with deep-set oculus windows, an intimidating porch and a dense dark interior) serves as a medium through which possibilities of crime are evoked. Architecture of a crime site plays an important part in gaining knowledge about the procedure and economy of crime. Thus, invading, interpreting, and surveying the architecture of a crime site can be seen as effective weapons to prevent crimes in future. *Psycho* (1960) is a part of a world without an all-pervading surveillance of a cyber-world. In such a world, the setting becomes all-important.

"She Wouldn't Even Harm a Fly", Mother, Norman, and Mann's "Sousveillance"

The penultimate prison scene with its stark walls, barred window, and Norman at the centre of it all draped in a blanket acutely conscious of watching eyes is the ultimate expression of minimal architecture that becomes an apt set for the staging of a docile body that Foucault speaks of. It is a scene where both mother and son address the viewer directly. We hear the enigmatic voice of mother, while the son stares maniacally at the camera. The prison scene reminds us of the Orwellian world where the apparent demeanour, the body movement, and the gestures of Norman conform to what is expected by Big Brother, while the rebellion seethes within. The moralising and the self-monitoring voice and the immobile body that refrains from swatting a fly seem almost like a parody, a mockery of those who are "watching". Norman's stare and mother's voice directed at the camera may be termed as Norman's and his mother's "sousveillance", reminding us that power that emanates from surveillance has its counterpoint in resistance. The penultimate scene of *Psycho* (1960) brings forth the idea that while surveillance technology proliferates, there is also an increasing tendency to observe those in positions of authority. Steve Mann (2002) terms this "inverse surveillance" as "sousveillance", that is, the use of surveillance technology to reflect back and defy the monitoring processes of those in authority. The last look of Norman/Mother may thus be read as a form of resistance or defiance of containment.

Conclusion

The Thief and the Hermit, the Swamp and the Cell

Psycho (1960) and its protagonists are still relevant in this age of hypersurveillance. Zygmunt Bauman may well be speaking of Norman and Marion when he states, "men and women of our times are haunted by the spectre of exclusion" (2004, p. 47). Marion feels marginalised in an increasingly prosperous city of Phoenix as her dreams of marriage and a home, all parts of the American Dream, seem more and more elusive. It is her desperation to belong to this culture of "settling down" within the bounds of marital institution that makes her steal. She is afraid of being left out. On the other hand, Norman has already been "flushed out" of the mainstream. Failure both as a service provider and as a consumer, he needs to be "weeded" out in an already competent consumer culture of late twentieth-century America. Bauman suggests that at present panopticon functions in reverse, "flushing the undesirables away and keeping the regulars in" (2007, p. 4). Speaking of contemporary consumerism, Bauman describes the excluded ones as "weeds in the consumerist garden, people short of cash, credit cards and/or shopping enthusiasm and otherwise immune to the blandishments of marketing"(2007, p. 4). And Alfred Hitchcock in 1960 shows how both these "undesirables" end up as "exclusions": Marion in a swamp and Norman in a cell. Both the swamp and the cell become significant part of the cinematic space of *Psycho* suggesting, at once, incarceration, illness, death, claustrophobia, insanity as well as resistance: recipes of a perfect panopticon.

Bibliography

Bauman, Z. (2004). *Identity*. Cambridge: Polity Press.

Bauman, Z. (2007). *Consuming Life*. Cambridge: Polity Press.

Benjamin, W. (2004). *The Arcades Project* (trans: Eiland, H. & McLaughlin, K.). London: Cambridge.

Bentham, J. (1843). In J. Bowring (Ed.), *The Works of Jeremy Bentham* (Vol. IV). London: Simpkin, Marshall, and Co.

Bloch, R. (2014). *Psycho* (1st ed.) [Kindle ebook]. London: Orion Publishing Group.

Clarke, R. (1988). *Information Technology and Dataveillance* [Online]. Available at: http://www.rogerclarke.com/DV/CACM88.html. Accessed 27 Mar 2018.

Durgnat, R. (2002). *A Long Hard Look at Psycho*. London: British Film Institute.

Foucault, M. (1991). *Discipline and Punish: The Birth of the Prison*. London: Penguin.

Giddens, A. (1985). *The Nation-State and Violence: Volume Two of a Contemporary Critique of Historical Materialism*. Cambridge: Polity Press.

Haraway, D. (1989). *Primate Visions: Gender, Race, and Nature in the World of Modern Science*. New York: Routledge.

Jacobs, S. (2013). *The Wrong House: The Architecture of Alfred Hitchcock*. Rotterdam: nai010 publishers.

Liebs, C. H. (1995). Motels. In *Main Street to Miracle Mile: American Roadside Architecture* (pp. 169–189). London: JHU Press.

Lyon, D. (2003). Surveillance as Social Sorting: Computer Codes and Mobile Bodies. In D. Lyon (Ed.), *Surveillance as Social Sorting: Privacy, Risk and Digital Discrimination* (1st ed.). London: Routledge.

Lyon, D. (2007). Surveillance, Power, and Everyday Life. In R. Mansell, C. Avgerou, D. Quah, & R. Silverstone (Eds.), *Oxford Handbook of Information and Communication Technologies* (1st ed., pp. 449–465). Oxford: Oxford University Press.

Mann, S. (2002). *Sousveillance* [Online]. Available at: http://wearcam.org/sousveillance.htm. Accessed 27 Mar 2018.

Mondal, S. (2017). *"Did He Smile His Work to See?"—Gothicism, Alfred Hitchcock's Psycho and the Art of Taxidermy* [e-journal]. London: Palgrave Communications, *3*, 17044. https://doi.org/10.1057/palcomms.2017.44.

Poliquin, R. (2012). *The Breathless Zoo: Taxidermy and the Cultures of Longing*. University Park: Pennsylvania State University Press.

Poster, M. (1995). *The Second Media Age*. Cambridge: Polity Press.

Rebello, S. (1990). *Alfred Hitchcock and the Making of Psycho* (1st ed.) [kindle ebook]. New York: Integrated Media.

Sparke, P. (2008). *The Modern Interior*. London: Reaktion Books.

Stamp, J. (2014). *From Turrets to Toilets: A Partial History of the Throne Room* [Online]. Available at: https://www.smithsonianmag.com/history/turrets-toilets-partial-history-throne-room-180951788/. Accessed 18 Mar 2018.
Sullivan, J. (2006). *Hitchcock's Music*. New Haven/London: Yale University Press.
Truffaut, F., & Scott, H. G. (1985). *Hitchcock: The Definitive Study of Alfred Hitchcock by Francois Truffaut* (Revised ed.). New York: Simon and Schuster

Films Cited

Frenzy. (1972). [DVD] Los Angeles, Universal: Alfred Hitchcock.
North by Northwest. (1959). [DVD] Beverly Hills, MGM: Alfred Hitchcock.
Psycho. (1960). [DVD] New York, Paramount: Alfred Hitchcock.
The Trouble with Harry. (1955). [DVD] Los Angeles, Paramount: Alfred Hitchcock.
Vertigo. (1958). [DVD] Los Angeles, Universal: Alfred Hitchcock.

CHAPTER 7

Architecture and *American Horror Story*: Reading 'Murder House' on Murderous Bodies

Antonia Mackay

Introduction

Previous studies on *American Horror Story (AHS)* (2011–present) have attested to the power of the first season ("Murder House") in ingraining established gendered cultural stereotypes, such as the "wicked" female and the flawed but "forgivable" man (Janicker 2017). However, the formation and manipulation of identity appears to be less concerned with the continuation of established familial cultural norms set up by the domestic space, and more to do with the home's (and by extension, Los Angeles') influence on the body. The aforementioned research, for example, has failed to take into account the reason for the family's relocation—Vivian Harmon's miscarriage and Ben Harmon's affair. As such, the mansion in "Murder House" is less concerned with extending existent identities, and more about creating a "new beginning". The architectural space of the home is therefore intended to eradicate the family's old identities and instil new ones—something the narrative insists the home is capable of

A. Mackay (✉)
Oxford Brookes University, Oxford, UK
e-mail: antoniamackay@brookes.ac.uk

S. Flynn, A. Mackay (eds.), *Surveillance, Architecture and Control*,
https://doi.org/10.1007/978-3-030-00371-5_7

doing as previous inhabitants "haunt" the Harmon's after being transformed into ghosts, destined to remain within its walls. This chapter will investigate and argue for the architectural (the literal space of the home) importance of the home in "Murder House" which possesses the ability to transform bodies and manipulate their identity. This chapter therefore concludes that a reading of the architectural environment in *AHS'* first season provides the home with impetus for both seemingly gender normative and also non-normative behaviour (murderous, demonic and disfigured), suggesting it is the architectural space of the renovated Victorian mansion which can maim, morph and manipulate bodies into conforming to familial normality, or else transgress into heterogeneous (and potentially non-human) identities.

The Home

Homes are capable of being both "unhomely" and familiar, but the home is also capable of representing a site of surveillance by blurring the division between inside and outside, public and private. Beatriz Colomina's research identifies the space of the home as one which encourages the "watchedness" of its inhabitants, for "it is impossible to abandon the space… without being seen by those over whom control is being exerted" (1992, 82). Domestic architecture, with its large picture windows and its fetish for transparent surfaces, open planning and communal living spaces does indeed offer itself up as a space of surveillance. The picture window of 1950s American suburban designs have frequently been analysed for their ability to let the occupants observe others in their street, as well as allowing others to observe *them* in an effort to "keep up with the Jones" and also to observe and identify any Communist sympathisers (see *Cold War Hothouses* and *Pursuing Privacy in Cold War America*). Contemporary domestic design, with its glass walls and attempt at bringing the outside in, similarly offers a space to be viewed as well as one by which to view others. It is perhaps therefore unsurprising to identify the home as a space designed for watching, for houses themselves are active in transforming the views of the landscape surrounding them, collecting "views and in doing so, classifying them" (113). As Colomina notes, the home is an architectural frame which can be interpreted as akin to Bentham's panopticon, opening up interiors for the encouragement of the gaze: "the house is a system for taking pictures. What determines the nature of the picture is the window" (113). In doing so, the home becomes a space with no clear public or private division—what was once hidden may be unveiled, and what was once visible could be concealed.

Elizabeth Grosz's theories of feminist corporeality demonstrate such bodily marking at the hands of architecture. In *Volatile Bodies* (1994) she argues for bodies which are active, capable of "generat[ing] what is new, surprising, unpredictable" (xi). For Grosz, the body is therefore not a static entity, but rather capable of acting and reacting to "representations of spatiality and temporality" (90). Space here can be understood to encompass not only social and physical space, but also the space of architecture, where "space is understood by us as a relation between these points and a cultural organising perspective" (90). Essentially, we require points of information which can indicate our position and provide the body with direction thereby allowing us to grasp our sense of situation. A built architectural space is one such space which can enable the body to grasp a situation, providing the body with a frame within which to act and react. For Grosz, this space is fundamental to our perception of identity, for it provides the body with a frame and with it, markers of behaviour, sensation, body image and culture (80). In *Architecture from the Outside* (2001), Grosz further connects bodies to architectural space, where "the body's infinite pliability is a measure of the infinite plasticity of the spatio-temporal universe in which it is housed and through which bodies become real, are lived and have effects" (33). According to Grosz's theories, bodies cannot be "real" without a frame, and our frame is required in order for the body to have an "effect".

Haunted Houses

The horror genre has long been fascinated by the domestic unit—from haunted houses to possessed and murderous families—it is the home which has often been harnessed as a site for the bizarre and uncanny in literature and film. Whilst the haunted house filled with ghouls has been a fundamental ingredient in thrillers, slashers and pop culture gore, its origins reveal far more architectural autonomy than on first glance. Edgar Allan Poe's "The Fall of Usher" (1839) features a haunted home that is itself, embodied: "[I] gazed down – but with a shudder even more thrilling than before – upon the remodelled and inverted images of the grey sedge, and the ghastly tree-stems, and the vacant and eye-like windows" (Poe, 1). H.P. Lovecraft's "The Shunned House" (1924) and Henry James' *The Turn of the Screw* (1898) also point not to homes which are haunted, but haunted *homes*, where the occupants are exposed to the home's previous inhabitants who still reside within its walls. Contemporary examples of the haunted house, from Mark Z. Danielewski's *House of Leaves* (2000) to Stephen King's *The Shining* (1977), similarly suggest not the haunting of a space, but a haunted space in and of itself. Our fascination with such spaces could perhaps be explained by the symbolic associations we draw from the concept of "home"—a space of familiarity and nurturing, family and safety. In "'Honey, I'm Home!' Splintering the Fabrication in Domestic Horror", Gina Wisker argues for a haunted home as a form of "domestic horror" which conjures up feelings of "entrapment, engulfment, monstrous parents and equally monstrous children, skeletons in closets and chopped messes on the kitchen table…the sickening flip side of 'domestic bliss'" (2002, 108). Indeed, as Wisker argues, by replacing traditional associations with the home with that of horror, established divisions are blurred exposing us to "the hidden fears and lurking perversities derived from disgust at difference, the body, the Other, the abject, the 'not I'" (109). Stanley Kubrick's adaptation of King's *The Shining* (1980) is a fitting example of such "lurking perversities" which are unveiled by a home's space. Kubrick's film, through the gradual mental dissolution of Jack, attempts to fragment the home and with it, the domestic space. Jack's supposed psychotic break, at the hands of the hotel's previous inhabitants, fractures the figurative space of the "home" by seeking to destroy his wife and child, but another fracture occurs in the physical space along spectral lines where labyrinths intersect between exterior (the maze), interior (the layout of the hotel) and its furnishings (carpets which look like mazes). The blurring of inside and outside suggests the hotel is a space which is active in its agency—capable of shaping Jack's identity along with its own, fracturing Jack's mental state. It is also worth remembering that the hotel is called "Overlook", further reinforcing the notion of a space which has agency, and one which can watch, look and oversee its inhabitants. As Wisker notes, "spaces erupt and split, allowing in what one hoped to keep hidden" (109); only *The Shining* splits Jack's selfhood allowing the hotel in. According to Colomina's analysis above, *The Shining's* mazes, corridors and secreted spaces become open for infiltration, offering Jack to the hotel's ghostly inhabitants, and beginning the process by which his public identity shifts into ambiguity. Put another way, built structures are capable not only of surveilling their inhabitants, but also of inflecting some part of that structure's identity, onto those inhabitants. Coupled with Grosz's theories, without Overlook, Jack would not have had (murderous) "effects" and thus *requires* the space of the home in order to carry out his maniacal acts—is the framing of the hotel which directly provides Jack with a new identity—one where he may become "Other" for "the body is not merely matter but a continual and incessant materialising of possibilities" (Butler 1988, 521). It is precisely this notion—that the haunted house is capable of agency and can mark bodies under its watchful gaze in order to create effect, that this chapter investigates, analysing one such type of haunted house—the "Murder House" of *American Horror Story's* (2011–present; referred to as *AHS*) first season.

In understanding the home as a site of horror, Sigmund Freud's theory of the *unheimlich* or the uncanny, manages to underscore the uneasiness with which these two concepts collide: "an uncanny experience occurs... when primitive beliefs which have been surmounted seem once more to be confirmed" (Freud 1955, 249). Our "primitive beliefs" associated with the home are those of familiarity, safety and nurture; yet those alluded to in Freud's uncanny transform into those of fear, distress and dread, resulting in a subject which we perceive to be frightening. In combining the confirmation of primitive beliefs with a familiar setting, the experience is upended, inverted and subverted—any comfort we seek to derive from the space of the home is redundant, and it becomes, quite literally *unheimlich* or "creepy". It is perhaps for this reason that the "unhomeliness" of Freud's uncanny works so successfully in creating a sense of fear, for it is more than a sense of not belonging, but rather, as Vidler argues, a "fundamental propensity for the familiar to turn on its axis, suddenly to become de-familiarised, de-realised" (1994, 7). The haunted house works so incredibly effectively in creating a sense of fear precisely because it has been turned on its axis, and what was once familiar is now entirely "Other".

American Horror Story's "Murder House"

In *AHS*' first episode, entitled "Pilot", the opening shots see the house as it was in 1978, appearing run down and in disrepair. The Victorian-styled home looms over the children (Addie and the, now deceased, twin boys) playing in its grounds, seemingly peering down on them from an endless multitude of windows, and also from its lofty turret.

Within the first few minutes of "Pilot" we are introduced not only to the home as a site which is architecturally imposing, but also to a building which is characterised as a site of surveillance. The collegiate gothic style turret echoes Bentham's panopticon and Foucault's theorisation of spatial visibility as a form of power (*Discipline and Punish*, 1975), whilst the basement is designated as the site of the home's secrets. The suggestion of a closeting of objects or bodies in the basement renders the home as fragmented from the outset much like King's Overlook, opening up the possibility for the fragmentation of bodies. A duality of surveillance is therefore implied between Murder House as a site which surveils its premises and thereby keeps intruders out, but also a site which keeps hidden its secretive identity—as a space which can maim, activate, deactivate and reconfigure the bodies residing within it. As the theories of Grosz and Colomina demonstrate, Murder House appears capable of blurring public and private divisions, and in doing so, opening up the possibility for the creation of new identities for its inhabitants.

Despite previous studies which have attested to the Murder Houses' primary function to be the re-establishment of normative social roles (*Reading American Horror Story* (2017)), reading the series as a commentary on architecture demonstrates the existence of a relationship between the body and the home. In "Pilot", Vivian's doctor offers her medication in order to help her regain "control over her body" to which she responds: "I'm not a house". The clear intersectionality between the home and the body emerges from the show's outset, positioning the two as interchangeable and in clear dialogue with one another in ways which negate the possibility of *AHS* as seeking to re-establish social homogeneity. Murder House is demonstrably not a space of normative social roles, and if bodies and the home are synonymous with one another, then *AHS*' first season suggests the reverse—an establishment of identity heterogeneity and with it, non-normative bodily forms. Indeed, "home" as a concept is in fact central to season one's narrative. After meeting with the doctor, Vivian returns to their Boston home and hears noises upstairs; believing the noises are the result of a home invasion, she discovers her husband (Ben) having an affair with one of his students (Hayden). Of course, for Vivian, this is not a home invasion in the typical sense, for the house is not under attack from burglars or thieves; and yet, her discovery of the affair is a form of home invasion of sorts—it is quite literally being invaded by the entrance of another woman, transforming Ben's and Vivian's relationship and resulting in their desire to move to Los Angeles where they might be able to rebuild their familial identities.

Contemporary criticism of the show (*Reading American Horror Story* and "The Monstrous Makeover: 'American Horror Story', Femininity and Special Effects") argues for the "constraints of the heteronormative social construction of gendered sexes" (2017, 86) and for a "critical commentary about femininity" (2013, 113) yet Murder House represents more than simply versions of gendered identity. Certainly some episodes do appear to reinforce aspects of gendered stereotypes, such as the conversation between Nora and Vivian in "Rubber Man" which references female types—the ghosts of the mad woman in the attic, the whore, the virgin—who are trapped in death into domesticity and patriarchal systems (e.g. Moira). Further Moira's reference to Charlotte Perkins Gillman's *The Yellow Wallpaper* works to instil a sense in which the house is capable of enforcing female domestic identity as maternal, deranged, trapped and misunderstood. The need for children also appears to drive much of the narrative, for it is Nora's desire for a child which results in the initial murder suicide of Charles and Nora—an event which prompts the home's endless historic cycle of death. Tate's murder of Patrick and his lover is also prompted by a desire for children, acting on their reneged decision to adopt a child, whilst Tate's rape of Vivian is directly motivated by a need to make Nora happy and produce a child for the home. Yet, in "Murder House" the reproduction of life mirrors the reproduction of death in ways which do not reflect those of the traditional or established domestic unit. Rather, the most potent form of reproduction which occurs in the house is not that of mother and child, but rather living and undead once more aligning the home with the uncanny and the haunted houses of Poe and James. Children are also incapable of existing within the home as "living". All of Constance's children born within the house die either prior to the narrative or during; Larry's children are murdered by their father in their sleep, whilst only the anti-Christ twin survives Vivian's labour. Whilst reproduction and children are part of the season's narrative, it is clear that the supposed heteronormative structures are themselves, rendered uncanny. Furthermore, the traditionally safe space of the domestic home is rendered uncanny in as much as conventional parenting is replaced by the house—no longer is it parents who watch over their children, but rather a horror house which watches and controls. The children of Murder House are relegated to the inverse realm of the maternal—to that of deceased, ghostly, deranged, inhuman, and deformed.

Further, contrary to the argument for *AHS'* establishment of normativity, many of Murder House's inhabitants are either already dead, or die during the season, only to be reincarnated as ghosts trapped by the house. Rather than suggesting the house is a space concerned with establishing domesticated female and masculine roles, "Murder House" in fact offers the opposite—a space where death can create a new identity, free from social and cultural constructions. The deathly freedom on offer may also help to explain why all the children born in the house die, for traditional domestic roles only offer "literal and metaphorical traps" (118). The Victorian mansion therefore comes to represent more than a site or sight, but rather takes on an autonomous role which is capable of shaping those it houses and views, inverting the conventional domestic space into one which quite literally haunts the traditional. The home's autonomy is furthered by the constant insistence on its life-like qualities. Much like Vivian's earlier refusal to be "a house", Constance (their eccentric neighbour and a previous resident of the house) reassures the Harmon's that the previous owners cared for the home "like a child". Similarly, Moira (the Harmon's undead maid) forcefully informs Vivian that the house "has personality, feelings – mistreat it and you'll regret it". The house is also capable of "speaking" to its occupants, as evidenced in "Pilot" when Larry (a disfigured prior occupant) claims the house encouraged him to murder his family by burning it down, and he again restates the home's apparent life-like qualities in "Home Invasion" confronting Ben over his past indiscretions: "What dream is chasing you? It's the house isn't it… What's tearing you apart? The house knows about it and will use it against you". Much like in *The Shining*, the home does not appear to be a haunted house, so much as a house which can haunt; and further, a house which is active in instilling identities—as murdered, murderer, ghost—onto its inhabitants through the gaze. As Jean-Paul Sartre stated: "my body is everywhere: the bomb which destroys my house also damages my body insofar as the house was already an indication of my body" (Vidler 1994, 34); in "Murder House", the house is an active part of the bodies who are trapped in its walls.

It is clear from "Murder House's" narrative that ghosts not only help to shape the house's identity, but are also the house's agents, aiding in the transformation of new inhabitants' identities. Acting as the home's collective, they can injure, maim, wound and kill others, transforming them from living to dead, and from dead to undead in order to join the ranks of existing ghouls: "It's not your house. We know it; you know it; and the house knows it". But the ghosts can also influence the living. As a ghost, Hayden plays an active part in the breakdown of Vivien and Ben's relationship by exposing the truth of his ongoing affair; ghost Tate influences Violet by encouraging her to scare the local high school bully by luring her into the basement where Thaddeus (the dismembered child of the home's first occupants) is lying in wait ("Halloween Part 2"). The death of the living can also be influenced by those in the house, such as the death of Addie. Addie, Constance's disabled child dies when she is hit by a car outside the gates of Murder House. Blamed for her death, Violet encouraged her to be a "pretty girl" by wearing a mask, which ultimately impaired her vision. Larry is similarly influenced by the ghosts in the house, recalling past events when he was a resident in the hope of warning Ben, leading directly to Hayden's murder and the setting fire of the house in "Halloween Part 2". In effect, Murder House is representative of an "in-betweenness"—being neither a traditional home nor wildly unconventional, housing the living and the dead, actively shaping identities but doing so through death—where the framing of structures can create bodily affect or Deleuzian "becoming".

Contrary to the belief posited in *Reading American Horror Story*, where "the evil ghosts in Murder House as positioned outside looking in" (393), the analysis thus far suggests ghosts are very much part of the home and its identity. They are further inside—not outside—and far from simply "looking", it is my contention that the house looks whilst the ghosts act. This theory is furthered by Grosz's theories of architectural mobility, where "a building is made up of other spaces within it that move and change, even if its own walls remain fixed" (2001, 7). At the start of "Pilot" the Harmon's move into Murder House and begin to peel back wallpaper, repaint the interior, move furniture, and transform spaces into new spatial categories (Ben's office space for instance). The walls of the home remain fixed, but interior spaces are mobile. Such a mobility and fluidity of space contravenes the traditional divisions set up by architectural design—rather than offer fixity, according to Grosz, it is this mobility of spatial identity which can enable the bodies inhabiting it to similarly shift. Indeed, if bodies are an active part of the home's structure, then a shift in space can be equal to a shift in bodily identity compounding Grosz's theory where "the boundary between the inside and the outside, just as much as between self and other... must not be regarded as a limit to be transgressed, so much as a boundary to be traversed" (65). In Tate's words, death allows you to take people to a place which is "clean" away from the "filthy" world filled with pain. Far from view death as an end, death within the limits of Murder House is a process which can enable a rejection of the past and an embrace of newness (as the undead), which appears to be true in both Tate's own death (revealed in "Piggy Piggy") and Violet's suicide enabling her to join the ranks of the other dead inhabitants of the house. According to Gilles Deleuze, this process of becoming suggests a particular path along which an entity might be transformed into something else, for "movement affects both space and the bodies moving through it. To move is… to become the other than itself" (1996, 84). According to both Grosz and Deleuze, it is therefore the framing of structures which creates bodily affect or "becoming" where "it is the architectural force of framing that liberates the qualities of objects or events that come to constitute the substance" (Grosz 2008, 11). In *AHS* this "becoming" demonstrates the possibility not of the establishment of norms but instead, the rejection of the past and the possibility of newness (the creation of the undead) from within the home's watchful frames.

Los Angeles, Surveillance and the Spectral Home

By extension, the home's location (in Los Angeles) is further suggestive of a space for transformation and watching, actively engaging in the creation of new identities through the gaze. As an urban space, Los Angeles is frequently viewed as fragmented and diffuse for "Los Angeles has no urban form at all" (Banham 1971, 57). Indeed, Los Angeles is a heterogeneous city space with no clear centre or urban boundary, rather encompassing 88 cities within its county. Unlike other American cities such as New York City or San Francisco, Los Angeles appears widely dispersed and unregulated, a space Reyner Banham describes as "a dynamic systems of flows" (xvviii). Such "flows" call to mind the earlier argument about fractured architectural space and the mobility of domestic interiors, opening up the city space of *AHS* as one which similarly encourages change and mutation for both the urban space itself and those residing there. Such a space may appear relatively free from the surveillant gaze, yet as is the case with Murder House's frames, Los Angeles does emerge as one of the active surveillance. Edward Soja argues in *Postmodern Geographies* (2011) for the city as a specifically surveillant space where the centre (in his argument, City Hall) monitors and defends the status quo, essentially maintaining power where old "nodalities" are reinforced. Soja's argument suggests a space which is "contained" and bounded, despite its seemingly fractured architectural nature. Hence, much like the house, the city which frames the Harmon's home is also a space which attempts to maintain power and control over its citizens. As Grosz argued, if the home frames not only its inhabitants, but also the landscape surrounding it, Murder House is framed by watchful walls and a system of power which extends past its perimeter. The possibility, however, of transformation can be found precisely in the city's "fragmented and fragmenting" (243) character, for the city "will never be fully understood by those who cannot move fluently through its diffuse urban texture" (Banham 1971, 5). Hence mobility of space, of temporality and of identity, transgressing the gaze, is what determines the occupants' ability to traverse into the new—what Banham describes as a form of "penetrability" (39).

Throughout season one of *AHS*, there are several site-specific nods to Los Angeles' establishment of such penetrability, blurring the lines between pre-existing boundaries. One such instance is the case of the Black Dahlia, whose murder in 1947 gripped the Los Angeles' media. The body of a 22-year-old female was found nude in an empty parking lot in Leimert Park; she had been tortured with cigarette burns and bisected at the waist. Her murder made headlines daily, in all of the city's newspapers, sparking one of the biggest manhunts in Los Angeles police history. Black Dahlia (Elizabeth Short) was frequently referred to in the media, inaccurately, as a prostitute, an "adventuress" and a slayed "sex fiend". The manner in which the media categorised her in death through the gaze and the further insistence on her latterly mythical and unreal status is compounded by the episode "Spooky Little Girl" which plays on Short's transformation at the hands of Los Angeles. In the *AHS* episode, Short appears as a patient wishing to gain an appointment with Ben (now practicing psychiatry from his home office). Over the course of the episode it is revealed that Short died at the hands of Dr David Curran—a dentist living in the house in the postwar period, who had caused her to overdose. As a ghost, Short's appearance prompts Hayden (now undead) to murder Travis (Constance's young lover) in order to prevent him from returning to Constance, and in the hope that he will join the undead trapped in the house and remain with Hayden in the afterlife. True to form, the house reproduces identity and births Travis as the undead, leaving his body behind. Rather than bury his body or dispose of it by other means, Dahlia's presence in the house prompts the undead to pose him as Black Dahlia, bisecting his body and dumping it in an unused parking lot. In the following episode "Smouldering Children" Travis is thrilled to learn that he has received the title of Boy Dahlia in death clearly indicating that despite his death, the murderous actions which take place within the home enable bodies to "become" (or in Travis' case, to become "someone" famous). Bodies are therefore transformed by the space of Los Angeles, rewriting the very real history of Black Dahlia, interweaving it into the narrative of

AHS' Victorian mansion, as well as inverting Short's dehumanised body into a male form which actively provides identity to the (un)dead.

Given that Los Angelenos' architecture mirrors "the illusions and destructive fantasies of those who dwell in them" (Fine 2004, 11), it is perhaps unsurprising that reality and illusion are blurred in the same way as architectural and urban boundaries. Many of the inhabitants are neither fully dead nor fully alive, trapped within the home's pervasive gaze where they are "disguised to look like something else" (173). Homes in Los Angles are therefore not unlike Disneyfied simulacra—representing desire and externalising performativity at the expense of authenticity. It is precisely the negation of this externalisation which renders the Murder House as capable of traversing established boundaries, for it eradicates such performativity by insisting on the stripping away of cultural and social norms, to reveal only internal bodily identity as spirit, ghost and spectre.

Such limitlessness is further enforced by the constantly shifting perception of Moira in the eyes of Vivian and Ben. When Vivian views her, she is an old and haggard maid, whilst Ben (and indeed, other men) sees her as beautiful, young and overtly sexual: "men see what they want to see, women see into the soul". Indeed, bodies and the perception of bodies housed in the mansion are capable of almost limitless shift and mutation, for it is the space of the home which acts as a panoptic site capable of directing a gaze in multiple directions—up, down, across and into bodies. Furthermore, the open space of the home's interior renders it as a space for viewing, where "he who is subjected to a field of visibility… inscribes in himself the power relation" (Foucault 1975, 202). Only here, the power relation is one which imbues power upon submission—where internalising power results in "constant, profound and permanent… effects" (202). Whilst the effects of this form of surveillance result in death, "Murder House" insists upon the positivity of such interior rebirth into new selves; though it is the pervasive nature of surveillance from *outside* the home which persists as negative and ultimately destructive.

In the episode "Murder House", the Eternal Darkness Tour bus stops outside the home on its journey around the sites of famous deaths and murders in Los Angeles. In the scene, the tour occupants are seen photographing and filming the house, gazing at it through a tourist lens inflected with an identity provided by the tour guide: "most famous houses of horrors in the city of angels – better known as the murder house". Notably, this is the first time the house is given a name—that of the Murder

House—prompting Vivian (who is pregnant) to start bleeding. There is a sense that the house (and its occupants) is being penetrated by the external gaze, wounding them by attempting to administer an identity which is at odds with the interior. This is compounded by the fact that Vivian's bleeding promptly stops the moment she re-enters the house, thereby advocating the house to position of protector and defender of its inhabitants.

Furthermore, in "Halloween Part 1", we learn that the "dead can walk freely" every Halloween—and walk beyond its perimeter. It is also the night we learn of Thaddeus' inception. As the child of Nora and Charles, Thaddeus was kidnapped by a disgruntled partner of one of Charles' abortion patients, only to be returned dead and dismembered. Driven mad by an addiction to chloroform, Charles determines to reassemble his child and bring it back to life, resulting in the creation of the demonic creature "infatata", otherwise known as Thaddeus. Nora, similarly driven mad by Charles' inhuman creation murders Charles and commits suicide. In another instance of blurring between fictional and non-fictional, the story of Thaddeus resembles that of the Lindberg baby in 1938, further suggestive of both the gaze of the media, and the distinction between interior reality and external sensationalism. However, it is the connection between the space of the home and the creation of identity which is of interest here. Nora's and Charles' story is centred around loss—the loss of other women's unborn children and that of their own child—but it is also focused on reconstruction and rebirth, piecing together their own dead child. This blurring of death, loss, life and birth results in a spatial marking which is characterised by both loss and an attempt to reconstruct that loss in ways which actively reshape subjectivity, albeit into grotesque and uncanny bodily forms. The Murder House is therefore the means by which to maim, disfigure and mutate bodies, maintaining their identity within the frames of the house; and it is also its position as the site of the uncanny which renders it a "sight" to be repeatedly surveilled by those from the outside who threaten to destabilise such identity creation. A victim of its own mythological position, violent past and location (in Los Angeles), the home is repeatedly gazed at by tourists, new residents taking the place of the dead proprietors and estate agents. What the series suggests, therefore, is not that the home is only capable of transforming identity, but is capable of doing so in a way which whilst trapping bodies within its walls, and marking them endlessly and repeatedly in ways which foreground the watching of bodies by way of ghosts and ghouls, they are also those who act out the home's desires thereby maintaining the status quo.

Conclusion

The haunted houses of *AHS*, Poe, King and James attest to the ongoing popularity of the uncanny and its place within our cultural psyche for "nothing is more horrifying to us than those unseen mysteries, terrors and wonders that lurk in the anatomical locked room, to which only the medical profession hold the key" (Armitt 2014, 177). "Murder House" remains one of the most celebrated seasons of *AHS*, and its appeal likely lies in its ability to both engage with and subvert the norms of traditional horror, where the ghosts can transgress boundaries and enter into our world—rupturing the boundaries of the traditional notion of safety within the home. Such an inversion of the home's appeal and transgression of bodies results in a house which watches, controls and disciplines in ways which rewrite the familial narrative. *AHS'* popularity is also, as Jervis states, bound up with our desire to look "at the screen [so that we are] reminded… of the reality of the medium that disseminates suffering as spectacle and fiction" (2015, 195); yet in this case, what emerges is a suffering which "is differentiated from chaos. An incandescent, unbearable limit between inside and outside, ego and other" (Kristeva 1980, 140). This process of differentiation is almost surely the product of the double gaze inflicted on the inhabitants of Murder House—being both "Other" and familiar—where "the twisting defines the 'flesh' beyond the body" (Deleuze 1986, 91) and thereby enabling a gaze which offers an escape from the abject and frightful. As evidenced in the season's final two episodes ("Birth" and "Afterbirth") Violet and Tate, now both ghosts, recognise their potential to create a future together, away from his mother's influence and the responsibilities of adulthood. The titles of the penultimate and final episode similarly mirror the implied positivity of this coupling, as well as foreshadowing Vivian's own death during childbirth and Ben's hanging. Reborn as ghosts, along with Ben's child who died at the hands of its twin the anti-Christ, the final episode mirrors the first, with new inhabitants entering the home. The Harmon family now fully reunited in death, having cast off their troubled past and made "new", is finally liberated from their sins and gaze eerily on from the home's shadows.

Bibliography

American Horror Story. (2011–present). "Murder House", Season 1. Fulchuk, B. Murphy, R.

Armitt, L. (2014). *Twentieth Century Gothic*. Cardiff: University of Wales Press.

Banham, R. (1971). *Los Angeles: The Architecture of Four Ecologies*. Berkeley: University of California Press.

Butler, J. (1988). Performative Acts and Gender Constitution: An Essay in Phenomenology and Feminist Theory. *Theatre Journal.*, *40*(4), 519–531.

Colomina, B. (1992). *Sexuality and Space*. Princeton: Princeton Architectural Press.

Deleuze, G. (1980). *A Thousand Plateaus*. London: Athlone Press.

Deleuze, G. (1986). *Foucault*. London: Bloomsbury Academic.

Deleuze, G. (1996). *A Critical Reader*. Oxford: Blackwell.

Fine, D. (2004). *Imagining Los Angeles: A City in Fiction*. Reno: University of Nevada Press.

Foucault. (1975). *Discipline and Punish*. London: Random House.

Freud, S. (1955). *An Infantile Neurosis and Other Works*. London: The Hogarth Press.

Freud, S. (2003). *An Outline of Psychoanalysis*. London: Penguin Modern Classics.

Godfrey, N. (2015). Into the Maze: Stanley Kubrick's the Shining. *Screen Education, 78*, 124–128.

Griffin, R. (2016). Dreams, Nightmares and Haunted Houses: Televisual Horror as Domestic Imagery. *A Journal of the Social Imaginary, 6*, 86–104.

Grosz, E. (1994). *Volatile Bodies: Toward a Corporeal Feminism*. Indianapolis: Indiana University Press.

Grosz, E. (2001). *Architecture from the Outside: Essays on Virtual and Real Space*. Cambridge: MIT Press.

Grosz, E. (2008). *Chaos, Territory, Art: Deleuze and the Framing of the Earth*. New York: Columbia University Press.

Janicker, R. (Ed.). (2017). *Reading American Horror Story*. Jefferson: McFarland and Company, Amazon Kindle e-book edition.

Jervis, J. (2015). *Sympathetic Sentiments: Affect, Emotion and Spectacle in the Modern World*. London: Bloomsbury Academic.

Jurca, C. (2001). *White Diaspora: The Suburb and the Twentieth Century American Novel*. Princeton: Princeton University Press.

Kristeva, J. (1980). *Powers of Horror: An Essay on Abjection*. New York: Columbia University Press.

Marks, P. (2015). *Imagining Surveillance: Eutopian and Dystopian Literature and Film*. Edinburgh: Edinburgh University Press.

Murphet, J. (2001). *Literature and Race in Los Angeles*. Cambridge: Cambridge University Press.

Murphy, B. (2009). *The Suburban Gothic in American Popular Culture*. London: Palgrave Macmillan.

Schissel, W. (2006). *Home/Bodies: Geographies of Self, Place and Space*. Calgary: University of Calgary Press.

Soja, E. (2011). *Postmodern Geographies: The Reassertion of Space in Critical Social Theory*. New York: Verso.

Subramanian, J. (2013). The Monstrous Makeover: "American Horror Story", Femininity and Special Effects. *Critical Studies in Television, 8*(3), 108–123.

Vidler, A. (1994). *The Architectural Uncanny: Essays in the Modern Unhomely*. Cambridge: MIT Press.

Wisker, G. (2002). 'Honey, I'm home!' Splintering the Fabrication in Domestic Horror. *Femspec, 4*(1), 108.

CHAPTER 8

Surveillance, Sousveillance, and the Uncanny Domestic Architecture of *Black Mirror*

Luke Reid

Introduction

Charlie Brooker's anthology series *Black Mirror* (2011–present) addresses the extent to which screen culture and social media have become enmeshed with corporate and state-run surveillance technologies, often depicting the uncanny effects of identity formation in societies of control. Brooker has said in several interviews that he wanted to make an updated *Twilight Zone* where "technology took the place of the supernatural" (CNNMoney 2017, 00:46). Exploring the relationship between technology and subjectivation, the series inflects its dystopian futures with gothic tropes, suggesting an affinity between the ghostly and the virtual. As a "spectral" technology in itself, surveillance recurs throughout the series as a frequent preoccupation. Several episodes allegorise the "unhomely" effects of surveillance in contemporary society, dramatising voyeurism and exhibitionism as not only corrosive to but also constitutive of the construction of the self. For such "construction" often involves data-mining and sousveillance as the materials and processes of what might be described as a new kind of "architecture," where the subject is transmuted into streams of

L. Reid (✉)
Université de Montréal, Montreal, QC, Canada
e-mail: lureid@dawsoncollege.qc.ca

S. Flynn, A. Mackay (eds.), *Surveillance, Architecture and Control*,
https://doi.org/10.1007/978-3-030-00371-5_8

information "dwelling" within devices and on social media platforms. As such, the series implies that, for many, participatory surveillance now gothically "houses" identity. If, as Michel de Certeau has said, "haunted places are the only ones people can live in" (1988, p. 108), then *Black Mirror* posits technology and surveillance as new forms of the unhomely, haunted places in which we are all learning to live.

The series invokes modernist architecture as a "site" upon which these issues converge and are brought into relief. After all, architectural modernism is itself a discursively haunted place, its repressed histories spectralising the present in legacies which continue to "come back." And yet modernism is the moment when the uncanny, reaching its fullest articulation in the nineteenth century as the "quintessential bourgeois kind of fear" (Vidler 1992, p. 4), was meant to be dispelled by a radical and socially progressive architecture of transparency and openness. It is also the moment when, as Beatriz Colomina has pointed out, the private home became "a media center" (1994, p. 210), not only incorporating technology but *becoming* technology—to use Le Corbusier's famous phrase, "a machine for living in" (1986, p. 4). A still-contentious series of debates arises here over architecture's part in facilitating the construction of the private individual through the construction of the private home. Elucidating what he calls the nineteenth century's "emergence of the interior," Charles Rice has argued that the domestic architecture of the time acted as a spatial organisation consolidating "acceptable norms" and "practices of self-representation," such that "domestic arrangements" became interlinked with specific "gendered and familial roles" (2007, pp. 2–3). The "interior" was thus "a new topos of subjective interiority" (Rice 2007, p. 2), whereby domestic space could be said, both literally and figuratively, to situate identity.

In their Utopian vision of architecture *as* revolution, Le Corbusier and the modernists sought to open up this interior to light and air, to declutter "the oppressive aesthetic of Victorian architecture" which, in their eyes, had become symptomatic of "an unproductive repetition of tradition and trauma" (Thorne 2012, p. 22). To do so, they turned to glass architecture. From Walter Gropius to Mies van der Rohe, modernist architects embraced glass as a defining material in the curative belief that literal transparency would translate to the political and the psychological, that the "[e]xposure of the hidden" and the "bringing to light of the repressed" would have "a healing function" (McQuire 2008, p. 11). And yet, as early as Colin Rowe's and Robert Slutzky's 1963 essay "Transparency: Literal and Phenomenal," some critics saw this conflation of the physical and the psychic as simplistic and naïve, constituting what Anthony Vidler has called modernism's "myth of transparency" (1992, p. 217). Promising to break from the repetitions of the past, modernism tried to do away with privacy and the interior altogether. In the process, it ironically demonstrated the ways in which a glass architecture of so-called total exposure can nonetheless breed "new impenetrable zones, new invisibilities" (Steiner and Veel 2011, p. 224), offering instead "a game of confusing semi-transparencies, suggesting exclusion, control, [and] framing" (Widrich 2015, p. 43). Imagining transparency would lead to clarity and openness to freedom, modernism arguably "turn[ed] the problem of repetition into one of repression" (Thorne 2012, p. 23).

Black Mirror takes up these debates, foregrounding a highly stylised and often modernist architectural aesthetic in order to delineate the continuities and interconnections between architecture, surveillance, and control. It thematises the chiastic relationship between architecture's demand for the transparency of the private home and surveillance's demand for the transparency of the private individual. The series furthermore suggests that, in societies of control, these demands have become normalised, with surveillance "not just a particular practice or form of organisation but…a condition" (Dernbach 2018, p. 48) of everyday life, a condition which in turn liquidates identity to a function of "non-place" (Augé 2008) and place to a function of state-verified "identity." This chapter explores these issues through a consideration of the home not only as a "media centre" but as itself a form of media, arguing that *Black Mirror* invokes domestic architecture as both a metonym for surveillance technologies and a technology of surveillance in its own right.

"Crocodile" (2017), the third episode in the show's latest series, revisits the controversial history of modernist architecture's "myth of transparency," dramatising its promises and failures in order to imagine the dystopian effects of cultures of monitoring. Suggesting the reversible gaze of both glass architecture and sousveillance, "The Entire History of You" (2011) explores subject formation in societies of so-called moral transparency. By way of conclusion, I turn briefly to "Fifteen Million Merits" (2011), arguing that its dystopian architecture of electronic screens instantiates what Rafael Dernbach has recently described as a new "uncanny of surveillance" (Dernbach 2018). These episodes remind us that architecture and surveillance have a shared history and that the legacies of architectural modernism continue to haunt the uncanny constructions of selfhood in control societies.

"Crocodile": Surveillance, the Myth of Transparency, and the Corbusian "Picture-Window"

As with most *Black Mirror* episodes, "Crocodile" constructs its plot around the practical and ethical implications of a futuristic technology, in this case "the Recaller," a device which, when hooked up to a subject's mind via a small chip placed on the temple, can view and record the visual contents of specific memories. The device is initially used to investigate an insurance claim. After a driverless pizza delivery van accidentally strikes a pedestrian, the investigator, Shazia, uses the Recaller to probe the memories of a handful of witnesses in order to corroborate the claimant's account. The episode implies that the Recaller not only surveils individual memory but that, by extension, it necessarily conditions a society of constant sousveillance. As one witness's perspective captures and files away the memory of other witnesses, Shazia is able to piece together these various sightlines and reconstruct the event. In effect, the Recaller turns visual memory, and thus every sighted individual, into a CCTV camera.

A problem arises when one witness captures the image of another witness, Mia Nolan, looking out at the accident from her hotel room where, seconds before, she has murdered her ex-partner, Rob. This murder is meant to prevent Rob from coming forward about a shared crime from 15 years earlier—namely, the accidental death but intentional disposal of a cyclist whom Rob and Mia hit while driving under the influence. Once the Recaller is inevitably turned on Mia's memory, the episode snowballs into a frenzy of murders committed by Mia to conceal her crimes: first Shazia and then, after Mia herself utilises the Recaller, Shazia's husband and, in one of *Black Mirror*'s darkest moments, the couple's infant son whom Mia believes is yet another witness. In the first of two perversely ironic twists, the viewer learns that the boy was blind; in the second, that his pet hamster is not—ultimately, Mia is felled by the hamster. The episode considers what can and cannot be hidden or repressed in societies of near-total transparency and how surveillance breeds insecurity and anxiety as much as, if not more than, security and peace of mind.

If "Crocodile" casts forward into the future to write a cautionary tale about surveillance, then it does so by casting back into the past to frame the history of modernist architecture as itself cautionary. Like the Recaller, the episode probes memory, revisiting the cultural memory of glass architecture and its "myth of transparency." It does so through the character of Mia, a successful architect, her house a sleek, contemporaneous ode to modernism. Opening out onto a cluster of rigid, snow-capped hills, Mia's windows are floor-to-ceiling "walls of light." They are recognisably "window-walls," a hallmark of Le Corbusier's work which enabled him to "*get rid of walls completely*" (Le Corbusier 1991 cited in McQuire 2008, p. 172). As Colomina argues, Le Corbusier's interiors are meant to push the subject to the periphery of the house (1992), such that the house becomes "a mechanism for viewing" (Colomina 1994, p. 7). In this way, the "window-wall" does not simply "open out" onto nature; it frames, captures, and converts it to an image akin to that of a postcard (Colomina 1992; McQuire 2008).

The connection to photography is explicit and deliberate. In the Corbusian home, "the window is a lens, the house itself is a camera pointed at nature" (Colomina 1992, p. 113). Le Corbusier intended photography to "provid[e] one means for architecture to achieve a kind of 'post-interior' domesticity," whereby the plush furnishings and soft wall-hangings of the Victorian era were "seemingly obliterated" (Rice 2007, p. 104). And yet, as Rice argues, the bourgeois interior's sense of enclosure was in large part constructed through the use of the image, "whether it be a two-dimensional representation such as a painting, a print in a portfolio of decoration, or a flat backdrop that could conjure up an interior as a theatrical scene" (2007, p. 2). As "a system for taking pictures" (Colomina 1992, p. 113), the Corbusian home does much the same. A problematic irony emerges within the aesthetic and discursive foundations of modernist architecture. Whereas glass was meant to usher in a "post-interior" of *light, air, and openness*, it simply transformed the house into "a frame for a view" (Colomina 1992, p. 119). Framing the exterior and rendering it an "image"—a two-dimensional backdrop—the "window-wall" becomes "a gigantic screen" (Colomina 1992, p. 119) and the so-called emancipatory potential of glass (Rice 2007, p. 104) remains unrealised. Propounding glass walls that would embody and embolden progressive change, modernism instead produced "picture-windows" which turned "the threatening world outside into a reassuring picture" (Colomina 1994, p. 7), recreating the repressive interiors of the past.

"Crocodile" exploits this irony to thematic effect. Mia symbolises an architecture that in theory promises progressive openness while in practice it is a technology of stagnant repression. Introduced at a talk she has been asked to give on her "vision of the future," she is described as "not just an architect of buildings but of communities" ("Crocodile" 2017, 08:23). And while her remarks pay lip service to the responsibility of "building a better tomorrow" in a world of "injustice and intolerance" ("Crocodile" 2017, 05:34), we later watch as she sneaks onto the construction site of one of her own projects to dispose of Rob's body ("Crocodile" 2017, 20:33). The ironies of architectural modernism are here dramatised as criminal hypocrisies, and the implication could not be clearer. Despite the bromides of a better tomorrow, embodied by a supposedly forward-looking and transparent architecture, Mia does not break with the past, she merely represses it. As with Rob's body, the past may be kept hidden out of sight but it is nonetheless *in the foundations* of both Mia and her architecture. Bleakly satirical in its formulation of this theme, the episode dwells on a sign outside the mass housing site where Mia is in the midst of burying Rob's body—it reads, "Affordable Living for All" ("Crocodile" 2017, 20:11).

Moments such as these are pointed allusions to what many critics have seen as modernism's failed Utopianism, its history of good intentions followed by, at best, little social progress and, at worst, adverse and even unjust living conditions (Brolin 1976; Coleman 2014; Rowe and Koetter 1978; Urban 2012). They also open up a further dimension to the episode's treatment of the "myth of transparency," namely, the notion that, for architectural modernism, "glass carried with it a mystical ideal of redemption" (Widrich 2015, p. 49). For example, it is clear that Mia sees her architectural work as compensatory, as somehow "making up" for her participation in the disposal of the cyclist's body. And yet she pursues this redemption by "constructing" both private and public selves which profess a transparency that is actually repressive and, as such, cannot help but repeat the patterns of the past.

This notion of Mia's identity as a projected image meant to conceal hidden depths is visually tied to the ambiguity of glass as at once transparent *and* reflective. In turn, it furthermore develops a motif whereby the ambivalence of the Corbusian picture-window gestures towards the repression of both the threatening nature of the outside world and the threatening "nature" of Mia's inner self.

Framing "Nature": Repression and the Ambivalence of the Modernist Interior

Steiner and Veel point out that an often overlooked but important property of glass is how, at certain times and in certain weather conditions, it can look "like a screen or even an impenetrable surface" (2011, p. 219). The episode makes use of this effect. In an early scene, as Mia plans her day with her husband and son, the camera films her from the exterior of the house, through the floor-to-ceiling windows, such that her image becomes obscured by, and even confused with, the reflection of the dramatic landscape outside, suggesting she is neither as "transparent" nor as *self-contained* as she might otherwise appear ("Crocodile" 2017, 27:42). This motif extends to Mia's construction of a public self as well. Before leaving for her talk, we see her in the bathroom of the house practising her speech before the mirror, the superficiality of her remarks visually linked to the two-dimensional "Mia" reflected in yet another glass surface which is nonetheless opaque ("Crocodile" 2017, 05:44). As the culmination of this trope of "Mia-as-image," the scene then cuts to a brief montage of her office, tellingly located in the basement of the house, where, with Mia's speech continuing in voice-over, the camera lingers on a framed copy of the architecture magazine *Dwell*, a photograph of Mia on its cover ("Crocodile" 2017, 05:47).

The episode suggests that Mia's crimes reveal a true "nature" that can barely be contained beneath the "reassuring picture" of an identity she has worked so hard to construct. To this end, it draws parallels between Mia's nature and the nature that surrounds her, between Mia as a constructed self and the architectural constructions which render the interior "a system for taking pictures" (Colomina 1992, p. 113). The performance and styling of Andrea Riseborough, the actor who plays Mia, reflect this dynamic. Riseborough is exhausting to watch. A frenetic steeliness energises her every move while her pale-skin, ice-blue eyes, and close-cropped platinum hair are clearly meant to mirror the menacingly austere Icelandic landscapes where the episode was filmed. John Hillcoat, the episode's director, has said that shooting in Iceland was "a constant reminder of how powerful nature is" (Delahaye 2018). "It adds energy," he continued. "The world is right in front of you, and you have to deal with it" (Delahaye 2018).

If "dealing with" nature is what Mia and modernist architecture do when confronted by the immediacy of its power, then Hillcoat's camera attempts much the same as well. The extensive diegetic use of modernist-styled windows which, throughout the episode, produce a Corbusian "gaze of domination over the exterior world" (Colomina 1992, p. 112), is paralleled by the camera's extradiegetic gaze, which masters the natural landscape and delivers it into the viewer's home flattened and tamed on computer and television screens—"window-walls" and "picture-windows" of a sort. And yet in the triangulation of these tropes and motifs, a more complex interplay of framing devices emerges, from Mia's framing of the self to architecture's framing of nature to the camera's framing of the narrative. Several scenes put glass architecture in tension with abrupt and thematically suggestive establishing shots of nature—the black mirror of a lake, a ribbon of treacherous road, snow-flecked outcroppings of basalt. In some, the camera slowly "slips inside" without edit to reveal the same landscape but now behind glass and framed by a window ("Crocodile" 2017, 07:50). The technique gestures towards the ambivalent effect of the Corbusian interior. On the one hand, it clearly positions the window as a kind of lens which "refocuses" the menace of nature, arranging it and collecting it as an image in order to relieve its troubling depths; on the other, the camera seems to pull the exterior world inside, reminding us that only a thin layer of glass sits between a view that has been framed and a view that, as Colomina emphasises, "*enters* the house" (1992, p. 119).

This sense of the interior's porosity corresponds with the precariousness of Mia's interiority and its ability to repress the menace of its own "nature." The ambivalence of the "picture-window" as a visual trope thus persists in key scenes related to Mia's murders. Talking to Rob as he confesses his plan to come forward with their criminal past, Mia leans against her hotel room wall, a mural which, spanning the full length of the room, depicts an outsize tree, its branches, flowers, and leaves all perspectivally warped and disproportionately large ("Crocodile" 2017, 10:36). The mural's unrealistic scale is a subjective rendering of nature's ability to threaten interior space, as well as a suggestion of architecture's ability to distance nature, to keep it at arm's length. As the idea of killing Rob takes "root" in Mia's mind, we watch as her own nature is at once flattened to the surface of the wall *and* brought into hideous "bloom". This motif recurs later when, as Mia stands before Shazia's infant son in his crib, the camera pans away, concealing the murder with a shot of the wallpaper, a hectic rain of flowers cast in the same colour palette as Mia's hotel wall ("Crocodile" 2017, 54:15). Whereas Mia intends her windows at home to be "walls" that keep nature out, the walls described above are "windows" that reveal the ways in which nature nonetheless manages to get in.

Nowhere is this dynamic of the picture-window's ambivalence made clearer than in the use of the Recaller. Bringing together the episode's twin preoccupations of glass architecture and surveillance, Shazia sits in Mia's living room, its "walls of light" framing a stunning view of mountains and sky, just as the Recaller's viewing screen frames Mia's shocking memories ("Crocodile" 2017, 42:08). Moments before, Mia has returned from the bathroom where, in a direct reference to the scene discussed earlier, she attempts to fabricate false memories in order to mislead the Recaller, standing in front of the mirror and, so to speak, "constructing interiority" ("Crocodile" 2017, 41:20). And yet, when subjected to the Recaller, her "opacity"—that is, her ability to utilise the ambiguity of glass to construct a surface image of the self and to immure an interior self—collapses into total transparency. Meant to secure the interior and repress the threatening gaze of the outside world, Mia's glass walls end up framing the scene's explicit parallel between an outward view of a clear and endless horizon and the Recaller's penetrating view of Mia's past.

The episode thus ironises the hypocrisy of modernism's failure to deliver on the promise of glass architecture's moral transparency. And then, in the form of the Recaller, it delivers on that promise, only to suggest that such transparency was itself a hypocritical "myth," neither socially progressive nor politically ethical. Captured in its portable box and visible on its square screen, identities are "housed" in the Recaller in much the same way as in the Corbusian interior, with the modernist home "a mobile box" and its picture-window a "view-finder" (McQuire 2008, p. 173). The implications of the Recaller's power to surveil and "frame" identity raise a host of legal and civil liberties issues which, significantly, go unaddressed in the episode, suggesting how seamlessly participatory surveillance integrates itself into control societies. In a complex symbiosis between architecture and surveillance, the episode thematises the Recaller as "[t]he point at which the 'openness' necessary for legitimate political scrutiny spills into an authoritarian demand for visibility" (McQuire 2008, p. 173). As such, it calls into relief the "structural ambivalence inhabiting architectural and political transparency" (McQuire 2008, p. 173).

Nothing to Hide: Glass Architecture's "Two-Way Window" and the Performance of Identity in "The Entire History of You"

A similar ambivalence informs an episode from *Black Mirror's* first series, "The Entire History of You." The episode involves a couple, Liam and Ffion, whose marriage dissolves after Liam begins to suspect Ffion of infidelity with a former partner, Jonas. Set in a futuristic though recognisable society where a majority of the population has an electively implanted chip known as the "grain" recording everything they see and hear, the episode concerns issues of trust and transparency in cultures of generalised sousveillance. After seeing Ffion and Jonas together for the first time at a dinner party, Liam obsessively retrieves and analyses "footage" from his own memory until he confirms his suspicions and forces Ffion to confess. Highlighted by the episode's foregrounded use of modernist houses, the "grain" is a futuristic analogue of the Corbusian picture-window. Its ability to play back memories in what are called "re-dos" allows characters to project video onto the walls of their home or to view it directly in front of their eyes. Like the Corbusian interior, the "grain" is a "mechanism for viewing": it suggests openness but effects enclosure.

At the same time, where "Crocodile" depicts the picture-window as dominantly framing the exterior world, "The Entire History of You" reminds us that "[t]he picture window works two ways: it turns the outside world into an image to be consumed by those inside the house, but it also displays the image of the interior to that outside world" (Colomina 1994, p. 8). Drawing a parallel between the "grain" and modernist architecture, the episode demonstrates how "[t]he reversibility of the gaze… splits the subject in a perpetual oscillation between viewer and viewed" (McQuire 2008, p. 177). A tension then persists throughout "The Entire History of You" where, on the one hand, the "grain" claims to effect a culture of moral transparency and authenticity while, on the other, it elicits the near-constant performance of identity, transforming individuals into "images" or simulacra of themselves, a tension thematised by the episode's use of glass architecture and the "two-way window."

Despite architectural discourse's disparaging reconsideration in the 1990s, glass continues to be associated with "light, clarity and democratic models of transparency" (Widrich 2015, p. 43). Citing a 2006 anthropological survey of people living in contemporary examples of glass architecture, Steiner and Veel point out that, for residents, "visual openness…

reflects a set of values" such as "open-mindedness and tolerance" (2011, p. 220). Inhabitants, furthermore, say that they regard people "who ensconce themselves behind curtains and plants...as being less accessible, old-fashioned, limited in their perspective...and even suspicious" (Steiner and Veel 2011, p. 220). Concisely summarising a pervasive attitude towards transparency and surveillance in general, one respondent "states explicitly that living this way signifies 'that you have nothing to hide'" (Steiner and Veel 2011, p. 220). Such comments revisit one of architectural modernism's central tenets—namely, that "clearly visible interiors" imply "a kind of courageous interior activity that requires no architectural cover" (Widrich 2015, p. 48). And yet, with the walls of the home "display windows" and domestic space "part of public life," inhabitants react to such exposure by developing what Steiner and Veel call "the performative aspects of interior decoration," whereby staging and dissimulation become "mode[s] of living" (2011, p. 222).

In other words, glass architecture prompts the *performance* of moral transparency. As a space which brings "the individual in contact only with another image of himself" (Augé 2008, p. 64), glass architecture might be said to instantiate a domestic iteration of what Marc Augé terms "non-place." Subjecting identity to total visibility and innocence to constant verification, "non-place" and glass architecture insist on the axiom "if you've nothing to hide, you have nothing to fear." "The Entire History of You" exemplifies this sense of the home as a "non-place" by dramatising the modernist interior as a technology of sousveillance similar to the "grain." Using architectural sightlines as frames, domestic space facilitates horizontal forms of visual monitoring and, like the "grain," problematises the twinned concepts of self/interiority and home/interior.

Taking Pictures: Architectural Modernism and "Unhomely" Subject Formation

Colomina has argued that the camera-like abilities of Le Corbusier's interiors unsettle notions of dwelling and inhabitation. "For Le Corbusier," she writes, "'to inhabit' means to inhabit the camera. But the camera is not a traditional place, it is a system of classification, a kind of filing cabinet. 'To inhabit' means to employ that system" (Colomina 1992, p. 120). In "The Entire History of You," the "grain" and the modernist interior are image-based "systems of classification." A number of scenes show characters watching "re-dos" directly in front of their eyes. In effect, they become absented from the immediate space, "dwelling" so to speak within the "grain." As such, they "inhabit the camera," a "non-place" where an archive of recorded memories, collected and classified, stands in for both interior *and* interiority. The episode gothicises these moments with the visual motif of a character's demonically glazed-over eyes, as though to inhabit the "grain" is to be inhabited by it, transmuting the posthuman subject into an uncanny double ("The Entire History of You" 2011, 34:43).

If the "grain" unsettles embodiment by replacing the individual with an "image of himself," then it produces a similar dislocation when it comes to the home. Towards the end of the episode, Liam walks through the house in playback mode transposing "re-do" memories of specific rooms onto these same rooms in the present, moving through both physical and photographic space at the same time ("The Entire History of You" 2011, 44:37). The scene suggests the capacity of the "grain" to displace the home as the subject's private interior. Recognising as much, Liam gruesomely cuts it out with a razor blade in the episode's final moments ("The Entire History of You" 2011, 47:14).

Signalling a continuity between architecture and sousveillance, the episode implies that the modernist house is an image-making technology complicit in the subject's uncanny alienation. In several instances, the episode's architectural spaces are seen "taking pictures." Coupled with modernism's distinctively open floor plans, the clean lines of the interiors become camera-like perspectives, narrowing in on certain characters and framing their arrangements as thematic tableaux. This is most significantly achieved as Liam arrives at the dinner party and, through the "telescoped" perspective of a long hallway suggestively flanked by floor-to-ceiling windows, sees Ffion and Jonas in conversation ("The Entire History of You" 2011, 05:35–05:57). It is this "image," captured and filed in his digital memory bank, which plants the first seed of doubt in Liam's mind, causing him to revisit and analyse it endlessly. Embellishing this theme, the motif recurs in various forms, from shots of Ffion framed by the built-in transparent screen where the couple watches "re-dos" ("The Entire History of You" 2011, 21:02) to the blurred reflection of a suspicious Liam returning his own gaze in a kitchen window ("The Entire History of You" 2011, 21:50). These particular examples develop a pointed trope. Where Ffion is reduced to an image from a "re-do," subjected to a detective-like gaze that must penetrate the surface and reveal some hidden mystery, Liam, plagued by spiralling insecurities, is depersonalised as a gothic alter ego, the indistinct mirror-image of himself.

As depicted in "The Entire History of You," surveillance becomes a system of space and space a system of surveillance, each disorienting, dislocating, and defamiliarising home and self. With the house complicit in the taking and filing of images, the episode suggests a set of structural affinities between architecture, surveillance, and the uncanny. Distinguishing between "house" and "home," Sarah Thorne comments that the latter is "a purely fantasmatic object of our desire," whereas the former is "that physical space in which this fantasy is staged, and through which we attempt [to] realize our desire for home by manipulating its aesthetic and interior configuration" (2012, p. 5). Following Freud, our sense of the *unheimlich*—the uncanny, the unhomely—originates with our departure from the womb, the first "dwelling-house," such that "the origin of the house is a consequence of loss" (Thorne 2012, p. 6). We are then always in search of the lost object, the "home," remaking it unsuccessfully in the "house." In this way, we return to "houses" without ever arriving "home" (Thorne 2012). For Liam and Ffion, the modernist house and the "grain" are technologies which, due to their surveillant capabilities, exacerbate this sense of ontological "homelessness." Both are "machines for living in" which, as we have seen, not only share an immediate capacity to replace the real with images (McQuire 2008) but also call to the surface that which was always there, forcing Liam and Ffion to confront an uncanny sense of "*augmented familiarity*" that now "resists domestication" (Trigg 2012, pp. 27–28).

The episode is an unambiguously critical allegory of screen culture and social media. However, it also depicts self-surveillance and sousveillance as forms of what Hille Koskela has called "empowering exhibitionism" (2004 cited in Steiner and Veel 2011, p. 226). Characters "show off" their memories, offering them up for public consumption and commentary ("The Entire History of You" 2011, 04:39), suggesting how the "grain" both constructs and verifies self-identity. The episode implies that for some people taking charge of surveillance means "tak[ing] charge over the way in which their lives are represented—turning (daily) living into an identity project" (Steiner and Veel 2011, p. 226). As one of the traditional spaces in which identity is "constructed," the domestic interior is depicted as facilitating such a project. During the episode's dinner party, as characters socialise at the table, "re-dos" of their various memories play in the background, projected directly onto the "wall-screens" of the house ("The Entire History of You" 2011, 13:49). In an article on "smart homes" and participatory surveillance, Albrechtslund and Ryberg contend that, just as "self-surveillance is a positive basis for socializing practices on the web," the "social surveillance of the intelligent house" can be "the basis for personal empowerment and social interaction" (2011, p. 44).

Both "Crocodile" and "The Entire History of You" invoke the legacy of modernist architecture precisely to satirise, in the bleakest terms possible, such arguments. And yet, while it is clear where its sympathies lie, *Black Mirror* nonetheless depicts worlds wherein constant surveillance is taken for granted as a generalised condition of everyday life, implying that, in one way or another, there is now no such thing as empowerment or sociality *without* the subject's participation in systems of surveillance. Writing on Jennifer Ringley, the creator of the website JenniCam, which from 1996 to 2003 "lifecasted" Ringley's day-to-day existence, Victor Burgin argues that thinking of Ringley's camera as a window "privilege[s] our own point of view" (2002, p. 230). By judging her "to be an exhibitionist," Burgin writes, "we have done no more than acknowledge our own voyeurism" (2002, p. 230). For Burgin, Ringley accepts and then harnesses the camera's surveillant power, using it to construct identity, such that from "our side of the screen, the camera is a window," whereas from "Ringley's position, her camera is a mirror" (2002, p. 230). Mechtild Widrich applies such thinking to the legacies of architectural modernism and its use of glass. "[I]t is the task of politically engaged art and architecture of our present time," she writes, "to question [the] ideology of [modernism's rationality and control]; to replace the false clarity of transparent glass with the clear disorientation, so to speak, of a system of mirrors" (2015, p. 51). To use Deleuze's phrase: "There is no need to fear or hope, but only to look for new weapons" (1992, p. 4).

Conclusion: "Fifteen Million Merits" and the Uncanny Architecture of Control

If certain forms of surveillance have the "potential to empower the watched" (Albrechtslund and Ryberg 2011, p. 43), then it is easy to imagine how subjects might seek out opportunities to construct identity through willing and participatory observation. Given the constant need to update one's Instagram and Facebook accounts, it is more than possible that we have already passed this point. As Zizek argued nearly two decades ago, "anxiety seems to arise from the prospect of NOT being exposed to the Other's gaze all the time, so that the subject needs the camera's gaze as a kind of ontological guarantee of his/her being" (2002, p. 225). As a strategy of control, the dystopia in "Fifteen Million Merits" exploits this need, withholding the gaze and commodifying the individual's sense that "I exist only insofar as I am looked at all the time" (Zizek 2002, p. 225). The episode depicts a futuristic society in which subjects are forced to pedal on stationary bikes while consuming endless streams of visual content, their exercise regimens tied to a system of "merits" which serve as currency for food and other necessities. At the cost of 15 million merits, the subject can buy an audition on *Hot Shots*, a competition-based reality show, securing at worst a few minutes of exposure and at best the offer of their own show. In a satirical take on binge-TV and screen ubiquity, the episode portrays "watching" as a form of hard labour that can only be escaped by becoming the "watched."

The dystopian architecture and mise-en-scène are complicit in this system. Making a pointed reference to modernism's ideological history of glass architecture, the episode represents "domestic space" as box-like rooms in which the walls are electronic screens displaying constant content ("Fifteen Million Merits" 2011, 00:08:08). We need look no further than Colomina's description of the inhabitants of Le Corbusier's houses to see how pointed this reference truly is: "they cannot fix (arrest) the image...[T]hey inhabit a space that is neither inside nor outside, public nor private...It is a space that is not made of walls but of images. Images as walls" (1994, p. 6). As Scott McQuire writes, "it is only a short step [from the Corbusian picture-window] to the contemporary horizon of electronic windows" (2008, p. 173). The episode takes the notion of the home as a "media centre" to its furthest extreme. Consuming media becomes not only the primary but the only domestic activity, while the interior becomes—if the resident/contestant is lucky—a broadcast centre unto itself. With the "solidity of [the] walls...giv[ing] way to the restless luminosity of electronic screens" (McQuire 2008, p. 9), there is no distinction between interior and exterior: screens can open out onto anything anywhere at any time, "disturbing the spatiality of the world at large" and rendering the home "no longer continuous with site" (McQuire 2008, p. 3).

The world of "Fifteen Million Merits" exemplifies what Rafael Dernbach has recently characterised as "the late-modern uncanny of surveillance" (2018, p. 51). While Freud's "uncanny" gestures towards dislocation, alienation, and the unhomely, Dernbach delineates an "uncanny" of "hyperactive incapacity" (2018, p. 47), whereby glass architecture and the "financial gazing" (2018, p. 50) of systems of observation compel the subject to replace action with activity. Inducing the subject's "uncanny complicity with a controlling gaze" (Dernbach 2018, p. 62), surveillance and architecture engender societies wherein "disruption and otherness are anticipated and pre-empted" (2018, p. 53). With its "merit" system, its near-constant physical activity, and its screen architecture, "Fifteen Million Merits" embodies just such a society. In the episode, the main character, Bing, refuses to be passively complicit any longer. Ultimately, however, his resistance only proves the flexibility of the system in place. After storming the *Hot Shots* stage and threatening to commit suicide with a shard of glass from one of his room's "screen-walls," Bing is offered his own show ("Fifteen Million Merits" 2011, 00:54:44). Co-opting and thus neutralising his rage and anger, the surveillant gaze of late-capitalism *re*-presents Bing and his activism as simply more content, the daily monologue of his new show a spuriously cathartic performance which incapacitates both himself and his viewers.

Where "Crocodile" and "The Entire History of You" cast backward through the histories of architectural modernism in order to suggest their continuities with surveillance and the uncanny, "Fifteen Million Merits" projects forward to an uncanny surveillance deeply informed by modernism's still lingering legacies. Concluding the episode, Bing finishes up a broadcast and walks around his now much larger room. Recognisably modernist, it is sparse and minimally appointed, with an openness and visibility suggestive of Bing's compliance and transparency ("Fifteen Million Merits" 2011, 00:59:19). After depositing his glass shard in a protective case, he moves to a set of double-height floor-to-ceiling windows and, in the episode's closing shot, looks out onto a view of forest and sky so lush and vivid we cannot help but wonder if it is real or if it is an image—if, sitting at home watching on our TVs and laptops, we are looking through a window or at yet another screen within a screen.

Bibliography

Albrechtslund, A., & Ryberg, T. (2011). Participatory Surveillance in the Intelligent Building. *Design 27*(3), 35–46. Available at: http://www.jstor.org/stable/41261942. Accessed 1 Jan 2018.

Augé, M. (2008). *Non-Places: An Introduction to Supermodernity* (2nd ed.). Translated from French by J. Howe. London: Verso Books.

Brolin, B. C. (1976). *The Failure of Modern Architecture*. London: Studio Vista.

Burgin, V. (2002). Jenni's Room: Exhibitionism and Solitude. In T. Y. Levin, U. Frohne, & P. Weibel (Eds.), *CTRL [Space]: Rhetorics of Surveillance from Bentham to Big Brother* (pp. 228–235). Cambridge, MA: MIT Press.

CNNMoney. (2017). *Black Mirror Creator: We Replaced the Supernatural with Tech.* [Online Video] Available at: https://www.youtube.com/watch?v=ggwCdrX-QYU. Accessed 26 Mar 2018.

Coleman, N. (2014). The Problematic of Architecture and Utopia. *Utopian Studies, 25*(1), 1–22. http://www.jstor.org/stable/10.5325/utopianstudies.25.1.0001. Accessed 15 Apr 2018.

Colomina, B. (1992). The Split Wall: Domestic Voyeurism. In B. Colomina (Ed.), *Sexuality and Space* (pp. 72–128). New York: Princeton Architectural Press.

Colomina, B. (1994). *Privacy and Publicity: Modern Architecture as Mass Media.* Cambridge, MA: MIT Press.

Corbusier. (1986). *Towards a New Architecture.* Translated from the French by F. Etchells. New York: Dover Publications, PDF (Online). Available at: https://monoskop.org/images/b/bf/Corbusier_Le_Towards_a_New_Architecture_no_OCR.pdf. Accessed 19 Mar 2018.

"Crocodile". (2017). *Black Mirror*, Streaming Video, *Netflix.* Available at: https://www.netflix.com

de Certeau, M. (1988). *The Practice of Everyday Life.* Translated from the French by S. Rendall. Berkeley/Los Angeles: University of California Press.

Delahaye, J. (2018, January 8). Black Mirror 'Crocodile' Location Revealed as Viewers Floored by the Breathtaking Snowy Landscapes. *Mirror* [Online]. Available at: https://www.mirror.co.uk/travel/europe/black-mirror-crocodile-filming-location-11791798. Accessed 3 Mar 2018.

Deleuze, G. (1992). Postscript on the Societies of Control. *October, 59,* 3–7. http://www.jstor.org/stable/778828. Accessed 18 Mar 2018.

Dernbach, R. (2018). The Uncanny of Surveillance: Architectures of Hyperactive Incapacity in Nikolaus Geyrhalter's *Abendland* and Falk Richter's *Unter Eis.* In A. Ring, H. Steiner, & K. Veel (Eds.), *Architecture and Control* (pp. 46–64). Boston: Brill. Available at: https://ebookcentral.proquest.com. Accessed 17 Mar 2018.

"Fifteen Million Merits". (2011). *Black Mirror*, Streaming Video, *Netflix.* Available at: https://www.netflix.com

McQuire, S. (2008). *The Media City: Media, Architecture and Urban Space.* London: Sage.

Rice, C. (2007). *The Emergence of the Interior: Architecture, Modernity, Domesticity.* Abingdon/Oxon: Routledge.

Rowe, C., & Koetter, F. (1978). *Collage City.* Cambridge, MA: MIT Press.

Steiner, H., & Veel, K. (2011). Living Behind Glass Facades: Surveillance Culture and New Architecture. *Surveillance & Society, 9*(1/2), 215–232. http://www.surveillance-and-society.org. Accessed 18 Mar 2018.

"The Entire History of You". (2011). *Black Mirror*, Streaming Video, *Netflix.* Available at: https://www.netflix.com

Thorne, S. (2012). *The Cleaving of House and Home: A Lacanian Analysis of Architectural Aesthetics.* Master's Thesis, The University of Western Ontario. Available at: http://ir.lib.uwo.ca/etd/1014. Accessed 27 Jan 2018.

Trigg, D. (2012). *The Memory of Place: A Phenomenology of the Uncanny.* Athens: Ohio University Press.

Urban, F. (2012). *Tower and Slab: Histories of Global Mass Housing.* Abingdon/ Oxon: Routledge.

Vidler, A. (1992). *The Architectural Uncanny: Essays in the Modern Unhomely.* Cambridge, MA: MIT Press.

Widrich, M. (2015). 'I'll Be Your Mirror': Transparency, Voyeurism and Glass Architecture. In: H. Steiner & K. Veel (Eds.), *Invisibility Studies: Surveillance, Transparency and the Hidden in Contemporary Culture* (pp. 43–59). Bern: Peter Lang AG, International Academic Publishers. Available at: http:// web.b.ebscohost.com. Accessed 18 Mar 2018.

Zizek, S. (2002). Big Brother, or, the Triumph of the Gaze over the Eye. In T. Y. Levin, U. Frohne, & P. Weibel (Eds.), *CTRL [Space]: Rhetorics of Surveillance from Bentham to Big Brother* (pp. 224–227). Cambridge, MA: MIT Press.

PART III

International Spaces, Performativity and Identity

CHAPTER 9

The Birds: Public Art and a Narrative of Surveillance

Joel Hawkes

Introduction

Built on the last area of undeveloped waterfront—once a location of sawmills and shipbuilders—the Olympic Village in Vancouver (2010 winter games) is now residential housing, touted by the city and the Millennium Development Group as "one of the greenest communities in the world" (Vancouver.ca 2018). At its centre lies the Olympic Village Square, a public space walled on two sides by buildings of steel and glass that seems to conform to Richard Sennett's reading of the modern city space as "safe because it is empty" (1990). Such precise design of neutral space makes surveillance easy, but you often forget the web of private and public cameras that capture every movement. And there are many cameras in Vancouver, as a mapping of camera's in the downtown area in 2010 revealed—a count taken before those added for the Olympics (Vancouver Public Space 2010). You forget the assemblage of surveillance because "empty" space encourages easeful movement (Sennett 1990). The pedestrian is always moving on, flowing like water, unhindered, to be somewhere else.

J. Hawkes (✉)
University of Victoria, Victoria, BC, Canada
e-mail: jhawkes@uvic.ca

S. Flynn, A. Mackay (eds.), *Surveillance, Architecture and Control*,
https://doi.org/10.1007/978-3-030-00371-5_9

Yet, in the Square you are invited to stop and look—to look at a place that was an Olympic television spectacle (beamed around the world to our screens), to look at the concrete framed vision of nature in the water beyond, to look at a Square "delineated by steel 'rib' lights which represent the shipbuilding that once took place on the site" (Cdm2 2018) It is, though, not this history, nor these modern framing devices of design, nor the "heritage" of the site that invites the pedestrian to pause. The programmable LEDs of the "rib" lights illuminate not only the Square at night but also *The Birds* sculpture—two giant sparrows, around five metres high, designed by Myfanwy MacLeod to peer menacingly down at passers-by. Inspired by Alfred Hitchcock's 1963 film of the same name, this public art disrupts the "empty" space and asks you to, for a moment at least, stop and look. The sparrows allow a "discovery"—not the kind that Sennett suggest gives "value" to space, creating an inhabitable "narrative" (1990), but rather alerting you to a narrative of surveillance—to a threatening space that owes more to horror and science fiction film than comforting heritage and "green" design. We no longer look at art; it looks at us. This is part of the artist's playful intent. But then, we look about us. And the space seems to look back. I will argue that through *The Birds* sculpture we see how the out-of-placeness of public art can alert the viewer to the reality of a carefully controlled and monitored city space. Drawing from the theory of Richard Sennett, Michel Foucault, and Gilles Deleuze, I will examine how the sculpture draws attention to the constructed, assemblage-nature of the environment that contains the viewer, and to the surveillance assemblage that is a half-seen component of this space. I will go onto to suggest that *The Birds* sculpture, like its film counterpart, alerts you to a narrative of surveillance and control that underpins the social spaces we inhabit. The sculpture even goes some way to establishing Hitchcock's narrative as part of the Village Square assemblage. The moment of "looking" at *The Birds* sculpture compounds the emptiness of the Square, draws attention to the site's isolation from the natural world, and removes the sense of safety found in the city. You are aware of a surveillance narrative and space.

Some of the Assemblage(s) of the Olympic Village Square

So, what do we look at? What is seen? Pedestrians unaware of the deliberate Hitchcock reference in the sculpture might still be jolted by its gigantic presence to recall the director's iconic birds and his "surveillance" film.

And if they are not, the sculpture is a spectacle offering its own narrative as well, the type of art that for Cher Knight does not blend into its surroundings, but rather "screams for attention" (2008). It seems out of place in the Square. It "opens up" space to our notice, and to a reading: there is spectacle throughout the components of the Square's design, from framings of the natural world (sky above and water beyond); to the towering, dominating apartment buildings; through the "space-aged" ribbed lights. And all of this was once the centre of the Olympics. There is spectacle at the heart of this urban assemblage. It should be a space that makes you look, but almost paradoxically the Olympic and urban design is disguised by the muted tones of brick and glass—the banality of modern urban planning. We are so used to the arrangements of this manufactured space that we forget to look; but of course, following Sennett's reading, looking is not required in a space that is after all designed to keep people as a regulated flow within its borders (Sennett 1990). The only looking supported here is that needed to police and monitor the space and those moving within. Indeed, the design of the Square and buildings appears to conform to recommendations made by Jane Jacobs in her hugely influential *The Death and Life of Great American Cities* (a book that still inspires urban design today) as to what makes for a safe street: that public and private space must be clearly demarked and that there "must be eyes upon the street" (Jacobs 1961). The flow of people must be continuous to add to the collective of watching eyes and to "induce people in buildings along the street to watch the sidewalks" (Jacobs 1961). The wide space of the Square, the clear demarcation of street and apartments, and the apartments of windows—blocks not too high so that watching is easy in all directions—are all eyes not enjoying space but policing it, making it "safe" in the words of Jacobs. But, then, shouldn't a Square be a location that encourages you to stop, and to look, not at those who might pose a risk but at those you might talk to and at the space itself, which should make you want to linger—in the tradition of the agora? It is *The Birds* that ultimately make you stop here. They draw attention to the overlooked quality of spectacle but also highlight the over-manufactured nature of a "safe" design. The viewer becomes more spatially aware.

Even without knowledge of Deleuze and Guattari's theoretical "assemblage" (1987), pedestrians are alerted by the giant sparrows to the movement and flow of the space they inhabit. Feeling watched, you look about the Square and become aware of at least part of the "machinic assemblage" or rather assemblages of "material and immaterial processes" (Staples 2014), of "bodies, of actions and passions" and the "acts and statements, of incorporeal transformations attributed to bodies," which at once create a territory and a process of "deterritorialization" in the Olympic Village Square (Deleuze and Guattari 1987). The viewer sees the parts of the physical assemblage, the quick movement of people through the Square, the Square as an empty, uninviting space, and also the less material parts of the whole: the narratives of heritage (birds, lights, and waterside), money, and political power, and even Hitchcock. With a sense of being watched in this space, there is a sense you, too, become spectacle and part of the assemblage—you move on but aware now that you are moving on. And perhaps you wonder, are you, too, also manufactured? Are you regulated by the design of this space? And if part of the spectacle, who is watching you and from where—from windows, coffee shop, water front, CCTV? Or is it just *The Birds* that stare?

If *The Birds* open up the Square to a consideration of surveillance and assemblage, the assemblage also opens to other theoretical interpretations of space, which are welcome in a space of multiplicity—theories that similarly both demark and blur the territory. Foucault's theory of heterotopia is a reading not unlike the assemblage—locations that are a "system of opening and closing that [both] isolates … and makes them penetrable at one and the same time" (Foucault 1997), while having "the power of juxtaposing in a single real place different spaces and locations that are incompatible with each other" (1997). Here we seem to have a Square that should encourage people to stop, but whose design encourages the opposite; and into this site we see reflected the past glories of the Olympics (All past Olympics?). Foucault, though, suggests only certain spaces as heterotopias, such as the theatre, garden, cemetery, or cinema. There is, or was, at least, something theatrical about this site with its connection to the heritage of the Greek games. But, through the sculpture we are introduced to film space—the sparrows acting like a screen or mirror (Foucault 1997), reflecting Hitchcock's *The Birds* into, and so altering, the "reality" of the Village Square. In a sense, the heterotopia is itself an assemblage—made from pieces of space, time, and narrative. "Narrative" is, then, also introduced to the Square, firstly through the allusion to film, but secondly, by introducing something unexpected into the space—developing what Sennett calls "properties of narratives" (Sennett, 190). *The Birds* blurs the clearly defined borders and walls of architectural design: with the sculpture not everything is explained; and, contrary to John Steil and Aileen Stalker's suggestion that public art (in Vancouver) should be accompanied by a sign to make clear the artist's "intent" (2009), Sennett understands that "only in bad art everything makes sense" (Sennett 1990), and that sharply designed spaces of the city might be read as bad art. *The Birds* offer a "displacement" (Sennett 1990): it challenges the traditional ordering of city space. For Sennett, this "unknown," in a city allows people to interpret and use space differently, outside of codified norms (1990)—offering what Deleuze and Guattari would call (appropriately, considering the sculpture) "lines of flight," or "lines of deterritorialization" (1987). Following this "line of flight," and embracing it as metaphor, we "fly" to Hitchcock's film *The Birds* (or it "flies" into the Square), introducing possibilities of thought and movement that would not usually be found in such a bland city space. *The Birds* and *The Birds* create a narrative that helps us recognise other narratives at play in this space, and the dominant narrative of the modern city—surveillance.

Hitchcock's Surveillance Narrative Reflected Through Vancouver's Giant Sparrows

In its disruption of city space, the sculpture's reference to Hitchcock's film is appropriate. The film also looks to disrupt, questioning "rationality" (McCombe 2009), fascinated with acts of seeing, and obsessed, like many Hitchcock films, with the artificiality of time and space (Sprengler 2014) and the role surveillance plays in this dynamic. Like the sculpture, *The Birds*, Hitchcock' film, *The Birds*, makes you look. Cinema is, in a sense, itself a narrative created through surveillance—the camera tracks individuals through time and space long before the birth of modern surveillance in the city (Zimmer 2015); Hitchcock is conscious of this, and *The Birds* plays with these qualities and techniques of film making. From the start, the film draws attention to its characters' movement, creating a sense of "social awkwardness produced by a loss of direction," which seems, as John Bruns notes, to produce a "comic tone in the movie early on" (2013), establishing a safe narrative space, well-known to the viewer. Numerous references, acts, and puns of seeing and not seeing in the film add to the sense of romantic-comedy, with a number of men looking admiringly on at socialite Melanie Daniels (Tippi Hedren), while lawyer Mitch Brener (Rod Taylor) clashes with her, flirtatiously, in what appears to begin the will-they-won't-they relationship of the genre. Negotiating (through some effort) her way to his family home, to play a trick on the object of her interest, Melanie is spotted covertly crossing the water by Mitch through a pair of binoculars. This is a film about watching and being watched. As Melanie disembarks the small boat, the first bird attacks, upsetting the comedy-romance and the image of an idyllic, safe, close-to-nature small town. Seeing suddenly becomes a threat as the birds watch ready to attack, and the townspeople must cover their eyes or risk losing them, as the film switches genres to horror, and explores the terror of being seen. Characters and viewers now inhabit a paranoid space. *The Birds* sculpture likewise elicits an uneasy sense of being watched, as a more threatening narrative is introduced to the neutral space of the Square—a space (like the romantic-comedy genre of the film) that we think we know—through sculpture and horror film association. The safe space is gone: the sky appears wide overhead, not crowded with attacking birds, but, could someone be watching? The all-seeing eye does not come through nature here but is located and concealed in the cameras of city and private industry that hover, tucked away above your head.

Through this "eye in the sky," both works of art establish a framing device and draw attention to acts of framing. The "frame" demarks and presents "reality;" it is a way to see "reality," but it is also a way to control and restrict what is seen, and how one "moves" (physically or in thought) in a space. The eye of the birds in film (the eye is a central motif) makes you not only conscious of the film camera but also the set and scene—that which frames. The eye of the sculpture alerts us to the potential of cameras as part of the assemblage sensed in the Square, whose architectural design also produces frames of "reality." Viewers of both film and sculpture discover an environment that seems manufactured, as you are asked to *watch* and *see*—something that is spectacle, something that is art, something not quite right or "real." Arguably, both works reject the order and structure of the immediate environment by making you aware of it. The attack of the birds on screen has been read as an attack on civilisation, a "rejection of human rationality and the institutions that serve the cultivation of reason" (McCombe 2009)—many of the attacks are against the local school. This idea of human-made order is epitomised in the high angle shot of the birds massing in the sky, gliding above the whole town, which appears like a (logical) clearly designed grid, or map. This is observed and scrutinised by the birds before they launch their precision attacks. The order down below is questioned, but even the birds themselves are not outside this critique as they raise awareness of the camera and the director's gaze and intent. Can you every escape the watched, manufactured and controlled environment?

Hitchcock's films are noted for their use of sets and screens that add an unreality to the watching experience—they further draw attention to the "art" of film and society. Robert Boyle, set designer for *The Birds*, comments that Hitchcock would have done "everything in studio without ever going outside" if he could (Païni 2001). As Sprengler points out, the director's use of rear projection creates, but also draws attention to, "spatial and temporal disjunctions" and a sense of "artificiality" (Sprengler 2014). The contrived nature of film set but also everyday reality is highlighted, and this heightens the viewer's spatial awareness. You not only become conscious of the camera lens and cinema product, but the fourth wall begins to break down so that you witness the power of your screen: the film world, and ours, which the film reflects, is manufactured, and observed, and you are its voyeurs. This is more evident in *Rear Window* (1954), where photographer L. B. Jefferies (James Stewart), trapped in his apartment convalescing, watches his neighbours through a telephoto lens. Filmed almost entirely on set, with Jefferies's view further mediated through the frame of his apartment window, the spaces of everyday life are deconstructed. Garrett Stewart detects through the film's various frames (rear window, camera lens, etc.), a "structuring absence" of the television screen linked to the film's surveillance theme (Stewart 2015). The rise of the television screen across America in this period transformed how we see the world, and anticipates the dominance of the screen as part of a future surveillance society. Intriguingly, Stewart notes the "boxed-off neighborhood is reduced to a 'cone' of vision with only one private 'apex' in the eye of the hero" (2015). He seems to be describing Bentham's panopticon, with Jefferies as unseen guard of the secrets of his neighbours. In this location, local residents are trapped by, but unaware of, Jefferies's (and our) gaze, but when the murderer realises he is being watched, he begins to alter his behaviour and resists, as a prisoner might. The assemblage of film and set, and the screen on which it appears in our own home, furthers this sense of the unseen viewers caught in but also using the mechanism that mediates and frames everyday life.

If Hitchcock's birds draw attention to a series of frames in film and social order, then the Vancouver sculpture also draws attention to the manufactured nature of the immediate environment—other frames of control. The frames of concrete design that looks to connect and highlight sky above and the water beyond, on closer observation demonstrates the forced removal from the natural world that design effects here. There is a sense of city "grid" pattern, which Sennett suggests moves upward in high-rise building (1990), unbounded in North-American design, denying "complexity and difference" (Sennett 1990). Trees stand in the Square but do not detract from the large paved area—the feeling of being exposed but also trapped in the city grid and between the steel and glass apartment blocks. The waterway beyond appears as if projected on a backscreen—at a distance—a reality that at best infringes upon the present space, creating a heterotopia of the Square, as if screen time and space, or some lost time and space are reflected into the glass and concrete arena. This reading would suggest complexity of space but the experience is anything but. The building of glass—glass that can open space, "make space into action" (Sennett 1990)—is used here to create the "sealed box" of modern urban design, which "devalues the tactile reality of what one sees" (Sennett 1990). This is exquisitely controlled space, where the pedestrian is meant to feel "in-touch" with nature while also connected to the site's "heritage," but the site is in fact increasingly removed from these in its modern design and materials. Like those caught in the society of Hitchcock's *The Birds*, with nature turning against them for what might be humanity's crimes or increasing distance from the natural world, those in the Square are also disconnected from the natural world. The unnatural, movie-like giant sparrows point (itself of prefabricated design) to a hollowness behind the facade of building that you would normally be oblivious of. The sculpture also points to apartments that are much reported in the Canadian media as being "shoddy" in construction, assembled too quickly in time for the Olympics (Mason 2014)—"hollow" in another sense. The Square takes on the eerie quality of an empty film set, and again you wonder, who is watching?

From the Bird's Eye to the God's Eye of Surveillance

In "The All-Seer: God's Eye as Proto-surveillance," Astrit Schmidt-Burkhardt maps the history of the all-seeing eye in art as a form of proto-surveillance: the eye of God, or the eye of the state—watching, reminding you to behave (Schmidt-Burkhardt 2002), reminding you of the divine or state panopticon; it also draws attention to the power invested in those in control (those people who actually watch). The eyes of the birds attacking in Hitchcock's film fall into this tradition of art. As if to remind us, a drunk proclaims the birds a divine act of an angry God (*The Birds*). The eye might also be Hitchcock's—another god in his role as auteur. But you are also reminded of the power of those in control of society—government, the church, other authorities, who create, or attempt to create the "narratives" of day-to-day life. The film acknowledges not only God and Hitchcock but also the author of the novella that is the film's source—another all-seeing eye, Daphne du Maurier. In the novella, we witness a greater system of control behind the attack by the birds—a metaphor for governments and war. Set in England shortly after the Second World War, the novella's bird attacks recall the bombings of England, the mechanical and technological domination and bombardment from the air. Characters constantly check the radio for news and wonder if the Americans will again come to their aid (du Maurier 2003). The film, released shortly after the Cuban missile crisis, might be seen to reflect a similar fear of aerial bombardment: characters also check the radio for news, while the noise the birds make sounds not only unnatural but mechanical, like the static of a radio or television (*The Birds*). Book and film offer manufactured, entrapping worlds, the metaphoric-surveillance of the bird's eye reflecting a society watched, planned, and manipulated from afar—from the air, as part of a surveillance assemblage of war.

In the Olympic Village, those with power to shape and control the space are the government and private real-estate developers (Millennium Development). If, as Sennett suggests, space is designed to engender easeful movement of people through an empty but safe space, then under the "eye" of government and real-estate developer, a different form of narrative can be utilised by those in power to control space and movement through it. Rosalyn Deutsche's critique of public art in Battery Park City in New York argues the art "fractures the social picture" and "conceals domination" of development that is "exclusionary," legitimising the city by delegitimising the homeless (Deutsche 1991). Does the heritage narrative of the Olympic Square and *The Birds* similarly seek to conceal and control? Both sculpture and lights in the Square are popularly seen to reflect the shipyard history—a connection encouraged by city and developer. The "rib" lights represent the shipbuilding that once took place on the site. Sparrows were introduced here as an invasive species by homesick settlers, and sailors once sported sparrow tattoos. The sculpture is then read as tapping into a sanitised reimagining of the past in celebration of immigration and inclusivity, when the past was, of course, not such a welcoming space, especially for non-white immigrants. Tellingly, the sculpture and the rosy heritage narrative were put in place even as the homeless of Vancouver were bussed out of the city to "clean up" Vancouver ready for the Winter Olympics (Hyslop 2010). Today, the heritage connection might be read as an attempt to synthesise another bland piece of city development into an ever-increasing assemblage of almost identical assemblages, while the story of inclusivity again distracts from the lack of social housing in the development project, which had promised much more. Those who remain in the limited social housing feel isolated, and many have moved out from a waterfront community increasingly a place of privilege (Vulliamy 2013). Such a space requires regulation and observation—some are welcome in the Village, others are not. Does then *The Birds* sculpture collude in this heritage construction of place, or point to (consciously or unconsciously), and so disrupt, the powers that mobilise such narratives of control?

Conclusion

To move towards answering these questions, you must return to a consideration of the pedestrian movement in the Square, around *The Birds*. If Hitchcock's film landscape confuses navigation, then the Vancouver sculpture has a similar effect. It asks you your place in this environment. Aware of the space you inhabit, you are not sure whether to linger in the Square or move on. You feel exposed, but you tell yourself that this is meant to be a square, a traditional gathering place, at the centre of urban design since Greek and Roman cities of antiquity. Here though, the Square is a not a centre—it is not an inviting space of gathering. It is empty; it's carefully designed with radiating walkways to keep you moving on. Is this intended, or poor design? Did developers want the Square to be used? *The Birds* seem to encourage the need to move, removing the sense of safety from the space. Are you being watched? From which window, which hidden camera, from where? Does the line of flight produced by the sculpture merely enforce the movement of pedestrians encouraged by what Sennett would call empty and safe city spaces? But movement at the expense of a sense of safety. Public art appears to clash with its environment even as justifications are found for it in the theory behind its placement, even as it appears to fit the location (in theory; in heritage). Does the sculpture make you question the design and purpose of this space, which you were oblivious to before? Does it make you resist? At the very least it makes you ask a question of it.

At the time of writing, *The Birds* has been removed for repair. Damage from skateboarders jumping up onto the tails of the birds is cited as part of the cause. This "line of flight" appears to open up space, initiating what Deleuze and Guattari would read as a process of "deterritorialization" (1987), resisting the systems of structure and control. Sennett would suggest the space has a new narrative, that time has been let in, where people can get to work finding new ways to use the space they inhabit (1990). Perhaps, then, the narrative of the Square is not created by Myfanwy MacLeod, Alfred Hitchcock, the developer or politician, nor by the machines and people who watch the city from CCTV cameras. If the narrative relies on how you choose to move through the Square, *The Birds* at least makes you stop and look at what you are moving through and might make you conscious of your movement. You pause for a moment in, and conscious of, the assemblage of self, city, and surveillance.

Bibliography

Bruns, J. (2013). 'The Proper Geography': Hitchcock's Adaptation of Daphne den Maurine's "the Birds". *Class: A Journal of Detection, 31*(1), 88.269–88.290.

Cdm2. (2018). *Southeast False Creek Olympic Plaza*. [Online]. http://cdm2lightworks.com. Accessed 10 Mar 2018.

Deleuze, G. (1986). *Cinema 1: The Movement-Image* (trans: Tomlinson, H., & Habberjam, B.). London: The Athlone Press.

Deleuze, G., & Guattari, F. (1987). *A Thousand Plateaus: Capitalism and Schizophrenia* (trans: Massumi, B.). Minneapolis: University of Minnesota Press.

Deutsche, R. (1991). Uneven Development: Public Art in New York City. In D. Ghisardo (Ed.), *Out of Site: A Social Criticism of Architecture* (pp. 157–219). Seattle: Bay Press.

Du Maurier, D. (2003). *The Birds and Other Stories*. London: Virago Press.

Foucault, M. (1997). Of Other Spaces: Utopias and Heterotopias. In N. Leach (Ed.), *Rethinking Architecture: A Reader in Cultural Theory* (pp. 350–356). London: Routledge.

Hyslop, L. (2010). Winter Olympics on Slippery Slope After Vancouver Crackdown on Homeless. *The Guardian*. [Online]. https://www.theguardian.com. Accessed 10 Mar 2018.

Jacobs, J. (1961). *The Death and Life of the Great American Cities*. New York: Random House.

Knight, C. (2008). *Public Art: Theory and Practice and Populism*. Malden: Wiley-Blackwell.

MacLeod, M. (2010). *The Birds*. [Sculpture] Vancouver: Olympic Village Square.

Mason, G. (2014). Olympic Village Proves to be a Costly Lesson for Vancouver. *The Globe and Mail.* [Online]. https://www.theglobeandmail.com. Accessed 10 Mar 2018.

McCombe, J. (2009). "Oh, I See. . .": The Birds and the Culmination of Hitchcock's Hyper-Romantic Vision. In M. Deutelbaum & L. Poague (Eds.), *A Hitchcock Reader* (2nd ed., pp. 264–279). Oxford: Wiley-Blackwell.

Miles, M. (1997). *Art, Space and the City: Public Art and Urban Futures.* London: Routledge.

Païni, D. (2001). The Wandering Gaze: Hitchcock's Use of Transparencies. In D. Païni & G. Cogeval (Eds.), *Hitchcock and Art: Fatal Coincidences* (1st ed.). Montreal: Montreal Museum of Fine Arts.

Rear Window. (1954). [Film] Hollywood. Alfred Hitchcock.

Schmidt-Burkhardt, A. (2002). The All-Seer: God's Eye as Proto-Surveillance. In T. Levin, U. Frohne, & P. Weibel (Eds.), *CTRL [SPACE]: Rhetorics of Surveillance from Bentham to Big Brother* (1st ed., pp. 7–31). Cambridge, MA: MIT Press.

Sennett, R. (1990). *The Conscience of the Eye: The Design and Social Life of Cities.* New York: Alfred A. Kopf.

Sprengler, C. (2014). *Hitchcock and Contemporary Art.* New York: Palgrave Macmillan.

Staples, W. (2014). *Everyday Surveillance: Vigilance and Visibility* (2nd ed.). Lanham: Rowman & Littlefield.

Steil, J., & Stalker, A. (2009). *Public Art in Vancouver.* Vancouver: Touchwood Editions.

Stewart, G. (2015). *Closed Circuits: Screening Narrative Surveillance.* Chicago: University of Chicago Press.

The Birds. (1963). [Film] Hollywood. Alfred Hitchcock.

Vancouver Public Space. (2010). VPSN Surveillance Map. [Blog] Vancouver Public Space Network. http://vancouverpublicspace.ca. Accessed 10 Mar 2018.

Vancouver.ca. (2018). *Olympic Village.* [Online]. http://vancouver.ca. Accessed 10 Mar 2018.

Vulliamy, C. (2013). Last Low-Income Tenants at Olympic Village Are Being "Forced Out." *The Mainlander.* [Online]. http://themainlander.com. Accessed 10 Mar 2018.

Zimmer, C. (2015). *Surveillance Cinema.* New York: New York University Press.

CHAPTER 10

Ireland's Magdalene Laundries and the Psychological Architecture of Surveillance

Jennifer O'Mahoney, Lorraine Bowman Grieve, and Alison Torn

Introduction

Just as the mental asylum was at one time perceived as the panacea for the mentally ill (Brown 1980), so too were the Magdalene Laundries of Ireland seen as the solution to the problems of "loose morality" and deviant behaviour of young women. This chapter will use the site of a former Magdalene Laundry in Waterford as a case study to consider both the psychological architecture of surveillance and how the physical site operated to enforce a sense of containment.

Schutz and Wicki (2011, p. 49) have argued that, "architecture can convey the natural existence of psychiatric structures within our society";

J. O'Mahoney (✉) • L. Bowman Grieve
Waterford Institute of Technology, Waterford, Ireland
e-mail: jomahoney@wit.ie; lbowmangrieve@wit.ie

A. Torn
Leeds Trinity University, Leeds, UK
e-mail: a.torn@leedstrinity.ac.uk

S. Flynn, A. Mackay (eds.), *Surveillance, Architecture and Control*,
https://doi.org/10.1007/978-3-030-00371-5_10

thus, both the outer architecture of a facility, as a representation of outside people's fears of those contained within, and the internal architecture (and the changes in these structures) may be representative of the prevalent views of "othering" of patients (in the case of psychiatric facilities) and women (in the case of Magdalene Laundries) and their treatment over time. Post-independence Ireland contained what it perceived as sexual immorality by locking it away across a range of interconnected institutions, including mother and baby homes, industrial and reformatory schools, mental asylums, adoption agencies, and Magdalene Laundries. Smith (2007) describes this system as Ireland's architecture of containment, which functioned to remove troublesome women from society. As a result, the Magdalene women existed in a dichotomous state of constant surveillance behind high walls and locked doors, while being hidden from view from the rest of society, lest they corrupt it.

Taking a psychological lens, this chapter will frame the Magdalene Laundry as a cultural phenomenon, and consider how the behaviour of the incarcerated women and girls is framed and manipulated by the constant surveillance of the Religious Orders within the physical site of the Laundry, whereby it is theorized that even subtle cues of surveillance can impact behaviour (Bourrat et al. 2011). This analysis will be contextualized within the frame of Foucault's (1979, 2006) discussions on the enactment of disciplinary power through architecture and Bentham's principle of Panopticon order.

Ireland's Magdalene Laundries

The Magdalene Asylums were founded in the nineteenth century as a result of societal and political concern regarding the interrelated issues of prostitution and venereal disease. These institutions formed with the ethos of public philanthropy of "rescuing" women who had fallen into prostitution. Magdalene Asylums were common institutions in societies in the nineteenth and early twentieth centuries; by 1900 there were more than 300 asylums in England, at least 20 in Scotland, and at least 40 in Ireland (Finnegan 2004). Institutions also existed in France, Australia, Canada, and North America. However, the Irish Magdalene Laundries are notable for their comparative longevity, remaining in existence until 1996 while similar Laundries in other countries were closing in the early to mid-twentieth century (Smith 2007). As institutions focused on social control, analysis of the Magdalene Laundries has global resonance to other institutions with similar ethoses.

The late nineteenth century saw a decline in prostitution in Ireland, due to improved educational and employment opportunities for women and high levels of emigration from Ireland (Titley 2006). Levels of prostitution saw further deep decline after Ireland gained independence from Britain in 1922, due to the removal of British soldiers. In order to maintain their survival, the Magdalene Asylums needed to reformulate their mission. The institutions began to focus their efforts towards unmarried mothers; referrals from the criminal justice system, social services, and other institutions; as well as girls who were "sexually aware" or "demonstrating marked tendencies towards sexual immorality" to maintain their clientele base (Department of Justice 2013; Raftery and O'Sullivan 1999, pp. 27–28; Titley 2006). The formation of the Independent Irish State in 1922 was heavily influenced by the Catholic Church and doctrine, which targeted these women who did not fit strict puritanical notions of womanhood and motherhood. Ten institutions existed after Ireland's independence, existing from 1922 to 1996; during their time these institutions accommodated fewer voluntary entrants, and became increasingly punitive, detaining girls and women for longer periods (many for life, who died behind Laundry walls).

The Church and the newly formed Irish Free State cooperated increasingly throughout the 1920s to police and surveil the nation's moral climate. In particular, the Catholic Church enforced moral control over women's bodies and sexuality through a social and legal establishment of power, which managed domestic life, education, health, the arts, welfare entitlements, and religious participation (O'Mahony and Delanty 2001). Women were restricted in behaviour and role to enforce the outward image of Ireland as a sexually pure and moral nation (Finnegan 2004). The control of women's sexuality, in both practice and discourse, became one of the main strategies by which the Catholic Church maintained its power, with severe consequences for those considered to have transgressed (Inglis 1998; Luddy 2007). The institutions bore the title of "Magdalene" in reference to Saint Mary Magdalene, described in contemporaneous Catholic doctrine as a reformed prostitute who was rewarded for her penitence and service to Jesus with love and compassion (although readings of the four gospels of the new testament offer little support to the prostitute narrative [BBC 2011]). Life in the institutions reflected this belief of penitence and servitude to facilitate forgiveness and redemption. The incarcerated women served penance through systematic prayer, silence, and hard labour laundering and ironing soiled sheets from hospitals, hotels, and other businesses (Department of Justice 2013; O'Donnell 2011; Smith 2007). Some of these women did so for decades without financial compensation, while denied freedom of movement.

This chapter will begin with a consideration of the psychological theories of social control and surveillance, followed by an analysis of how these culturally embedded notions of control and surveillance are manifested in the physical architecture of a former Magdalene Laundry.

The Psychology of Social Control

Fundamentally, the ethos of the Catholic Church and its relationship to social control (and, more specifically, its control of women's sexuality) frame cognitive schemas to justify and validate the surveillance of women's bodies. This surveillance of women is culturally embedded in Irish social life through the shaping of rhetoric by the Catholic Church, and is reinforced by the physical buildings associated with the Church. Institutions like the Catholic Church must be understood as part of the historical evolution and broader context of social action and cultural traditions, from which it emerged (Melossi 2001).

Social control refers to the regulation and enforcement of social norms to maintain social order, and can be defined as an organized action intended to change people's behaviour (Innes 2003). In the Magdalene Laundries, girls were often transferred between industrial schools and the laundries without warning or explanation (Raftery and O'Sullivan 1999). The girls were kept in a constant state of emotional and psychological turmoil, often unaware of why they were there, how long they would remain, or whether they would be transferred elsewhere. The girls were under constant control of the Religious Order and deprived of an education, rest, and privacy, and were assigned new names and uniforms (O'Rourke 2011). Social control was achieved using positive and negative sanctions, reinforcing acceptable behaviour, and punishing unacceptable behaviours that violated promoted social norms.

Closely related to notions of social control are actions of "watching" and surveillance. Individuals who violate the social norms are seen as deviants, with women who break the rules often looked at as doubly deviant, breaking not only social norms or societal laws but also the gender norms of acceptable behaviour. In the case of the Irish Magdalenes, the Irish State and Religious Orders have been complicit in portraying these women as deviants to justify their incarceration (O'Mahoney-Yeager and Culleton 2016). Historically, women's sexuality has been targeted in order to portray an external image of Ireland as a moral and pure nation. Extramarital sex contradicted a national identity which emphasized conformity and Catholic morality.

McCullough and Carter (2013) hypothesize that religion fosters the development and exercise of self-control and self-regulation. They argue that changes in religion, in particular an increased focus on entities that possess preferences about human behaviour and morality, and who monitor, reward, and punish those behaviours, reflects a belief in the efficacy of these entities to control behaviour. Furthermore, according to Raven (1999) to implement power strategies of social control, various devices can be used including the notion of an omnipotent deity with the power to reward or punish; reward and coercive power is enhanced by omnipotence and where omnipresence establishes necessary continual surveillance (real or perceived). Thus, religious cognitions, in particular those featuring moralizing Gods, and a belief in the afterlife, are particularly useful for promoting social control. The idea of being watched and punished by a deity, or its representatives, should promote prosocial behaviour (Bering 2006; Johnson and Bering 2006; Norenzayan and Shariff 2008). The supernatural monitoring hypothesis suggests that thinking about God might make believers think their behaviour is being monitored. Various studies find support for changes in behaviour when participants are primed to think they are being watched by some "other" (Gervais and Norenzayan 2012; Bering et al. 2005; Piazza et al. 2011). The ability to measure these results in a lab setting only indicates how simple it is to achieve the sense of "being watched". Unfortunately, the actual history of the Magdalene Laundries speaks to what can be achieved through the systematic promotion of a watchful God both culturally (in Ireland) and institutionally (in the Laundries), coupled with actual behaviour monitoring by members of the Holy Orders who ran the institutions. This was further exacerbated by the Nuns in the Laundries encouraging the women to report on each other's behaviour, thus creating a system of high-level social control and in-group monitoring, with detrimental effects. This in-group monitoring acted as an informal sanction, ensuring the reinforcement and punishment of behaviour by in-group members.

Social Control and Surveillance

Intuitively, we can know that being watched changes our behaviour, however this intuition is also empirically supported in research. For example, the Hawthorne Effect refers to the modification of behaviour (person or group) in response to knowledge of being observed, similarly the Spotlight Effect (Gilovich and Savitsky 1999) is the tendency for us to think that people notice our actions more than they do and that this impacts our behaviour. Thus, from the perspective of social accountability we have evolved to follow group norms, particularly under group observation—to not do so would lead to discomfort similar to that experience by those who did not conform in Asch's (1951) infamous conformity experiments. Additionally, it may not simply be the real presence of others that can influence our behaviour, but also the implied or imagined presence of others. This is exemplified in research by Bourrat et al. (2011) who found that humans pay close attention to the reputational consequences of their behaviours and that even very subtle cues that one is being observed can affect, for example, cooperative behaviours. In investigating how even subtle cues of being watched would affect moral judgements, Bourrat et al. predicted that participants exposed to these subtle cues (in this case an image of eyes) would affirm their endorsement of prevailing moral norms by expressing greater disapproval of moral transgressions. Bateson et al. (2013) found similar results in their study where they found that images of eyes induce more prosocial behaviour, independent of local norms. These studies illustrate that even in cases where people are not being watched, but the perception of being watched is primed, it has a measurable impact. Also indicated is the relevance of reputation to engagement in behaviour, with an evolutionary link to cooperative reputation identified in Engelmann et al. (2016). A small number of contemporary studies suggest that even at preschool age children show reputational concern and choose to modify their behaviour when in the presence of a peer observer (Engelmann et al. 2013; Leimgruber et al. 2012; Shaw et al. 2014).

The significance of this in relation to the Magdalene Laundries is particularly relevant—where the institution was built on the premise of reputation management and change in line with the professed Catholic moral of the time. Irish women were historically constructed as the biological and moral representatives of the Irish State; sexual immorality was the most extreme act of deviance and was dealt with by locking it away.

Ireland's architecture of containment (Smith 2007) allowed for women's sexuality (and their sexual abuse) to be hidden from society and written out of Irish history.

The psychological theories explaining the phenomenon of social control and surveillance can aid in understanding how social control was maintained in these institutions. However, to more comprehensively consider surveillance in the Magdalene Laundries, it is essential to consider how the physical architecture of the Laundries also contributed to this experience of being constantly monitored. To illustrate this point, the chapter will consider how architecture plays a role in the psychology of surveillance and social control through the case example of the former Magdalene Laundry in Waterford, Ireland.

Architecture, Surveillance, and Social Control: St Mary's Good Shepherd Laundry, Waterford

Historically, the rapid growth of industries and technologies in the eighteenth and nineteenth centuries meant that society was no longer able to carry perceived deviants (Scull 1993). Consequently, there was increased demand for those deemed extraneous to society to be institutionally accommodated and separated as surplus to the capitalist economy, thus maximizing the labour force and removing the threat to social order (Scull 1993). Asylums turned no one away; anyone whose behaviour was judged intolerable was likely to be incarcerated. So lay definitions of acceptable and unacceptable behaviour gained influence in demarcating the sane from the insane, moral from immoral.

In relation to asylum construction, there were grand political ideals from reformers of constructing architecturally pleasing buildings with a stimulating environment of galleries, music, and artists' rooms. However, with the compulsory erection of asylums throughout England, for example, as a result of the 1845 Lunatics Act, asylums became expensive to build, run, and staff, becoming an unnecessarily costly means of managing deviants ostensibly from the lower classes (Scull 1993). Thus, the emergence of asylums was paralleled by the creation of other institutions such as prisons, workhouses, juvenile reformatories, and Magdalene Laundries, with which there are obvious similarities. As Scull describes them, such institutions turned out to be "museums for the collection of the unwanted" (Scull 1993, p. 370). Not only did they become a depository for deviants, critically these institutions also became a disciplinary space, with a movement from physical to psychological forms of power and restraint as Foucault (1979) describes, "it is the transition from one art of punishing to another, no less skilful one. It is a technical mutation" (p. 257).

Whilst asylum-type institutions were products of the philanthropic reform movement, all were organized around the order of surveillance and control, and all reinforced the reformative powers of labour, religion, and routine (Ignatieff 1983). Isolation from the outside world was a key feature of these institutions, premised on avoiding the antecedents of deviance and restoring the spirit. In relation to the Magdalene Laundries, isolation and solitude provided space for spiritual reflection, so that the institution was not solely an administrative apparatus but "a machine for altering minds" (Foucault 1979, p. 125). Such isolation became a disciplinary enclosure, a means of preventing the spread of immorality in society, thus the institution was a societal instrument used for the maintenance of social order. Incarceration and partitioning were therefore motivated by the twin desires for a pure community and a disciplined society (Foucault 1979).

Coercion was used within the reform institutions, and the Magdalene Laundries in particular, to mould the inmates through techniques, such as timetables, compulsory activities, silence, and repetition (Foucault 1979). Within the Waterford Institution, the business of the laundry itself functioned to establish the rhythms and control of activity to serve multiple purposes: to eliminate idleness; to avoid preoccupation (e.g., with immoral, criminal, or mad thoughts); and to transform the individual via occupation towards a fixed norm. The most powerful tool in coercion however was observation and the material manifestation of this was evident in the architecture of the reform institutions of that time.

The Panopticon design that embodied this all-seeing architecture, whilst devised in the eighteenth century, came to fruition in the nineteenth century. Its designer, Bentham, sourced the idea of the Panopticon from a visit to his brother's factory, which had been set up around a centralized unit from where his brother could keep a watchful eye on his workforce. Bentham describes the Panopticon not as a schema or template for institutional architecture, but as a mechanism, which, for Foucault, means a mechanism of disciplinary power (Foucault 2006). The building had corridors of locked and barred rooms circling around a central building or tower, from which inmates could be seen at all times, with minimal staffing (two or three at the most). The tower was a central point of surveillance, which illuminated all that had to be seen, whilst providing a single gaze. This central observation cell was often constructed in such a way that the observer could not be seen by the inmates. The power of surveillance on the bodies of the inmates was therefore exercised irrespective of the actual presence of the observer. Conversely, the cells of the inmates were constructed to make them permanently visible, therefore the power exercised, whilst ever present, was only ever an optical and psychological effect (Foucault 2006). Crucially, the architecture of asylums enabled power to be distributed, an all-pervasive continuous control, whose premise was internal governance and, as such, was essentially embodied. The inmate of a Panopticon was therefore at the receiving end of asymmetrical surveillance, policing the self for fear of punishment.

There is no question that the literature on the Panopticon is omnipresent in surveillance studies, as the leading scholarly model and metaphor for considering surveillance. Haggerty (2006, p. 27) goes as far as to suggest that, "Foucault continues to reign supreme in surveillance studies and it is perhaps time to cut off the head of the king". However, much criticism has been written about the desire to move towards post-Foucauldian studies of surveillance (e.g., Caluya 2010; Wood 2007). Wood (2007) suggests that Actor-Network Theory is the only viable option for post-Foucauldian studies of surveillance, which combines both a genuine methodological advance borne through genealogy, which does not allow for moral assumptions to determine resulting analyses. However, these writings and calls to move beyond Foucault's analysis of the Panopticon focus on examining the links between life and technological surveillance; the current chapter examines the role of surveillance in Ireland's Magdalene Laundries, which experienced its zenith prior to the 1970s (and, therefore, prior to electronic or virtual surveillance technologies). For this reason, Foucault's pre-technological considerations of surveillance are much more relevant to the present chapter than post-Foucauldian studies of surveillance.

Further, we must consider that Foucault's primary theoretical focus in *Discipline and Punish* is to analyse power. Foucault uses Bentham's Panopticon as "an architectural diagram" as a metaphor from which to consider power in Foucault's disciplinary society (Caluya 2010, p. 624). Caluya (2010, p. 625) reminds us that the core principle of the Panopticon is not the surveillant gaze, but the "automatisation and disindividualisation of power", where the analysis of the Panopticon is part of a larger analysis to understand power. Through this lens, scholars have called for following Foucault's method, by tracing the evolution and genealogy of punishment, power, and object relations (Caluya 2010; Wood 2007). Foucault (1979, p. 307) completes *Discipline and Punish* with the statement that "I end a book that must serve as a historical background to various studies of the power of normalization and the formation of knowledge in modern society". In other words, Foucault was writing a genealogy of modern punishment (and not a history of prisons and incarceration), where the Panopticon is presented as an architectural diagram and metaphor, and not as a "summative theory" (Wood 2007, p. 250).

The applicability of the Panopticon to the Magdalene Laundries is apparent on many levels, as a method for understanding how surveillance and power manifested in this specific context. While the Laundry in Waterford was not built architecturally speaking, in line with the concept of the original Panopticon, they nevertheless retain features of the broad concept of Panopticon surveillance (and its supposed merits in containment), as well as the broader diagram of power as described by Foucault. The very design of the site of the Waterford laundry facilitated the control exerted over the women held on site, who are also referred to as inmates in contemporary analysis of the Laundries (e.g., Finnegan 2004; Luddy 2007; Smith 2007).

The College Street Campus of the Waterford Institute of Technology, purchased in 1994, is the former site of a convent of the Congregation of Our Lady of Charity of the Good Shepherd of Angers (commonly known as the Good Shepherd Sisters), as well as the St Mary's Good Shepherd Laundry and St Dominick's Industrial School. In 1842 Reverend Timothy Dowley established an institution for homeless girls and women in Waterford. Bishop O'Brien approved Reverend Crotty's request to the Good Shepherd Sisters in France to send sisters to facilitate the running of the institution, and five sisters arrived in 1858 (Department of Justice 2013). Building work on the Convent and other buildings began in 1882 and was occupied in 1884. The Laundry operated on site until its closure in 1982 (Department of Justice 2013).

Figure 10.1 depicts the Convent building. There are no known pictures of the functioning laundry, which would have been located to the left of the Convent (but still physically attached to the Covent building), where the Nuns' "cells" were located. The interior of this building is adorned with patterned tiles and handcrafted woodwork (see Fig. 10.2); the incarcerated girls and women were not permitted in this part of the complex, except to clean. The girls' sleeping areas were located in a separate part of the complex, on the second and third floors of the building, above the

Fig. 10.1 Good Shepherd Convent, Waterford postcard. (The Poole Photographic Collection, National Library of Ireland)

Fig. 10.2 Interior of Convent building

Fig. 10.3 Former Magdalene Laundry building (right) with connecting hallway (centre of image) leading to Convent building

laundry, which was located on the ground floor (see Fig. 10.3). Survivors of the laundries report being monitored constantly in the building, with at least one Nun keeping watch on the shared dormitories to ensure the girls did not speak to each other or leave the room for any reason. While the Convent and Laundry buildings were connected through a hallway (see Fig. 10.3), this hallway was barred to the girls by locked doors at either end.

Similarly, the Panopticon perfected the exercise of disciplinary power, providing a constant pressure whilst simultaneously reducing the number of those who exercise the power and increasing the number on whom it is exercised (Foucault 1979, p. 206). Bentham glorifies the Panopticon for its ability to exercise this form of power: it "gives a herculean strength to those who direct the institute" and constitutes a "new mode of obtaining power, of mind over mind" (Bentham 1843; as cited in Foucault 2006, p. 74). The Nuns had supreme control over the behaviours of the inmates of the Laundries through the physical design of the building; however, it

Figs. 10.4, 10.5, and 10.6 The main corridor connecting the former Laundry building to the Convent (Fig. 10.4; see also Fig. 10.3). Halfway down the corridor is the "penitent's" entrance to the Chapel on the right (Fig. 10.5). At the end of the penitent's entrance are the double doors (Fig. 10.6) leading directly into the left side of the Chapel where the Magdalene girls would have sat for Mass

was the power of mind over mind that was most effective. Being able to control when and where the inmates of the Laundry went and maintaining watchful eyes (real or perceived) on them at all times facilitated high levels of social control.

Within asylum architecture, inmates became a productive source of knowledge on, for example, the causes of immorality, criminality, insanity, its control, and cure and skill. The formation of knowledge and exercise of power form a symbiotic relationship with a mutual reinforcement of the other:

> The Panoptican functions as a laboratory of power. Thanks to its mechanisms of observation, it gains in efficiency and in the ability to penetrate into men's behaviour, knowledge follows the advances of power, discovering new objects of knowledge over all the surfaces on which power is exercised. (Foucault 1979, p. 204)

This constant monitoring of the girls by members of the Holy Orders who ran the institutions was facilitated by the Nuns promoting some of the "more penitent" or obedient girls to the status of "Sister". The Sisters were encouraged to report any deviant behaviour to the Nuns, creating what Foucault described as "a laboratory of power".

As part of the Good Shepherd complex in Waterford, a Chapel was built adjacent to the Convent. The Chapel in Waterford depicts a physical a representation of Jesus on the cross, the prevailing model of Church architecture until the second half of the twentieth century (Fig. 10.7; Schloeder 1998, p. 30).

> Christ's head is at the apse, which is the seat of governance represented by the bishop's cathedra; the choir is his throat, from which the chants of the monks issue forth the praise of God; the transepts are his extended arms; his torso and legs form the nave; since the gathered fruitful are his body; the narthex represents his feet, where the faithful enter the church; and at the crossing is the altar, which is the heart of the church.

The gothic Revival style Chapel in Waterford was built ca. 1880 (National Inventory of Architectural Heritage n.d.). Gothic revival design emphasized the continuity between the established church and the pre-Reformation Catholic Church (Curl 1990). The Waterford Chapel is constructed from limestone, with an exposed solid timber roof, creating a sense of proportion and durability. The Catholic Church placed great

Fig. 10.7 Good Shepherd Chapel, ca. 1901–1908. (Poole Photographic Collection, National Library of Ireland)

emphasis on permanence in design, both externally and internally. The edifices and buildings were designed to represent Christ's presence in this permanent structure, by drawing metaphorical links between the physical firm foundation of the site with the firm foundation of the Catholic faith. In this way, the buildings themselves bear silent witness as a survivor of time and change, transcending time and place as Christ does (Rose 2001). Designers of Catholic architecture were tasked with conveying a sense of "permanence that speaks of reverence due to sacrament", echoing Hebrews 13:8 "Jesus Christ is the same yesterday and today and forever" (Schloeder 1998, p. 123). Similarly, Foucault describes the primary effect of the Panopticon was "to induce in the inmate a state of consciousness and permanent visibility that assures the automatic functioning of power" (Foucault 1979, p. 201). The most powerful tool in coercion was observation and the material manifestation of this was evident in the architecture of the reform institutions. The building itself was a carceral mechanism which aimed to transform individuals through a combination of coercion, reward, and punishment. Foucault (1979, p. 172) describes institutional architecture thus;

> architecture ...is no longer built simply to be seen..., or to observe the external space..., but to permit an internal, articulated and detailed control – to render visible those who are inside it; ...an architecture that would operate to transform individuals: to act on those it shelters, to provide a hold on their conduct, to carry the effects of power right to them, to make it possible to know them, to alter them.

The exercise of power via surveillance is further manifested in the Waterford Laundry through religious symbolism and iconography embedded throughout the building. Schloeder (1998, p. 145) maintains that Catholic buildings, like the Waterford Chapel, have important value "as a symbol... it should in some way speak of what it is: not a secular building surmounted by a cross, but a sacred building: a place set aside for God and his people... we must look beyond the functional arrangements so even the language and grammar of the building might contribute to our understanding of the things of God".

In addition to the physical structure of the Chapel, religious imagery was displayed throughout the Waterford complex of buildings (e.g., pictures and statues of Jesus, the Virgin Mary), contributing to the sense of constant surveillance of the girls and women. Iconography or the sacred image of God has been important throughout the history of Christianity. Schloeder (1998) maintains that the most important role of this iconography is to "depict the truths of the Gospel in material media" (p.145), where the import and symbolism of these icons "lies not in the object, but in its subject" (p. 148). The Catholic Church has long valued the symbolism of unity between Christ, the message of the Gospels, and their conveyance of these values through icons.

Religious icons are embedded with meaning, conveying a sense of a permanent and omnipotent surveillance in the physical space of the Laundries. The icons are often depictions of Jesus, Saints, or the Virgin Mary in human form. In this way, "surveillance has particular significance because it can invoke audiences that are not immediately present and hence bring to bear constraints upon action from elsewhere in space and time" (Reicher and Haslam 2002, p. 14). These physical icons and artefacts assume the role of "a physical symbol of God's or Christ's presence itself" (Hart 2013, p. 172). These symbols, coupled with regimes of prayer, labour, and silence, served to fuel the message of an omnipotent God, and the sense that the Magdalene girls and women were under constant surveillance. The girls were surrounded by spiritual images of "eternal verity" where "the best the transient viewer on earth can hope to do is to glimpse a fragment of the eternity that awaits the souls of the redeemed" (Antonava 2010, p. xi); their role of "penitent" and "sinner" was reinforced by their incarcerated status and physical and verbal degradation from the nuns.

Conclusion

Foucault's (1979) Panopticon describes a system of power that resulted in people monitoring and disciplining their own behaviour in response to the sense of being continually surveilled by a central watchtower where prisoners were unable to see the guard through the obscured watchtower. In this sense, the omnipotent gaze of the guard is both visible and invisible. The inmate must therefore assume they could be watched at any moment, and begin to control and discipline their own behaviour (Foucault 1979). The girls and women in the Laundries were similarly monitored by the physical gaze of the Nuns and Sisters, as well as the omnipotent gaze of Catholic icons. As with the early asylums, coercion was used to control both asylum and Magdalene Laundry inmates. Similarly, the most powerful tool in coercion was surveillance, and the material manifestation of this was evident in the architecture and physical environment of the Magdalene Laundries.

Although Magdalene Laundries existed in Ireland for much longer than other countries, they were initially common institutions in societies in the nineteenth and early twentieth centuries in the United Kingdom, the United States, Canada, France, and Australia (Finnegan 2004; Smith 2007). The consistencies and similarities in surveillance in these institutions (along with mental asylums and other institutions of social control, such as workhouses and industrial schools) suggest that the theories and examples discussed here can be extrapolated to other contexts internationally. Surveillance permeates the environment of the Laundries in multiple forms: their own in-group; the out-group of Sisters and Nuns; and by the physical icons and structures of the buildings. The physical institution of the Magdalene Laundry creates group inequality by restricting the movement and behaviour of girls and women in and through the building complex.

Foucault's Panopticon is a method for considering social order and social control through surveillance via two methods. The first involves training people through "hierarchical observation exemplified by the military camp" where the Panopticon is a diagram of power enacted through its very visibility (Foucault 1979; Wood 2007). The second method is enacted through the process of normalizing codes of behaviour, which can be found across most institutions (e.g., schools) (Wood 2007). It is only through the combined reality or suggestion of hierarchical observation and generation of social norms that social order and control can be enforced. Foucault (1979) speaks of how time is needed to create a generation of sameness, which allows for a boundary between normal and abnormal and worth and unworthiness to be created. In social psychology, this process of the creation social norms has been empirically described as the customary rules that govern behaviour in groups and societies. Social norms provide a robust method for understanding social influence and conformity.

In the Magdalene Laundries, this dual approach for considering social order and control, as conveyed through Foucault's Panopticon, manifests in both the physical architecture of the buildings (which often echo a prison setting with locked doors, high walls, the removal of the girls' names, and wearing of uniforms, along many other cruelties); and in the generation of social norms, which enforce social order. The Magdalene girls are not permitted to speak, except in prayer, and the norm of penance through systematic prayer, silence, and hard labour governed their daily behaviour.

As such, Foucault's (1979) Panopticon is both a system of visual surveillance and linguistic control; "a system of optic surveillance that is predicated upon – and reinforced by – the documentation and distribution of personal information" (Elmer 2003, p. 234). Foucault's concept of the Panopticon considers both what is visible and what is expressed through this architecture of surveillance. Part of the system of control and power is visible (in the physical structures), while also being expressed through the classification and separation of people. The Magdalene Laundries functioned via a similar mechanism of overt displays of control through the presence of the Nuns and Catholic iconography, and strict regimes of control (through silence and prayer), reinforced through the separation of Magdalene girls and women from other areas of the complex through locked doors by incarceration. Like the Panopticon, the Magdalene Laundry is a permanent structure, where the inmates are visible to an assumed gaze from those in power (the Nuns and/or God). As such, the "architectural apparatus" of both the Panopticon and Magdalene Laundries "induce in the inmate a state of conscious and permanent visibility that assures the automatic functioning of power" (Foucault 1979, p. 201).

The Magdalene Laundries were institutions focused on social order and control. Using the former Magdalene Laundry in Waterford as a case study to consider both the psychological architecture of surveillance (as well as how the physical site operated to enforce a sense of containment) has global resonance for institutions focused on social control worldwide, while giving due consideration to the Irish cultural context. Foucault's (1979) Panopticon has provided an internationally relevant paradigm from which to understand how the behaviour of incarcerated women and girls is framed and manipulated by the constant surveillance and physical gaze of the Nuns and Sisters (as well as the omnipotent gaze of Catholic icons of the Religious Orders), within the physical site of the Laundry.

Bibliography

Antonava, C. (2010). *Space, Time, and Presence in the Icon: Seeing the Word with the Eyes of God*. Farnham: Ashgate.

Asch, S. E. (1951). Effects of Group Pressure Upon the Modification and Distortion of Judgments. In H. Guetzkow (Ed.), *Groups, Leadership and Men; Research in Human Relations* (pp. 177–190). Oxford: Carnegie Press.

Bateson, M., Callow, L., Holmes, J., Redmond Roche, M., & Nettle, D. (2013). Do Images of Watching Eyes Induce Behaviour That Is More Pro-social or More Normative? A Field Experiment on Littering. *PloS One, 8*(*12*), e82055.

BBC. (2011, July 20). Mary Magdalene: The Clichés. *BBC Religions*. Retrieved February 15, 2018, from http://www.bbc.co.uk/religion/religions/christianity/history/marymagdalene.shtml

Bentham, J. (1843). The Works of Jeremy Bentham (Vol. 4). *Panopticon, Constitution, Colonies, Codification*. Retrieved November 1, 2017, from http://oll.libertyfund.org/titles/bentham-the-works-of-jeremy-bentham-vol-4

Bering, J. (2006). The Folk Psychology of Souls. *Behavioral and Brain Sciences, 29*, 453–498.

Bering, J., McLeod, K., & Shackelford, T. (2005). Reasoning About Dead Agents Reveals Possible Adaptive Trends. *Human Nature, 16*(*4*), 360–381.

Bourrat, P., Baumard, N., & McKay, R. (2011). Surveillance Cues Enhance Moral Condemnation. *Evolutionary Psychology, 9*(*2*), 193–199.

Brown, T. (1980). Architecture as Therapy. *Archiveria 10: Archives and Medicine, Summer*, 99–124.
Caluya, G. (2010). The Post-Panoptic Society? Reassessing Foucault in Surveillance Studies. *Social Identities, 16*(5), 621–633. https://doi.org/10.1080/13504630.2010.509565
Curl, J. (1990). *Victorian Architecture*. London: Newton & Charles.
Department of Justice. (2013). *Report of the Interdepartmental Committee to Establish the Facts of State Involvement with the Magdalene Laundries*. Dublin: Department of Justice and Equality.
Elmer, G. (2003). A Diagram of Panoptic Surveillance. *New Media & Society, 5*(2), 231–247.
Engelmann, J., Over, H., Herrmann, E., & Tomasello, M. (2013). Young Children Care More About Their Reputations with Ingroup Members and Potential Reciprocators. *Developmental Science, 16*, 952–958.
Engelmann, J., Herrmann, E., & Tomasello, M. (2016). The Effects of Being Watched on Resource Acquisition in Chimpanzees and Human Children. *Animal Cognition, 19*(1), 147–151.
Finnegan, F. (2004). *Do Penance or Perish: Magdalen Asylums in Ireland*. Oxford: Oxford University Press.
Foucault, M. (1979). *Discipline and Punish: The Birth of the Prison*. New York: Penguin Books.
Foucault, M. (2006). *Psychiatric Power: Lectures at the College De France 1973–1974* (trans: Burchell, G.). Basingstoke: Palgrave Macmillan.
Gervais, W., & Norenzayan, A. (2012). Like a Camera in the Sky? Thinking About God Increases Public Self-Awareness and Socially Desirable Responding. *Journal of Experimental Social Psychology, 48*, 298–302.
Gilovich, T., & Savitsky, K. (1999). The Spotlight Effect and the Illusion of Transparency: Egocentric Assessments of How We Are Seen by Others. *Current Directions in Psychological Science, 8*, 165–168.
Haggerty, K. (2006). Tear Down the Walls: On Demolishing the Panopticon. In D. Lyon (Ed.), *Theorising Surveillance: The Panopticon and Beyond* (pp. 23–45). Devon, UK: Willan Publishing.
Hart, T. (2013). *Between the Image and the Word: Theological Engagements with Imagination, Language and Literature*. Burlington: Ashgate.
Ignatieff, M. (1983). State, Civil Society and Total Institutions: A Critique of Recent Social Histories of Punishment. In S. Cohen & A. Scull (Eds.), *Social Control and the State: Historical and Comparative Essays* (pp. 75–104). Oxford: Martin Robertson.
Inglis, T. (1998). *Moral Monopoly*. Dublin: UCD Press.
Innes, M. (2003). *Understanding Social Control: Deviance, Crime and Social Order*. Berkshire: Open University Press.

Johnson, D., & Bering, J. (2006). Hand of God, Mind of Man: Punishment and Cognition in the Evolution of Cooperation. *Evolutionary Psychology, 4*, 219–233.

Leimgruber, K., Shaw, A., Santos, L., & Olson, K. (2012). Young Children Are More Generous When Others Are Aware of Their Actions. *PLoS One, 7*, e48292.

Luddy, M. (2007). *Prostitution and Irish Society: 1800–1940*. Cambridge: Cambridge University Press.

McCullough, M., & Carter, E. (2013). Religion, Self-Control, and Self-Regulation: How and Why Are They Related. In *APA Handbook of Psychology, Religion, and Spirituality* (Vol. 1, pp. 123–138). Washington DC, US: American Psychological Association.

Melossi, D. (2001). The Cultural Embeddedness of Social Control: Reflections on the Comparison of Italian and North-American Cultures Concerning Punishment. *Theoretical Criminology, 5*(4), 403–424.

National Inventory of Architectural Heritage. (n.d.). *Main Record – County Waterford*. Dublin: Department of Arts, Heritage and Gaeltacht. http://www.buildingsofireland.ie/niah/search.jsp?type=record&county=WA&regno=22830232

Norenzayan, A., & Shariff, A. (2008). The Origin and Evolution of Religious Prosociality. *Science, 322*, 58–62.

O'Donnell, K. (2011). *Justice for Magdalenes*. Paper presented at the Irish Human Rights Commission and Law Society of Ireland Ninth Annual Human Rights Conference, Dublin.

O'Mahoney-Yeager, J., & Culleton, J. (2016). Gendered Violence and Cultural Forgetting: The Case of the Irish Magdalenes. *Radical History Review, 126*, 134–146.

O'Mahony, P., & Delanty, G. (2001). *Rethinking Irish History: Nationalism, Identity and Ideology*. London: Palgrave Macmillan.

O'Rourke, M. (2011). Ireland's Magdalene Laundries and the State's Duty to Protect. *Hibernian Law Journal, 200*(10), 200–237.

Orwell, G. (1949). *1984*. London: Secker & Warburg.

Piazza, J., Bering, J., & Ingram, G. (2011). Princess Alice Is Watching You: Children's Belief in an Invisible Person Inhibits Cheating. *Journal of Experimental Child Psychology, 109*, 311–320.

Raftery, M., & O'Sullivan, E. (1999). *Suffer the Little Children: The Inside Story of Ireland's Industrial Schools*. London: Continuum.

Raven, B. (1999). Kurt Lewin Address: Influence, Power, Religion, and the Mechanisms of Social Control. *Journal of Social Issues, 55*(1), 161–186.

Reicher, S., & Haslam, S. (2002). Social Psychology, Science, and Surveillance: Understanding the Experiment. *Social Psychology Review, 5*. 7–17.

Rose, M. (2001). *Ugly as Sin: Why They Changed Our Churches from Sacred Places to Meeting Spaces – And How We Can Change Them Back Again*. New York: Sophia Institute Press.
Schloeder, S. (1998). *Architecture in Communion: Implementing the Second Vatican Council Through Liturgy and Architecture*. San Francisco: Ignatius Press.
Schutz, B., & Wicki, L. (2011). Architecture for Psychiatric Treatment. Énoncé théorique for the Master Thesis in Architecture. Available at: http://archivesma.epfl.ch/2011/051/schue_wicki_enonce/Wicki_Schuetz_Enonce%20theorique_architecture%20for%20psychiatric%20treatment.pdf/
Scull, A. (1993). *The Most Solitary of Afflictions: Madness and Society in Britain 1700–1900*. New Haven/London: Yale University Press.
Shaw, A., Montinari, N., Piovesan, M., Olson, K., Gino, F., & Norton, M. (2014). Children Develop a Veil of Fairness. *Journal of Experimental Psychology: General, 143*, 363–375.
Smith, J. (2007). *Ireland's Magdalene Laundries*. Notre Dame: University of Notre Dame Press.
Titley, B. (2006). Heil Mary: Magdalen Asylums and Moral Regulation in Ireland. *History of Education Review, 35*(2), 1–15.
van der Leeuw, G. (2006). *Sacred and Profane Beauty: The Holy in Art*. Oxford: Oxford University Press.
Wood, D. (2007). Beyond the Panopticon? Foucault and Surveillance Studies. In J. Crampton & S. Elden (Eds.), *Space, Knowledge and Power Foucault and Geography* (pp. 245–264). Aldershot: Ashgate.

CHAPTER 11

Performing the Repentant Lover in the Courtroom: An Analysis of Oscar Pistorius' Recreation of Hegemonic Masculinity

Alexandra Macht

Introduction

Paula Meth (2017) argues that the pervasive culture of violence in South Africa is borne out of social inequalities across racial, gendered and classed lines, and augmented by the design of domestic spaces in urban areas. In her view places and spaces have a constitutive role in everyday relations of power and the perpetuation of violence. In large urban settings such as Cape Town, the high rate of crimes has led to the development of a programme for Violence Prevention through Urban Upgrading (VPUU) seeking to reconstruct public spaces, to reduce violence and increase public safety. However, the boundaries between public violence and private violence are permeable in South Africa, as the home is the main site for the perpetuation of gendered abuse, mostly instigated by the design of certain spaces (such as shabbily built homes which attract predatory behaviours in poor areas). Yet public spaces can also be used as sites for intimacy and redemption, through social agents' emotional performance of their personal troubles, in situations when the safely protected homes of the rich

A. Macht (✉)
Oxford Brookes University, Oxford, UK
e-mail: amacht@brookes.ac.uk

S. Flynn, A. Mackay (eds.), *Surveillance, Architecture and Control*,
https://doi.org/10.1007/978-3-030-00371-5_11

become publicly scrutinized due to gender-based violence. Such acts indicate how love and power contribute in the creation of permeable boundaries between the two spheres.

To illustrate the links between architectural design and emotions as constitutive elements in the production of power (Heaney 2013), I focus in this chapter on the highly mediatized case study of the athlete Oscar Pistorius, accused of the murder of his girlfriend, the model Reeva Steenkamp, which took place on 14 February 2013. According to press releases, the case was summarized in lyrical terms by Judge Eric Leah, who in December 2015 reconvicted Pistorius of murder, after the initial sentencing was overruled:

> A young man overcomes huge physical disabilities to reach Olympian heights as an athlete. In doing so he becomes an international celebrity, he meets a young woman of great natural beauty and a successful model, romance blossoms, and then, ironically on Valentine's Day, all is destroyed when he takes her life.

Paradoxically the events that took place in Oscar Pistorius' home on 14 February 2013 echo the themes of martyrdom and redemption present in the original story of the formation of Saint Valentine's Day (Schmidt 1993). What is particularly significant about this case is that it serves as a canvas to explore the intersections of racial, gendered and class-based privilege in a specific setting. The South African courtroom is particularly interesting as it provides the space for the temporary emotional containment of the endemic violence that forms part of everyday life in the region. The trial of Oscar Pistorius, a South African public icon and amputee athlete who competed in Olympic championships, began in the North Gauteng High Court in Pretoria in April 2014, one year following his conviction. The trial was streamed online through SABC NEWS (a South African public broadcaster) and SkyNews (a general broadcaster) and was therefore easily accessible worldwide to members of the public with an internet connection or access to a television. The material I use for analysis in this chapter relies on online videos of the trial, and on my reading of several news pieces about the trial, published between February 2012 and January 2018.

Theoretical Backdrop

The framework I employ to support my reflections is Michel Foucault's theoretical consideration of Jeremy Bentham's Panopticon (1977) and also his later development of the concept of *technologies of the self* (1988).

In this analysis I follow Foucault in considering the panopticon as a symbol of power and control, but I transpose it from Bentham's specific architectural prison model to the space of the modern South African courtroom, panoptically constituted through digital surveillance. As such, in the South African courtroom, on the one hand the architectural space is designed to enact control and order, while on the other hand the insertion of filming cameras which broadcast the trial to the wider public enacts a form of mass surveillance. The power of the legal institution is therefore enacted through a combination of architectural and technological modalities. In addition, I offer a reconsideration of the architectural space as it contributes to the containment of violence in the South African setting, establishing links between the exercise of power and the expression of emotions (Heaney 2013). My main argument is that in interactions with these processes, Pistorius used his body alongside his emotionality as technologies of self, to construct a repentant lover performance that helped him transform from an *object* of power to an *agent* of power and manipulate the disciplining force of the gaze to achieve a privileged sentencing.

A Virtual Panopticon

The word *panopticon* stems from Greek and means "all seeing." Applied to surveillance technologies it refers to the act of making the controlled subject "seen" while taking away his power to "see," turning him into an "object of information, never a subject in communication" (Foucault 1977, p. 200). But before becoming a prisoner, the accused, privileged by his race (White), gender (man) and above-all social status (famous), might use digital surveillance to resist the power of the court. From this perspective and following on from Foucault, power in the courtroom is reconstituted through perceptual *visibles* and *invisibles*. In the present example, the *visibles* are the courtroom, Pistorius' body and his displays of emotion (crying), while the *invisible* is represented by the observant public gaze, physically present in the courtroom only through cameras, and therefore enhancing the court's power through the unseen and unexpected potential of multiple moral gazes, those of the audience.

The courtroom is an architectural system of control, and in this specific case it is symbolic of the functioning of South African power. This power relies materially upon the architecture, which supports it, and is reflected in its design. Unlike the Constitutional Court in Johannesburg, built to reflect an inclusive and democratic society following the conflicts of the apartheid era (Noble 2011), the North Gauteng High Court in Pretoria was not built to have a self-standing identity, but forms part of the fragmented apparatus of judicial power currently operating in the reformed South African landscape. Information on its original architect is scarce (Ellis 2010); it is likely the commissioned work of the local public administration. Frequently in the media, it appears "compiled" together with its other branch, the South Gauteng court in Johannesburg. The North Gauteng High Court in Pretoria was not designed in the Dutch Architect Sytze Wierda's colonial style exemplified in the Palace of Justice nor does it completely emulate Gordon Leith's round dome imperial architecture depicted in the South Gauteng High Court in Johannesburg. To my eye, it appears as a *hidden* hybrid, a mix of the imperial style of the South Court with a functional and modern finish (Noble 2008). This aspect of the hidden is also reemphasized by its location, as the building is placed right behind the Palace of Justice.

The Emotional Elements of Architecture

In this context, I propose that even as he is constrained by the disciplining aspect of legislative power, Pistorius uses his agency, at key moments in the trial either through controlling or releasing his emotions, to *maintain* a set of privileges, previously conferred to him by his status, his race and his gender. His performance was enhanced by the courtroom design meant to architecturally symbolize the application of reason and order, with the aim of containing violence (Spaulding 2012).

The pervasive nature of crime in South African culture influences how safety is understood and how urban buildings are designed (Awol 2016). The North Gauteng Court in Pretoria has a rectangular shape, made of massive dark wood, with neatly organized silos, symmetrically delineating the side of the law and the side of public, that of the defence and the prosecution. Even if this design reflects the Foucauldian principle of *partitioning* as "each individual has his own place; and each place its individual" (1977, p. 143), one is left to consider what makes this particular courtroom special? My interpretation is that the space, not initially designed according to a panoptic structure, becomes as such due to the presence of the cameras colluding with the fame of the accused, and thus brings the audience into the courtroom. This creates a hyper-real environment that magnifies the space of the South African court to a wider and international audience. The North Gauteng courtroom became widely known precisely because of the presence of Pistorius within it, as his own individual power in relation to his status and popularity influences the space; it is not simply the case that the space exerts exclusively power over him as a prisoner.

In addition, a fortified structure, such as the North Gauteng court, does not only repudiate criminal access, but it can also serve to hermetically contain it, and reinterpret it for the public, through trial and sentencing. The space of the courtroom is not a hyper-permeable one but one which claustrophobically contains a lot of the tensions that exist in South African society across class, gender and race (Meth 2017). If Paula Meth discusses how informality and insecurity shape domestic housing, I am concerned with the *formality* and *security* that the architecture of the North Gauteng court symbolizes. My reading is that even if the courtroom attempts to keep order and emotional control through ritualized proceedings, it is not the neutral place that it attempts to be as emotions are contained but also performed within this space. This emotional containment is evidenced by the architectural elements of the courtroom designed to support the enactment of the means of correct training (Foucault 1977) and thereby materialize the production of power.

The Judge's Power and Position

Firstly, the judge, Thokozile Masipa, sits with two assessors on a podium, overlooking the court and through this she performs *hierarchical observation*. In addition, the decolonized space of the courtroom, symbolically linking back to the indigenous origins of the space, is represented (Barnard 2010) by coat of arms of ancestral South African heritage which stands directly above the judge. The coat of arms promotes the motto "!Ke e: /xarra //ke", which translates as "Diverse people unite." This symbol reminds of the unity and persistence of indigenous populations even as they were subjected to West-European colonizing forces, but also about the supremacy of some African tribes over others; such complex social forces left behind a legacy of violence that nowadays forms part of everyday life in the South African society (Meth 2017). This architectural element is emotionalized by its placement behind judge Masipa's body, framing her as the person with utmost decision-making power in the room, meaningfully increased along tense racial and gendered lines, as this power is represented here by an educated Black woman, contesting through her embodiment the privilege of White Afrikaners. Another particularity of the South African courtroom is that the judge's power is also increased because juries were abolished under the apartheid regime (Awol 2016).

This case could have also been part of judge Masipa's transformation of her public role, famously tough on male sex offenders and domestic violence cases, but surprisingly lenient in Pistorius' case (Chibba 2014). Through online streaming, the audience can see that the camera is focused mainly on the advocates and the judge, who holds the control over the representation of the witness, obscured from sight. For example, the judge asks on the first day of the trial for the camera to not film the witness; on another occasion, Masipa prohibited the live tweeting and broadcast of the post-mortem report of Gert Saayman. This presents a selective model of the transparency of justice, which is *being done* and *seen* as being done through screens in real time (whether televised or computerized), but only in the selected moments that the judge allows. But were these attempts to protect or to control? Although it can be argued that Masipa wanted to protect the witness in case and to not mediatize the images of the dead victim's body, a carefully orchestrated surveillance served to increase the judge's power through selectively presenting the trial in the televised/online representation of the courtroom. In this space, according to Foucault "the judge – magistrate or juror – certainly does more than 'judge'" (1977, p. 21). As public viewers were left to imagine the rest, while the judge prioritized the ethic of protecting participants, the potential to include the public into a transparent process of justice was diminished.

Intimate Hybridization

Furthermore, the intimate drama of Oscar's love relationship with Reeva, and her subsequent murder, is brought into the courtroom through material devices, such as the reconstitution of the bathroom door from Pistorius' apartment during the ballistic report test, the presentation of their private text messages and of their home environment through the architectural scrutiny of their domestic place. In this manner, private elements of their relationship before and after the incident were reconstructed through legislative power in the space of the courtroom and disseminated under the gaze of the public.

This reshaped and hybrid space of the courtroom (material and televised) is essential therefore in the creation of Oscar Pistorius' repentant lover identity but also in how the viewer's gaze is influenced to feel certain emotions. In this setting, Oscar Pistorius manipulates the reforming power of the gaze with the moral weight it carries, to create an alliance with the public. He thus presents a lover's discourse which challenges the discourse of power of the courtroom. Such a strategy asks for public forgiveness through image rehabilitation and is sufficiently resistant to contribute to the reduction in his sentence, even if temporarily. The contextual aspects that help produce his performance are multiple and intersectional: on gendered lines, Pistorius' masculinity interacted with judge Masipa's femininity; on racialized lines, a Black civil servant interacted with a famous White Afrikaner athlete; and finally, along the lines of ability, Pistorius' prosthetic legs contrasted with most of able-bodied presences in the courtroom. Several social forces thereof collided in the South African courtroom in problematizing Oscar Pistorius' trial.

Architectural Order and the Limits of Emotional Containment

In front of the judge sit in rows other members of the judicial system and technicians who operate computers. These rows demarcate a line between the accused and the judge, isolating the former and enhancing the power of the latter. This row, situated in the centre of the courtroom, is flanked on all sides by an array of television monitors, all pointing in different directions. The monitors do not broadcast all the time but are left switched on during the trial, to be used by experts for the ***detailed examination of proofs*** (Foucault 1977). In front of the accused (situated in a low-level gated section that blends into the wooden carpentry of the room) is the defence lawyer Barry Roux and at a relative distance on the same row is the prosecuting lawyer Gerrie Nell, both standing behind lecterns. Behind the accused are the members of the public and supporters (family and friends) and parallel to these are the family of the victim and supporters of the prosecution.

The witness booth, situated to the right of the judge and diagonally from the accused, serves as the place for expert depositions which construct power/knowledge (Foucault 2007). As an interesting detail, the online viewers do not see the witnesses at the request of judge Masipa; only the experts are shown through the online streaming of the trial. According to Foucault, the people who embody the legal and moral apparatus of the court (psychological experts, members of prison service, etc.) are meant to "fragment the legal power to punish" (1977, p. 143).

What the viewers are presented with is a cohesive yet selective image of the functioning of the apparatus of power, which I shall return to in the second section of this chapter. However, even if the proceedings are televised, their broadcasting is frequently interrupted by court breaks, reminders of housekeeping rules and judge's requests to leave witnesses out, which often disrupted the power and the reverence imposed by the space of the courtroom. For example, before the beginning of the trial, at one moment, judge Masipa used the media to remind spectators in a stern message that they should respect not only the law but the building within which it is enforced by not treating it as their "picnic place." The judge was left to maintain order in a case that, because of its mediatization and the fame of the athlete, would overwhelm the boundaries of the building, as people climbed over the gates to see the accused, or sit for hours waiting outside. This episode denotes the limits of the architecture in containing the intense emotions and actions of the public, in relation to the trial.

If the accused and members of the public are incited through the design of the room to exert emotional control, the perceived messiness of emotionality disturbs the order of the room upon which the constitution of power relies. Moreover, the control of emotions is enhanced through surveillance strategies. The space of the courtroom also controls the acts of *looking-out* and *looking-in*, of *seeing* justice function; therefore, it is to my mind significant when the only direct windows of the room are those available through the cameras of the filming crew, positioned close to each entry into the courtroom. Only certain select members of the public are invited to *watch on* the trial proceedings. As the ceiling is low and there are no windows, the room conveys a claustrophobic atmosphere and other citizens are obstructed from spontaneously *looking in*; confirmed by the fact that it recently received public complaints of submitting its attendants to overheating, as doors had to be shut because of poor acoustics and the air conditioning system malfunctioned during the warm season (Venter 2018). These elements when considered in their entirety present the High Court in Pretoria as a space of order and oppression, rather than civic gathering on equal terms; this sense of oppression is digitally augmented on a panoptic dimension, through the presence of the broadcasting cameras.

Agency, Architectural Surveillance and Processes of Othering

As Foucault posited, institutional surveillance shapes bodies, recreating them on docile terms through disciplining practices; but through bodies emotions are also controlled and released. Panoptic surveillance adds to the institutional power of the court because according to him this "schema makes any apparatus of power more intense" (Foucault 1977, p. 206). Furthermore, as Piro (2008) adds, in a society that privileges the visual, then the visual environment "intensifies power" (p. 31). Therefore, architectural elements such as those presented above that echo the violent history of the country and the visual elements, such as the surveillance of the filming cameras, work together to confer legal institutions like the High Court in Pretoria, their power. Moreover, a reformed judicial system is concerned not only with punishing perpetrators but also curing them, and this is reflected in judge Masipa's final ruling:

> Thankfully *healing* has already started as both Mr. Steenkamp and Mrs. Steenkamp have stated that they have forgiven the accused. The life of the accursed shall also never be the same. He's a *fallen hero*, who has lost his *career* and is *ruined financially*. The worst is that in having taken the life of a fellow human being, in the manner that he did, he cannot be at peace. It came as no surprise therefore when both Mr. Nell, his pastor and professors described him as *a broken man*. *Recovery* is possible, but it will depend mostly on *the accused's attitude towards the punishment* imposed on him. This court is aware that the accused through his past has shown a willingness and expressed a wish to do community work as punishment (...) However punishment is not what you choose to do, it is something that is imposed on you. By its very nature punishment is unpleasant, uncomfortable, it is painful and inconvenient (...) Although a custodial sentence is the proper sentence, I am of the view that a long term of imprisonment will not serve justice in this matter. The accused has already served a sentence of 12 months imprisonment, he is a first offender and considering the facts of this matter, *he is not likely* to re-offend.

In this context, one questions remains: what made Pistorius choose emotional release in the public setting of the courtroom, when in other public circumstances such as the Olympic stadium, he relied on emotional control and agility? According to previous interviews that the athlete gave to the press before his conviction, he considered himself as able-bodied as any other sportsman (Perry 2013). While in court this discourse changed. Simultaneous with a change in discourse came a transformation of the body, which shifted from an agile and self-disciplined one to a docile and vulnerable body. It has been previously claimed that institutions create and legitimate certain masculine roles (Connell 2002). Therefore, I argue that Pistorius' exemplary masculine role could not be performed under the control of the court and public surveillance.

To assert his innocence, Pistorius had to transform under the demands of docility and discipline; he, therefore, took on a repentant lover role, which both incurred for him new privileges under the guise of a *caring form of masculinity* while also complying with the power of the court. One emotion played a central role in this transformation: love. Since he had murdered the person he loves, the only manner through which romantic love could be used in his favour was through publicly expressing *regret*. These processual operations between love and power worked to create his repentant lover performance, denoting the embodied and gendered links between emotions and power (Heaney 2013).

From the Exemplary Athlete to the Repentant Lover

First of all, Pistorius used his emotions and body in court to manipulate the gaze; seemingly spontaneous outbursts of emotional release occurred at pivotal moments when the evidence seemed to point against him. For example, in 2014, during a neighbour's description of the moment he attempted to save Reeva's life and again during the pathologist's report, Pistorius held his head in his hands and started weeping, distracting the attention of court members from the witnesses' deposition. On another occasion, in 2016, during an appeal for leniency on his sentence, he takes off his prosthetic legs and walks in front of the court on his stumps, visibly on the brink of tears and barely walking upright. Through such actions, Pistorius became "more than just a body to be watched" (Flynn and Mackay 2017, p. 3). The episodes disrupted the discourse of power in the courtroom, as the audiences watched the unravelling of a powerful White man contravening the features of exemplary masculinity (Messner 1995) through an intense display of emotions. As an athlete, Pistorius was undoubtedly familiar with the power of disciplinary practices. However, he enacted the role of the repentant lover to secure forgiveness, and thereby used the courtroom to construct a new role for himself, as forensic details reconstructed the reality of the murder.

Agent Regret

One way to interpret Pistorius' crying in court is through Amelie Rorty's (1980) concept of agent regret, as the emotional reaction to a situation of wanton and harm. Although the prolonged crying combined with instances of physical disgust, such as vomiting in court, might point towards and experience of remorse or guilt which are the higher intensity forms of regret:

> Shame tends to involve obsessive imagistic replays of the moment of exposure, to be expressed in the focused remembering of the event, as if time were arrested (…) The condition of publicity can be internalized when the shamed person is his own witness; private shame is derivative from imagined public shame. In culture or contexts where a person's sense of his agency is his sense of how he is perceived, regret and shame can coincide. (p. 498)

It is difficult to assert what he might have been *feeling*, but the focus of the analysis is to show that Pistorius' display of emotional and physical instability was devised to earn the court members' and the cameras' (and through this the public's) forgiveness. For example, Pistorius' request to be forgiven by Reeva's parents, Barry and June Steenkamp, formed part of this redemptive performance. The victim's parents displayed the sadness and grief ordinarily expected of loving parents in such circumstances. But by *matching* his grief to theirs, Pistorius could become *likeable* again and reinstate his public power.

In addition, the images that appeared in the media were predominantly focused on Reeva and Oscar's before-the-murder bliss, and after the murder were zoomed in on Pistorius' face and his body, depicting his moments of crying or vomiting in court. These images were pitted against June and Barry Steenkamp's reactions and displays of mourning in court, such as during Barry' intense description of the pain of losing his daughter (Burke 2016b). The photos in online and paper magazines told a different visual story than the one taking place in court. For most of the trial, Pistorius stood singularly with his head bent down, quiet and subdued, taking notes or listening.

Embodying Vulnerability in a Legal Setting

Since the architecture of the courtroom holds together all the political investments of the body, my interpretation of the situation is that it also contains its emotions, which Pistorius has used to subvert legal power, by being himself a man in a powerful position due to his fame but also helped in this context, by his race and disability. Consequently, as part of his performance of vulnerable masculinity, by representing his body as vulnerable and disabled he emphasized his plea for *earning forgiveness* (Lippitt 2017). According to this framing, he is worthy of forgiveness because he is visibly repenting for his actions, he is not the able murder but the frightened lover who tried to protect his girlfriend from an intruder. Pistorius then reforms his image as that of a disabled athlete who is a victim of circumstance in South Africa's tense racialized and gendered socio-political conditions (Meth 2017); he is also a *crying* (to be read as emotionally sensitive) disabled man in the rigid if ordered atmosphere created by the architecture of the courtroom, which helps him produce a striking visual contrast; in a different setting his performance would have garnered a different meaning.

However, the public gaze reacted differently than the intended effect. Public opprobrium was not secured through this emotional performance, and many railed in front of the building against the initial sentencing of culpable homicide (Burke 2016a), claiming that he should be convicted to murder as the legislation stipulates a punishment of 15 years, which would have normally been applied to ordinary South African men. This shift occured in my thinking because there was a division between the courtroom gaze, which could be observed by the accused while the mind was seeing, and the public gaze, unidirectional aimed at Pistorius, but nonetheless divided in its belief of his culpability. Many public voices claimed that he incurred racial and status-bound privileges in receiving less time in prison. These critical voices and the subsequent appeals of Gerrie Neil and the Steenkamps were powerful enough to contest Judge Thokozile Masipa's initial conviction and submit the accused to a resentencing. And it is here where judge Leah (quoted at the beginning of the chapter) intervened convicting him of murder, an action which then led to him receiving a sentence of 15 years in prison (Cowell 2017).

The cameras in the courtroom form an optical system of control which is distributed to the larger population not physically present in the courtroom at the time of the trial. Through allowing the televisation and online streaming of the trial, panopticism functions in this media environment as the combined collection of the public's eye, magnifying the gaze of surveillance. But this gaze is not only disciplining and moral, it is also gendered. The accused's identity, performance, body and emotions are *othered* through technological devices. As such Pistorius is not only the repentant lover, the accused and athlete but also an object of desire, which can be eroticized: viewers participate in the emotional unfolding of his identity from the exemplary masculine role to the repentant lover role, enacted under the material constraints of the courtroom, but also in relation to themselves as bearers of the moral gaze.

Othering Pistorius

There are gendered aspects to emotional performances in designated spaces (Gorman-Murray and Hopkins 2014), which highlight how transitions between public and private environments are laced with power and control. For example, a man does not enter a courtroom in the same way that a woman does. He is *seen*, he *occupies* and can *use* the space of the room differently due to the unconscious power of gender stereotyping and the structure of the courtroom itself, which promotes patriarchal values through the structure and ordering of legal settings (Smart 2002). Gendered performances matter in how the public gaze surveys an individual and asserts its power over the body, and in this case contributes to its sentencing verdict. Following from this, I argue that the trial shows the viewers (a) how Oscar Pistorius' public image transformed from *exemplary* masculinity (shown through physical prowess and a socially rewarded emotional and physical discipline) (Messner 1995) to the *toxic* masculine trope (evidenced through Pistorius' obsession with guns and excessive risk-taking which lead to murder), and (b) that Pistorius is using his emotionality to shift the discourse and perform an appealing form of vulnerable masculinity (Scott 2014), in his attempts to influence the public gaze to his advantage and reinstate his hegemonic role.

As a sociologist, a woman and a White viewer learning about the South African judiciary system, I also played a part in this analysis. My feminist standpoint (Ramazanoğlu 1993) compels me to reflexively consider my own gaze and its capacity to *other*. While watching the trial I kept wondering, how does Foucault's idea of disciplining power work to control an already self-disciplined body that would not remain docile? Oscar Pistorius was constructed in media discourses as a hero, as a South African symbol of national pride, whose fame was compared to that of Nelson Mandela (Gibson 2013). And yet during the trial Pistorius' body suffered a transformation, and devolved from what was according to him, the body of a prototypical able-bodied athlete, into a vulnerable body in the space of the courtroom.

I'm particularly interested in how his body became *cathected* (Connell 2002), in relation to the courtroom as a discourse of power, but also in terms of the *affective atmosphere* (Griffero 2014) that the accused created to influence the moral gaze of the judge and the public. In this sense, his episodes of emotional release were intensified as they contrasted with the simplistic yet heavy wood-panelled and claustrophobic architectural elements of the room (a lack of windows, for example). However, I argue in this chapter that his body far from being docile reconstructed itself in front of the public gaze in an empowering way to first ask for his freedom, and as this became limited, to negotiate leniency. In the following section, I turn my analytical focus in tackling their implications, first the space of the courtroom as a discourse of power, then in the second section I describe how the public gaze can function as a digital apparatus of surveillance and consider issues which appear when the gaze is reversed.

Reversing the "Gaze"

As a spectator of the trial, I was complicit in the spectacle of Pistorius' powerlessness and appeals to forgiveness. My gaze however was a female one. Initially, Simone de Beauvoir introduced the female as the object of the *male gaze*, as the object of desire produced in the act of "othering." However, current conceptualizations of the gaze have *inverted* it. For example, men "other" each other on racialized and classed lines in the constitution of privileged forms of identity (Stahl 2017). Moreover, Ruth Waterhouse described how there is a positive pleasure experienced when taking control of the gaze (1993). Although unlike her analysis mine does not imply that I extend the female gaze on the female body, but rather on the male body and its emotionality. Surveillance as control and surveillance as eroticization of the male body are thus blurred. If Laura Mulvey, who initially coined the term, described the gaze as serving the creation of "the function of woman in forming the patriarchal unconscious" (p. 833), then what is the function of *man* in the female viewer's unconscious? Mulvey argued that the power of the gaze functions trough an optical sorting: "Power is backed by the certainty of legal right and the established guilt of the woman (…) the man is on the right side of the law, the woman on the wrong" (1999, p. 841).

In my viewing of the Pistorius trial, by reversing the gaze, the male as *spectator* becomes the male as *spectacle*. Through streaming his trial online, I become the bearer of the look, which is both moralizing and libidinal, fulfilling unconsciously a voyeuristic phantasy which implies temporary and clandestine omnipotence over a famous man who murdered a woman. I along with the rest of an unseen audience, broadcasting the trial in their homes, become participants in a pathological fantasy, which fascinates in connection to the juxtaposition of a social taboo (murder) with a powerful ideology (romantic love). There was indeed a certain kind of pleasure involved, a voyeuristic phantasy in seeing this man's intimate life come undone in the controlled hermetically sealed confines of the courtroom: "looking itself is a source of pleasure, just as in the reverse formation, there is pleasure in being looked at" (Mulvey 1999, p. 835). I was complicit in the eroticization of a hegemonically normative body and it gave me a sense of satisfaction in visualizing his final verdict.

Due to the context and its representation in the courtroom I experienced conflicting feelings, having to match my moral outlook of analytical disbelief with the types of masculine performance on display: My concern was how does the disciplined and attractive body of an athlete become a strategy meant to diminish a sentence? How did he employ the discourse of love and his role within it as a repentant lover to emotionally manipulate the people who were judging him, and diffuse the operations of power? And what does the temporary success of his repentant lover performance say about surveillance? Based on my reading of this case, I tentatively assert that rather than being a tool for producing docile bodies, and therefore acting against the freedom of the individual, surveillance can be a tool asserting the agency of the subject, as a tool for liberation.

From a feminist perspective concerned with the gendered aspects of discourse of power (Ramazanoğlu 1993), I am aware that I have written a chapter focused on the male role in the trial, and not that of his partner: Reeva Steenkamp, who continues to be the sidelined agent in this whole story, the other presence in the courtroom, visible only through the acts performed on her by Pistorius' reinstatement of power, to which the viewers both myself and the audience are complicit. As a female viewer, I emotionally reverberated with the unfolding of her story, aware that in my role as a woman, such forms of gender-based violence do not exclude me. What I witnessed was a media story focused on the perpetrator and not on the victim, where *his* journey, *his* story of loss and redemption are described, while she is merely a daughter to a mourning family, a presence reconstituted from evidence. This gendered myopia was enhanced in combination with the critical backlash on Judge Thokozile Masipa's sentencing, deemed inadequate by the angry public and members of the victim's family, which appealed against her judgment.

The restrained and claustrophobic space of the courtroom serves to contain Pistorius' performance of emotional control and emotional release; this is repackaged and redistributed to the voyeuristic viewer, instilling doubt and fascination. The emotional holding that the space of the courtroom provides is to my mind significant, as it produces the question:

"Could it have been as well, that Pistorius is using the courtroom not only to perform a vulnerable role that could reduce his sentence, but also as a public space for redemption and healing?" To my mind his acts in the courtroom described what Connell (2002) has named accessing the ***patriarchal dividend***, by appealing to the public gaze to reward him the privileges he had lost through his actions but hoped to regain through a public acknowledgement of regret, discursively enriched by the humanizing effect of upholding the ideology of love (Evans 2003). In this manner, it is not only that the court shapes his performance of vulnerable hegemony (Scott 2014) but that the courtroom is reinterpreted though the emotional and bodily characteristics he brings into the room: it becomes a place of healing, of cathecting the stoic body of an athlete into that of a vulnerable lover and setting the stage for his redemptive performance, enhancing in this way the symbolic meaning of the application of justice.

Spatially Amplifying Race, Gender and Emotions

As previously mentioned, the space of the courtroom is also a hyper-real one (Kellner 2015), amplified by its televisation, and widespread in its mediatization for a number of years, which also polarized the viewers as the bearers of the gaze, engaged in this multi-level experience. In this context, the gaze dominates, objectivizing the subject and operating as a *technology of power* (Foucault 1988). Considering this analysis, Foucault's description appears eerily premonitory of the Pistorius trial in underlining how others but also how the individual acts upon himself through moral dissemination:

> The meaning of this mourning must be clear to all; each element of its ritual must speak, repeat the crime, recall the law, show the need for punishment and justify its degree. Posters, placards, signs, symbols must be distributed so that everyone may learn their significations. (1977, p. 111)

The mediatization of the event is significant across gendered and racial lines: here was a White couple in love, which each acceded to the emphasized femininity role—a beautiful blonde homely model—and the exemplary masculinity role—a successful, competitive and sexy athlete (Gibson 2013). In court, their idealized public images contrasted sharply to the portrayals of the predominantly impoverished Black ethnic majority in the Pretorian landscape.

However, and unlike Awol Allo (2016), who describes the context of the Black man in a White court room, Pistorius' performance was that of a White disabled rich man in a South African court of law ruled by a Black, female judge; their public images were juxtaposed, creating polarized public interpretations about *her competence* and *his innocence*. The social circumstances of a trial, which was about establishing intent in a situation suffused in emotions and out-of-courtroom drama, were magnified through their interaction with the televised broadcast and its spread across the media in newspapers and Twitter feeds. Televised surveillance, through my gaze (and that of the public), replaced the role of the supervisor, although viewers were granted less power since they were remote and could not physically access the courtroom and the perpetrator, akin to a Deleuzian concept of surveillance as "control at a distance" (Galič et al. 2017, p. 20). This also strengthens the idea that even though Pistorius was trialled for murder nonetheless fulfilled his hegemonic reconscription, which happened once as a disabled Olympic athlete in his role as a blade runner—a nickname earned because of his carbon-fibre prostheses, serving to accentuates his Otherness (Sokolovejan 2012)—and again through his conscription as the repentant lover during the murder trial.

Oscar Pistorius employs a *technology of the self*, which according to Foucault permits individuals to:

> effect by their own means or with the help of others a certain number of operations on their own bodies and souls, thoughts, conduct, and way of being, so as to transform themselves in order to attain a certain state of happiness, purity, wisdom, perfection, or immortality. (1988, p. 18)

In summary, Pistorius deploys his self, his body (represented this time, as a vulnerable and docile body) and most importantly his emotions to subvert power and reattain public recognition and reminding us through this case study of the links between emotion and power (Heaney 2013). He achieves this through the performance of the repentant lover, which enables him to not only appeal to the judge's gender-assumed emotional leniency, but by following from Foucault, it enables him to reconscribe himself under the gaze of the public as a moral actor. Furthermore, Foucault posited that the technologies of self which evolved from Christian theology (*exomologesis* and *exagoreusis*) crystalized into verbalization, but the accused's use of the emotions and his body creates in certain moments of the trial, a dramatic performance breaking through those normative confines of verbal and reasonable disclosure, reaching the audience emotionally and unconsciously.

Oscar Pistorius was aware that the world was watching his trial, since there was a row of cameras and a group of journalists ever present at the entry to the courtroom throughout the duration of the trial. Paralleling this experience of being seen with that of Foucault's interpretation of Bentham's panopticon, unlike Pistorius, the panoptic prisoner is not under constant surveillance, but merely thinks that they *might* be under surveillance at any given time. That's why the prisoner is refused the ability to look back: the curtains in the central tower are closed so that the prisoner does *not* know whether someone is indeed watching. This is different from a camera, which would give the prisoner the certainty of having an audience/being watched. Therefore, the possibility of manipulation in the Pistorius case is not equivalent to the potential for manipulation afforded to the Panopticon prisoner. This manipulation remains in my argument, a visual and emotional one: the accused asks the public to *know* him and *see* him based on a performance of vulnerable masculinity, and through this to *take care* of him, as the last remaining partner of a wounded duo of star-crossed lovers. Resisting then the objectification of the gaze, the accused acts as an agent in the courtroom asking to be transformed and *subjectified* (Friesen 2017), both through conscious interactions with the space and actors in the courtroom, and by making a powerful and mediatized representation on the viewers at an unconscious level, teletechnologically impressing the gaze (Clough 2000).

Conclusion: The Architectural and Emotional Reshaping of Hegemonic Masculinity in the Courtroom

Oscar Pistorius' emotionally oppressed performance in the North Gauteng courtroom, whether veridic or not, in the process of atoning for his actions through visible displays of intense sorrow, hybridizes his image with that of his victim's, becoming the victim of the system. This image recalibration is reliant upon not only the institutional order of the judicial South African system but publicly mediated by plays between progressive and naturalized understandings of gender, confined and contained by the space of the courtroom, and broadcasted in the homes of the viewers.

This case study is significant because it demonstrates as Jonathan Heaney has argued that emotions and power are deeply intertwined (2013), in reminding us that loving and killing can co-exist and that love and power mediate the transfer of experiences from the private sphere into the public, and vice versa, helping a privileged man transforms his masculine role in front of an audience. This role transformation was supported by the architecture of the place, meant to exercise the rational application of justice and of emotional containment, and through this inadvertently functioning as a scene for the emotional release which allowed Pistorius to perform his repentant lover role. He achieved this through a combination of emotional regret and physical vulnerability in reconstructing hegemonic masculinity on new terms, helped by surveillance devices and the public's gaze.

Spatially determined performances of gender and emotionality as they collude with the institutionalization of power are relevant in the age of "dataveillance" (Galič et al., 2017), defined by the constant monitoring of human interactions through mobile phones, drones and the spread of Closed Circuit Television cameras (CCTV). This new, constructed social environment is one of constantly *watching* and being *watched*. In this context, surveillance fulfils a double function: as something external to individuals and connected to the institutionalization of power, and as a self-inflicted activity, in the process of which the physical and (as I have argued) the emotional is merged with the digital.

Interestingly, the public's collective voice is resituated as a powerful agent, helping us reflect on how much things have changed since Foucault's analysis of 18th century public violence with direct moral messages. Events might be more progressive nowadays through teletechnological mediation, comprising unconscious flows between agency, televised technology and ad hoc processes of making sense of the world (Clough 2000), that can limit the power of institutionalized mechanisms of justice and reshape the architecture of the courtroom. But this also reminds that the fate of the agent under surveillance and institutional control escapes complete rationality and fairness but is decided at the unconscious and emotional conference of multiple and unequal intersectional advantages: those of gender, race, status and ability, contained in specific architectural spaces.

Bibliography

Awol, A. (Ed.). (2016). *The Courtroom as a Space of Resistance: Reflections on the Legacy of the Rivonia Trial*. Farnham: Ashgate.

Barnard, A. (2010). Coat of Arms and the Body Politic: Khoisan Imagery and South African National Identity. *Ethnos, 69*(1), 5–22.

Burke, J. (2016a). *Oscar Pistorius Sentenced to Six Years in Jail for Reeva Steenkamp Murder*. https://www.theguardian.com/world/2016/jul/06/oscar-pistorius-jailed-for-xx-years-reeva-steenkamp. Accessed 25 Mar 2018.

Burke, J. (2016b). Emotional Barry Steenkamp Says Pistorius Must Pay for Reeva's Murder. https://www.theguardian.com/world/2016/jun/14/reeva-steenkamps-father-says-oscar-pistorius-must-pay-murder. Accessed 25 Mar 2018.

Chibba, S. (2014). *Judge Thokozile Masipa: Reserved and Astute*. http://mediaclub.co.za/democracy/3735-judge-thokozile-masipa-reserved-and-astute. Accessed 25 Mar 2018.

Clough, P. T. (2000). *Autoaffection: Unconscious Thought in the Age of Teletechnology*. Minneapolis: University of Minnesota Press.

Connell, R. W. (2002). On Hegemonic Masculinity and Violence: Response to Jefferson and Hall. *Theoretical Criminology, 6*(1), 89–99.

Cowell, A. (2017). *Oscar Pistorius's Murder Sentence Is Increased to 15 Years*. https://www.nytimes.com/2017/11/24/world/africa/oscar-pistorius-sentence.html. Accessed 25 Mar 2018.

Ellis, P. (2010, April). A Short History of the North and South Gauteng High Courts. *Advocate*. pp. 48–49. http://www.sabar.co.za/law-journals/2010/april/2010-april-vol023-no1-pp48-49.pdf. Accessed 25 Mar 2018.

Evans, M. (2003). *Love: An Unromantic Discussion*. Cambridge: Polity Press.

Flynn, S., & Mackay, A. (Eds.). (2017). *Spaces of Surveillance: States and Selves*. Cham: Springer/Palgrave Macmillan.

Foucault, M. (1977). *Discipline and Punish*. London: Penguin Books.

Foucault, M. (1988). Technologies of the Self. In L. H. Martin, H. Guttman, & P. H. Hutton (Eds.), *Technologies of the Self: A Seminar with Michel Foucault* (pp. 16–50). London: Tavistock Publications.

Foucault, M. (2007). *Security, Territory, Population: Lectures at the College De France, 1977–78*. Basingstoke: Palgrave Macmillan.

Friesen, N. (2017). Confessional Technologies of the Self: From Seneca to Social Media. *First Monday, 22*(6). http://firstmonday.org/ojs/index.php/fm/article/view/6750/6300. Accessed 25 Mar 2018.

Galič, M., Timan, T., & Koops, B. J. (2017). Bentham, Deleuze and Beyond: An Overview of Surveillance Theories from the Panopticon to Participation. *Philosophy and Technology, 30*(1), 9–37.

Gibson, O. (2013). Oscar Pistorius: The Golden Boy with an Edge of Steel. *The Guardian*. https://www.theguardian.com/sport/2013/feb/14/oscar-pistorius-golden-boy-edge-steel. Accessed 25 Mar 2018.

Gorman-Murray, A., & Hopkins, P. (2014). *Masculinities and Place*. Farnham: Ashgate Publishing.
Graham, S., & Wood, D. (2003). Digitizing Surveillance. *Critical Social Policy, 23*(2), 227–248.
Griffero, T. (2014). *Atmospheres: Aesthetics of Emotional Spaces*. Farnham: Ashgate.
Heaney, J. G. (2013). Emotions and Power: A Bifocal Prescription to Cure Theoretical Myopia. *Journal of Political Power, 6*(3), 355–362.
Jones, R. (2007). The Architecture of Surveillance. *Criminal Justice Matters, 68*(1), 33–34.
Kellner, D. (2015). Jean Baudrillard. In: E. N. Zalta (Ed.), *The Stanford Encyclopedia of Philosophy*. https://plato.stanford.edu/archives/win2015/entries/baudrillard. Accessed 25 Mar 2018.
Lippitt, J. (2017). Forgiveness: A Work of Love? *Parrhesia, 28*, 19–39.
Messner, M. A. (1995). *Power at Play: Sports and the Problem of Masculinity*. Boston: Beacon Press.
Meth, P. (2017). Informal Housing, Gender, Crime and Violence: The Role of Design in Urban South Africa. *The British Journal of Criminology, 57*(2), 402–421.
Mulvey, L. (1999). Visual Pleasure and Narrative Cinema. In L. Braudy & M. Cohen (Eds.), *Film Theory and Criticism: Introductory Readings* (pp. 833–844). New York: Oxford University Press.
Noble, J. A. (2008). Architecture, Hybridities and Post-Apartheid Design. *South African Journal of Art History, 23*(2), 71–88.
Noble, J. A. (2011). *African Identity in Post-apartheid Public Architecture: White Skin, Black Masks*. Farnham: Ashgate.
Perry, A. (2013, March 1). Pistorius and South Africa's Culture of Violence. *The Times Magazine*. http://content.time.com/time/magazine/article/0,9171,2137420-1,00.html
Piro, J. M. (2008). Foucault and the Architecture of Surveillance: Creating Regimes of Power in Schools, Shrines, and Society. *Educational Studies, 44*(1), 30–46.
Ramazanoğlu, C. (Ed.). (1993). *Up Against Foucault: Explorations of Some Tensions Between Foucault and Feminism*. London: Routledge.
Rorty, A. O. (1980). Agent Regret. In A. Rorty (Ed.), *Explaining Emotions* (pp. 489–507). Berkeley: University of California Press.
Schmidt, L. E. (1993). The Fashioning of a Modern Holiday: St. Valentine's Day, 1840–1870. *Winterthur Portfolio, 28*(4), 209–245.
Scott, J.-A. (2014). Illuminating the Vulnerability of Hegemonic Masculinity Through a Performance Analysis of Physically Disabled Men's Personal Narratives. *Disability Studies Quarterly, 34*(1). http://dsq-sds.org/article/view/3570/3526%20. Accessed 25 Mar 2018.
Smart, C. (2002). *Feminism and the Power of Law*. London Taylor & Francis.

Sokolovejan, M. P. (2012). The Fast Life of Oscar Pistorius. *The New York Times.* http://www.nytimes.com/2012/01/22/magazine/oscar-pistorius.html?pagewanted=1&_r=1&hp. Accessed 25 Mar 2018.

Spaulding, N. W. (2012). The Enclosure of Justice: Courthouse Architecture, Due Process, and the Dead Metaphor of Trial. *Yale Journal of Law & the Humanities, 24*(1), 16, 311–343.

Stahl, G. (2017). The Practice of 'Othering' in Reaffirming White Working-Class Boys' Conceptions of Normative Identities. *Journal of Youth Studies, 20*(3), 283–300.

Venter, Z. (2018). Feel the Heat When You Go to City Courts. *Pretoria News.* https://www.iol.co.za/pretoria-news/feel-the-heat-when-you-go-to-city-courts-13108636. Accessed 25 Mar 2018.

Waterhouse, R. (1993). The Inverted Gaze. In S. Scott & D. Morgan (Eds.), *Body Matters: Essays on the Sociology of the Body* (pp. 105–121). Washington, DC: The Falmer Press.

PART IV

Technological Cultures of Surveillance

CHAPTER 12

In the Drone-Space: Surveillance, Spatial Processing, and the Videogame as Architectural Problem

Nathaniel Zetter

Introduction

Games have long offered military strategists a means of picturing the world. "War games" may be designed to simulate battles, but they also present a perspective on warfare's spatial dimensions. For strategists, games and the techniques of vision are connected; together, they represent both a way of thinking through problems and a problem in itself. In 1812, Georg Leopold von Reisswitz, a war advisor to the Prussian crown, presented a new kind of *Kriegsspiel* (war game) that addressed these problems with models—a board divided into a grid to stand for territory, counters for units, and a set of dice to roll for chance. Where older games associated with military strategy, such as chess, had employed an abstract mode of representation, *Kriegsspiel* took cartography as its semiotic framework for rendering military campaigns. In creating a perspective that viewed the battlefield *from above*, the game offered training not only in battlefield tactics but also in a specific form of visualisation. Ever since, war games have framed strategy as an eagle's-eye view on the territory of warfare. The correspondence between this perspective and contemporaneous

N. Zetter (✉)
University of Cambridge, Cambridge, UK
e-mail: nmz21@cam.ac.uk

S. Flynn, A. Mackay (eds.), *Surveillance, Architecture and Control*,
https://doi.org/10.1007/978-3-030-00371-5_12

technology is striking: von Reisswitz invented *Kriegsspiel* in the wake of the first tactical uses of aerial surveillance in warfare, the use of balloons during the Napoleonic Wars. More striking still, today's military strategy videogames first emerged in the context of the Cold War's systems of global air power, and they continue to develop in the present context of "surgical strikes" and unmanned aerial surveillance "drones".

If the aerial perspective, military thought, and games have collocated for at least two centuries, the distinctiveness of the present "military-entertainment complex" (Lenoir 2000; Der Derian 2001) can be located in the way videogames and military surveillance have directly converged in both aesthetics and technology. Infamously, the US military employed Xbox 360 controllers to operate small drones of various kinds on the battlefields of Iraq and Afghanistan. This was not a mere technological convenience. In 2008, the arms manufacturer Raytheon publicised its "Universal Control System" for unmanned aerial vehicles (UAVs) as being "based on the same technology that drives" videogames such as "*Halo* and *Splinter Cell*" (Hambling 2008). As Mark Bigham, Raytheon's development director for "tactical intelligence systems", explained: "Gaming companies have spent millions to develop user-friendly graphic interfaces, so why not put them to work on UAVs? […] The video-game industry always will outspend the military on improving human-computer interaction" (Hambling 2008).

Such unions between game design and militaries are certainly both culturally and politically significant, but it is also worth observing the frequency with which videogames represent military surveillance drones in mimetic terms. A common gameplay trope in the "first-person shooter" genre is to play one level from a drone operator's point of view. The player trains their eye in surveillance skills, observing enemy movements from the sky and performing targeted missile strikes. The trope signals a deep connection between videogames and drones which will be the focus of this chapter. I claim that game design and military surveillance converge in the way they construct vision and frame its relation to spatiality. To understand this convergence, I examine the ways in which "shooter" and "strategy" games mediate architectural forms, and how this mediation has come to reflect the contemporary apparatus of military observation and annihilation. On the one hand, the shooter form—the focus of the chapter's first section—is organised according to a linear mode of vision, employing optical targeting and the architecture of *enfilade*, of spaces sequentially arranged to extend the vista. On the other hand, the strategy form—the focus of the chapter's second section—is organised according to a distributed mode of vision, employing a network of data points and the architecture of the urban sprawl.

My approach examines both the representation of architectural forms and the construction of an architecture within videogames. Although abstract, this latter usage—common in computational discourse—suggests an interface between architectonic thinking in digital design and contemporary architectural theory. As many recent thinkers have noted, it is not only the case that post-war architecture has been inseparable from the computer as a guiding metaphor, but that the convergence of architecture and computation has itself reorganised spatiality since 1945 (Martin 2003, 2010; Halpern 2014; Galloway 2018). Indeed, as Beatriz Colomina (1994, p. 7) influentially claimed, modern architecture has always been "the space of media, of publicity", in which inside and outside are divided by the distribution of visibilities: "To be 'inside' this space is only to see. To be 'outside' is to be *in* the image". Since the rise of computation, digital media have entangled with architectural forms in the way they reorganise the spaces of everyday life. McKenzie Wark (2007) has called this spatial redistribution "gamespace": a mode of interfacing with digital media that no longer observes boundaries between mediated and unmediated zones of interaction. Instead, space itself is assembled by the materiality of the communication media that run through it. The convergence between architecture and digitality, therefore, must be examined as both a metaphor and a materiality. In what follows, I examine videogames' representation of architectural forms as "in-game" objects alongside their architectonic construction of a space of "human-computer interaction". The two aspects work together, I will argue, in rendering military surveillance an aesthetic property in videogame design.

This kind of convergence between digital media and architecture is also embedded, if obliquely, in the paradigmatic model of surveillance studies—Michel Foucault's (1995, p. 200) reading of the "Panopticon" as an "architectural figure" (both materiality and metaphor) for the "composition" of disciplinary mechanisms. Suggestively, the digital enters Foucault's vocabulary in his description of the individual who is always observed, but cannot observe their surveyor nor their fellow prisoners: "he is the object of information, never a subject in communication" (p. 200). Information extraction is one-directional: only the guard can collect it and employ its communicative potential. The panoptical organisation is thus a "network of mechanisms" that achieves power through the centralisation of information; in this network, discipline "programmes" social functions (p. 209). For Foucault, the relationship between surveillance and architecture is never only a matter of coordinating visual observation; it also involves constructing a communication system that conceives of the visual field as an informational apparatus.

With the rise of information technology, Philip E. Agre (1994) reflected on these informational apparatuses by proposing two theoretical models for the relationship between privacy and technology. The traditional "surveillance model", based on "visual metaphors", was to be supplemented by a newer form, the "capture model"—the "prototype" of which is "the deliberate reorganization of industrial work activities to allow computers to track them in real time" (p. 101). Thus, it can be seen "principally in the practices of information technologists" (p. 101). Today, this latter mode, if often going by other names, plays a major role in debates concerning the form of surveillance enacted by the extraction and processing of data. I use Agre's terminology specifically throughout this chapter, since the correlation between videogame genres and his two models represents a compelling frame for the relationship between military surveillance technology and the videogame as a cultural form.

Indeed, videogames offer a useful means of discussing computational and data-based developments in surveillance culture, since, formally speaking, their *appearance* is based on the production of images, while their *logic* is based on the computation of data (Manovich 2001). Thus, in certain iterations, videogames can be seen to combine the visual dynamics of Agre's surveillance model with the informational dynamics of the capture model—a feature I will draw on throughout my analysis.

In employing this confluence, I have in mind something similar to the way Gilles Deleuze and Félix Guattari (1987, p. 352) took the "theory of games" as their model to "compare the war machine and the State apparatus". Since Go "is war without battle lines", they wrote, it represents the "smooth" space of the "*nomos*", of the war machine; whereas, Chess is "an institutionalized, regulated, coded war, with a front, a rear, battles", and so represents the "striated" space of "the State"; thus, their contrast presents an analogy of "*nomos* against *polis*" (p. 352). My comparison is more specific in searching for a formal opposition with which to examine the epistemic constellation of surveillance, architecture, and control in war games. I will contrast the linear architectural mode of the shooter against the distributed architectural mode of the strategy game. On the one hand, the shooter presents a directed optical targeting that proceeds from surveillance to violence; on the other hand, the strategy game presents a distributed informational capture that controls by reorganising the space in which subjects are disclosed. These features, I argue, represent two possible architectural figures, in Foucault's sense, for thinking about surveillance under what Deleuze (1995) later called "societies of control". Indeed, it is possible to parse the two game genres together as a kind of *dronology*—a formal property presenting different, but collectively coded, iterations of the relationship between surveillance and architectonics that is, today, articulated through computation.

Drone Missions in the Military Shooter

Drones and other surveillance aircraft are ubiquitous in military shooter videogames. The trope I mentioned above appears to have been popularised by the "Death from Above" level in *Call of Duty 4: Modern Warfare* (2007), in which the player took on the role of the gunner in an "AC-130 gunship", raining down machine-gun and artillery fire onto anonymous enemy soldiers below. The AC-130, as Roger Stahl (2010, p. 101) has noted, "had received significant public exposure during the Afghan and Iraq invasions", and *Modern Warfare* convincingly reproduced the "infrared gunsight footage" shown on American news networks.

The drone mission trope is suggestive not for its distinctness from typical gameplay, but for the way it isolates the key features of shooter game design. These scenes hark back to the genre's roots in arcade "shoot-'em-ups", which were played "on rails", a term referring to the avatar's predetermined movement through the game-world. As in arcade games, the drone mission grants the player control only over panning or tracking the camera, which serves to aim the gunsight, and over firing their weapon. It also condenses the shooter's interface design. Stripping away the visual representation of the gun, which is typically extended before the camera, drone missions leave only the "reticule" or "crosshairs" that is projected onto the screen. In this way, no separation remains between the game's interface and that of the weapons system. That so few changes need be made to convert the shooter's interface into a drone piloting system reveals their formal similarity, and it makes visible the ways in which the shooter interface always visually rhymes with that of surveillance systems. Drone missions are not the exception to, but the essential form of the genre: all military shooters are played from within what Stahl (2013, p. 559) has called the "drone vision".

A note on historical trajectory is necessary at this point. I am not suggesting that the shooter interface is simply a result of drone technology; rather, they share a genealogy in the apparatus of military, camera-based surveillance technologies. But it is notable that shooter game interfaces have increasingly converged with the aesthetics of the drone vision since images of air strikes from the drone operator's camera have become widely distributed on television and online. Indeed, this trend has proved popular with consumers. Since *Modern Warfare*'s release, military shooters set in contemporary conflicts have consistently out-sold their historical competitors (Caldwell and Lenoir 2016).

Surveillance as Optics

Before analysing architectural form in particular, it is worth assessing the way the shooter's aesthetic properties guide in-game action. For Wark (2007, ¶127), shooters are fundamentally about the "*act* of targeting", an act which represents the basis for every interaction between the player and in-game objects. According to Alexander R. Galloway (2007, p. 88, 89), this targeting is "essentially optical", employing the material properties of the gunsight such that "ballistics and optics merge". It "is a line-of-sight environment, and nothing more", he writes; "encounters are strictly symmetrical: one target, one bullet" (p. 89). Whether opening a door or initiating a conversation, the player may only act through the mechanism of optical targeting—as if every action were firing a rifle. The game-world is thus enframed by the properties of military surveillance and weapons targeting: vision is structured by optical observation, and the only way to interact with those observed is to fire a weapon—to kill.

This distribution of vision and agency corresponds to Agre's (1994, p. 101) "surveillance model", which is built "upon visual metaphors" and based on the politics of observation, personal privacy, and the spatial boundaries that frame each category. As I noted of Foucault's analysis, the surveillance model conceptualises information transfer only in one direction: the "assumption [is] that this 'watching' is nondisruptive and surreptitious (except perhaps when going astray or issuing a threat)", and its spatial organisation constitutes a "[c]entralized orchestration by means of a bureaucracy with a unified set of 'files'" (pp. 105, 106). This model is useful in conceptualising the shooter's mode of vision and interaction. Firstly, the optical register is purely linear: observation, communication, and interaction may only be directed *at* a target, since they are all of the same form. As Foucault (1990, p. 136) wrote of sovereign power, the player may act only "to *take* life or *let* live". This binary application of violence is synthesised with the panoptical mode of observation. Had Bentham envisioned his prison as a shooting gallery, he might have produced a diagram of the shooter videogame. In this conceptualisation, surveillance is not identical to power, but represents the precondition or epistemological framing from which it proceeds. This is because surveillance is perceived to offer the information necessary to determine whether or not violence should be enacted: to kill or let live, to shoot or to ease off the trigger.

Enfilade: Shooting through Walls

These relationships between observation and violence are mirrored significantly in game architecture. Indeed, I believe that the organisation of in-game space represents a predicate for this mode of interaction—an ontology that makes it possible to process the world through surveillance optics. The term *enfilade* arose in Baroque architecture to designate a suite of rooms whose doors are placed opposite each other, such that, when opened, they create an uninterrupted vista down their length. In essence, enfilade is an architectural form employed to arrange vision as if it were optics—lineated, narrowed, and directed. Understanding geometry as the basic tool for spatial concepts, it was related to Baroque architecture's more general use of "spatial *extension*" to create the feeling of "*movement* and *force*" (Norberg-Schulz 1986, p. 8). In capturing and re-deploying the spatial extension of hallways and corridors, enfilade represents an architectural feature that treats rooms as the sort of mediational tools of vision that hallways and corridors are.

In the early eighteenth century, the term began to refer also, in infantry tactics, to positioning troops in formation according to the optimal strafing angles of rifle fire. An infantry formation is "in enfilade", according to John Kersey's *Dictionarium Anglo-Britannicum* of 1708, if its angle of fire "can discover and scour all the Length of a straight Line". The idea thus processes the spatial dynamics of the battlefield as if they were geometrically calculable—a matter of angles, lines, surfaces; the determinations of topology. The term has persisted into more recent iterations of infantry tactics, such as the U.S. Marines' "Rifle Squad" doctrine, in which enfilade fire is "[f]ire delivered so that the long axis of the beaten zone coincides [...] with the long axis of the target" (U.S. Marine Corps 2007,

¶2305). Enfilade is thus part of a general architectonic theory of the battlefield, which holds that individual infantrymen must, at all times, think of space as a matter of superior and inferior optical angles that represent greater or lesser ballistic exposure to the enemy's position.

The architectural and military senses of enfilade, taken together, conceptualise the spatial organisation of military shooter games. Their conjunction also clarifies the relationship between the features of interface design I have already described and those of game architecture. This is because shooters employ the passageway as their basic spatial form. Since the only mode of interaction possible is that of linear optics, space must be laid out before the player according to lineated visibilities. Enemies are arrayed down the extension of pathways, and approach the player, or are approached by them, through these vistas. Level design thus operates as a series of intersecting hallways which provide greater or lesser openings onto the field of vision. The hallways often connect and overlap, but in doing so they create forms that mirror the spatial extension of the labyrinth, rather than the spatial distribution of the network (Aarseth 1997). Military shooter games, in this way, process all space according to the principle of enfilade, in both architectonic and military senses. Architectural units are chained together to create spatially extended vistas, and in this way architecture is activated to negotiate the tactical courses of gunfire.

The design of military shooter videogames, resultantly, must always mediate between the necessity of linear direction and the ideal of openness. The trick in designing a specific shooter's architecture is to guide the player's optical progression through the level smoothly and efficiently, while still avoiding a vision so narrow as to elicit the sensation of being led down identical hallways. Games such as those in the *Call of Duty* series, which preference the former over the latter, are often criticised for feeling as if they are "on rails"—merely narrow and entirely directed. Yet I suspect their great pleasure lies in the feeling of efficient movement through a smooth chain of viewpoints: the conversion of optics into the programmed consumption of space. If this design is accomplished, the architecture of the game space can feel as if it has been mapped to the linear optics of the game's visual perspective in an intricate formal symmetry.

There is a remarkable reflection between these gameplay dynamics and the theory of vision in general, and of surveillance in particular, in the recent transformation in urban warfare tactics. According to Stephen Graham (2012, p. 137), "it is necessary to talk of a 'new military urbanism'" in "state security and military thinking". Where traditionally "[c]ities were seen as targets, not battlefields [...] today, the cityscapes of the global South have emerged as paradigmatic conflict zones" (Graham 2007, p. 121). In this context, as Eyal Weizman (2017) has shown, the Israeli Defense Forces (IDF) experimented with post-structuralist concepts of spatiality to reconceive the architectural properties of the urban battlefield. This spatial revolution in military tactics has involved re-thinking interiors as interlocking systems of lines of sight. Urban architecture no longer represents a fixed space in which battle might take place, but a complex of possibilities through which the reconfiguration of optics might lend an advantage over the enemy. Thus, in the IDF's reinterpretation of "both architectural and urban syntax", the "tactics of 'walking-through-walls' involved a conception of the city as not just the site, but as the very *medium* of warfare – a flexible, almost liquid matter that is forever contingent and in flux" (Weizman 2017, p. 186). As the space of visibilities, architecture becomes the medium for reorganising vision towards optical, and thus ballistic, superiority. In short, surveillance has become not only an intelligence gathering tool but also the foundation for all urban warfare.

Military shooter games have not only paralleled this mode of thinking but continually adapted in pace with its intensification. The mantra of *Modern Warfare* players in 2007 was the imperative to "watch your corners", to see architectural features as potential points of exposure to enemy fire. Architecture was reconceived through *lines of sight*. In 2015, *Tom Clancy's Rainbow Six: Siege*, a game entirely composed of urban warfare scenarios, made its environment destructible such that, as in the IDF, the tactics of "walking through walls" could become the basis for urban warfare. Architecture was reconstituted as a material component within combat—as its medium. To interact with spatial boundaries through the shooter's only mode of interaction—*to shoot*—is to re-imagine all architectural forms as possible enfilade, as possibilities for the production of shooting galleries. Weizman (2017, p. 208) writes that "new methods have been devised to allow soldiers not only to see, but also to shoot and kill through solid walls [...] practices and technologies [which] will have a radical effect on the relation of military practices to architecture". These are, he continues, "the main components in the search to produce a military fantasy world of boundless fluidity, in which the city's space becomes as navigable as an ocean (or as in a computer game)" (p. 209). *As in a computer game* has come to mean not only walking through walls but shooting through them.

The surveillance model, for Agre (1994, p. 106), employs "territorial metaphors" that register the transgression of privacy as "the 'invasion' of a 'private' personal space". Thus, the "rights" of the individual are understood through an "opposition between 'coercion' and 'consent'" that is framed by its spatial properties (p. 106). In the military shooter's architectural form, every player action is configured in this way—as a spatial transgression that discloses interaction only as a form of coercion. The principle of enfilade converts every movement through space into a destruction of boundaries and an invasion of interiors—a transgression of privacy. In this way, the conflation of optics with ballistics in the shooter game offers a picture of a military fantasy for which surveillance vision is understood to proceed rationally down the "kill-chain" to annihilation. So long as a space can be transgressed by observation, violence can be manifested there.

Commanding from Above in the Strategy Game

The appearance of drones is less regular and perhaps more oblique in the strategy game than in the shooter. *StarCraft II* (2010), for example, features flying units such as the "Raven" and "Overlord" which have surveillance functions, while *XCOM: Enemy Unknown* (2012) features the "Drone" as an opposing unit. Unlike in the shooter, however, these drones are not accompanied by modifications to the game's interface. When featured, drones are simply another unit to be commanded or fought against—from the same perspective that is used for any other gameplay. If the drone vision in the shooter was a revealing trope on account of the minimal changes it made to the main game's interface, the representation of drone units in the strategy game is revealing for the fact that it requires no changes to the game's interface or gameplay mechanics.

Such modifications are unnecessary because strategy games are typically already played from a free-floating aerial perspective. Tethered neither to an avatar nor to a single location, this perspective observes the gameworld from above. In this sense, it is always played with the perspectival features associated with drone surveillance. This view, however, differs significantly from those moments of drone vision in the shooter, since it does not employ the gunsight interface as its organising principle. Instead, a mouse-pointer is used for all interactions across the plane of vision, enabling the camera to move along multi-linear axes and rotations. If the shooter employs the optical register of drone vision, but not its aerial perspective, the strategy game employs its aerial perspective, but not the optics of its weapons technology.

Suggestively, this practice of untethering releases the player from some of the restrictions of space, but not from those of optics as such. Strategy games follow the typical videogame design principle of simulating the lens optics of a camera's capture of light, rather than the dynamics of ocular vision. For this reason, classifying the game interface as a sort of "God's-eye-view", as industry terminology often terms it, is insufficient. In fact, the interface draws on a number of technological aesthetics to create a coherent optical vision. A starting point to address this feature lies in the way it mirrors what Grégoire Chamayou (2015, p. 38) has described as the ideal conception of drone observation: the "*principle of a totalization of perspectives or a synoptic viewing*". This principle understands the elimination of spatial restrictions from aerial observation to be the goal of surveillance, and it seeks to achieve this by viewing the territory from numerous perspectival positions simultaneously. I will return to this "totalization" in a moment; for now, it is worth analysing the representational schema that frames it.

Surveillance as Representation

Strategy game-worlds are laid out according to two common formal principles. The first is a simulation of the tabletop game-form—today popularly embodied in *Warhammer 40,000* (1987–), the science fiction miniatures game which inspired the first *StarCraft* (1998). This mode employs a kind of synecdoche to represent units, with one soldier standing in for the role of many or a few trees standing in for an entire forest, and a panorama to represent territory, with a visual sweep compressed to arrange the topic of a singular landscape. I refer to this as the *panoramic mode*, and it is most common in "real-time strategy" games. The second is a simulation of the map-based board game, which inherited its representational mode from cartographic systems of military planning. This *cartographic mode* integrates economic and political concerns into its geographic schema, rendering these as correlative strategic factors to those of territory in a general register of spatialised information. This mode is more common in "turn-based strategy" games, in which the playing of "grand strategy" tends to be preferred over individual battles. Although it is conceptually useful to separate the panoramic and cartographic modes, it is worth noting that many strategy games today integrate both in their design; other games, such as the long-running *Total War* (2000–) series, split gameplay between the two—geopolitical strategy is played on a map, and battles are separately played out on a tabletop.

Whether primarily cartographic or panoramic, however, the precondition for each mode's particular functions lies in gameplay mechanics that are consistent with the register of data-based surveillance. Since the player typically does not take the role of an in-game avatar, all of their interactions are mediated through objects that they observe, select, and order. In *StarCraft*, a "marine" is selected with a mouse-click and then ordered to move, to "attack", and so on, with a second mouse-click. The player has continuous control only over the mouse-pointer which directs these clicks. The game's drone-eye-view enables the player to navigate space quickly and efficiently in order to select any unit under their command. For this gameplay mechanism to function, however, units must be visually discrete such that they appear, on the one hand, as immediately recognisable, and, on the other, as autonomous yet subject to modulation. David Golumbia (2009) has theorised this feature of strategy games as programming discrete types which cause concepts such as culture and history to be rendered incidental or mere surface effects. In the *Age of Empires* (1997–) series, peoples—"Britons", "Koreans", "Aztecs", "Mayans"—are compressed into categories defined by their "characteristics" and the forms of interaction these produce: in the former sense, processed as classifications—"Archer civilisation"—and, in the latter, as informatic modifiers—"Resources last 20% longer" (p. 138). This representational schema employs a form of surveillance procedure, in the sense of a "social sorting" through codes that produce classifications. As David Lyon (2003, p. 20) has influentially argued, these techniques of sorting, placed in the register of the social rather than private realm, obtain "personal and group data in order to classify people and populations". These classifications organise power relations by identifying those "who should be targeted for special treatment, suspicion, eligibility, inclusion, access, and so on" (p. 20). By embedding social sorting at the base of its representational mode, the strategy game takes surveillance as the foundation for the strategic view as such. To see from the strategy perspective is to understand the polity as always/already compressed into categories. Since these categories are based on informational variation, datasets precede aesthetics in producing game mechanics; thus, the game's visual form corresponds to pre-rendered informatic classifications. The register of data surveillance, which identifies subjects according to their typological traces and patterns of behaviour, operates in this way as an organising principle for interactivity in the strategy game. Surveillance makes possible the selection and ordering mechanisms that the aerial view articulates in gameplay.

If it were stripped of visual representation, selecting a marine and ordering them to attack could be parsed as formally equivalent to the selection of two data entries in a spreadsheet, and the calculation of one value against another. This is the great phenomenological mystery of videogame culture: the gulf between the aesthetic and spatial constructions the player experiences and the subterranean level of information through which such systems function. This dichotomy is also central to surveillance, which makes visible by being invisible, and it is all the more prevalent in today's vast systems of data capture and accumulation. Such systems enable, as Joseph Pugliese (2016, p. 5) notes, drone operators to use metadata to hunt after phones as if their users are "entirely coextensive with the technology they use"; a practice he evocatively calls, "killing by metadata". Indeed, reflecting on the problem of visibility in relation to drones in 2013, Zygmunt Bauman (p. 20) remarked that the "new generation of drones will stay invisible while making everything else accessible to be viewed". This corresponds to drones' particular form of violence: "they will stay immune while rendering everything else vulnerable", thus moving further "towards making the war itself all but invisible to the nation in whose name the war is waged" (p. 20).

To address this dichotomy, it is useful to turn to Agre's (1994, p. 107) second concept: the "capture model", which specifies data surveillance's formative procedure. This mode of privacy's transgression by technology employs the "linguistic 'parsing' of human activities", translating them into "the constructs of a computer system's representation languages" to make possible the "active intervention in and reorganization of those activities" (p. 107). Capture functions through a "[d]ecentralized and heterogeneous organization" in which a "process is normally conducted within particular, local practices", but will accumulate with other processes to "involve people in the workings of larger social formations" (p. 107). We can thus locate capture among those practices Bernard Stiegler (2010) calls "grammatization", which proceed through the discretisation of social behaviours, and also alongside Golumbia's (2009, p. 8) redefinition of "*computationalism*" to name "the view that a great deal, perhaps all, of human and social experience can be explained via computational processes". Indeed, Agre (1994, p. 109) wrote that capture describes the application of "*grammars of action*"—accounting systems and user interfaces are two of his examples—to "human activities", and the resulting effect "when the newly reorganized activities are represented by computers in real time".

If marines fighting "Zerg" in *StarCraft* presents a visual analogy of numerical values calculated against one another, it also offers a structural analogy of the representational system that makes it possible to visualise the interplay of numerical values as a battle between space marines and aliens. Through capture, the attack has been discretised into a calculable property, but so too has the grammar of action that *commanding to attack* represents. Sending a marine to fight represents a series of interlocking systems of representation founded upon capture. Galloway (2007, p. 95) writes that *StarCraft* "highlights the problem of how to 'control' that which is uncontrollable, or how to shift from top-down control to organic, bottom-up control". In the context of surveillance, this is a problem of what form data may take in an interface that enables it to be subject to exterior manipulation and control.

Architectronics: The City as Surveillance Apparatus

Architectural forms offer a path to unlocking this problem of data's scaling-up into representation. In strategy games, all production takes place within "buildings" that are constructed to expand the player's ability to train troops, upgrade weapons, and so on. Yet these buildings contain no interior rendering of space; they collapse the interior/exterior dyad, since their function is only to operate as components in a system that consumes resources and produces units. Architectural in form yet spatially vacant, they operate as architectonic black-boxes, describable in terms of data input and output alone. The problem of visibility, however, remains crucial. What takes place inside the building need not be addressed—since it is assumed to have been revealed entirely by the data output—but its spatiality within the urban distribution of the player's "base" is, nevertheless, a significant feature of gameplay. This is because the buildings' exterior form and spatial distribution determines the base's defensibility, and typically the destruction of the player's base means losing the game. Whether domestic, military, or industrial, in-game architectures thus disclose interiority as an operation only, and exteriority as a spatial formation oriented towards the problem of urban defence.

Peter Galison (2001) has influentially suggested that the typical account of post-modern architecture should be supplemented by the history of the Second World War's "Strategic Bombing Survey". The "architectures of dispersion, counter-urbanization, and nonhierarchical grids" present in post-war architecture and urbanism turn out to have their roots in a militarised aerial perspective: "the pounding, repetitive process of planning, delivering, and analysing strategic air strikes along with the destructive functionalism of economic life that accompanied it" (p. 31). Distributing individual buildings across the network involves describing them primarily in the terms of their operation within that network, and not their interior properties. Accordingly, the architectural network can be re-designed to strengthen connectivity and thus protect such operations against an attack from the skies.

We can observe this same sequence, from defence to urban planning to distributed architectural networks, in the strategy game. Real-time strategy games such as *StarCraft*, in particular, encourage players to disperse their productive buildings according to their function and defensibility within the base, forming de-centralised zones of production and security around resource sites and other territorial features. This follows the collapsing of distinctions between the territory (as a network) and the city (as an "island of architectonic forms") that Reinhold Martin (2010, p. 184) has observed "to produce complex topologies in which insides and outsides are multiply enfolded". While such a feature relies on the black-boxing of in-game buildings, it is worth clarifying, following Martin, that such a mode does not render interiors irrelevant, but enfolds them into the network as informatic operations alone. In this sense, the representation of architecture in-game mirrors the game's own architecture: informational black-boxes reside below the player's perception, but nevertheless form units in a larger distributed system of management that is represented, spatially and aesthetically, in the network form. This system is not so much architectonic, then, as *architectronic*—a method of reorganising urbanism according to the needs of the network, which is built upon computation as both a metaphor and a formal model.

I suggest, therefore, that it is useful to conceptualise three levels of architectural form present in the strategy game: buildings, which operate as black-boxes; cities, which operate as distributed urban and territorial networks; and topics—in the sense of *topos*—which operate as localising forms that construct the game itself as an interior architectural space. This last point is crucial. If tabletop and board strategy games required a flat surface laid out in front of the player, their videogame descendants have constructed three dimensions of space within which the player is involved as if within a building. Earlier, I described the aerial perspective as a form that loosens spatial restrictions, and this is true of individual movements, but in the wider game space the player is limited by boundaries on all sides. Since the world has been defined in three dimensions, it is now expressed in the terms of these interior proportions.

In the Drone-Space

How might these three levels of architectural form help us to understand the strategy game's disclosing of military surveillance and control? Writing on drone warfare, Chamayou (2015) has described the theory of the "kill box", which defines a three-dimensional space of air and land within which all objects are conceived to be available for observation and thus rendered potential targets for slaughter. The concept relates to a wider shift from the "battlefield" to the "*battlespace*" in military thought (Graham 2009), which has re-defined spatiality among multiple scales in the attempt to integrate "a conception of military matters that includes absolutely everything" (Agre 2001, quoted in Graham 2009, p. 279). Weizman (2017, p. 7) offers an evocative description of this kind of thinking: laid out "under a blanket of aerial Israeli surveillance",

> the territory of Palestine emerged as a hologramatized "hollow land" [... in which] the imaginary spaces of conflict have seemingly fully adopted the scale of a building, resembling a complex architectural construction, perhaps an airport, with its separate inbound and outbound levels, security corridors and many checkpoints. (p. 15)

These theories of battlespaces, kill boxes, and hollow lands characterise strata of the "new military urbanism" (Graham 2012) at the strategic level equivalent to that which I described at the local, tactical level in the shooter videogame. They represent a system of military-strategic thinking designed to enclose the land within a spatial form that makes it constantly accessible to observation and violence from the air.

A distributed architecture, in looking to nonhierarchical grids for formal inspiration, also tends to form a field of discrete units. To be dispersed is to be available to perception as objects spread out on a table. *Distribute* and *disperse* share an etymology with this sense of *discrete*, which leads back to the Latin *distribuo*, "to divide", and *discernere*, "to discern"—as in the sense of *to comprehend*, but also that of *to perceive a distinction*. The distribution of architecture may be said to have this feature of distinction-making, which, by spreading out, makes architectural forms increasingly divisible, and thus proliferates connections among entities that have been arranged by relation rather than form. The *Civilization* (1991–) grand strategy series makes this principle particularly clear. Territory, in *Civilization VI* (2016), is divided into hexagons—each formally identical to, internally discrete from, and externally interactive with their neighbours. Arranged under zones of management by "cities", each hexagon may contain either the city's central "settlement", which contains administrative, educational, and cultural buildings, or one productive building—a "farm", "factory", "barracks", and so on. Where strategy board games have long employed this crystalline structure, *Civilization* also renders a three-dimensional space extending above it. The hexagons are laid across the horizontal plane, while the vertical axis enables the player to roam across multiple camera angles and motions. Thus, the discreteness and distribution of architecture on the ground places individual buildings within a system of information flow that is controlled from above. Spatial form maps informational connectivity.

Chamayou (2015, p. 55) writes of the theory of the kill box: "One should imagine a theater of operations portrayed on a screen in 3-D as a set of cubes laid out on a surface divided into squares". This form of division considers each kill box discrete, and each zone within it a further discretisation. Such logic converges two principles that are central to the military's justifications for the legitimacy of drone warfare: "*precision* or *specification*" with "*globalization* or *homogenization*" (pp. 56–57). The foundation for this contradictory convergence lies in the formal property I have described, of discrete units connected in a network of identical zones. It represents the rationale behind the view that a surveillance form based on integrating optics with data can be simultaneously precise, because it is located in a discrete entity, and also globalised, because it is infinitely repeatable. In this way, we have an analogy for how the procedure of capture scales-up into integrated systems of surveillance. Capture here is articulated at architectural, urban, and territorial levels simultaneously, and it discloses a fantasy of surveillance that imagines identification as if it were precision, and homogenisation as if it were globalism.

The mode of thinking I earlier termed *architectronics* can, I believe, describe the logic that interlocks these levels of the surveillance apparatus.

In a basic sense, the term would simply designate the view that spatiality can be re-thought according to the principles of computational and informational architectures. In a larger sense, it would designate the form of thinking—military, managerial, or governmental rationality—that understands information and computation as the tools with which multiple levels of spatiality and zones of interaction can be integrated into one system. In short, it represents the view that the digital makes all spatial scales subject to the same principle of organisation. As it becomes visible in the strategy game, this *architectronics* articulates some of the principles by which data surveillance (capture) and optical surveillance (observation) are integrated into a military fantasy of a world wherein informatics enables all subjects to be tracked, and thus, to be annihilated.

Conclusion

In this chapter, I have presented two architectural figures which disclose the contemporary military surveillance apparatus and address some of the epistemic relations through which this apparatus operates. The contrast between the shooter and strategy genres presents a play of oppositions that is useful in examining this particular epistemic constellation. In Table 12.1, I lay out some of these oppositions as they have emerged from the preceding analysis; but the central dialectic is also worth re-stating. I have argued that the shooter constructs an idealised drone vision. This vision frames a univocal progression from surveillance to annihilation based upon the smooth and unequivocal presentation of optics. The strategy game also constructs an idealised drone vision, but one that renders a distributed system of militarised spatiality wherein every object is accessible to observation. The former represents a kind of solipsism, since it assumes the interiority of the aggressor alone, and thus interaction exists within it only in the projection of ballistics towards a target. The latter, by contrast, represents a political rationality that enables *points of contact*—identification, selection, command—to emerge as an integrated system of control between multiple levels of spatial organisation. Taken together, the shooter and strategy games present a *dronology*—a phenomenology of the drone vision as situated within systems of computational command and control. My analysis has demonstrated that the remediation of architecture within these games is inseparable from the surveillance apparatus that is embedded in their design.

Table 12.1 Table of aesthetic, architectonic, and military-strategic relations

Shooter	*Strategy*
Panoptics	*Synoptics*
Lines of sight	Points of contact
Topology	Topography
Solipsism	Politics
Enfilade	*Architectronics*
Corridors	Networks
Visibilities	Black boxes
Domestic	Urban
Tactics	*Strategy*
Battlefield	Battlespace
Targeting	Datasets
Ballistics	Kill boxes

If the novelty of this apparatus lies in its technological specificity, it is nevertheless worth remarking on the continuity with older surveillance forms that remain rooted in its cultural imaginary. Chamayou (2015) has noted the panoptical fantasies that continue to be embedded in the language of drone warfare:

> The names given to these devices are very revealing: Argus and Gorgon Stare. In Greek mythology, Argus, the figure with a hundred eyes, was also known as Panoptes, "the one who sees all." [...] We are entering into the era of winged and armed panoptics. As for the gaze of the Gorgon, it turned to stone all those unfortunate enough to encounter it. It was a gaze that killed. At this point, it is a matter no longer of surveillance and punishment but of *surveillance and annihilation*. (pp. 43–44)

It is important not to slip into generalisations concerning a homogenous "surveillance society", as David Murakami Wood (2009) has argued, since its forms are variable across the social field. Nevertheless, the epistemic properties of what Chamayou calls the "era of winged and armed panoptics" can, in the specific convergence of videogames and drones, be located in a military fantasy of total observation and its projection into annihilation. The videogames I have examined present an insight into this fantasy by replicating its logic at the structural level of game design. That this mirroring is so thoroughly integrated into ordinary game aesthetics places it among those "efforts to rebrand and reconfigure drones as banal entertainment" that Caitlin Overington and Thao Phan (2016, p. 149) have observed in drones' civilian use. As they note, this "banalisation" must be "critiqued as part of the disciplinary efforts within control societies to perpetuate the discourse of global war" (p. 149). Thus, it may be the case that some of the most significant examples of the military-entertainment complex are offered by those videogames that obscure surveillance in general, and the drone vision in particular, by their very ubiquity.

Games have long offered military strategists a means of picturing the world; they may do the same for the critical theorist analysing the fantasises of militarism today. When Xbox "peripherals" control drones in both the battlespace and the living room, it is the apparatus and not the peripheral which must be placed under critical pressure. All play and no work in the drone-space.

Acknowledgements I am grateful to Trisha Banerjee and Hunter Dukes for their insightful comments on drafts of this chapter; the research period that formed it was generously supported by Peterhouse, University of Cambridge.

Bibliography

Aarseth, E. J. (1997). *Cybertext: Perspectives on Ergodic Literature*. London: The Johns Hopkins University Press.

Agre, P. E. (1994). Surveillance and Capture: Two Models of Privacy. *The Information Society, 10*(2), 101–127.

Bauman, Z., & Lyon, D. (2013). *Liquid Surveillance: A Conversation*. Cambridge: Polity.

Caldwell, L., & Lenoir, T. (2016). Wargaming Futures: Naturalizing the New American Way of War. In P. Harrigan & M. G. Kirschenbaum (Eds.), *Zones of Control: Perspectives on Wargaming* (pp. 253–279). London: MIT Press.

Chamayou, G. (2015). *Drone Theory* (trans: Lloyd, J.). London: Penguin Books.

Colomina, B. (1994). *Privacy and Publicity: Modern Architecture as Mass Media*. London: MIT Press.

Deleuze, G. (1995). *Negotiations, 1972–1990* (trans: Joughin, M.). New York: Columbia University Press.

Deleuze, G., & Guattari, F. (1987). *A Thousand Plateaus: Capitalism and Schizophrenia* (trans: Massumi, B.). London: University of Minnesota Press.

Der Derian, J. (2001). *Virtuous War: Mapping the Military-Industrial-Media-Entertainment Complex*. Boulder: Westview Press.

Foucault, M. (1990). *The History of Sexuality, Volume 1: An Introduction* (trans: Hurley, R.). New York: Vintage Books.

Foucault, M. (1995). *Discipline and Punish: The Birth of the Prison* (trans: Sheridan, A.). New York: Vintage Books.

Galloway, A. R. (2007). *StarCraft*, or, Balance. *Grey Room, 28*, 86–107.

Galloway, A. R. (2018). Informatic Brutalism. In A. Ring, H. Steiner, & K. Veel (Eds.), *Architecture and Control*. Leiden: Brill.

Galison, P. (2001). War against the Center. *Grey Room, 4*, 5–33.

Golumbia, D. (2009). *The Cultural Logic of Computation*. London: Harvard University Press.

Graham, S. (2007). War and the City. *New Left Review, 44*, 121–132.

Graham, S. (2009). The Urban "Battlespace". *Theory, Culture & Society., 26*(7–8), 278–288.

Graham, S. (2012). When Life Itself Is War: On the Urbanization of Military and Security Doctrine. *International Journal of Urban and Regional Research, 36*(1), 136–155.

Halpern, O. (2014). *Beautiful Data: A History of Vision and Reason since 1945*. London: Duke University Press.

Hambling, D. (2008, July 19). Game Controllers Driving Drones, Nukes. *Wired*. https://www.wired.com/2008/07/wargames/. Accessed 30 Mar 2018.

Kersey, J. (1708). *Dictionarium Anglo-Britannicum: Or, A General English Dictionary*. London: J. Wilde.

Lenoir, T. (2000). All but War Is Simulation: The Military-Entertainment Complex. *Configurations, 8*, 289–335.

Lyon, D. (2003). Surveillance as Social Sorting: Computer Codes and Mobile Bodies. In D. Lyon (Ed.), *Surveillance as Social Sorting: Privacy, Risk, and Digital Discrimination*. London: Routledge.

Manovich, L. (2001). *The Language of New Media*. London: MIT Press.

Martin, R. (2003). *The Organizational Complex: Architecture, Media, and Corporate Space*. London: MIT Press.

Martin, R. (2010). *Utopia's Ghost: Architecture and Postmodernism, Again*. London: University of Minnesota Press.

Murakami Wood, D. (2009). The "Surveillance Society": Questions of History, Place and Culture. *European Journal of Criminology, 6*(2), 179–194.

Norberg-Schulz, C. (1986). *Baroque Architecture*. London: Faber and Faber.

Overington, C., & Phan, T. (2016). Domesticating Drone Technologies: Commercialisation, Banalisation, and Reconfiguring "Ways of Seeing". In H. Randell-Moon & R. Tippet (Eds.), *Security, Race, Biopower: Essays on Technology and Corporeality*. London: Palgrave Macmillan.

Pugliese, J. (2016). Death by Metadata: The Bioinformationalisation of Life and the Transliteration of Algorithms to Flesh. In Randell-Moon & Tippet, *Security, Race, Biopower*.

Stahl, R. (2010). *Militainment, Inc.: War, Media, and Popular Culture*. London: Routledge.

Stahl, R. (2013). What the Drone Saw: The Cultural Optics of the Unmanned War. *Australian Journal of International Affairs, 67*(5), 659–674.
Stiegler, B. (2010). *For a New Critique of Political Economy* (trans: Ross, D.). Cambridge: Polity.
U.S. Marine Corps. (2007). *Marine Rifle Squad*. New York: Cosimo Classics.
Wark, M. (2007). *Gamer Theory*. London: Harvard University Press.
Weizman, E. (2017). *Hollow Land: Israel's Architecture of Occupation* (New ed.). London: Verso.

Gameography

Age of Empires. (1997). Ensemble Studios.
Call of Duty 4: Modern Warfare. (2007). Activision.
Sid Meier's Civilization VI. (2016). Firaxis Games.
Shogun: Total War. (2000). The Creative Assembly.
StarCraft. (1998). Blizzard Entertainment.
StarCraft II: Wings of Liberty. (2010). Blizzard Entertainment.
Tom Clancy's Rainbow Six: Siege. (2015). Ubisoft Montreal.
Warhammer 40,000. (1987). Games Workshop.
XCOM: Enemy Unknown. (2012). Firaxis Games.

CHAPTER 13

Sensurround: 4D Theatre Space and the Pliable Body

Stacy M. Jameson

Introduction

Going to the movies seems at first glance an act of innocuous escapism that offers a brief freedom from our own realities, both in the sense that we can forget our lives in favour of the film narrative, and in the physical sense in which attention is directed to the lights on the screen, not the materiality of the space and the flesh of the film goers. Indeed, we tend to think of movie theatres as spaces of distanced watching in anonymity, where our individual bodies are hidden in darkness and thus from public view and scrutiny. In this way, movie theatres seem antithetical to the topic of surveillance and any form of monitoring beyond the discourses within the film texts themselves. However, this chapter demonstrates how one new form of movie theatre facilitates comparable outcomes to the panopticon—specifically, the internalization and incorporation of modes of power and control—but through very different structures. Four-dimensional (4D) theatres, a growing international phenomenon, add environmental and sensory effects to three-dimensional (3D) film screenings inculcating both the movie theatre space and the corporeal spectator in the cinematic spectacle in meaningful ways. The 4D movie theatre is not a venue of surveillance as we know it, in which the gaze is central to a

S. M. Jameson (✉)
University of Rhode Island, South Kingstown, RI, USA

S. Flynn, A. Mackay (eds.), *Surveillance, Architecture and Control*,
https://doi.org/10.1007/978-3-030-00371-5_13

paradigm of control. Rather, this chapter suggests that by manifesting a form of spectacle that galvanizes the physical senses as equal modes of engagement with the world and by enacting a programme of sensory management, 4D movie theatres encourage a comparable but unique mode of social management to the technologies and architectures of visual surveillance.

In 4D cinema, the architecture of the theatre no longer functions to facilitate simple sight of the film, but instead the space works directly on the bodies of the moviegoers. Like Maurice Merleau-Ponty's discussions of a blind man's cane, the material of the theatre becomes an extension of our embodied perception. Vibrating chairs, lights, sprayers, air jets, fans, and ticklers are not separate distinct things or tools. The technologies and objects of the space expand the individual body's "area of sensitivity, extending the scope and active radius of touch, and providing a parallel to sight" (Merleau-Ponty 1962, p. 142). Thus, while popular discourse understands the 4D experience as an expansion of the cinema diegesis, this chapter conversely explores the theatre as an arena of interface with the corporeal spectator, whose perception is—very unlike the blind man with his cane—managed from a control room. Beyond enabling cinema viewing, the 4D theatre with its programmable infrastructure, functions in ways comparable to Michel Foucault's understanding of Bentham's prison design of the panopticon: "to permit an internal articulated and detailed control—to render visible those who are inside it; in more general terms, an architecture that…[operates] to transform individuals" (Foucault 1977, p. 172). Instead of bodies laid visibly bare, 4D theatres condition bodies as known quantities, whose nerves and feelings are calculated and disciplined. By exploring the historical development, the material space, and the spectator experience of contemporary 4D cinema, we can begin to understand how such an easily dismissed entertainment practice functions as a lens into the sensory side of surveillance and the practices and meanings of forms of complicit management that operate unseen through air bursts, smells, and vibrations. In this close reading of the 4D movie theatre, I am concerned with the logics inherent in the space—how design, function, and use position spectators in troubling ways. If the old era of visual surveillance has given way to new modes of monitoring at the level of digital cookies, the 4D theatre operates as a locus of impulse mapping, where the seemingly intimate/automatic/physical senses are systematized and regulated.

4D Origins and Evolutions: Towards the Sensory Collective

The 4D movie theatre is not altogether new, but rather draws on a long history of experimentation with materiality in relation to both narrative and spectacle. The augmentation of a visual display—usually one that in form or substance suggests a sense of physical motion or travel—with contextual effects has pre-film origins. Nineteenth-century panorama shows in the United States and in Europe provided accompanying effects to enliven static images, taking the form of theatrical lecturers or musical performances, but also multisensory stimulations. For example, the panorama display *Paris By Night* presented at the New York Colosseum in 1875 was enhanced by "storm, lighting, wind, and rain effects" (Huhtamo 2013, p. 305). The often travel themed displays encourage an additional sense of transport and travel; by utilizing environmental effects, the show maintained that audiences could at some level "embody" these locals. Similarly, 4D theatres construct a comparable sense of cinema as a material "place" we can visit. As one 4DX (the brand technology of the CJ 4D PLEX company) advertisement suggests in the form of a text message exchange: "where are you?" "I'm in the movie" (CJ 4DPLEX 2011).

Short-lived film versions of this sort of physical attraction have emerged over the years; these tended to contribute an additional singular sensory experience to the privileged audio-visual. Smell-O-Vision, for example, was introduced at the world's fair in 1939 by Hans Laube and released smells to individual seats in movie theatres (Brownlee 2016). Forgotten for many years, the technology was enacted for the 1960 film *Scent of Mystery*, in which Laube's "smell brain"—a series of perfume bottles—was synchronized to release smells automatically into the theatre during the movie via tubes along each theatre seat. One such featured odour was that of the assassin's pipe smoke, functioning as a clue in aroma form. Likewise, there have been comparable exhibitions over the second half of the twentieth century that presented other modes of film "feeling." A theatre notice for the 1974 film *Earthquake* warned:

> ATTENTION! This motion picture will be shown in the startling new multi-dimension of Sensurround. Please be aware that you will feel as well as see and hear realistic effects such as might be experienced in an actual earthquake. The management assumes no responsibility for the physical or emotional reactions of the individual viewer. (Konow 2013)

Not demanding major theatre renovations, Sensurround harnessed the physical powers of sound to simulate the rumbling and shaking of an earthquake. Here sound becomes a corporeal thing that extends cinema off the screen into the material realm of the theatre. As the advertisement for Sensurround warns, the result of these singular extensions of cinema beyond the screen is a unique spectator experience. The spectator is not afforded emotional or intellectual distance from the film, but rather becomes physically invested in the systematization of feeling. This is an exceptional kind of "immersion," and one that is not in fact about absorption into a narrative as is typical of the address of the classical Hollywood film style.

If early experiments in multisensory cinema tended to focus more on singular senses such as smell or motion, the promise of 4D is the construction of a complete sensorium that encircles the viewer in a total "touchable" realty. With 4D, the significance of the material space of the theatre and physical presence of the body are intensified by the kinesis of the theatre seats, blowing air, and so on as an organized infrastructure to engulf and move the viewer in coordinated and choreographed ways. According to the industry leader, their 4DX technology "changes the cinematic paradigm from just Watching to Experiencing" (CJ 4DPLEX n.d.). This notion builds on the tradition of the earliest films as entertainments of amusements parks and vaudeville rather than movie theatres. A case in point is offered by the ground-breaking *Captain EO* (Frances Ford Coppola 1986) created for Disney Theme parks, in which the actions of the sci-fi and musical film are extended into the theatre matching 3D visuals with in-theatre laser effects, hydraulics under the seats, water sprayers, and even leg ticklers.

I had the pleasure of experiencing *Captain EO* as a child in the 1980s and again in 2009 when the show was reopened at Epcot Center following the death of the film's star Michael Jackson. My memories of this attraction as a child at Disney Land are telling in contrast to my experience of *Captain EO* as an adult, fully cognizant of both the constructed park context of Future World in Epcot and the communal theatre space rigged as specified by the original film makers to shake, spray, and ultimately allow you to feel the "major love" Jackson sings about. The film suggests the transformative, magical effects of music which is not just auditory, but rendered material, with implications for the dystopian world the hero visits but also for the audience members who are equally referenced and incorporated in Jackson's new reality. As suggested by the original song titled "Another Part of Me," the film promotes universal inclusion and collectivity by way of the figure of Jackson, who functions not just as messenger of truth to a new planet but as a material conduit to that sense of unity. Indeed, as implied by the last lines of the chorus, "Can't you see? / You're just another part of me" (Jackson 1987)—and augmented by the multisensory nature of the show that makes us feel along with the characters—*Captain EO* posits the individual's place in a broader society as an embodied appendage attuned to the sensory climate and physical context in time/space with the unified whole.

My childhood recollections of this sensory spectacle are more intimate, primal, and terrifying. I remember neither the characters nor the narrative from this visit but rather the experience, which my young brain registered as a human/machine interface. I actively recall the body slapping, shaking, and spraying as if, instead of being in a theatre with sensory effects, I was actively/actually fused with a machine like a Borg in *Star Trek: The Next Generation*, a television fixture of our house at the time. I recall my position as a corporeal spectator as a reflection of the spectacle of the terrifying antagonist—the supreme leader, hanging from a net of wires part flesh, part cyborg—made manifest. My own body in memory seemed infused to an infrastructure that sprayed, poked, and made me part of a system in which it seemed unclear where my organic body and that of the artificial machine (and through it the Borg like "collective") began or ended. As I reflect back on both encounters with *Captain EO*, I think there is something quite truthful in the easily dismissed memory of my childhood self: the idea of the mass audience reified through popular culture, refashioned via 4D into the sensory cy-Borg inculcated (or we might say "assimilated"), into a centralized systematized collective of feeling.

The "Attractions" of a Space That Feels for Us

The new 4DX experience is innovative in terms of scope and scale, relocated from the theme park to the multiplex, its treatment no longer singular but applicable to the mainstream blockbuster. It has become a practice and a technology adaptable to any film in 3D rather than a singular construct located and fixed in the Future World of a theme park. Opening its first theatre in Seoul in 2009, the South Korean company CJ 4DPLEX has adapted this entertainment oddity for a mainstream consumer, and further for a global society with theatres from Mumbai, India, to New York, United States, creating a two-hour homogenized sensory experience (not unlike the McDonald's Hamburger).

Conventional wisdom posits Hollywood cinema as a medium that encourages (through film form, etc.) modes of "escapism," which privilege the diegesis of the film over the space of the theatre and over the individual concerns (physical and mental) of the bodies that inhabit it. Building and intensifying the classical paradigm, contemporary 4D audience goers regularly state that 4DX makes you feel as though you are "in the scene" (4DX 2017) and cinema effects scholars describe how changing technologies that provide "greatly intensified sensory experiences" are moving the medium towards a more "immersive aesthetics" (Prince 2011, p. 183). However, such claims do not account for the ways in which the environmental effects of the medium seem to function antithetically to both escapism and immersion by drawing attention away from the screen and back to the theatre space and the physical body, implicating the corporeal spectator in the prescribed programme.

This mode of engagement is not (as we have shown) altogether new, but the contemporary 4D model galvanizes innovative cinematic technologies in the augmentation of extra-narrative aspects of the film. There has been a renewed interest in the concept of "cinema of attractions"—coined by Tom Gunning and André Gaudreault in the 1980s to describe the structures and styles of pre-narrative cinema—in the analysis of contemporary special effects cinema (or in my case special effects theatre spaces). Forms of moving image spectacle and their contexts of consumption in the early years of the twentieth century before narrative takes primacy, functioned, according to Gunning, to "continually remind the spectator of the act of watching by a succession of sensual assaults" (Gunning 1994, p. 127). The earliest examples of moving image spectacle suggested a self-reflexive readiness to "rupture a self-enclosed fictional world for a chance to solicit the attention of the spectator" (Gunning 2011, p. 71). Contemporary blockbuster action films such as *Spider-Man* and *The Matrix*, especially when presented in 3D, seem in their own ways "dedicated to presenting discontinuous visual attractions, moments of spectacle rather than narrative" that are not unlike this early theorization of spectatorship (Strauven 2006, p. 11). Referring to a new "almost fairground cinema" advanced by such godfathers as George Lucas and Steven Spielberg in the eighties and continuing to evolve four decades later (Tomasovic 2006, p. 309), film scholar Dick Tomasovic outlines a contemporary new mechanics of cinema inherited from this historical tradition of "attractions" including: exhibitionism, ride sequences, augmentation of cinematic motion, autonomous emblematic shots, and the direct address of the spectator in the form of often aggressive visual assaults such as projectiles (Tomasovic 2006, pp. 313–317). I suggest that 4D further augments the qualities of attractions in such cinematic spectacles, by, for example, making 3D projectiles material through burst of air.

Most helpful for our understanding of 4D, are the ways in which "attractions" are thought to encourage distinct modes of spectator experience and engagement with film form and film space. Describing the title credits for *Spider-Man*, for example, Tomasovic notes how in this sequence "the gaze is not allowed to linger: it is excited, provoked, exhausted even before the beginning of this film." Like an "autonomous visual prosthesis" the purpose of such displays is to "disrupt the spectators' perceptions, to give him the sensation of vertiginous mobility" (Tomasovic 2006, p. 314). In this way the film spectacle and, in the case of 4D, the theatre space are not so much vehicles of storytelling but overriding prosthetic mechanisms of physical, sensory, and perceptual experience that extend and expand the bodily feeling of the movie goer (recall the blind man's cane). Indeed, the "cinema of attractions" concept was originally adapted from Sergei Eisenstein's theory of "montage of attractions" which suggests that "the spectator constitutes the basic material of the theatre" and "attractions" were understood as "aggressive aspects" or any element "that subjects the spectator to a sensual or psychological impact" (Eisenstein and Gerould 1974, p. 78). Not far from 4D, one proposed example by Eisenstein was to create "a salvo under the seats of the spectators" (1974, p. 78). Combining film spectacle with a range of live performances and extra-film engagements in the theatre, the qualities of the "cinema of attractions" remind us that film has always been at some level concerned with modes of audience "contact" that do not fit within the mantel of illusionistic absorption, and with new technologies such modes of "contact" are becoming both more intimate, and, at the same time, more expansive, comprehensive, and panoptic.

The ways in which 4D specifically transfers attention from the world of the film to the theatre space begin with a process true of all 3D films. As film scholar Philip Sandifer explains, 3D projection violates the strict delineation of space engendered by the screen as a window into another world (Sandifer 2011, pp. 66–67). This is done in a number of ways. For instance, 3D effects, while projected universally, are realized at the sight of the human eye, where physical location in the theatre—distance and angle from the screen—is not arbitrary (as they are in the case of the vision of the screen world). More complex 3D films such as *Avatar* make use of effects of depth (positive parallax) that augment the illusion of space behind the screen plane, but traditionally the staple of the medium is the effects of negative parallax that create the sense of protrusion of objects outward towards the spectator. As the tagline for the 1952 film *Bawana Devil* proclaims: "A LION in your lap! A LOVER in your arms!" Indeed, by privileging images that seem to extend from screen towards the viewer, the material and physical relationship between screen, theatre, and body of the spectator is augmented. "Rather than being immersive," Sandifer explains, "3D film is profoundly bound up in an act of spectatorship whereby the theatre, instead of disappearing, is even more conspicuously visible" (ibid., p. 69). 4D builds on this foundation and additionally renders the space more conspicuously sensible, drawing the dynamism of the cinema text from the screen and localizing it in the material space.

With its addition of environmental effects, 4D thus goes beyond drawing visual attention to the theatre space, and in doing so further erodes the possibility of autonomous perception. More than pleasure in the visible and the act of watching the screen, the enjoyments of 4D are material and multidirectional, surrounding the "spectator" in air, water, and texture. In this way, the emergent cinema breaks with the mainstream formula of scopophilic pleasure as described by film theorist Laura Mulvey that "portray a hermetically sealed world which unwinds magically, indifferent to the presence of the audience, producing for them a sense of separation and playing on their voyeuristic phantasy" (Mulvey 2011, p. 717). The conditions of the traditional theatre, principally the darkened environment, "isolates the spectators from one another," while "the brilliance of the shifting patterns of light and shade on the screen helps," according to Mulvey, "to promote the illusion of voyeuristic separation" (ibid., p. 717). In effect, the identities and desires of the spectator are "repressed" and instead "projected on the performer" (ibid., p. 718). In contrast, the 4D theatre violates the traditional rule of darkness, extending events happening in the film such as explosions, lights, and camera flashes into the physical world of the movie goers by way of strobe lights that line the theatre ceiling. There is no complete absorption into a film, as the entertainment itself is largely extended into the space of the theatre. Rather than locating the object of attention and fantasy in the body on the screen, it is instead our own bodies that are the subject of this cinema. And what becomes "repressed" is our individual sensory experiences overwritten by the programme of 4DX.

Theme Park Cinema: The "Docile Body" Behind the Unruly Body

The "pleasure" afforded by this sort of cinema is still in keeping with its roots in the amusement park. Enjoyment is not grounded completely in the visual spectacle, but in the elemental, the physical, and sensory stimulation and exertion. The theatre space functions not unlike the attractions described by John Kasson of Coney Island that attempted to encourage and reproduce an "impulse toward childish release" (Kasson 1978, p. 59). Games and rides in the park emphasized vertigo, splashing water, and the "whirling and sprawling" pressure of centrifugal force (ibid., p. 60). The very act of entering the park demanded visitors release their self-control, and instead give into the demands by the space over their bodies and likewise their proprieties. For example, a "Barrel of Fun," a rotating cylinder, sent visitors rolling off their feet and into intimate contact with strangers; or the "Blowhole Theater," used concealed jets of compressed air to send skirts billowing and hats flying. The offered pleasure of the space was a pleasure in altered perceptions, disorientation, intimate contact, loss of equilibrium—an unruly body that was out of one's individual control and likewise out of the bounds of civility. Despite the availability of benches within the park, steps were taken (in the form of musicians and such to consistently rouse tourists to their feet) to prevent visitors from becoming too detached a critical audience (ibid., p. 82). Similarly, the possibility of intellectual detachment (like escapist absorption) is denied by the blowing jets on the head rests of 4D theatre seats.

The Coney Island rides and entertainments—and their 4D extensions we shall see later—"were based upon the ability to coordinate the mass activity through technology, to assemble and disperse crowds at will without making such efforts oppressive" (Kasson 1978, p. 82). This was the production of a "sense of spontaneous gaiety through calculated means" (ibid., p. 82). Yet, rather than a true if temporary revolt from social constraints of the progressive era or the demands of urban industrial life, the Coney Island model of carnival "fun," "play," and "revelry" used an engineered environment constantly shaped and controlled by its managers (ibid., p. 106). I draw from the early amusement park example then, both a comparable structure of pleasure to 4D and a comparable effect or consequence. As Kasson explains, "Dispensing standardized amusement, [Coney Island] demanded standardized responses. Beneath the air of liberation, its pressures were profoundly conformist, its means fundamentally manipulative" (ibid., p. 105). The 4D film comparatively encourages a sense of increased entertainment through an augmentation of audience "engagement" with the film, which we now not only see but touch and feel. In doing so, 4D takes the senses, which we perceive as automatic and instantaneous, and submits them to a digitized schedule designed to move the masses in time to the unfolding show.

The 4DX company programmers design the effects to accompany what have overwhelmingly been blockbuster Hollywood films. As a cinematic structure, Hollywood film style has largely been the scapegoat of the passive cinematic spectator. Building on the systemic structures of film form implemented in the studio era, the Hollywood film promotes narrative absorption and regulates the rhythm of emotional response via such things as the musical score. Comparing the mainstream American film to fast food, Philosophy Professor Dennis Rothermel has suggested that the "designed outcomes of the respective industries of food and film" is "to create the reliability of desire for the same products repeatedly" (2009, p. 265). What he calls "fast film" is easily and instantaneously digested with a formulaic infrastructure that dictates when and what to feel, through industry standards of style: "bite sized" units of display exemplified by the close-up (p. 267). The new programming of multisensory effects seems particularly applicable to a cinema whose form is already one that prescribes experience through formal structure. Yet the realm of the physical senses—as opposed to the world of intellect—is privileged as a site of the seeming "automatic" response. The programming of the sensuous response suggests a mechanical view of the corporeal spectator. This is not merely a passive body but a body guaranteed to respond in ordered ways.

The standard 4D film experience offers the digitized version of the pathways through the park at Walt Disney Land, which "represent the programmed assimilation of the spontaneous" (Willis 1999, p. 184). Pathways were laid down only after Immagineers watched the crowds pass through the park on opening day—solidifying the spontaneous in prescribed routes. There is no room for variation, nor authentic play but instead controlled and scripted amusement, where in "spontaneity itself has been programmed" (ibid., p. 184). In the case of 4D, it is physical impulses—the skin responding in goose bumps or the automatic flinch away from impact—rendered indexical. Through the digital programme, the sensual and organic becomes the systematized and the automatic becomes the disciplined (to use the Foucauldian term).

In the opening sequence of the film *Ready Play One* (Spielberg 2018), seats move pulling the audience in a meandering downward motion as the camera tracks the protagonist Wade in his climbing, jumping decent from the trailer park skyscraper. At the same time, the thumping impact of Wade's landing is felt as a vibration under our own feet—the spectator feels the effect of his body as contact. The haptic quality of 4DX—to feel the film as touch and to feel the solidity of the characters passing as vibration—seems central to the distinction of the medium as more "real" then traditional 2D cinema. I am interested, however, in the tension between material bodies in the theatre and those in the film or virtual world and the ways touch passes between and through these bodies not so much to understand how this affects our experience of the film, but rather to consider how such touches ultimately resonate in the regulation of lived experience.

Ready Player One seems an appropriate case in point, with its construction of a seeming complete escapist experience, that allows the dystopian future citizens of the world to depart their economically and environmental depleted reality for the OASIS (Ontologically Anthropocentric Sensory Immersive Simulation). There is a similarity between the use of virtual reality in this film and the function of other mass media such as Hollywood film in the lives of audience goers, but the parallelism is made blatant in 4DX where "escapism" is rendered corporeal. Throughout the film, images abound of bodies moving in time to unseen stimuli, their faces obscured by visors, and their bodies covered by varying degrees of "immersion" gear from haptic gloves that allow them to manipulate objects in the OASIS to full body haptic suits that allow them to "be touched" by what they encounter in the virtual. Complete from toe to fingertips, this sleek tightfitting suit is technology, clothing, and skin all in one. An interwebbing of sensors covering the bodysuit appears to glow blue and red while transferring touch (both pleasure and pain) from virtual contact back to the physical flesh underneath. Rig variations in *Ready Player One* suggest a two-way material feedback loop via omni-directional treadmills that convey motion to the virtual and "smell towers" that produce aromas back in the physical world. It is the rig of the antagonist of the film, Sorrento—CEO of the corporation attempting to gain control of the virtual for marketing—that most resembles that of the spectator in 4DX. He enters the OASIS from a high-tech form fitting haptic chair that seemingly transfers sensation from the virtual into the backside of the recliner. Yet where

Sorrento's chair is blatantly singular we are ranked and lined in rows our chair identical in form, motion, and affect to the one next to us.

The distinction is one of agency and individuality. From the opening scene of the hero descending the stacks, we see numerous neighbours wearing goggles, dancing in their own worlds. One mom jumps up on the back of a couch engaged in her own action adventure, while her daughter pulls helplessly on her robe attempting to get her attention. The physical motion of trying to brush off her daughter in the flesh leads to the "death" of her avatar in the OASIS. As this example illustrates, there is a back and forth feedback of sensory information, where contact and action reverberate between the real-world body and the virtual space. Like these characters, 4D spectators don goggles and are outfitted with a haptic rig but our bodies in the real world are docile ones carried along en masse with a scripted paradigm. There is no agency in the form of interactivity available to the film spectator; their corporeal bodies are the locus of the spectacle ("basic material" described by Eisenstein) and as such spectators are pliable not dynamic forms.

Taken for a Ride: Reinserting Physical Aggression in the Panoptic Schema

The specific film display is significant as the content against which our physical experiences are charted. Films must already be available in 3D—a technology largely utilized for films of certain genres: action adventure, horror, sci-fi, animation. 4D is thus applied to and best used in association with certain sorts of scenarios and modes of feeling. This is largely a reproduction of action, motion, and violent conflict rather than sensuality or emotionality. Because of the reliance on 3D films, 4DX precludes application to genres such as "weepies" as well as independently produced lower budget films. Within the standard action film fare of 4D, the slower segments of films that foreground conversation over activity tend to be conversely jarring in their very stasis. Given the normalized ways in which 4D is implemented, 4DX becomes largely complicit in the aestheticization of violence and in the displacement of individual action and motion of the body into the machine.

A common feature of the 4D precursors from the moving panorama to early cinematic theatres was "vehicular amplification" in which the theatre or auditorium itself was fashioned into a vehicle (trains, boats, or even hot air balloons) (Huhtamo 2013, p. 309). These spaces were sometimes stationary, but were additionally built on platforms that rocked and pitched in time to the visual display. Hale's Tours, for example, was a large chain of turn of the twentieth-century theatres for moving pictures which serves as a case in point for how space and film spectacle join to create a controlled multisensory experience of travel/motion. The non-narrative film sequences presented fit the model that has come to be known as "the phantom ride," featuring images from moving vehicles, most often trains. The theatre itself mimicked the train car complete with conductors and sound effects creating the clack of metal wheels and the hiss of air in the brakes (Gunning 2011, p. 72). Both the ride film structure and the multisensory and physical effects are paramount examples of a film tradition in which the experiential dominates over storytelling. The standard 4DX Regal movie theatre is visually understated and even uninteresting, in comparison to Hale's Tours or the 4D experiences based in theme parks such as Disney World, where the more continuous shows/rides allow for elaborately designed viewing spaces that match the performances (the space transport in "Star Tours" or the underground theatre beneath the Tree of Life for "It's Tough to be a Bug"). Yet the ways in which the contemporary theatre space "comes alive" during the film continues to exemplify the prominence of the phantom ride and the ways in which it its facilitated by the ubiquitous hidden mechanics of the space that functions instead of context of viewership as our cyborgian sensory prosthesis.

Before launching into the feature presentation, you are given a "preview" of 4DX in practice. An intensified version of the full spectrum of effects on offer is highlighted during a screening of one of several 4DX promo trailers, each of which demonstrates the primacy of the "ride" trope. In one, the quintessential car chase complete with high-speed flight from the crest of hill is supplanted by a driving/flying man in a theatre seat whose "car" dodges gunfire from the getaway vehicle and smashes into a construction barrel sending water flying. Our own chairs in the theatre are of course synchronized with the one we see giving us motion through the "space" of the film. The theatre space is no longer the static stadium but a technological chameleon, which, though visually understated, conforms to the order of the show, while our bodies go along with the ride.

Experiencing a film in 4D demands complete pliancy as your body is subtly blown, pushed, and moved to mimic the figures and kinesis of the film. The viewer is at once put in the place of the apparatus—the motions of the chair match the tracking motions of the camera. The chaotic shifts in angle and rapid cuts of an action sequence are experienced likewise as choreography of air blasts from the seat beside your head and a tilt or shake beneath you. But if we are made to embody the apparatus of cinema, we are also, at the same time, made to inhabit divergent bodies within the diegesis from human to machine. The "phantom ride" in 4D produces more than the experience of the characters on the screen carried away in a high-speed car chase or in the cockpit of the *Star Wars* TIE fighter. Additionally, the nature of the effects makes our bodies at times align with those of the vehicle and machines themselves, manifest by the wind in our faces even while the human characters appear protected and enclosed inside and thus incapable of such feeling. The programming of the theatre effects prioritizes contextual cues and action over narrative and identification, such that our physical point of view shifts with the active figures in the film, which may at times be animal, machine, object, or human.

Interestingly, when the 4DX effects seem most violent and most transparent are when the sensory effects are synchronized with the sensory context of the human bodies on the screen and what is being done to and with them in those environments. When characters are thrown to the ground, against walls, or generally knocked about, the spectator receives a punch in the back from the theatre seat. As Rey and Kilo Ren join forces against the Praetorian Guard after the death of Snoke in *Star Wars: The Last Jedi*, the spectator experiences the action in bursts of air, shaky seats, and swipes from the seat back and the leg "ticklers." "Watching" this scene in 4DX suggests a conflict between visual and physical point of view. The camera invites us close to the action but does not necessarily align us with first person perspective. The thumping our bodies receive in tandem with the screen suggests an intimacy and proximity that at times departs from the visual and/or narrative perspective. What results is not a clear or simple immersion in the fight sequence, but a push and pull between the physical body we inhabit and that produced on the screen. Indeed, 4DX effects have no allegiance to character identification. In fact, we are just as often physically aligned with the antagonist receiving the punches as with the hero. Rather, what dominates is a general state of sensory "identification" forged with mechanical motion instead of any human emotional connections.

Indeed, emotional connections and sexual pleasures are distinctly absent in 4DX. Despite the "lover in your arms" advertisements of early 3D, the contemporary technology instead prioritizes punches. Beyond vehicular motion, the most common use of the effects in 4DX is the material experience of physical destruction and violence. In the film *Ready Player One*, when Wade's haptic suit lights up in response to another avatar's sensual touch within the OASIS and his body shudders in pleasure, there is no corresponding sensation for the spectator. The haptic chair of the theatre does not render material the lover's caress but rather concerns itself most often with pain and brutality. Violence, as a paramount subject of 4DX effects, is offered as gratification. But this is violence sanitized and softened. Bullets are experienced as compressed air; body blows are thumps in the seat more akin to the massage chair at a pedicurist. We are granted corporeal engagement in battle and destruction but experience it instead as the fun of a roller coaster. Ironically, given the multisensory promises of the medium, this is violence desensitized and desensitizing.

There is, however, one significant though limited exception to the affinity of 4D and action/violence. 4D shows at theme parks such as "Shrek 4D" at Universal Studios Theme Parks and "It's Tough to be a Bug" at Disney World, each demonstrates the potential of the medium to comedy—especially "body humour" categories that use odour aesthetics for flatulence and stink bugs. Though these moments that might present a more "distasteful" movie going experience might be more rare in the mainstreaming of 4DX, the exploitation of "physical spectacles" in the service of comedy or horror draws attention to the intimacy at the heart of "touching film." Two water effects used during a screening of *Ready Player One* reify taboos about contact with bodily fluids. Paying tribute to *Alien*, a creature busts forth from the chest of an avatar spraying the characters and the audience with gore, while a recreation of a segment from *The Shining* drenches us in a river of blood rushing forth from a hotel elevator. More so than the chair motion, sprayers and smells seem to violate the perceived autonomy of our bodies. As one audience member responds to the horror film *It* in 4DX where covering ones face or eyes during scary scenes does little to dispel the fear: "here you can't do anything about it, your completely helpless" (4DX 2017). While surveillance is characterized by a distanced/nonviolent model of social control, the model of 4D suggests a reinsertion of the physical into the panoptic schema at some level. Yet, because these "effects" are perceived as entertainment and precisely because they are of the seemingly organic world of the senses, we do not necessarily notice the ways in which such choreography might suggest forms of physical coercion.

4D Cinema as Laboratory of Social Practice

These multisensory entertainments of the theatre are not isolated and neutral experiences of enjoyment (or even the cathartic pleasures offered by horror). Rather, I understand the 4DX theatre much as Kasson understands the significance of Coney Island: not merely as a space of escapist entertainment, but "as laboratories of [a] new mass culture, providing settings and attractions that immediately affected behaviour" (Kasson 1978, p. 8). Indeed, the programming of touch, smell, and the like typical of 4DX is part of a broader practice of monitoring, tracking, and manipulation of individual behaviour through sensory information that is being applied broadly to arenas of consumer culture, health, and even security. Comparable to the 4D theatre is the application of smell to spaces and gadgets that prime, direct, and boost conduct. Nike, for example, filed a patent for a device that would pump scent through a user's headphones or glasses to improve athletic performance. Similarly, I have written elsewhere about the branded scents disbursed through casinos and stores in Las Vegas. Such scents are designed specifically to encourage increased gambling and consumption, regulating behaviour through incorporation of and eventual acclimatization to the unseen aroma architecture (Jameson 2015). This control of sensory experience as a way to shape action or performance—the most comparable to the 4DX experience—is just one side of the coin, however.

The counterpoint to such systems of sensory programming and implementation is the area of aroma sensors, or sensory detection. Though far from reality, given, for example, the complexity of aromas, inroads are being made into handheld devices (with an eye for incorporating them into personal devices like smartphones or watches), to detect smells with applications for health or even safety (Wagstaff 2016). Or consider new research being done out of Universidad Politécnica de Madrid, into development of a new biometric technique that identifies individuals through their unique personal odours. Despite personal care products and the like, individual patterns of body odour have a constancy that would allow for identification of a single person within a group at 85% accuracy (an error rate lower than facial recognition). This is the police dog turned robotic architecture, where development of odour capture and analysis systems could be applied to spaces like airports or train stations, while getting around the need for individual consent (Science Daily 2014). But consider also the applications of odour detection technologies to register disease in hospitals, or mood swings in interrogation situations, or detect fear in the potential terrorist lost in a crowd. This is 4DX turned on its head; instead of programming our experience of film, we map the senses to detect variation and to maintain discipline in health and society.

The slogan for the international company Sensoptics is "we detect what you cannot see." In 2007, Sensoptics teamed up with the company Qinetiq to develop and implement a technology for monitoring security perimeters and border fences. Rather than visual surveillance, the resulting OptaSense technology uses sensors to track acoustic vibrations along fibre-optic cables buried underground to detect and identify breaches in barriers by moving vehicles, individuals, or unknown figures (animals, for example) passing nearby, each with its own unique signature (*The Engineer* 2007). OptaSense recalls the entertainment applications of Sensurround—the acoustics with material touch—in this case applied to regulate and control access to nations, industries, or facilities. As these examples suggest, the new horizon of surveillance technologies is not the seen but the sensed, and the 4DX theatre functions as model for a Sensopticon where disciplining feeling seems simple entertainment curiosity.

Conclusion

Our terms for describing theatre goers are limited by an audio-visual understanding of the medium. The etymology of "audience" is distinctly tied to the physical sense of "hearing" as well as an experience grounded in space, as in: to seek an "audience" with an official. In a movie theatre, an audience is "a body of hearers," a collective group organized and connected by a common sensory experience (*Oxford English Dictionary* 1989). Similarly, the term "spectator" is tied distinctly to the sense of sight as well suggesting connections to one's "presence" at a show or event: "A person who is present at, and has a view or sight of, anything in the nature of a show or spectacle" (*Oxford English Dictionary* 1989). Can we fully understand the functions and implications of the 4D cinema experience when our conceptualization so traditionally sublimated into the distanced senses alone? And, by extension, can we recognize surveillance practices strictly through technologies and vectors concerned with the gaze?

Indeed, what is unique about 4D is the more holistic physical presence of the movie goer, who is stimulated to touch, to smell, to feel. There is disruptive potential in the nature of the multisensory effects that augment attention both to the theatre space and the viewer's body (via the negative parallax of 3D, the activity of smoke and bubbles, tipping seats, etc.). As Dan North describes in his account of cinema special effects, there is inherently a "dynamic friction" operating between effects and the illusion of film (North 2008, p. 4). There is a dualistic motive embedded in this sort of "spectatorship," where on the one hand we revel in the cinematic fantasy while at the same time, as with a magic trick, we seek to understand how it is done (ibid., p. 2). In this way, 4D holds the possibility to nurture a critical distance from the film, to trouble standard modes of character identification and to disrupt simple modes of absorption into the continuity of the story. Yet, I am continually reminded of the ways in which the sensate "audience" in 4D is manifest as a piece or an appendage of another "body" (as in *Captain EO*); of the ways in which the theatre space functions as mechanical and digital prosthesis of the organic individual who is attuned to the programmed whole. The physical person in the theatre seat finds him or herself at the mercy of organized stimuli, responding consistently and unthinkingly. 4D generates a docile body responding automatically to a subtle physical choreography that is infused and diffused throughout the theatre and internalized by participants.

In this way, 4D seems part of larger unseen normalizing infrastructure of society, one that shapes or tracks the organic, the sensory, and the elemental for other ends. Mid-way through the book version of *Ready Player One*, Wade stares at his immersion rig with haptic chair and body suit which were previously his conduits of personal expression and escape and reflects: "I'd come to see my rig…as an elaborate contraption for deceiving my senses, to allow me to live in a world that didn't exist. Each component of my rig was a bar in a cell where I had willingly imprisoned myself" (Cline 2011, pp. 308–309). Here is a new sort of prison, in which power is internalized and surveillance is not an apparatus of an outside gaze, but rather a state of sensory "immersion" with no distinction between inside and outside and thus no escape.

Bibliography

Cline, E. (2011). *Ready Player One.* New York: Broadway Books.

Eisenstein, S., & Gerould, D. (1974). Montage of Attractions: For "Enough Stupidity in Every Wiseman". *The Drama Review: TDR, 18*(1), 77–85.

Foucault, M. (1977). *Discipline & Punish: The Birth of the Prison.* Translated from French by A. Sheridan. New York: Vintage Books, Random House, Inc.

Gunning, T. (1994). An Aesthetics of Astonishment: Early Film and the (In) Credulous Spectator. In L. Williams (Ed.), *Viewing Positions: Ways of Seeing Film* (pp. 114–133). New Brunswick: Rutgers University Press.

Gunning, T. (2011). The Cinema of Attractions: Early Film, Its Spectator and the Avant-Garde. In T. Corrigan, P. White, & M. Mazaj (Eds.), *Critical Visions in Film Theory: Classic and Contemporary Readings* (pp. 69–76). Boston/New York: Bedford/St. Martin's.

Huhtamo, E. (2013). *Illusions in Motion*. Cambridge, MA: MIT Press.

Jackson, M. (1987). Another Part of Me. In *Bad*. Los Angeles: Epic Records.

Jameson, S. (2015). Gaming the Senses. In *Strip Cultures: Finding America in Las Vegas* (pp. 184–214). Durham: Duke University Press

Kasson, J. (1978). *Amusing the Million: Coney Island at the Turn of the Century*. New York: Hill & Wang.

Merleau-Ponty, M. (1962). *The Phenomenology of Perception*. London: Routledge & Kegan Paul, Ltd..

Mulvey, L. (2011). Visual Pleasure and Narrative Cinema. In T. Corrigan, P. White, & M. Mazaj (Eds.), *Critical Visions in Film Theory: Classic and Contemporary Readings* (pp. 713–725). Boston/New York: Bedford/St. Martin's.

North, D. (2008). *Performing Illusions: Cinema, Special Effects and the Virtual Actor*. New York: Wallflower Press.

Oxford English Dictionary. (1989). Oxford: Oxford University Press.

Prince, S. (2011). Immersive Aesthetics. In *Digital Effects in Cinema* (pp. 183–220). New Brunswick: Rutgers University Press.

Rothermel, D. (2009). Slow Food, Slow Film. *Quarterly Review of Film and Video, 26*, 269–275.

Sandifer, P. (2011). Out of the Screen and into the Theater: 3-D Film as Demo. *Cinema Journal, 50*(3), 62–78.

Strauven, W. (2006). In W. Strauven (Ed.)., *The Cinema of Attractions Reloaded Introduction to an Attractive Concept*. Amsterdam: Amsterdam University Press.

Tomasovic, D. (2006). In W. Strauven (Ed.)., *The Cinema of Attractions Reloaded The Hollywood Cobweb: New Laws of Attraction*. Amsterdam: Amsterdam University Press.

Willis, S. (1999). Public Use/Private State. In *Inside the Mouse: Work and Play at Disney World* (pp. 180–198). Durham: Duke University Press.

Web Sources

4DX. (2017). IT in 4DX: Audience Reactions. Retrieved April 2, 2018, from http://www.youtube.com/watch?v=A3lBj2IklJE

Brownlee, J. (2016). A Brief History of Smell-O-Vision. *Wired*. Retrieved March 14, 2018, from https://www.wired.com/2006/12/a-brief-history-2-2/

CJ 4DPLEX. (2011). 4DX! This Is 4D!!. Retrieved June 2, 2018, from https://www.youtube.com/watch?v=l4FMm6Jntfg

CJ 4DPLEX. (n.d.). 4DX: Absolute Cinema Experience. Retrieved June 2, 2018, from http://www.cj4dx.com/

Konow, D. (2013). Before THX: The Cinema Shaking Technology of Sensurround. Retrieved March 14, 2018, from http://www.tested.com/tech/455667-thx-cinema-shaking-technology-sensurround/.

Science Daily. (2014). Identity Verification: Body Odor as a Biometric Identifier. Retrieved March 14, 2018, from https://www.sciencedaily.com/releases/2014/02/140204073823.htm

The Engineer. (2007). Border Patrol. Retrieved April 18, 2018, from https://www.theengineer.co.uk/issues/26-november-2007/border-patrol/

Wagstaff, J. (2016). Nose Job: Smells Are Smart Sensors' Last Frontier. *Reuters*. Retrieved March 14, 2018, from https://www.reuters.com/article/us-tech-smell/nose-job-smells-are-smart-sensors-last-frontier-idUSKCN0Z82SH

CHAPTER 14

Surveillance and Spectacle Inside *The Circle*

Brian Jarvis

Introduction

In an essay with the spiky title 'Why Bother?', the American author Jonathan Franzen grapples with the challenge of writing fiction about the contemporary. Novelists who seek to engage with present-day issues are confronted by the conundrum of 'how to design a craft that can float on history for as long as it takes to build it' (Franzen 2003, 65). In an accelerated culture where the pace of technological innovation appears almost exponential, the 'cutting-edge' novel can be bluntly obsolete almost immediately after publication. It might be contended that in some regards contemporary fiction has dodged the daunting task of staying afloat on the rapids of our current historical moment. One area where fiction is largely silent and where its voice is urgently needed is the viral proliferation of digital surveillance technology. A vast and intricate assembly of machines, institutions, social, and spatial practices has risen and rapidly penetrated all aspects of everyday life. Digital surveillance technology has been integrated into the built environment and become an essential component in social and economic relations: work and leisure, public and private life, communication and consciousness. A notable exception to the evasion by most authors of these momentous developments and the subject of this chapter is Dave Eggers' *The Circle* (2013).

B. Jarvis (✉)
Loughborough University, Loughborough, UK
e-mail: b.jarvis@lboro.ac.uk

S. Flynn, A. Mackay (eds.), *Surveillance, Architecture and Control*,
https://doi.org/10.1007/978-3-030-00371-5_14

At the start of the novel, a youthful protagonist, Mae Holland, arrives for her first day of work at the Californian 'campus' headquarters of the world's most powerful technology company. In this parallel universe, the Circle has 'subsumed Facebook, Twitter, Google, and finally Alacrity, Zoopa, Jefe, and Quan' (Eggers 2013, 23). Mae initially finds her work stressful and at times underwhelming. Stuck at a desk in an open-plan office in front of multiple screens (new ones keep appearing), she feels trapped on a digital hamster wheel of customer satisfaction surveys, social media updates, emails, texts, tweets, and blogs. By working 24/7, Mae achieves stellar progress in the corporate hierarchy. Her number of followers on multiple platforms proliferates to the point at which she is given the opportunity to go 'transparent' and have her every waking (and sleeping) moment made available to the world. *The Circle* begins as a postindustrial Horatio Alger tale, but then swiftly descends into dystopian sci-fi satire. Mae Holland's meteoric rise from lowly office drone to global social media celebrity is mirrored by her fall from ingénue to anti-heroine as the public face of an evil corporate empire intent on eradicating privacy.

According to the company's marketing slogans 'PRIVACY IS THEFT' and 'SECRETS ARE LIES' (Eggers 2013, 326). The Orwellian resonances are unavoidable, but Eggers replaces the Big Brother whose 'boot [is] stamping on a human face' with a sinister Big Sister whose disarming smile conceals the Circle's soft totalitarianism (Orwell 2004, 280). Like the corporations on which it is modelled, the *Circle* stages media events where casually dressed CEOs pose in front of giant screens to unveil shiny new products. Far from being mere commodities, these machines and software are pitched as technological fixes for social problems and the harnessing of human potential. Corporate mantras are chanted about 'changing the world' by fostering connectivity and community, creativity and communication. This is the 'new spirit of capitalism' 2.0. As Boltanski and Chiapello (2018) observed, the information technology industry that emerged in the 1980s and 1990s often evoked the emancipatory discourses of 1960s counter-culture. The Circle conjures an identical rhetorical smokescreen to obscure its cyber-capitalist imperative. As one of the company's few critics complains, the Circle 'monetized our utopia' (Eggers 2013, 484). All employees at the company are expected to use their online presence to promote products. Soon after her arrival, Mae is warned that her success in stimulating purchases will be closely monitored using in-house algorithms: 'the minimum expectation for high-functioning Circlers is a Conversion Rate of x250, and a weekly Retail Raw of $45,000' (Eggers

2013, 251). The circuit established here between the corporation, its employees, and consumers is just one example of the extent to which surveillance is the centre point of the Circle's operations. Eggers' fictional company functions as a paradigm for an emergent regime of accumulation which Shoshana Zuboff (2015) has termed surveillance capitalism. According to Zuboff, this regime depends on a 'global architecture of computer mediation' through which it generates '*surveillance assets*' and '*surveillance capital*' (Zuboff 2015, 75). This, precisely, is the corporate strategy of the Circle and it entails massive increases in the scale, speed, and synergies of computerised 'surveillant assemblages' (Haggerty and Ericson 2000).

Starting from a pioneering platform which revolutionises internet use, the Circle proceeds to introduce and integrate a range of devices into the workplace, the home, the city, and the human body. The initial commercial success is founded on the design of a universal operating system called 'TruYou' which

> combined everything online that had heretofore been separate and sloppy – users' social media profiles, their payment systems, their various passwords, their email accounts, usernames, preferences, every last tool and manifestation of their interests… Your devices knew who you were, and your one identity – the TruYou, unbendable and unmaskable – was the person paying signing up, responding, viewing and reviewing, seeing and being seen. (Eggers 2013, 21)

This unique identifier is marketed as a tool of transparency and consumer convenience, but is also instrumental in allowing the company to convert its users into surveillance assets. The second key technological innovation produced by the Circle is an inexpensive micro-camera which enables a prodigious expansion of the company's surveillance apparatus from online to the material world. 'SeeChange' is marketed as a device that allows consumers to maintain constant visual access to key locations in their daily life at home and work as well as traffic conditions and leisure destinations. The company also promotes the potential of this device for sousveillance of the police and military in repressive regimes. Users can position the SeeChange camera anywhere and then share live feeds with others in an exponentially expanded network. At the product launch, a CEO outlines an ambitious manufacturing plan: 'Within ten years, two billion cameras. There will be very few populated areas that we won't be able to access from the screens in our hands' (Eggers 2013, 69). To demonstrate and advertise the product's potential, SeeChange is installed throughout the Circle's corporate headquarters: 'the campus, to the eyes of a billion-odd Circle users, was suddenly clear and open' (Eggers 2013, 241). SeeChange has synergies with a range of other surveillance equipment designed by the Circle and deployed on the campus from smart buildings to health monitors worn by all employees. The Circle offers itself as a paradigm for healthy lifestyles, safe and hyper-efficient workplaces as well as domestic settings and landscapes of leisure. As corporate ambition swells, the Circle reveals grand designs for smart cities and ventures into the realm of security with a raft of crime detection and prevention tools: 'TruYouth' tracking chips inserted in the bones of children; 'SeeYou' filters on cameras and retinal implants that automatically identify and colour code the threat level posed by individuals; 'NeighbourWatch' and 'WeaponSensor' to make homes and communities safe. 'SoulSearch' is a crowdsourced social media dragnet which at the product launch is demonstrated in front of a live audience of over a billion people. A fugitive is chosen at random from a criminal database and hunted down in less than ten minutes. Following its success in other spheres, the Circle proceeds to extend its reach into government. Politicians and public officials are encouraged to go transparent and offer uninterrupted live feeds to their constituents. This becomes practically compulsory since anyone who resists is suspected of having something to hide. The Circle also develops plans to take over the running of elections ('Demoxie') and to introduce its own currency ('CircleMoney').

When 'Completion' is achieved, the Circle will be finally closed and the dream of a global apparatus of 24/7 total surveillance made real. The Circle's circumference stretches from satellites in orbit to drones mapping the Marianas Trench. At the close of *The Circle* itself, Mae visits a hospital to see a friend in a coma and is exasperated by the fact that she has no access to what the patient is thinking. Having inserted sensors inside the body a next logical step would be, to paraphrase a rallying cry from *The Truman Show*, putting a camera in everyone's head. *The Circle* offers a dystopian projection of current developments involving the encroachment of surveillance assemblages and concomitant erosion of privacy and interiority. In what follows below we will foreground the extent to which these surveillance practices are enframed by an architectural apparatus that integrates material and virtual components.

The importance of architecture is immediately apparent in the novel's opening pages as Mae (alongside the reader) is given a grand tour of the campus. The 400-acre site is elegantly landscaped with 'soft green hills', lemon and orange groves, organic gardens, fountains, and sculpture. There is an abundance of arts and recreational facilities including theatres, music venues, athletic courts, and picnic areas. The main buildings are streamlined 'brushed steel and glass structures' named after historical eras such as the 'Renaissance' and 'Enlightenment' (Eggers 2013, 1). This complex is configured so as to maintain a sense of open space. Airy atria are soaked in California sunshine and building interiors extend this design ethic with an emphasis on open plan and glass. Office furniture imitates organic shapes, but this is combined with an array of high-tech devices. Cameras and screens are omnipresent. Screens feature on desktops, in halls, on walls and elevator doors and often celebrate the campus not just as a place of work, but as a community. Mae's initial impression and the opening line of the novel is 'My God… It's heaven' (Eggers 2013, 1). During her tour of this techno-pastoral utopia, a discordant and prophetic note is struck when Mae's guide draws an analogy between the induction of new employees and the installation of new wood flooring which needs to 'acclimate': '[w]e'll hammer you with ten thousands tiny nails. You'll love it' (Eggers 2013, 16).

With its postmodern mash-up of themed zones including an 'Old West' and a 'TomorrowTown' alongside the presence of children and pets (the Circle provides day-care centres for both), the campus in part suggests Disneyland. Other architectural features are clearly modelled on the corporate headquarters of Disneyland's Californian neighbours in the information technology industry. Apple's former centre of operations at One Infinite Loop was replaced in 2017 by the perfect circle of the Apple Park campus development. Googleplex is another 'campus' HQ and it is hard not to see the vowels at the centre of this transnational brand name looming in Eggers' novel. Google's architectural aspirations are not confined to its own buildings. Sidewalk Labs, a subsidiary of Alphabet, have recently designed a $50 million urban renewal programme for part of the Toronto waterfront. The key design feature here maps Google's online practice of dataveillance onto the built environment. An integrated network of cameras, sensors, drones, mobile devices, and wearables will establish smart buildings in a smart city. The campus in *The Circle* is similarly seen as a prototype for the future in which urban design aspires to ambient intelligence. During her tour, Mae is informed that there are sensors everywhere interacting with devices carried by employees and guests. This technology is responsible for an unpleasant surprise during an elevator ride when Mae is suddenly confronted by a personalised greeting projected onto the door alongside her own image from a high school yearbook.

The enclosure of the elevator in Mae's workplace can be read as a microcosm of the Circle's goal of building a universal and automated digital Panopticon. Bentham was insistent in his blueprints for his ideal 'Penitentiary Inspection House' on the importance of an annular design: 'I cannot help looking upon every form as less and less eligible, in proportion as it deviates from the circular' (Bentham 1995, 44). In his various writings on the Panopticon, Bentham paid scrupulous attention to every aspect of architectural design: prime locations, building materials, the precise dimensions of cells and doors, walls and walkways, towers and stairs as well as matters of lighting, plumbing, air circulation, and sewage. The motivation for this conscientiousness is summed up succinctly in Churchill's famous aphorism: 'We shape our buildings; thereafter they shape us'. The key feature in this regard was visibility: 'Nothing and no one can be hidden inside the Panopticon – it is the most important point, that the persons to be inspected should always feel themselves as if under inspection' (Bentham 1995, 45). In 'Jeremy Bentham's Panoptic Device' (1973), Jacques-Alain Miller underscored this key relationship between power and sight lines: '[f]rom the central point the whole of the enclosed space is totally visible; nothing is hidden, everything is totally transparent' (Miller 1987, 3). Following Miller's pioneering study, Foucault explored the mechanisms by which this 'architectural apparatus' induced in its occupants 'a state of consciousness and permanent visibility that assures the automatic functioning of power… surveillance is permanent in its effects, even if it is discontinuous in its action' (Foucault 1995, 201). Foucault similarly foregrounded the core ideal of 'transparency' built into the Panopticon and traced its genealogy back to Rousseau's 'dream of a transparent society, visible and legible in each of its parts' (Levin 2002, 96). Bentham envisaged his Panopticon not merely as a penitentiary, but as a machine for promoting human perfectibility that had universal utility:

> Its great excellence consists in the great strength it is capable of giving to any institution it may be thought proper to apply it to… by the gradual adoption and diversified application of this single principle, you should see a new scene of things spread itself over the face of civilized society. (Bentham 1995, 95)

> *Morals reformed – health preserved – industry invigorated – instruction diffused, public burthens lightened – Economy seated, as it were, upon a rock… all by a simple idea in Architecture!* (Bentham 1995, 31)

This 'simple idea in Architecture' could provide the framework for a factory, school, hospital, asylum, or indeed any institution which wished to promote absolute transparency. Bentham proposed that a 'combination of inspection-houses' might be conjoined in an ever-increasing series of concentric circles or 'rotundas' so that 'the field of inspection might be dilated to any extent' (Bentham 1995, 42). Eventually, the expansion of this annular architectural assemblage would reach a state of 'ideal perfection' in which 'each person should actually be in that predicament, [under observation] during every instant of time' (Bentham 1995, 34).

Bentham's inspection-house was never built during his lifetime. Two centuries on from this original 'simple idea in Architecture', however, technological developments have enabled the realisation of a digital panopticon. In *The Circle*, a corporate CEO called Eamon Bailey is animated by a Benthamite vision. Following an indiscretion when she 'borrows' a kayak for a late night paddle and the act is caught on a SeeChange camera, Mae is summoned to Bailey's office. He starts by asking whether Mae would have behaved differently if she had known about the camera and then proceeds to underline the principle of panopticism: 'my point is, what if we all behaved as if we were being watched? It would lead to a more moral way of life. Who would do something unethical or immoral or illegal if they were being watched?' (Eggers 2013, 290). This conversation inspires Mae to go transparent. Clearly any criminal or even merely secretive activity is impossible when under observation by her followers, but she also finds herself making various subtle self-corrections: she thinks more carefully about her choice of clothes and diet and about mundane acts such as scratching and blowing her nose.

Transparency elevates Mae into a role model who has been 'liberated from bad behaviour' (Eggers 2013, 329). She feels blessed to know she is 'being watched, that the Circle was, overnight, the most-watched workplace in the world' (Eggers 2013, 329). Every aspect of architectural design on campus is designed to promote the aura of transparency. There are large open spaces between buildings and open-plan design within. During her tour Mae remarks that '[t]he designers really like glass, eh?' (Eggers 2013, 40). Most of the rooms are flooded by natural light due to extensive use of 'floor-to-ceiling windows' (Eggers 2013, 159). Mae encounters a 'blur of glass rooms' featuring 'glass ceilings', 'glass walls', and 'glass doors' connected by 'glass hallways' and 'plexiglass' elevators. On her way to a restaurant called the 'Glass Eatery', Mae momentarily experiences vertigo as she walks over a glass floor. At her induction, Mae is reassured that her desk is 'not far from all the more senior people. And here [her guide] swept her arm around, indicating about a dozen offices surrounding the open space. The occupants of each were visible through the glass walls' (Eggers 2013, 40).

The open-plan office with unimpeded lines of sight in every direction offers an architectural analogue with the rhetoric if not the reality of neoliberalism. The choice of materials and design principles suggest a lack of borders and freedom of movement, but Mae and her fellow workers are nonetheless fixed firmly in place. Bentham insisted on the efficacy of the panopticon design as a tool for labour control and envisaged inmates engaged for much of the day in productive work. At the Circle, the workforce are practically imprisoned at their desks in front of screens for protracted periods. On her first day, Mae's workstation features two screens, but over time this increases to nine plus a further two on wrist bracelets and her work smartphone. Despite the postindustrial trappings, Mae's office is essentially a factory in which the muscular movements of manufacturing industry are replaced by more nimble but nonetheless repetitive motions of hand and eye on a high-tech assembly line. The speed and quantity of information increases with the arrival of each new screen:

> The third-screen feed dropped forty new InnerCircle messages every few minutes, fifteen or so OuterCircle posts and zings, and Mae used every available moment of downtime to quickly scroll through, make sure there was nothing that demanded her immediate attention, and then come back to her main screen. (Eggers 2013, 105)

Whilst she is trying to work, Mae is also bombarded by live metrics on response time, volume of queries, customer satisfaction ratings, and her ranking within the organisation. During her induction, Mae is shown a 'cool new app, which sort of gives us a history of the building every day. You can see when each staffer checked in every day, when they left the building' (Eggers 2013, 96). The offices at the Circle also utilise motion sensor technology which detects 'any irregularity of movement or in the order of operations, and the computer either reminds you of what you might have forgotten, or it logs the mistake for management' (Eggers

2013, 424). Whilst leading information technology companies market themselves as offering creative working environments, the principles of Taylor's scientific management are vigorously applied to every aspect of individual and team performance. An array of devices and software are deployed in this regard, including active and sociometric badges, recording of phone and video calls, and the monitoring of workstations by webcam, screenshot, and mouse click. What appears to be an 'open plan' office, on closer inspection, more closely resembles Foucault's description of the Panopticon as an

> enclosed, segmented space, observed at every point, in which the individuals are inserted in a fixed place, in which the slightest movements are supervised, in which all events are recorded, in which an uninterrupted work of writing links the centre and the periphery, in which each individual is constantly located, examined and distributed. (Foucault 1995, 197)

Christian Fuchs' (2014, 228) study of working conditions at Google hones in on this dichotomy between a workplace that offers free food, cultural activities, sports facilities, and massage alongside anecdotes about employees routinely working 130-hour weeks and sleeping at their desks due to the pressure of performance targets. Recreation and leisure here are essentially a secondary form of labour: the provision of home comforts and downtime distractions is a means of ensuring subsequent productivity gains. At the Circle, employees are offered the chance to stay in amply stocked campus dorms and Mae ends up as a permanent resident. Whilst the presence of accommodation on campus appears to enhance its credentials as a progressive seat of learning, this practice is also reminiscent of the construction of small towns around factories in the nineteenth century such as in Lowell, Massachusetts, and Pullman, Illinois, to cut down on travel time and make sure the labour supply was close at hand.

In a study of literary representations of surveillance in the office, Graham Thompson suggests that

> [t]he architecture of Silicon Valley… has facilitated the flattening of the distinctions between the workplace and the home, between work and leisure, that have stood at the heart of the experience of work in American culture in the last hundred years. Once the architecture of code replaces the architecture of the built environment as the site for the creation of value in a capitalist economy, the need for the workplace to be discretely marked and separated becomes less and less important. (Thompson 2003, 178)

The transition from a 'visible architecture of material production to an invisible architecture of code' is central to *The Circle* (Thompson 2003, 183). The metaphor of architecture is prominent in computer science and especially network design. Users also routinely rely on architectural tropes to navigate the internet: 'walls' and 'windows', 'backdoors', and 'home pages'. According to Lev Manovich, '[c]omputer space is also the space of a human dweller… its architecture responding to the subject's movement and emotion' (Manovich 2002, 262, 269). Cyberspace in general and social media platforms in particular constitute a digital dwelling in which we can communicate intimately with family and friends, store treasured belongings, and curate life stories. When Mae accidentally destroys a hard drive on one of her mobile devices, it is compared to 'having your house burn down with all your belongings inside' (Eggers 2013, 43).

On day one at the Circle, it is made clear to Mae that her new home is a split-level structure featuring both material and virtual dimensions: 'being social, and being a presence on your profile and all related accounts – this is part of why you're here. We consider your online presence to be integral to your work here. It's all connected' (Eggers 2013, 95). The Circle requires its employees to work hard at improving their Participation Rank:

> PartiRank for short… It's just an algorithm-generated number that takes into account all your activity… zings, exterior followers of your intra-company zings, comments on your zings, your comments on others' zings, your comments on other Circlers' profiles, your photos posted, attendance at Circle events, comments and photos posted about those events – basically it collects and celebrates all you do here. (Eggers 2013, 100)

Sociability inside the *Circle* is compulsory and compulsive and Mae becomes neurotically obsessed with climbing to the top of this virtual ziggurat. Eggers presents social media as a huddled house of mirrors in which anxious users watch others and watch themselves being watched by others. The subjectivity shaped in and by the structure of social media is a digital magnification of the 'other-directed' personality type identified by David Reisman. In the preface to his seminal sociological survey of *The Lonely Crowd*, Reisman diagnosed a burgeoning psychopathology involving 'heightened self-consciousness about relations to people, and a widening of the circle of people with whom one wants to feel in touch' (Reisman 2001, xxiv). This social type is driven by a need to belong, to share, and receive updates as well as continual validation from others. Reisman argued that in the postwar era, these traits made the other-directed personality indispensable to the workforce of large corporations. *The Circle* offers a sketch of the Lonely Crowd 2.0 and highlights the extent to which social media can be decidedly anti-social. The rhetorical emphasis on community and constant communication might make the digital dwelling appear as an antipode to the Panopticon in which inmates are silently segregated. The example of Mae, however, underlines the extent to which members of the lonely crowd are confined to and by screens. Sociability here is largely a matter of interacting with what Virilio terms 'simulators of proximity' (Virilio 2002, 41). Mae feels as though '[n]on-communication in a place like the Circle was so difficult, it felt like violence' (Eggers 2013, 234). At the same time, in social media structures, violence is being inflicted on communication itself. Mae's exchanges with others are so fast and frequent that they are reduced to a blur of boiler plate banalities decorated with emojis. Eggers delivers a wry commentary on the decline of public political discourse and the rise of slacktivism with the image of Mae sending a smiley face to a woman in Guatemala who has escaped rape and prostitution by a paramilitary group and a frown to her captors.

At the end of her working day, Mae dutifully stays online: 'at five p.m. the chute closed and Mae worked on her PartiRank for forty-five minutes, bringing it from 1,827 to 1,430, a process entailing 344 comments, posts, and almost a thousand smiles and frowns' (Eggers 2013, 277). By plugging away every evening and weekend and at times all night, she manages to break into the 'T2K' and feels immediately [that] the fruits of her labours were evident (Eggers 2013, 192). *The Circle* includes a number of lengthy passages detailing Mae's exhaustive online efforts. Much of the digital economy is founded on unpaid work carried out by 'prosumers': '[t]he online work they perform on social media is informational work, affective work, cognitive work, communicative work, community work and collaborative work' (Fuchs 2014, 265). According to Fuchs, this entails an inversion of the commodity fetish: instead of social relations being hidden by the commodity, commodification is hidden behind social relations. The platform user is both consumer and product. In the process of uploading and watching content, they are also being watched and downloaded and sold as a data commodity. In her critique of surveillance capitalism, Zuboff notes that

> [n]othing is too trivial or ephemeral for this harvesting: Facebook 'likes', Google searches, emails, texts, photos, songs, and videos, location, communication patterns, networks, purchases, movements, every click, misspelled word, page view, and more. Such data are acquired, datafied, abstracted, aggregated, analysed, packaged, sold, further analysed and sold again. (Zuboff 2015, 89)

Social media is a huge contributory factor to the rise of big data. Inconceivably vast amounts of information exist in relation to every aspect of our life and environment: media and culture, business and consumerism, government and the military, science and technology, health and education. The surveillance of big data, or 'dataveillance' to use Garfinkel's (2000) portmanteau term, involves increasingly sophisticated information-gathering, management and processing tools and has become integral to business and government. In a prescient study from the early 1990s, Oscar Gandy referred to this process as the 'panoptic sort': 'a difference machine that sorts individuals into categories and classes on the basis of routine measurements' (Gandy 1993, 15).

The social sorting of our digital doppelgangers involves sophisticated algorithmic segmentation into forensically fine-grained systems of differential classification and personalisation. The two main corporations upon which the Circle are based, Facebook and Google, are at the leading edge of dataveillance and panoptic sorting. Facebook and its subsidiaries including Instagram and WhatsApp employ monitoring software and artificial intelligence that automatically monitors each connection and comment, photo, and video, right down to individual clicks and cursor movements. This is used to manufacture granular profiles of over two billion users worldwide which can then be 'monetized' as audience commodities to commercial and political interests who wish to precision target their messages. Whilst Facebook dominates social media, Google controls around 70% of the search engine market and monitors an estimated 3.5 billion searches per day. Since the first use of their product in 1997, Google has expanded exponentially. A range of software allows Google to mine data on a scale hinted at by the corporate brand name: the Google toolbar and Gmail, Google Calendar and Google News, Google Books and Google Docs, Google Checkout and Google Health, Google Earth, Maps, and StreetView. The acquisition of other online services such as YouTube in 2006 further extends the Google domain. The company's unrivalled access to data has inevitably led to covert collaboration with the surveillance industry. Google and Facebook are the infrastructure of the digital panopticon and possess far more information about individuals and populations than the most repressive surveillance state in history. The dimensions of big data are so astronomical that computer systems, databases, and software architecture are continually being torn down and rebuilt to accommodate its growth. The Chief Economist at Google, Hal Varian, notes the evolution of 'new types of databases that can store data in massive tables spread across thousands of machines [which] can process queries on more than a trillion records in a few seconds' (Zuboff 2015, 77). With the advent of quantum computing processing speeds will be reduced to zero. New technologies for the capture and analysis of data are becoming increasingly conspicuous in our everyday lives: smart homes with personal assistants (Alexa and Siri are merely the first generation), drones, wearables, and the so-called Internet of Everything will ensure that the behemoth of big data continues to be fed. Advances in artificial intelligence alongside behavioural and psychometric analytics promise more effective predictive technology: machines that will confidently tell us what we want and need to know *before* we have even realised.

In *The Circle*, TruYou is the key innovation for the company's expansion of dataveillance:

> And those who wanted or needed to track the movements of consumers online had found their Valhalla: the actual buying habits of actual people were now eminently mappable and measurable, and the marketing to those actual people could be done with surgical precision. (Eggers 2013, 22)

Not content with the online retail market, company CEO Eamon Bailey declares 'ALL THAT HAPPENS SHALL BE KNOW' (Eggers 2013, 67). The Circle's projects aim to make all places 'mappable and measurable' from the mysteries of the Marianas Trench to the number of grains of sand in the Sahara. People, too, will be known exhaustively. At a 'Dream Friday' presentation, the *Circle* presents 'the Transparent Man'. Every detail of 'Stewart's' life over a five-year period has been recorded and stored in underground units the size of double-decker buses. All employees at the Circle are expected to complete CircleSurveys. Throughout her working day and after hours, Mae listens through a tiny headset and responds to around 1000 questions. Mae wants to be an acolyte, but experiences moments of apostasy including a brief 'blasphemous flash' that

> the volume of information, of data, of judgments, of measurements, was too much, and there were too many people, and too many desires of too many people and too many opinions of too many people, and too much pain . . . and having all of it constantly collated, collected, added and aggregated, and presented to her as if that all made it tidier and more manageable – it was too much. (Eggers 2013, 410)

In key respects, the accumulation of big data in the digital panopticon constitutes a realisation of Bentham's architectural blueprint. Bentham dreamt of a proto-TruYou:

> new systems of branding, sorting and categorising individuals – tattoos, clothing, names: so that in each country every individual will have a proper name that belongs to him and to him alone… a proper name, a truly proper name, for everyone (in short the equivalent of a number)… this would spread the panoptic order throughout the world. (Miller 1987, 18)

According to Miller, the Panopticon was a grand 'house of calculation' designed to satisfy a compulsive utilitarian 'need to divide, to classify, to count, and to organize' (Miller, 8):

> products, population tables, stock inventories, health records, moral conduct records, requests, punishments (with a black cover), rewards (red cover)… And the entries will cover the entire nation: every event will immediately be recorded and broken down into its constituent parts, each of which will then be noted in the corresponding book… And on the horizon… looms planetary bookkeeping, the comparison of everything with everything, all of mankind entered in a ledger… 'The process of subdivision cannot be carried too far' – down to the very atoms of meaning, the very single digits of thought. (Miller 1987, 28)

The ones and zeroes of binary code and big data might then be counted back to Bentham's indefatigable book-keeping. Foucault takes this genealogy further by tracing the genealogy of the Panopticon back to when 'rulers dreamt of the state of plague' (Foucault 1995, 199). An epidemic enabled control over the populace through the establishment of extensive systems of registration, classification, and spatial partitioning. Foucault sees this early modern disciplinary apparatus as the inspiration behind the Panopticon. In this context, Bart Simon contends that as much as it is a vision machine, the Panopticon is also an 'ordering machine', or 'sociomaterial assemblage for sorting and arranging social categories and individual persons so that they can be seen and understood' (Simon 2005, 4).

In the latter stages of his career, Foucault extended his work on panopticism into an exploration of biopower as a disciplinary tool for the management of populations. Biopower aims to 'discipline the body, optimize its capabilities, extort its forces, increase its usefulness and docility, integrate it into systems of efficient and economic controls' (Foucault 1980, 139). Biodata is a burgeoning field in which we can detect a vigorous attempt to exercise control over life processes. Google is at the forefront of this field. As well was storing a vast quantity of health records, the corporation is also funding research into genetics and molecular biology. The use of activity trackers and apps for leisure and at work is on the rise. In 2015, the retail giant, Target, gave away 335,000 Fitbit trackers to its employees. This was promoted as an exercise in corporate well-being, but would of course also have potential benefits for productivity. During her medical at the Circle, Mae is issued with not one but two health monitor bracelets. After agreeing to sign-up for CHAD, the company's 'Complete Health Data' programme, Mae is also informed by her doctor that she has already ingested a microscopic sensor in a smoothie that will relay real-time biometrics to the cloud: '[i]t'll collect data on your heart rate, blood pressure, cholesterol, heat flux, caloric intake, sleep duration, sleep quality, digestive efficiency, on and on' (Eggers 2013, 154). When she logs on through her bracelet, Mae discovers 'dozens of layers to the information, every data point allowing her to ask more, to go deeper' (Eggers 2013, 157). CHAD enables the Circle to collect 'perfect and complete data' on its 11,000 employees. The Circle hosts a conference for 'all the major health insurance companies, world health agencies, the Centers for Disease Control, and every significant pharmaceutical company' with the intention of collecting all available medical data in one location (Eggers 2013, 335). The corporation is also keen to extend its biotech to the general population. The ChildTrack chip implanted in an infant's bones is initially seen as a security device, but is subsequently proposed as a compulsory procedure to ensure the health of the nation's youth. When Mae meets some biochemists on the campus and hears about 'Project 9', it seems as though the Circle is intending to move beyond merely collating biodata to resequencing its human subjects: 'a plan to embed and make accessible massive amounts of data in human DNA' (Eggers 2013, 218). Elsewhere in the novel, Eggers hints that fundamental changes to the human form have already occurred. Alongside the high-tech bracelets and nanotechnological sensor inside her body, Mae is practically integrated with an array of gadgets, screens, cameras, and earbuds. Many of her work colleagues are fitted with retinal devices that appear to have replaced smartphones. Outside the Circle, Mae is confronted by the messy materialism of the body. She has less than fond memories of a manager at her previous job who 'was an awful assault on the senses, his breath smelling of ham' (Eggers 2013, 10). When she visits her sick father at home, he soils himself. Off-campus Mae sees 'homeless people, and there were the attendant and assaulting smells, and there were machines that didn't work' (Eggers 2013, 370). Safely inside the Circle, Mae and her peers aspire to a cyborg ideal and spend most of their time in a hyper-optical and antiseptic cyberspace beyond the material world's assault on the chemical senses. By the end of the novel, Mae has lost contact with her family, female friends, and male lovers, but has millions of virtual followers and feels connected to a digital community. Mae appears to have internalised the Circle's posthuman imperative of downloading the body and human identity into the safely antiseptic architecture of the digital panopticon.

Before this downbeat denouement, Mae experiences doubt and attempts on occasion to retreat to spaces outside the Circle's architecture of surveillance. Self-denial and inauthenticity are suggested by moments when she recognises a disjunction between the 'ability to look, to the outside world, utterly serene and even cheerful, while, in her skull, all was chaos' (Eggers 2013, 322). When she goes transparent, Mae is allowed three minutes of downtime during bathroom visits and uses these for secret conversations. In his panopticon design, Bentham was insistent that toilets with appropriate plumbing were positioned in each cell to ensure no escape from the disciplinary gaze. Earlier in the novel Mae uses the bathroom for sex with a boyfriend in a covert act which reinvigorates those tactile and chemical senses the Circle seeks to suppress. In an earlier sexcapade, the same boyfriend takes Mae into an underground labyrinth far below the campus to a darkened cave beside a black water lake. Nature in *The Circle* offers a furlough from the digital panopticon. Mae kayaks across lakes at night to remote islands. She experiences 'the strong smell of [...] animals, a cross between tuna and unwashed dog' and sees but does not photograph, video, or disturb the wildlife (Eggers 2013, 81). The darkness, solitude, and mystery of these interludes position nature as an antipode to the campus and its fanatical project of enlightenment. Another character in *The Circle*, Mae's former boyfriend Mercer, writes (rather than using electronic communication) to tell her he is running away from the 'surveillance dome ... moving north, to the densest and most uninteresting forest I can find' (Eggers 2013, 431). 'Alone in some cabin' in the woods, Mercer resembles a modern-day Thoreau (Eggers 2013, 435). The nineteenth-century transcendentalist was a keen kayaker and retreated to a life in the woods near Walden Pond to escape from the 'factory bells' ringing out across Jacksonian America. In *Walden* (1854), Thoreau crafted a critique of industrial capitalism as a society in which 'men have become the tools of their tools' (Thoreau 2012, 226). New technologies of production, transport, and telecommunication (the telegraph) resulted in a mass alienation from nature and the rich life of the senses. *The Circle*, however, is ghosted by a second *Walden*. In the wake of the Second World War, B.F. Skinner wrote *Walden Two* (1948) as a work of utopian fiction which was read by many as disturbingly dystopian. Skinner imagined the use of behavioural psychology to engineer a perfect community, but his critics objected that free will would be replaced by Pavlovian conditioning. *The Circle* might be read as *Walden 2.0*: a dystopian utopia in which woman has become the tool of her digital tools. Mae's participation in the endless questions of CircleSurvey echoes the scenario confronted by Pavlov's dogs: 'every time you hear the bell, you'll nod, and the headset will register your nod, and the question will be heard through your headphone' (Eggers 2013, 228). Mae customises her chime to whisper her own name and here we might detect another uncanny echo from the original panopticon. Bentham proposed the installation of

> a small tin tube [which] might reach from each cell to the inspector's lodge... By means of this implement, the slightest whisper of the one might be heard by the other, especially if he had proper notice to apply his ear to the tube. (Bentham 1995, 36)

Jacques-Alain Miller may not have had this particular extract in mind when referring to the panoptic style: '[t]he discourse you write will be flat, without depth, without semantic thickness, it will be Bentham's writing, which he strove to make "algebraic"' (Miller 1987, 28). In a similar vein, the literary critic D.A Miller proposes a fundamental alignment between realist fiction and the panoptic gaze: 'the genre of the novel belongs to the disciplinary field that it portrays' (Miller 1987, 15). It is necessary to consider, albeit briefly, aspects of literary form and style in *The Circle*. Eggers' novel aims to critique contemporary developments in surveillance society and yet, in places, the writing might be said to intersect with a panoptic style. Communication by Mae and the Circlers is degraded by the stylistics of the perfunctory zing, meme, and emoji and this is unfortunately mirrored by a certain cartooning of character, transparency of message, and flatness of prose in *The Circle*. Tom Stenton, one of the CEOs, is described on first appearance as 'sharky' (Eggers 2013, 23). Stenton then proceeds to purchase a shark, place it in a tank with other sea creatures, and observe excitedly as the predator consumes its prey. The shark is repeatedly referred to as 'circling' its tank and the sledgehammer symbolism is unnecessarily underscored by another character who denounces the Circle as the 'fucking shark that eats the world' (Eggers 2013, 480). Circling back to the starting point of this reading of *The Circle*, we might conclude that whilst rudimentary in parts, Eggers has managed to design a 'craft that can float on history for as long as it takes to build it' (Franzen 2003, 65). If future writers and critics in these troubled waters wish, like Mae in her kayak, to stay afloat, it will be incumbent on them to recognise the extent to which the medium is also the message.

Bibliography

Bentham, J. (1995). *Panopticon Writings*. Verso: London.

Boltanski, L., & Chiapello, E. (2018). *The New Spirit of Capitalism*. London: Verso.

Eggers, D. (2013). *The Circle*. London: Penguin.

Foucault, M. (1980). *The History of Sexuality: Volume I: An Introduction* (trans: Hurley, R.). New York: Vintage.

Foucault, M. (1995). *Discipline and Punish: The Birth of the Prison* (trans: Sheridan, A.). New York: Vintage.

Franzen, J. (2003). Why Bother? In *How to be Alone: Essays*. New York: Picador.

Fuchs, C. (2014). *Digital Labour and Karl Marx*. London: Routledge.

Gandy, O. (1993). *The Panoptic Sort: A Political Economy of Personal Information*. London: Routledge.

Garfinkel, S. (2000). *Database Nation: The Death of Privacy in the Twenty-First Century*. Sebastopol: O'Reilly.

Haggerty, K. D., & Ericson, R. V. (2000). The Surveillant Assemblage. *The British Journal of Sociology, 51*(4), 605–622.

Levin, T. Y. (2002). *CTRL [Space]: Rhetorics of Surveillance from Bentham to Big Brother*. Cambridge, MA: MIT Press.

Manovich, L. (2002). *The Language of New Media*. Cambridge, MA: MIT Press.

Miller, J. (1987). Jeremy Bentham's Panoptic Device. *October, 41*, 3–29.

Orwell, G. (2004). *1984*. London: Penguin.

Reisman, D. (2001). *The Lonely Crowd: A Study of the Changing American Character*. New Haven: Yale University Press.
Simon, B. (2005). The Return of Panopticism: Supervision, Subjection and the New Surveillance. *Surveillance & Society*, *3*(1), 1–20.
Skinner, B. F. (1948). *Walden Two*. Indianapolis: Hackett.
Thompson, G. (2003). *Male Sexuality Under Surveillance: The Office in American Literature*. Iowa City: University of Iowa Press.
Thoreau, H. D. (2012). *The Portable Thoreau*. London: Penguin.
Virilio, P. (2002). *Ground Zero*. London: Verso.
Zuboff, S. (2015). Big Other: Surveillance Capitalism and the Prospects of an Information Civilization. *Journal of Information Technology*, *30*, 75–89.

CHAPTER 15

Wayfinding *re/dicto*

Graydon Wetzler

Introduction

The Academy of Neuroscience for Architecture (ANFA) formed in 2003 with a mission to promote and advance knowledge that links neuroscience research to a growing understanding of human responses to the built environment. Michael Arbib, an Emeritus Professor and University Professor at the University of Southern California's Departments of Computer Science, Neuroscience and others who currently leads ANFA's Advisory Council identifies three facets linking neuroscience and architecture: The first is the *neuroscience of the design process* that asks, "What can we understand about the brain of the architect as he or she designs a building?" Alternatively, and most addressed in ANFA's work, the *neuroscience of the experience of architecture* attends to brain processes in people experiencing a building. Finally, Arbib posits *neuromorphic architecture* as a third pursuit asking, "What happens if our knowledge of the structure and function of brains informs our design of perception, control and communication systems for buildings, so that these systems are based on brain operating principles rather than ad hoc computational designs?" (Dougherty and Arbib 2013). In this pursuit, Arbib suggests leveraging empirical studies

G. Wetzler (✉)
Department of Visual Arts, University of California, San Diego,
La Jolla, CA, USA
e-mail: gkw214@nyu.edu

S. Flynn, A. Mackay (eds.), *Surveillance, Architecture and Control*,
https://doi.org/10.1007/978-3-030-00371-5_15

of biological brains to reimagine brains *plus* built environments as "interactive infrastructures" with buildings designed as "inside-out" fields enabling social interaction between place and people, as well as, between places and things (Arbib 2012a). The very idea of space as a "perceiving, acting and adapting" *intraface* renders a number of conceptual registers and analytic objectives for the current collection. This chapter instead suggests another bead by double-leveraging Arbib's proposed methodological fulcrum for wayfinding "cross-border traffic" on currently reclusive disciplinary problems. The one considered here goes through the hippocampus, a region supporting spatial navigation and episodic memory, and therein an open challenge for neuroscientists resolve a structural/functional concurrence for wayfinding in time *and* space. Meditating on the good life (2016), Arbib stipulated an implicit criterion for non-trivial traffic beyond boundaries in neuroscience and architecture:

> Neuroscientists will engage with architects not only as a form of "translational science," where architecture rather than medicine provides the challenges for applications of neuroscience findings, but conversely the architects must pose questions that stimulate new basic research on cognition and the brain without demanding that every such effort have an immediate practical payoff. (31)

A particularly salient path for boundary crossing, Arbib points out, is by multiplexing the neuroscientific problem of hippocampus wayfinding with an architectural design problem. The aims of the current chapter are to traffic in the hippocampus as *method* in order to coax something more speculative out of Foucault's idea of "problematization" and his circumscription of this notion through the related concepts of "milieu" and "counter-conduct." In a 1984 conversation with Paul Rainbow just before his death 1984, Foucault suggested a speculative dimension within the critical aims of "problematization" as a "history of thought":

> It seemed to me that there was one element that was capable of describing the history of thought: this was what one could call the element of problems, or, more exactly, problematizations. What distinguishes thought is that it is something quite different from the set of representations that underlies as certain behavior; it is also something quite different from the domain of attitudes that can determine this behavior. Thought is not what inhabits a certain conduct and gives it its meaning; rather, it is what allows one to step back from this way of acting or reacting, to present it to oneself

> as an object of thought and question it as to its meaning, its conditions, and its goals. Thought is freedom in relation to what one does, the motion by which one detaches oneself from it, establishes it as an object, and reflects it as a problem. ("Polemics, Politics and Problematizations," 388)

By considering Foucault's notions of "problematization," "milieu," and "counter-conduct" through Arbib's move beyond "translational science," we might make a speculative project of Foucault's later work more perceivable. This is part of larger project that I here hope to modestly anchor through a pair of projects encountered in my research elsewhere. This chapter, and its larger project, does not manifest in a vacuum, but build upon the aims and share the ethos of previous work. One such resonance is found with Siegfried Zielinski's (2006) conceptual constructs of "anarcheology" and the subsequently reworked positive remedy "variantology." In his book *Deep Time of the Media*, Zielinski animated these concepts in contexts and modes the current chapter approximates:

> The concept of archaiologia, stories from history, comprises not only the old, the original (archaios), but also the act of governing, of ruling (archein) and its substantive archos (leader). Anarchos is the nomen agentis to archein, and it means "the absence of a leader," also "the lack of restraint or discipline." 30 Discussing Foucault's concept of an archaeology of knowledge, Rudi Visker used the term "an-archeologie" more than ten years ago to describe a method that evades the potential of identifying a "standardized object of an original experience." 31 A history that entails envisioning, listening, and the art of combining by using technical devices, which privileges a sense of their multifarious possibilities over their realities in the form of products, cannot be written with avant-gardist pretensions or with a mindset of leading the way. Such a history must reserve the option to gallop off at a tangent, to be wildly enthusiastic, and, at the same time, to criticize what needs to be criticized. This method describes a pattern of searching, and delights in any gifts of true surprises. (26–27)

Out of a similar trajectory, the current chapter shares the analytic contexts and methodological ethos with the works of Orit Halpern (who eloquently bridges the histories of science, computing, and cybernetics with design and art practice), Mara Mills (who assertively unearths co-evolutions across epistemic and material practices of media, disability and engineering), and David Trippett (taking a lateral path on the sonic as an irreducibly effective and affective field). In step with these thinkers and others, my aims for the current chapter will be to emphasize how *æffect/æffective* enables one to perceive a constellation of discourses assembling on a series of contingencies, overlapping epistemic frames, and cultural practices. At the same time, this constellation congeals a set of adjoining contextures perhaps differently dampened but exchangeable.

I begin the chapter discussing how one university lab has reimagined the vibrating surround as a method for "clandestine listening." To animate the technical details of this research, I offer a media archaeology to suggest how it can be traced to mid-twentieth-century cybernetic research around problems of sensory prosthesis. This latter research also made important contributions to pattern recognition that advanced contemporary surveillance technologies. I also draw on Alvin Lucier's score, *I Am Sitting in a Room* (1969)—a score and an act that provoke the architectural surround into a Janus-faced prosthesis, de dicto/de re (about the said and the sensed), as well as, in locus sin quo (but if there is, where?).

After summarizing recent calls for reassessing the potentials of Foucault's later idea of "problematization" and the empirics of "milieu" and "conduct"/"counter-conduct" alongside his better-known work on discipline, I then suggest a contemporary fulcrum coming to us through Arbib's cross-trafficking challenge for "interactive infrastructures" with special attention to his manifesto's positing wayfinding as a vibrant anti-disciplinary spur for coaxing Foucault's later ideas into more speculative territories. With wayfinding as a prompt, I unpack how "artivist" collective Electronic Disturbance Theater (EDT) 2.0/bits, atoms, neurons, and genes (b.a.n.g.) Lab positions a concurrency of effect and affect as a design principle for the "Transborder Immigrant Tool" (TBT)—a global positioning satellite (GPS) hack assisting immigrants navigating and crossing the Mexico/US border. I close the chapter to see how the same multimodal surveillance engineering research evolved to hunt untapped perceptual modalities enabling the visually impaired to feel and navigate (otherwise) invisible space.

The chapter hopes to contribute each of these cases as both discursive and robust schema reimagining the concurrent modalities of surveillance, control, and architecture. I also hope in their sum; the cases evoke a mandala that follows Marshall McLuhan's definition of acoustic space as "centre everywhere and margin nowhere" (Findlay-White and Logan 2016).

Ada *Meets* SISL

Please meet Ada. Ada wants to play with you but cannot leave home. Her parents think she is an "an inside out robot" that is "like an organism," coherent and expressing unitary "sentience" (Eng et al. 2005). Ada is more a milieu. In 2002, over 550,000 people came to play with Ada during the Swiss national exhibition Expo.02. She likes controlled play:

Sleep: One tile color for all visitors
Wake: Visitors given different colored floor tiles
Explore: Probe for "interesting" visitors; deploy gazers (cameras which could be directed to attend to particular visitors)
Group: Try to direct visitors to a certain location in space, for example, by floor patterns or by deploying light fingers (beams of light for pointing at individual visitors or indicating different locations in the space)
Play: Play a game selected on the basis of number of visitors grouped together.
Leave: Show a path for visitors to exit the space.

Ada *meets* Serial Interception Sequence Learning (SISL). He secures against rubber hose attacks by emplacing your password in that inarticulate part of you. SISL's progenitors conceived him when it occurred to them how "[i]mplicit learning presents a fascinating tool for designing coercion-resistant security systems" (Bojinov 2012). SISL also likes to play—opponents are paced through a sequence of motor tasks with a covertly structured repeating sequence. SISL synchs with your residual pattern of play and buries your authentication within the dissociative information processing characteristics of the cortico-striatal memory system. This is your non-reportable password, *up in the cut*, between the basal ganglia and motor cortical areas where declarative (explicit) and implicit memory are mutually exclusive. Sit back and let SISL do the work to vet you.

In "Surveillance, Power and Everyday Life," David Lyon cautioned against an increasingly complex coupling of *control* with *care* in contemporary information and communication systems pervaded by surveillance discourse. Ada and SISL cannot meet one another in any conventional sense. But we might imagine their indirect encounter along Lyon's contagion of *control* and *care* where Ada and SISL marry in threes—surveillance, control, and built environments. Ada, however, disrupts conventional architectural discourse because she is, according to her designers, like "an inside out robot" seeking symbiosis with her inhabitants—whether living or themselves inhabited. SISL disrupts conventional discourses of security by replacing terms like "adversary," "secrets," and "tokens" with those of "dissociation" and "statistical averages." The current chapter hopes to contribute some other provocations of contemporary spatial culture through disruptive reimagining how surveillance, architecture, and control generate performative nexuses, and cross-trafficking "problematizations." To do so, I look to traffic in wayfinding as *affective* concurrence by going through a recent challenge for architecture to "problematize" the hippocampus.

Signal Control de/re

Bruce Nauman's "Video Surveillance Piece: Public Room, Private Room" (1969) is, in my opinion, one of the most succinct meditations and caustic interventions on how emerging communication technologies, security discourses, and built space seamlessly integrate to inflect spatial practice. Viewers enter a small room where Nauman has placed a monitor on the floor in one corner and a ceiling mounted a CCTV camera panning the room from the opposite corner. Viewers expect to find the current room screened on the monitor, but instead realize they only appear via a second monitor, embedded in the first. Zbikowski narrated the intended experience: "At this point things start to grate with customary perception for the experimentation with simultaneous transmission evolves into active observation and being under surveillance" (Zbikowski 2004). Nauman's staging of expectation and denial is explained by realizing the room's exterior is twice the interior of the room: "The video surveillance occurs in two rooms: a public and a private one." The second room is only accessible through the CCTV transmission. At one level, Nauman's work is a pun on "closed circuit" and broadcasting. At another level, it is a succinct implementation of built space with then emerging communication technology. Herein, the work has simple control logic of signal flow (input and output) and complementary pairs (cameras, monitors and rooms). I offer a bird's eye graphic of Nauman's piece intentionally confusing schematic with pictorial circuit diagrams in order to capture a viewer's subjective dissonance of surveillance and participation. Nauman's mise-en-abyme mutually incurring built space with signal control generates a more complex architectural experience formed upon the viewer's active error correction. User's need *wayfinds* a solution to the cognitive flutter by actively combining allocentric spatial memory (e.g., inferring one room is in fact two due to the mismatched scales between the exterior and interior) and egocentric space (interacting with your image on the monitor) (Fig. 15.1).

Nauman's controlled design of the signal transmission is effective. The piece's primary aim however is more a conjoint of æffect. Stephen Duncombe characterizes affect in the relevant sense as "a surplus of meaning: something we cannot quite describe or put our finger on, but which moves us nonetheless for a moment their perception is a surplus of signification" (Duncombe 2016, 118). Nauman's effective control of signal flow compels viewers to wayfind the complementary perceptual spaces. The EDT 2.0/b.a.n.g. Lab identifies a relevant principle defining their work as "being concurrently affective and effective" (Dominguez and Nadir 2012). As artists, the Lab aims for work that is "perceptive by feeling" (affective). As activists, Lab projects should also be effective in creating sustainable community spaces. In a way, Duncombe's ligature and the EDT 2.0/b.a.n.g. Lab's concurrency are inverses with deeply compatible aims. Surprisingly, both of these resemble how Michael A. Arbib has long made "action-perceptual schemas" at the center of his research in social neuroscience. More recently, Arbib has theorized "neuromorphic architecture" as a design strategy for developing interactive spaces based on a broader claim motivating "action-perceptual schemas" such that brains and bodies co-evolve together with "receptors and effectors and body architecture" mutually respond to and "constrain the brain and vice versa" (2012a, 3). There are

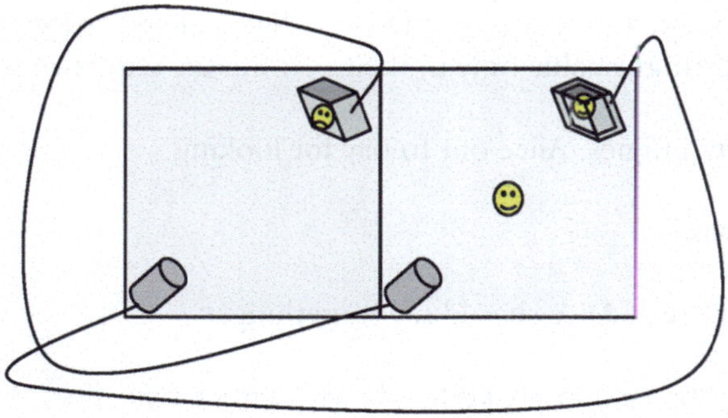

Fig. 15.1 Schematic/Pictorial rendering of Bruce Nauman's "Video Surveillance Piece" (1969). Image CC 2018, Graydon Wetzler (the author)

both critical and creative potentials in thinking these complex sums of affect and effect. Below I introduce some broader contexts for considering how.

Clandestine Listening Through the Mirror Countrawise

The Prussian born philosopher Gotthard Günther (1900–1984) spent much of his career attempting to establish trans-Aristotelian logic with a central aim to omit the law of excluded middle stating that either a proposition is true or its negation is true. In the context of seeking *tertium datur* ("a third possible"), Günther proposed a theoretical device, the "thought translator," enabling indirect spiritual communication between two mutually exclusive mentalities (e.g., a human-like Aristotleian binary logic and a non-human-like contra-Aristotleian binary logic). These mentalities are in fact exactly alike in every regard including being perfect denials of each other. To distinguish between them, one requires, he speculated, a three-valued machine-like logic for transposing their symmetrically binary exclusions into a third operator that faithfully tracks their simultaneous exclusions within a single AND. Günther's thought experiment sought to give his own ideas form through the American science fiction writer Jack Williamson's novel, *Seetee Ship*—itself a mash-up of two previous short stories by the author, "Minus Sign" (first published in the November 1942 issue) and "Opposites—React!" (two installments in January and February 1943). Günther further confesses that the thought translator has already been invented if more synoptically when Alice went *Through the Looking-Glass* and encountered the twins, Tweedle-dee and Tweedledum (Carroll 1998). Like the mutually exclusive mentalities, the twins are (except the names printed on their collars) materially alike in every way, distinguishable only in their continuous sequence of denial:

(α) If they are effigies, Alice out to pay for looking.

Contrariwise,

(β) If they are real, Alice should say something.

Realizing she cannot shake hands with either twin first, Alice takes a complementary hand of each boy and "soon the three were dancing in a ring." In Fig. 15.2, I have rendered Günther's reading of Alice's meeting the twins.

In 2008, I introduced myself to the City University of New York computer scientist, Zhigang Zhu who also directs the City College Visual Computing Laboratory (CCVCL) and Co-Director of the Center for Perceptual Robotics, Intelligent Sensors and Machines (PRISM). I wanted to learn more about his team's then ongoing research to develop novel sensing modalities for adaptive surveillance applications. He subsequently invited me to participate in an interdisciplinary seminar, "Multimodal Sentient Computing" that he was organizing to convene cross-disciplinary discussion for enabling computing systems "to perceive the world and relate to it in much the same way as people do using multimodal perceptions (seeing, hearing, touching, etc.)." The seminar also planned to look beyond engineering questions to relevant conceptual and methodological questions linking multimodal systems to cognitive science, architecture, and a broad array of social science. Given Zhu's current research, however, the seminar was empirically grounded in current challenges for surveil-

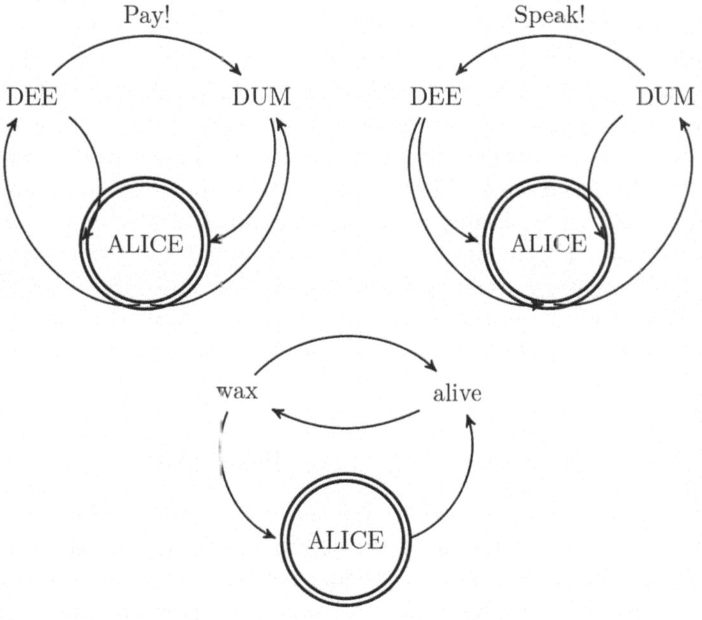

Fig. 15.2 Alice goes twinning with/in a syneches (continuous) circuit: Dee (top left), then Dum (top right), and, finally, together (bottom). Image CC 2018, Graydon Wetzler (the author)

lance and security applications where he was convinced multimodal sensor designs proving to be "finely sensitive in perception or feeling" are in great demand.

The particular challenges Zhu's lab set itself were designing systems for covert surveillance of non-cooperative subjects in potentially obtrusive environments. At the heart of their research novelty is laser Doppler vibrometer (LDV): an instrument for making non-contact vibration measurements of a surface. LDV is conventionally applied to test structural integrity of transportation and related civic structures like high-rises and bridges. Zhu instead reimagined laser Doppler vibrometry to enable "clandestine listening" (Weihong Li and Zigang Zhu 2007). Zhu and his team's multimodal system (hereafter simply, LDV) was thoroughly Do-It-Yourself comprising only of repurposed off-the-shelf hardware and software modules. The system's design theory was also canonically *cybernetic* in theory and execution. In one iteration, for example, the system design integrated three sensing units into a closed control loop: (1) a consumer PTZ (point, track, and zoom) camera mounted on a commercial LDV, (2) a mirror mounted on a pan-tilt-unit (PTU) (platform with panning and tilt capabilities), and (3) a reflective surface in the environment. It is not unproductive to recall Nauman's two rooms. Rather than directly characterizing the operational details of Zhu's multimodal platform, I'll attempt to evoke some of the epistemic and cultural conditions of its surveillant imaginary. In doing so, I will combine actual with possible conditions as an æffect recurrence placing surveillance, control, and spatial practice in spiraling circuit. This media archaeology begins with the 1950s cybernetic research into sensory prostheses, and then looks Janus-faced backward to World War II encryption advances and forward to Alvin Lucier's *I Am Sitting in a Room* (1969). But first we need go more or less concomitant through the mirror.

Designing Sensory Problems

In 1951, MIT professors Norbert Wiener (a colleague of Günther's) and J.B. Wiesner were collaborating on design problems related to sensory and muscular-skeletal prosthesis. Wiener believed cybernetics to enable a unique approach by assuming that the mouth, or its instantaneous speech as feedback, was as fundamental to the ear in designing sensory prosthesis for the hearing impaired.[1] If you've ever experienced an anechoic chamber (a room treated to eliminate all echo), you understand why. The experience of these acoustically "dead" rooms is most unsettling. One prefers a little distance, or drift, from oneself to effectively coordinate sensation with action. In a short report from 1951, Wiener explained that the problem with sensory afflictions is unboxing—"[t]he difficulties lie in the fact that for these people the act of conversation has been broken into two different parts." For problems of sensory prosthetics therefore, "we must consider the entire speech process as a unit," (26) and then,

> it appeared to us that it is perfectly possible to make the transition between sound in the outside air, and the semantic recognition of speech, by an artificial phonetic stage, making use of touch, and supplemented by adequate electrical tools. Having come to this conclusion, we started the detailed design of such apparatus. (32)

The influence of fellow cyberneticians Warren S. McCulloch and Walter Pitts' work on pattern recognition and the perception of universals is evident. A more concrete influence on Wiener's thoughts on sensory prosthesis was the "vocoder." A truncation of "voice" along "coder," the "vocoder" was developed at Bell's Telephone Lab during the 1930s as an early attempt to code speech and reduce bandwidth of its transmission. The vocoder was based on the following: (i) human speech involves a controlled motor process—opening and closing of the glottis by the vocal cords and then filtered by the nose and throat, and (ii) these processes affect localized vibrations falling into distinguishable frequency bands, vibrating at different speeds. Identifying a set of bands to be interest defines a model. Each speech-act fills the model with parameters (so in principle, spoken words that are acoustically identical produce identical model parameters). This means given a set of model parameters, recorded speech could be transmitted without the instantaneous frequencies of its performance. A receiver only needs the defined model to translate its parameters back into performed speech. As a compression technique, the vocoder exploited the fact that speech varies fairly slowly as the components of the throat move during the phonetic stage. These features led the "vocoder" to become a perceptible import into a more complex encryption architecture—the SIGSALY system (also known as the X System, Project X, Ciphony I, and the Green Hornet)—that encrypted high-level Allied voice communications during World War II.

From the hindsight of laser Doppler vibrometry surveillance, the conjoint of Wiener's hearing glove and the vocoder design that influenced it further curdles into discursive maps across control architectures and their spatial gestalts. Arbib describes the particular motivation for McCulloch and Pitts' (1947) work on pattern recognition that also grounded Wiener's glove:

> [The] system of visual-muscular feedbacks is not sufficient to completely account for our perception of universals like chairs, circles, etc. We must still account for the way in which our brains enable us to recognize a letter A, say, despite its being subjected to many transformations such as rotations, translations on the retina, shifts in perspective, etc. Pitts and McCulloch, 1947, provided the classic discussion of possible neural mechanisms that could account for this perceptual capability of our brains. Their designs show some interesting, although admittedly superficial, similarities to real brain structures. (49–50)

Wiener believed that sensory processes such as hearing and vision must not be treated as mere causal links between stimulus and effect, but rather in terms of finding their underlying gestalt relations. Under a discourse of the exchangeability of time and space, (McCulloch and Pitts 1947) demonstrated how "the detailed geometry of topographically mapped, layered, columnar cortices provided specific relationships among neurons in both time and space that could, in principle, allow them to calculate generalizations and invariances among sensory inputs." In the context of sensory prosthetics, Wiener argued, one must "treat scanning not so much as of a group [but] as of a group of transformations of energy" and "in this way [a human or machine] can recognize a figure independently of its orientation" (Masani, 226). The "hearing glove" was an artifact that emerged out of this discourse we might canonize under the principle of *an exchangeability of time and space*. The glove *vocodes* the instantaneous frequencies of a human speech-act into an energy signature divided into five frequency bands *modulo* the five digits on a human hand. His and McCulloch's work on pattern recognition and perception of universals convinced Walter Pitts would prove the operation of the nervous system amenable to purely logical explanation. He would later collaborate with Robert Gesteland to undertake foundational studies of sensory coding in the olfactory system. These studies led to an archive of smells generated by Gesteland and Pitts. Their subsequent collaboration on sensory coding in the frog retina would demonstrate the impossibility of Pitts' earlier conviction regarding the logic of perception-action circuits. Decades later all of this work would become a central foundational for today's ubiquitous computational surveillance and missile tracking systems.

Whispering in a Room

In 1969, the experimental musical composer Alvin Lucier could be said to transpose the hearing glove with a third value operator when he conceived "I am sitting in a room" as a performance for voice on tape. The work is a Janus-faced sensory prosthesis of sorts that extends Wiener's glove into the surround but shares with the vocoder to serve a sort of voice encryption. To perform Lucier's composition requires a room with resonance, one microphone, two tape recorders, amplifier, a room, one speaker, and one loudspeaker. The performance begins by the speaker reading and recording the following text (see Föllmer 2018):

> I am sitting in a room different from the one you are in now. I am recording the sound of my speaking voice and I am going to play it back into the room again and again until the resonant frequencies of the room reinforce themselves so that any semblance of my speech, with perhaps the exception of rhythm, is destroyed. What you will hear, then, are the natural resonant frequencies of the room articulated by speech. I regard this activity not so much as a demonstration of a physical fact, but, more as a way to smooth out any irregularities my speech might have.

The recording of the text is then played back while re-recording it, and this process is repeated (the first recording of the performance comprised of 32 repetitions of the text). In effect, the room convolves voice. With each iteration, the ongoing superposition, or oscillation, of the original recorded text is driven by the frequencies resonant to the room. More specifically, the resonant frequencies of the space and the original recording are amplified while their differences are attenuated. The phonetic upstage the semantic by amplifying the latter's deviation from itself. Rather than performing error correction by minimizing drift between script and its performance, "sitting in a room" is a case of what Magoroh Maruyama (1963) referred to as a "deviation amplifying" system. Somewhere along the way the boundaries between words disappear, and only a faint rhythm of speech remains. The declarative becomes performative, or perhaps equally apt, deformative: the voice fed back to itself (the converging series of room and voice) is increasingly sensed as modulated resonance. In the

DRAM notes for the original recording, Nicolas Collins describes experiencing the shift from effective to affective modes:

> What was once a familiar word has become a whistled three- note motif; what was once a simple declarative sentence has become a curiously tonal melodic fragment; what was once a paragraph of unaffected prose has become music. Some- how, somewhere in the course of 40 minutes the meaning of what we've been listening to has slipped from the domain of language to that of harmony.

Returning to Zhu and his team's work, how does the LDV system emerge from this archaeology? This multimodal sentient surveillance platform is comprised of three modules (see Zhigang Zhu and Huang 2007 and Tao Wang et al. 2011): (i) a visual module consisting of a Canon pan/tilt/zoom (PTZ) video camera, (ii) an acoustic module consisting of Polytec LDV and a mirror mounted on a PTU platform, and (iii) the human-computer interaction module consisting of a computer, custom Java software program and a human user. The operational heart is LDV working according to the principle of laser interferometry: a class of methods that make use of the interference of two energy waves by combining them into a third wave whose shape and size (superposition) depend on the patterns of the original two waves. The superposition gives the phase difference between the two waves that is meaningful as the amount of drift, or displacement gives the Janus-faced as much as Alice's solution to how the pattern changed. Laser vibrometry is a device that performs interferometry with a laser. A laser beam is passed through a beam splitter (at once both a window and mirror) that divides into an object beam and a reference beam. The object (or "thing") beam strikes a point on the moving (vibrating) object, while the reference beam simply *takes time*. The "thing" beam reflects its object light back to the beam splitter where it is superposed (interferes) with the reference (or do *no-thing*) beam. The drift, displacement, or superposition appears as light fluctuations and this "signal" is in turn converted to a voltage fluctuation. Laser vibrometry captures Gregory Bateson's definition of information as "a difference which makes a difference"—the difference between object and referent gives the phonetic stage. To optimize the laser doppler operation, a model is needed for optimizing the measured displacement. In Zhu's platform, just as in the "vocoder" and Wiener's, it is the human voice that matters. Zhu's model takes both object vibrational properties and the spectral structure of human speech as key parameters. To narrate the Laser vibrometer's operation, see that water glass in front of you? It hears you!

Here, the deformative drift through *scale* into non-identity is a semantic closure. The effective deficiencies of Lucier's speech (his stutter) find harmony (self-concord) in affect. My placing Lucier's composition/performance in the same context as Wiener's prosthetic glove and the LDV surveillance platform is not so ad hoc. For example, a formal and applied apparatus unites them in the study of Fourier transforms, or equivalently in their effective harmonies. My intention, however, is more to emphasize how *affect* enables one to perceive a constellation of discourses assembling on a series of contingencies, overlapping epistemic frames and cultural practices. At the same time, this constellation congeals a set of adjoining rooms perhaps differently dampened but exchangeable with the vocoder emphasizing control of instantaneous bulk while the "hearing glove" sought to control the translation of instantaneous speech into energy pulsed rectified along each of the five fingers. There is also a critical link across these sites: Wiener sought to develop cybernetics as a method based on the signifier "machine" as a Bergsonian discourse where the "present" acts as a buffer between the influencing "past" and the indeterminate "future" Masani (134). Bergsonian processes are irreversible: reversing their documentation in time and ordinary perception begins to *grate*. Such processes are more like what Foucault circumscribed in the "milieu" and should be contrasted with the stabilized asymmetry characterized by Bentham's panopticon.

In theory, laser vibrometry could reference the body of the speaker itself as a point for clandestine listening. Herein seems to be a hyperbolic distinction of surveillance from other spatial/relational discourses. A subject is both acoustically dead and the instantaneous superposition of referent and thing (de/re) informing in their difference. One might posit The Mystery Man in David Lynch's *Lost High- way* (1997) when he proves to Fred Madison (Bill Pullman) that he is both *here* and *in* Fred's home. So, the glass on the table in front of you suggests a Lacanian variation on a floating can—"You see that glass of water" Do you see it? Well, it [feels] you!"—where it is the body in superposition with itself that gives the difference, matters amplify and resonate such that what is all-seeing is also without accompanying provocation. Lacan's triangular schema is unintentionally evoked by the LDV platform, as an anamorphosis is also at work—an effect of the relationship between four different coordinate systems—two of which independently rotating along different axes. Given this, perhaps more suggestive are Caillois' remarks on mimicry (that Lacan, of course, cites) where:

> a dihedral of action whose horizontal plane is formed by the ground and the vertical plane by the man himself who walks and who, by this fact, carries the dihedral along with him; and a dihedral of representation determined by the same horizontal plane as the previous one (but represented and not perceived) intersected vertically at the distance where the object appears. It is with represented space that the drama becomes specific, since the living creature, the organism, is no longer the origin of the coordinates, but one point among others; it is dispossessed of its privilege and literally no longer knows where to place itself … The feeling of personality, considered as the organism's feeling of distinction from its surroundings, of the connection between consciousness and a particular point in space, cannot fail under these conditions to be seriously undermined; one then enters into the psychology of psychasthenia, and more specifically of legendary psychasthenia, if we agree to use this name for the disturbance in the above relations between personality and space. (28)

Caillois' passage equally describes Lucier's performance, but where the disorder gives harmonics (again Caillois): "the individual breaks the boundary of his skin and occupies the other side of his senses … [and] feels himself becoming space." Lucier's score, and its act, reimagines an oscillation of subject, sensory extension, and built space that is more suggestive of Jon McKenzie's theory of "machinic performance" and the challenges of efficacy, efficiency, and effectiveness; as well as what Andre Lepecki (2005) proposed with choreographing "kinetic refusals"—sitting in a room. One could also posit a Foucauldian "analytics," in the sense that Mitchell Dean (*Governmentality Power and Rule in Modern Society*) tasked as "an analysis of the specific conditions under which particular entities emerge, exist and change" (30). The next section looks to develop this by reconsidering Michel Foucault's underdeveloped ideas on counter-conduct as an equally critical and creative bead on that presence.

Counter-Conduct in a Milieu

Elsewhere, the scholars Xavier Guillaume and Jef Huysmans (2013) also refer to Dean's articulation of "analytics" as an important project attending to the situated "junctures" through which alternative forms of political being "emerge, exist and change" (Dean 2010, 30). They propose "interstitial" as an analytics of the points of contact between citizenship and security, and more specifically, as a method to make analyzable "the other politics" at the nexus between securitizing processes and their refusal. An interstitial approach presupposes an irreducible nexus binds security politics to citizenship and requires analysis of both their "conjunctive and disjunctive" dimensions—dominant political frames of those included in the realm of politics, as well as, those excluded (e.g., non-status migrants). In a sense, an interstitial is like Alice and the thought translator: a more complex "and."

In *The History of Sexuality: Volume I* (2013), and *Security, Territory, Population* (2009), Foucault advanced "analytics" as a collection of empirical methods for uncovering the "complexities and contingencies" that enabled our present to appear as a field of truth. In both works, he is more specifically interested in how present conditions came to harden a "grid of intelligibility" as a function of power to operate on as a regime of truth. In (2013), for example, Foucault's objective is to historically characterize how sexuality came to be constituted as a distinct field of discourse that scientific inquiry could both operate on and through as a "regime of truth." He thus asks, "If sexuality was constituted as an area of investigation, this was only because relations of power had established it as a possible object; and conversely, if power was able to take it as a target, this was because techniques of knowledge and procedures of discourse were capable of in- vesting it" (98). Toward this, Foucault explicitly characterizes his inquiry as an "analytics" of power rather than a "theory" of power in that the former aims toward, "a definition of the specific domain formed by relations of power, and toward a determination of the instruments that will make possible its analysis" (82). For this to be done, Foucault decisively departs from a representation of power insofar as this can only serve to bind inquiry to the "juridico-discursive." Theorizing power as co-extensive with the law and with sovereignty (legitimacy) characterizes only its negative, repressive mechanisms as centralized authorities and institutions—the negative and "terminal forms power takes" (92). The "juridico-discursive" representation of power cannot give its positive, productive, and emergent operations. Needed instead is "a definition of the specific domain formed by relations of power, and toward a determination of the instruments that will make possible its analysis" (82). Foucault argues that a historical analysis shows that in modern societies, power has not governed sexuality by means of law and authority, but rather has done so by "a veritable 'technology' of sex" rendering sexuality a sphere of inductive proposition: "whose operation is not ensured by right but by technique, not by law but by normalization, not by punishment but by control, methods that are employed on all levels and in forms that go beyond the state and its apparatus."

Dreyfus and Rainbow (1983) further elaborated Foucault's distinction of theory as propositional, while he deployed analytics in a more diagnostic mode. Building on these authors' work, Colin Koopman and Tomas Matza (2013) offered a taxonomy distinguishing Foucault's application of concepts from that of analytics. Analytics were strategies to modalize an inquiry into the historical contingencies that conditioned a truth to become apparent as such. Analytics are methodologically focused on the limits for coherent inquiry, and enabled Foucault's "rigor and mobility" across analytic contexts. Foucault solicited archaeology and genealogy as analytics "to critically excavate historical conditions of possibility that reveal the objects of our historical present as contingent (rather than necessary), complex (rather than simple), and composed (rather than merely given)" (826). Application of concepts alternatively provided Foucault to narrate a given site in terms of a "a complex plurality." They identify *discipline, biopower, security, governmentality*, and *care of the self* as vivid Foucauldian concepts.

With the concept of security, Foucault's key narrative construct was the "milieu" that he understood as a fundamental axis through which security deployed. Security does not react to a "milieu" as a discrete existential threat as much as the finding of "a project, a political technique" for its apparatuses to emerge in order to "work, fabricate, organize, and plan" its form (Security, Territory, Population 38). Whereas sovereignty operates on legal entities acting through volition and discipline operates through panoptic optics on some multiplicity of bodies performing normative rules, the milieu instead affects "precisely, a population" (37).

Foucault specified the milieu's conditions of possibility as "Lamarckian," and more importantly distinctly "Newtonian" insofar as needing "to account for action at a distance of one body on another" (36). These also operationally bind the milieu with the operation of security:

> let's say then that sovereignty capitalizes a territory, raising the major problem of the seat of government, whereas discipline structures a space and addresses the essential problem of a hierarchical and functional distribution of elements, and security will try to plan a milieu in terms of events or series of events or possible elements, of series that will have to be regulated within

> a multivalent and transformable framework. The specific space of security refers then to a series of possible events; it refers to the temporal and the uncertain, which have to be inserted within a given space. The space in which a series of uncertain elements unfold is, I think, roughly what one can call the milieu. (35)

More succinctly, the milieu is "the medium of an action and the element in which it circulates" (36). Security targets the milieu as an agglomeration of "natural" and "artificial" givens, and as "circular link" established between effects and causes. The milieu gives security its project as a phenomenon of "a certain number of combined, overall effects bearing on all who live in it." The milieu enables security to become self-referential. As an analytics, security focused Foucault on the micro-powers "not confined by definition to a precise domain" nor determined by a sector of the scale, but as "a point of view, a method of decipherment which may be valid for the whole scale, whatever its size" (Foucault 2008, 186).

Arnold I. Davidson (2011) argued that the Collège de France lectures "contains a conceptual hinge" for connecting the political with ethical axes of Foucault's work (27). A possible answer he believes lies with the emphasis of governmentality as the principal import in *Security, Territory, Population* with a consequence of obscuring "one of the richest and most brilliant moments in the entire course" (27)—Foucault's remarks on the notions of "conduct" and "counter-conduct." In "The Subject and Power," Foucault summarized his sustained objective for the last two decades as a historical enumeration of the different modes by which "human beings are made subjects" (77). To do so, he has not approached power as a phenomenon occurring, as it were, in different places, nor to establish a theoretical framework for characterizing power. Instead, he has sought to render the ways in which a subject emerges as a perceptible objective, addressable as it were, to, and for, power to operate. He identifies three different modes through which a subject is formed: (i) through a scientific mode of inquiry that objectifies a subject, (ii) through what he calls "dividing practices" that function categorically in objectivizing a subject, and (iii) those modes through which human beings turn themselves into a subject.

Wiener and colleague have similarly categorized a cybernetic discourse as an analytics of machines for comparative study of behavior as a circuit of control and communication. There were, in fact, two higher categories of subject: the cybernetic bestiary and the speciation of the purely theoretical automata—for example, sequential machines, linear control systems, tree automata, and stochastic automata. Among the earliest of subjects belonging to the first category was the "palomilla" created by Wiener, Wiesner, and Singleton. In fact, the Spanish word for moth only gives half of the creation's identity. It was, in effect, a moth-bedbug, palomilla comprising a small tricycle cart with a pair of photocells facing "front" and to the right and left sides of one another. An amplifier was connected to these photocells that upon loading power to either one or the other cell "reaches the tiller controlling the front steering wheel." Depending on which cell received the output voltage as input, palomilla either goes toward light (acting pro-phototropic) or turns toward darkness (acting anti-phototropic)—thus performing either a "moth" or "bedbug." In addition to "Bateson's Polyploid Horse," "Maturana's Frog," and "McCulloch's Rat" was the "colloquy of mobiles" that included Gordon Pask's televisions converting sound into visual patterns.

The third mode Foucault identified is where the notion of "counter-conduct" enters as a second-order empiric. Fundamental to this is Foucault's characterization of power as "not simply a relationship between partners, individual or collective" but is more important a modulation of relations and their relative flows, or a "way in which certain actions modify others" ("The Subject and Power," 789). Critical for Foucault is to attend to the way power acts indirectly and with delay on subjects. Alternatively, a relationship of violence "acts upon a body or upon things" in direct manner—"it forces, it bends, it breaks on the wheel, it destroys, or it closes the door on all possibilities," and because of this violence operates on passivity alone. When it meets resistance, its only recourse is to dampen it. "On the other hand," Foucault wrote:

> a power relationship can only be articulated on the basis of two elements which are each indispensable if it is really to be a power relationship: that 'the other' (the one over whom power is exercised) be thoroughly recognized and maintained to the very end as a person who acts; and that, faced with a relationship of power, a whole field of responses, reactions, results, and possible inventions may open up. (789)

He does not exclude relations of violence or the coercion of consent from the exercise of power but considers them the instruments or effects and not the principle. Power does not require an inimical subject to operate on. In seeking for the right term for organizing an analytics of power in this setting, Foucault suggests the term "conduct," for perhaps its "equivocal nature" as "one of the best aids for coming to terms with the specificity of power relations" (789). He is remarking on the available multiplicity of interpretations registered in the term that (more explicit in French) is at once "to drive" and "to behave," and as the translator notes, "whence la conduite, 'conduct' or 'behaviour'" (later we might attempt to fold "to bring in, or forth"). In the productive equivocation of "conduct," Foucault brings into focus that power is only mistakenly associated with confrontation, when it more accurately should be understood as the proper generality of governing action in terms of possibility. In this regard, for Foucault, "conduct" appropriately situates an analytics of not so much coercive but conducive mechanisms that conduct behavior and brings into presence "a more or less open field of possibilities" (789). It is in through both interpretations, but made more immanent in the second one, that even while Foucault stressed there is no "position of exteriority with respect to power" (Foucault 2013, 125–7), a notion of "counter-conduct" is possible that shares with "conduct," as Foucault writes, "a series of elements that can be utilized and reutilized, reimplanted, reinserted, taken up in the direction of reinforcing a certain mode of conduct or of creating and recreating a type of counter-conduct" (Davidson, 27).

Under the insightful title, "What the Frog's Eye Tells the Frog's Brain" (Lettvin and Pitts 1959), the authors anticipate the crowd sourcing trick of optimization by offloading work to the sensing periphery. They characterize how "the frog" (as a milieu) conducts itself: "A frog hunts on land by vision. He escapes enemies mainly by seeing them. His eyes do not move, as do ours, to follow prey, attend suspicious events, or search for things of interest. If his body changes its position with respect to gravity or the whole visual world is rotated about him, then he shows compensatory eye movements" (233). The frog is also *free from care* about whatever in its surround does not move. The frog's eye only tells the frog's brain either to *escape* enemies (*universally* large moving things), to snap at flies (*universally* small moving things), or *do* nothing. Consequently, when confronted with a sufficiently small moving stimulus, the frog snaps regardless of what it is. Not conducting itself to what doesn't move, a "frog surrounded by dead flies will starve to death." In the event of "two 'flies' encountering the snapping zone simultaneously," the frog's eye may transpose by snapping at "an" average fly between. By thinking of the frog's eye as power, we see how power operates, by the subject forming a relation to itself as something to conduct. These convenient reductions in frog behavior do lead to a place of more interest: in evolutionary terms, "circuitry for avoidance behaviour exploits circuitry for approach behaviour" (Arbib "Rana Computatrix to Human Language," 2349). In other words, in order to conduce avoidance, the frog visual system needed to exploit (breech or hack) its contrariwise, *to hunt*. Perhaps this gives new legs to Foucault's counter-conduct to bootstrap (and power) something more speculative in aim.

When reading Foucault on this constellation of concepts (power, force, resistance, conduct, counter-conduct, and governmentality), I cannot help but think of Oliver Heaviside's (1850–1925) work on electromagnetic theory. A productive affinity reveals itself in their privileging of analytics over theories of power. Perhaps Heaviside even suggests an extension of Foucault's analytic repertoire for the relations of "conduct" and "counter-conduct" with: *admittance, conductance, electret, impedance, inductance, permeability, reluctance,* and *susceptance*. Heeding Foucault's stipulation that, with an analytics, "one must go nominalistic" I leave these open.

Davidson suggests how some of Foucault's remarks on the gay movement provide a "conceptual hinge" linking the notions of "conduct" and "counter-conduct" to his earlier analytics of "power" and "resistance." Counter-conduct occurs not through "the sexual act" directly, but rather through a "culture that invents modalities of relations, modes of existence, types of values, forms of exchange between individuals that are really new, that are not homogenous to nor superimposable on general cultural forms" (Foucault 2009). Here Foucault invests in a potential for the gay movement that puts into play "relations in the absence of codes or established lines of 'conduct,' 'affective intensities,' [and] 'forms that change"' (Foucault 2001). In this, the movement "will create relations that are, up to a certain point, transposable to heterosexuals," but:

> One has to overturn things a bit, and rather than say what one said at a certain moment – "Let us try to reintroduce homo-sexuality into the general normality of social relations" – let us say the opposite: "No. Let it [homosexuality] escape as far as possible from the type of relations that are proposed to us in our society, and let us try to create in the empty space in which we find ourselves new relational possibilities." (33)

This allows me to entertain a possible analytics in the sense the chapter started with—as a project to develop "conceptual devices that turn the spectre of another possible politics into an immanent analytical presence" (Guillaume and Huysmans 2013). Quite simply: as a supplement to an interstitial method, an analytics of "vacant niches" for wayfinding unused resources and residual capacities to practice new forms of life. This suggests a possibility for developing Foucauldian analytics toward more speculative aims while remaining faithful to his rigorous empirical attentiveness. Nauman's "Two Surveillance Rooms" seems to be one compelling case of this kind of combination. Also evocative is how Jill Magid has deployed seduction as a relentless empiric of *care* in order to speculate encounter in *dicto* sensu *re* (in the real sense).

Wayfinding Interactive Infrastructures and Other Dislocative Positionings

In this section, I return to the EDT 2.0/bits, atoms, neurons, and genes (b.a.n.g.) Lab's "Transborder Immigrant Tool" (TBT) project with descriptive focus on the "artivist" collective's principle of producing work that is "concurrently effective and affective." At a tactical level, TBT is an ongoing project repurposing consumer technology into a platform for humanitarian aid. In *metal*, the tool comprises: "an inexpensive cell phone, with a Global Positioning Satellite (GPS) chip, and a custom piece of software" (Cárdenas 2009). In functionality, the tool's software component provides users with GPS information matching phone position to nearest water cache or first aid. At the techno-discursive levels of interest to the current collection of essays, TBT implements a kind of SISL and Private Room/Public Room signal control game of continuity, expectation, and denial: while TBT mounted phone accesses continuous GPS data, it only returns data to two of three satellites and thereby prevents triangulating the users location (Carcamo November 20, 2009). In other words, as Lab members muse, "TBT is not a locative media project but a dislocative media performance" (Dominguez and Nadir 15 April 2018). TBT is *dis* and not *de* locative insofar upon making a call, a user can be located.

A Global Poetic System

The TBT crosses discourse contexts: Simultaneously a user-driven design and a bold activist claim that a set of rights is in need for verification embodying Jacques Rancière's conception of politics in *dissensus*. It responds to a humanitarian (or an actually existential) urgency. At the user level, TBT is implemented with a simple compass navigation device, as well as, both aural, and haptic cues providing cross-border travelers a way-finding tool leading them to water caches placed in the desert by volunteer organizations. In addition to *locative-become-dislocative* procedural coding, another transposition is at work in the project's user interface where `GPS' realigns to "global poetic system" (Dominguez and Nadir, 2012).

The TBT is also place where code/code gives Janus-faced æffect. Amy Sara Carroll (poet, scholar, and visual artist) contributed poetry transmitted to the user on their journey. To compose, she asked herself what she would *want* as a user:

> I turned to texts about desert survival: handbooks, military manuals, a guide book for border-crossers briefly distributed by the Mexican government. ... I wrote pared down prose poems, ideologically neutral (Is any writing 'ideologically neutral'?), procedural, if you will– a poem about locating the North Star, a poem about what to do if you are bitten by a rattle snake or tarantula, poems that contained details about how to weather a sandstorm or a flash flood. I imagined one poem for every hour of the day, a series of twenty-four fragments in conversation with one another, in conversation with previous museum-gallery-university series of poems that I'd composed. (4)

A combination of academic, aesthetic, and technical glitching, the TBT bears its politics, theatrics, and ethics in intraface. In conversation with Nadir, Dominguez has described a queering of a "technological condition" to redouble the transboarding principle of the TBT in "the trans-body in relation to gender, class, race and desire," as well as, the project's calling "into question the northern cone's imaginary about who has priority and control of who can become a cyborg or 'trans' human." Beyond the TBT project, a larger methodological, or transempiric is at the root of the EDT/b.a.n.g. lab's work. Dominguez has succinctly stated that "activists break the law, while artists change the conversation theatrically, by disturbing the law," and elaborated in terms of the Lab's being "concurrently affective and effective." While activists "have traditionally, for good reasons, focused solely on the side of effective use of social technologies or actions"; members of the Lab also anchor themselves in "being and becoming as artists" and herein in the spirit of the Greek rendering of aesthetics, *aisthitikos*, which is affective in tone—that which is "perceptive by feeling." Going in the other direction, coding feelings (affect) should be effective poetry, or code that "works." He has also unpacked this concurrency from the perspective of the other sense of code—"Law" (Dominguez and Nadir 15 April 2018):

> These projects must have or at least be imagined as having strong, concrete outcomes to the conditions that have failed or are failing to create the spaces necessary for a community to be sustainable in any number of ways. And often power, as command and control, will respond to activists by targeting them as law breakers or potential law breakers and shut them down under the empirical weight of the 'Law.' (7)

Recall how SISL hacked a rubber hose resistant crypto-primitive by going *up in the cut* between online action-perception tasks and long-term declarative memory. TBT similarly goes *up in the cut* "into question the northern cone's imaginary" about priority and control, but SISL needs to be effective while TBT forces a new conversation. I would like to think Arbib's recommendation to import open challenges for the neuroscience of wayfinding into design challenges for designing "inside-out" cyborgs. This brings us to another borderland of threesomes that the EDT/b.a.n.g. Lab wayfinds: "relational, non-relational, and non-relational relationality" (Dominguez 2014). SISL *meets* the "thought translator."

Conclusion: Wayfinding Spaces Inside-Out

Please recall the laser Doppler vibrometry trick for clandestine listening discussed above. Its condition for thought, or field of problematization, emplaced something even more magical than listening to a glass of water. More recently Professor Zhu has brought together a multidisciplinary team to investigate devices for "alternative perception." More specifically, Professor Zhu's methodological assemblage is implemented as a basis for a wearable "multimodal sensing, display and learning" platform enabling visually impaired users to "see" with their hands, bodies, or faces. Like the LDV surveillance platform, Zhu's team lifts commercially-off-the-shelf sensors and stimulators, such as infrared rangers and vibrators, into wearable range-vibrotactile devices allowing a blind person to "feel" his or her environment without touching it (Khoo et al. 2013; Molona Diallo and Zhu 2013). To "see" that we are in cybernetic country, Zhu explains the larger basis of this work as a project serving, "as a starting-point for further research in benchmarking assistive technology for the visually impaired and to eventually develop a man-machine sensorimotor model that will improve current state-of-the-art technology, as well as a better understanding of neural coding in the human brain."

Please recall Ada—"an inside out robot" that is "like an organism," coherent and expressing unitary "sentience" through "visual, audio and tactile input, and non-contact light and sound effectors" (Eng et al. 2003). Among Ada's admirers is M.A. Arbib who we encountered earlier in the cybernetic contexts of pattern recognition and the frog visual system. More recently, Arbib has proposed *neuromorphic architecture* as a biologically grounded design theory putting operational principles of animal brains to work on "interactive infrastructures" trafficking in the speculation of a building with a brain, and borrowing the problematizations animating neuroethology (Arbib 2013):

> When we study an animal we are looking at a creature whose brain has evolved to support its exploration of the environment around it—its embodiment is external to its (again, physical and social) environment. Complementing this is the idea that if a building had a "brain," its embodiment would be internal. (50)

With problematization, Foucault situates critique in Bergsonian time:

> A certain problematization is always a kind of creation; but a creation in the sense that, given a certain situation, you cannot infer that this kind of problematization will follow. (*Fearless Speech*, 172–73)

Two, three, n+, or "less than one" problems seem to be curdling in this concurrence of a non-inferential with the intrafacial. I hope to have raised, by way of TBT but also SISL, a route worth taking in trafficking problems, and their discursive constructions, across otherwise reclusive problematizations.

Note

1. A significant number of people have chronicled this historical context. Two out-standing texts I am indebted to are Mara Mills' "Media and Prosthesis: The Vocoder, the Artificial Larynx, and the History of Signal Processing," *qui parle* 21.1 (Fall/Winter 2012): 107–149, and Orit Halpern's "Cybernetic Sense: Warren McCulloch and Norbert Wiener's Conception

of Perception," *Interdisciplinary Science Reviews* 37.3, pp. 218–236. I do however change the particular focus on many of the same tensions addressed by Mills' and Halpern's articles.

Bibliography

Arbib, M. A. (2003). Rana Computatrix to Human Language: Towards a Computational Neuroethology of Language Evolution. *Philosophical Transactions of the Royal Society A: Mathematical, Physical and Engineering Sciences, 361*(1811), 2345–2379.

Arbib, M. A. (2012a). Brains, Machines and Buildings: Towards a Neuromorphic Architecture. *Intelligent Buildings International, 4*, 147–168.

Arbib, M. A. (2012b). Why Should Architects Care About Neuroscience? In P. Tidwell (Ed.), *Architecture and Neuroscience: A Tapio Wirkkala – Rut Bryk Design Reader* (pp. 42–75). Espoo: Tapio Wirkkala Rut Bryk Foundation.

Arbib, M. A. (2016). When Brains Design/Experience Buildings: Architectural Patterns for a Good Life: East–West Connections. In Gulyas Balazs, Vasbinder Jan Wouter (Eds.), *Cultural Patterns and Neurocognitive Circuits: East-West Connections*. Singapore: NTU/World Scientific.

Bojinov, H. (2012). Neuroscience Meets Cryptography: Designing Crypto Primitives Secure Against Rubber Hose Attacks. *Communications of the ACM, 57*(5), 110–118.

Boone, J. V., & Peterson, R. R. (2016). *SIGSALY – The Start of the Digital Revolution*. https://www.nsa.gov/about/cryptologic-heritage/historical-figures-publications/publications/wwii/sigsaly-start-digital.shtml. Visited on 2016.

Caillois, R., & (translator) Shepley, J. (1984). Mimicry and Legendary Psychasthenia. *October, 31*, 16–32.

Carcamo, C. (2009). GPS Tool Will Help Immigrants Cross Border. *Orange County Register*. Last visited June 2018.

Cárdenas, M. (2009). The Transborder Immigrant Tool: Violence, Solidarity and Hope in Post-NAFTA Circuits of Bodies Electr(on)/ic. In *Proceedings of the 11th International Conference on Human-Computer Interaction with Mobile Devices and Services*. Bonn: ACM.

Carroll, L. (1998). *Alice's Adventures in Wonderland and Through the Looking-Glass* (Ed. P. Hunt). London: Wordsworth Collection.

Collins, N. (1990). DRAM: Notes for Alvin Lucier: I Am Sitting in a Room.

Crossing the Border Illegally? There's an "App" for That: A Q+A With Ricardo Dominguez (2011) 10.

Davidson, A. I. (2011). In Praise of Counter-Conduct. *History of the Human Sciences, 24*(4), 25–41.

Dean, M. (2010). *Governmentality: Power and Rule in Modern Society* (2nd ed.). Thousand Oaks: Sage. isbn:9781847873842.

Deleuze, G., & Guattari, F. (1987). *A Thousand Plateaus: Capitalism and Schizophrenia*. Minneapolis: University of Minnesota Press.

Dominguez, R. (2014). Threesomes+: Social Practice, Speculative Aesthetics, and Love. Couse Syllabus for UCSD Vis Arts Contemporary Critical Issues.

Dominguez, R., & (interviewer) Dunbar, A. (2011). Crossing the Border Illegally? There's an "App" for That: A Q+A With Ricardo Dominguez. *Motherboard, 10*. https://motherboard.vice.com/en_us/article/z44m53/the-transborder-immigrant-tool-helps-mexicans-cross-over-safely. Last visited June 2018.

Dominguez, R., & (Interviewer) Nadir, L. (2012). *Poetry, Immigration and the FBI: The Transborder Immigrant Tool, Hyperallergic*. https://hyperallergic.com/54678. Visited on 15 Apr 2012.

Dougherty, B. O., & Arbib, M. A. (2013). The Evolution of Neuroscience for Architecture: Introducing the Special Issue. *Intelligent Buildings International, 5*(sup1, 4–9). https://doi.org/10.1080/17508975.2013.818763

Dreyfus, H. L., & Rabinow, P. (1983). *Michel Foucault: Beyond Structuralism and Hermeneutics* (5th ed.). New York: Harvester Wheatsheaf.

Duncombe, S. (2016). Does It Work? The Æffect of Activist Art. *Social Research: An International Quarterly, 83*(1), 115–134.

Emory, M. (2018). *From Building Brains to Brained Buildings: An Interview with Michael A. Arbib*. http://brainworldmagazine.com/from-building-brains-to-brained-buildings-an-interview-with-michael-a-arbib/

Eng, K., et al. (2003). Ada – Intelligent Space: An Artificial Creature for the Swiss Expo.02. In *Proceedings of the 2003 International Conference on Robotics and Automation (ICRA 2003)*. Taipei: IEEE/RSJ.

Eng, K., Douglas, R. J., & Verschure, P. F. M. J. (2005). An Interactive Space That Learns to Influence Human Behaviour. *IEEE Transactions on Systems, Man, and Cybernetics—Part A: Systems and Humans, 35*(1), 66–77.

Findlay-White, E., & Logan, R. K. (2016). Acoustic Space, Marshall McLuhan and Links to Medieval Philosophers and Beyond: Center Everywhere and Margin Nowhere. *Philosophies, 1*, 162–169.

Föllmer, G. (2018). *Lucier's Classic: I Am Sitting in a Room*. http://www.medienkunstnetz.de/works/i-am-sitting-in-a-room/

Foucault, M. (1982). The Subject and Power. *Critical Inquiry, 8*(4), 777–795.

Foucault, M. (1988). The Concern for Truth. In *Michel Foucault: Politics, Philosophy, Culture (Interviews and Other Writings, 1977–1984)*. New York: Routledge.

Foucault, M. (1992). *The History of Sexuality: The Use of Pleasure: V. 2: The Use of Pleasure* (Ed. & Trans. R. Hurley). London: Penguin Books.

Foucault, M. (1998). Polemics, Politics and Problematizations (Interview with P. Rainbow). In *Essential Works of Foucault* (Vol. 1, 1st ed.). New York: The New Press.

Foucault, M. (1999). *Aesthetics, Method, and Epistemology* (Eds. J. D. Faubion & P. Rainbow). New York: The New Press.

Foucault, M. (2001). *Madness and Civilization: A History of Insanity in the Age of Reason*. London: Routledge Classics.

Foucault, M. (2008). *The Birth of Biopolitics: Lectures at the Collège de France, 1978–1979* (Trans. Graham Burchell). Basingstoke: Palgrave Macmillan.

Foucault, M. (2009). *Security, Territory, Population: Lectures at the Collège de France* (Ed. A. I. Davidson, 1st ed.). New York: Palgrave Macmillan.

Foucault, M. (2013). *Lectures on the Will to Know* (Ed. A. I. Davidson, 1st ed.). New York: Palgrave Macmillan.

GPS tool will help immigrants cross border (2009, November 20).

Guillaume, X., & Huysmans, J. (2013). Chapter 2: Citizenship and Securitizing: Interstitial Politics. In X. Guillaume & J. Huysmans (Eds.), *Citizenship and Security: The Constitution of Political Being, PRIO New Security Studies* (pp. 18–30). Oxfordshire/New York: Routledge.

Günther, G. (1955). The Thought Translator. *Startling Stories, 33*(1), 62–67.

Haggerty, K. D., & Ericson, R. V. (2003). The Surveillant Assemblage. *The British Journal of Sociology, 51*, 605–622.

Halpern, O. (2015). *Beautiful Data: A History of Vision and Reason Since 1945*. Durham: Duke Press.

Heaviside, O. (2013). *Electromagnetic Theory* (Vol. 1). New York: Cosimo Classics.

Khoo, W. L., et al. (2013). Designing and Testing Wearable Range Vibrotactile Devices. *Journal of Assistive Technologies, 7*(2), 102–117.

Koopman, C. (2011). Foucault Across the Disciplines: Introductory Notes on Contingency in Critical Inquiry. *History of the Human Sciences, 24*(4), 1–12.

Koopman, C., & Matza, T. (2013). Putting Foucault to Work: Analytic and Concept in Foucauldian Inquiry. *Critical Inquiry, 39*(4), 817–840.

Lab, EDT2.0/b.a.n.g. (2014). *Electronic Disturbance Theatre Transborder Immigrant Tool*. C-Theory.

Lepecki, A. (2005). *Exhausting Dance: Performance and the Politics of Movement* (1st ed.). New York: Taylor & Francis.

Lettvin, J. Y., Maturana, H. R., McCulloch, W. S., & Pitts, W. H. (1959). What the Frog's Eye Tells the Frog's Brain. *Proceedings of the IRE, 47*(11), 1940–1951.

Li, W., Molina, E., Wolberg, G., & Zhu, Z. (2007). LDV Sensing and Processing for Remote Hearing in a Multimodal Surveillance System. *IEEE Conference on Computer Vision and Pattern Recognition '07*. IEEE.

Lyon, D. (2009). Surveillance, Power and Everyday Life. In C. Avgerou et al. (Eds.), *Handbook of Information and Communication Technologies*. Oxford: Oxford Handbooks/Oxford University Press.

Maruyama, M. (1963). The Second Cybernetics. *American Scientists, 5*(2), 164–179.

Masani, P. R. (1989). *Norbert Wiener 1894–1964, Vita Mathematica*. Basel: Birkhauser Verlag AG.

McCulloch, W. S., & Pitts, W. (1947). How We Know Universals the Perception of Auditory and Visual Forms. *The Bulletin of Mathematical Biophysics, 9*(3), 127–147.

McKenzie, J. (2001). *Perform or Else: From Discipline to Performance* (1st ed.). London: Routledge.

Mills, M. (2012). Media and Prosthesis: The Vocoder, the Artificial Larynx, and the History of Signal Processing. *Qui Parle, 21*(1), 107–149.

Molina, E., Diallo, A., & Zhu, Z. (2013). Visual Noun Navigation Framework for the Blind. *Journal of Assistive Technologies, 7*(2), 118–130.

Pallasmaa, J., Mallgrave, H. F., & Arbib, M. (2013). *Architecture and Neuroscience: Volume 1, Tapio Wirkkala-Rut Bryk Design Reader*. Espoo: Tapio Wirkkala-Rut Bryk Foundation.

Sonami, L. (2006). On My Work. *Contemporary Music Review, 25*(5/6), 614.

Sonami, L. (2014). *And Now We Leave Gloves and Other Wearables to (Small) Dictators*. London: NIME, Goldsmith. http://sonami.net/writing-goldsmith/

Trippett, D. (2018). Music and the Transhuman Ear: Ultrasonics, Material Bodies, and the Limits of Sensation. *Musical Quarterly, 100*(2), 199–261.

Wang, T., Zhu, Z., Kraczek, R. S., & Rhody, H. E. (2011). A System Approach to Adaptive Multimodal Sensor Designs. In R. W. McMillan, R. Hammoud, G. Fan, & K. Ikeuchi (Eds.), *Machine Vision beyond Visible Spectrum, Volume 1 of Augmented Vision and Reality* (pp. 159–176). Berlin: Springer Science & Business Media.

Wiener, N. (1949). Sound Communication with the Deaf. *Philosophy of Science, 16*(3), 27–36.

Wiener, N. (1951). Problems of Sensory Prosthesis. *Bulletin of the American Mathematical Society, 57*(1), 26–36.

Zbikowski, D. (2004). *Media Art Net (2004): Nauman, Bruce: Video Surveillance Piece: Public Room, Private Room*. http://www.medienkunstnetz.de/works/video-surveillance-piece/. Visited on 2004.

Zhu, Z., & Huang, T. S. (2007). *Multimodal Surveillance: Sensors, Algorithms, and Systems* (Eds. Z. Zhu & T. S. Huang). Boston: Artech House Publishers.

Zhu, Z., Li, W., & Wolberg, G. (2005). Integrating LDV Audio and IR Video for Remote Multimodal Surveillance. *Computer Vision and Pattern Recognition – Workshops, 2005. CVPR Workshops*. IEEE.

Zhu, Z., Molina, E., Wolberg, G., & Li, W. (2007). LDV Sensing and Processing for Remote Hearing in a Multimodal Surveillance System. In *2007 IEEE Conference on Computer Vision and Pattern Recognition (CVPR)*, Minneapolis, MN, pp. 1–2.

Zielinski, S. (2006). *Deep Time of the Media: Toward an Archaeology of Hearing and Seeing by Technical Means*. Cambridge, MA: MIT Press.

CHAPTER 16

Epilogue: Control(ling) Space

Susan Flynn and Antonia Mackay

From the products we purchase to the ever-shifting notion of corporeality and consciousness, one aspect of our contemporary cultural moment is certain—we are bodies to be watched. The chapters contained in *Surveillance, Architecture and Control* illustrate not only the extent of such incessant surveilling but also—and more alarmingly—its ubiquitous invisibility. All of the contributors published in this collection allude to the built environment's subliminal power and control, and further, attest to the manner in which space itself is implicit in forming not only our topographical landscape but also framing our cultural and social territories. Expanding upon the discourses contained in our previous collections (*Spaces of Surveillance* (2017) and *Surveillance, Race, Culture* (2018)), this volume demonstrates the very tangible and interdisciplinary issue of architectural, spatial, and structural watching.

As this collection makes clear, the built environment and architectural space are complicit in the watching and overseeing of bodies, where a multitude of obscured and muted systems are at work. Contemporary architecture works as an armature to surveillance; the modern structures'

S. Flynn (✉)
School of Media, London College of Communication, University of the Arts London, London, UK
e-mail: s.flynn@lcc.arts.ac.uk

A. Mackay
Oxford Brookes University, Oxford, UK

S. Flynn, A. Mackay (eds.), *Surveillance, Architecture and Control*,
https://doi.org/10.1007/978-3-030-00371-5_16

provocations offer the promise of lateral surveillance and democratic "watching" while the buildings' contemporary elements, such as fingerprint recognition, control the buildings and their entry. Architecture evolves in response to security concerns; the increasing fear of the stranger arguably replaces the older fear of dissent. Architecture now incorporates social and cultural anxieties, the problem of control and physical barriers are replaced by "intelligent systems"; data-laden and information-rich, control is now sleeker and more aesthetically pleasing.

By bringing together scholars from urban planning, sociology, psychology, geography, film studies, art, literature and cultural studies, it is our intention to vocalise the interconnectedness of space and surveillance. Despite the large canon of work on surveillance studies, there remains much work to be done using such intersectional perspectives; and it is the editors' contention that these surveilling practices be voiced in order to better understand not only our current moment, but also our future.

While large canons of previous work in surveillance studies have confirmed that Foucault's panopticon has been a leading academic model for analysing surveillance, there has been a plentitude of arguments for the redundancy of the panopticon model, from Bauman, Latour, and others. Indeed, we agree that data use, connectedness, informability, and the global information economy have become entwined with social management. However, the history of surveillance in our societies, as well as in the popular imaginary, has impressed relations of power upon our cultural psyche through structures, places, and buildings where dissent and agency were constrained. Hence, by using new intersectional and nuanced approaches to Foucault's model, this collection reads a variety of iterations of surveillance and social control to illustrate the innate connection between surveillance, spaces, and structures. Examining a range of historic and fictitious built environments, the chapters in this collection aspire to illustrate the extent to which spaces and buildings have been implicated in enforced conformity and suppression.

* * *

Popular imagination has long been fascinated by the role of surveillance, such as films featuring the first electronic surveillance narrative in 1971s *The Anderson Tapes*. Much critique has been levied at the wide variety of film texts dealing with the surveillance phenomena; however, frequently the role of space and of the built environment is overlooked. In *The Anderson Tapes* Sean Connery's character Duke becomes embroiled in a burglary which both utilises the apartment block surveillance system and is hampered by the Federal Bureau of Investigation (FBI), Drug Enforcement Administration (DEA), and Inland Revenu Service (IRS)' use of it. Central to the film's plot is the apartment block's architecture—not its surveillance network—a spatial frame which operates to both enable the burglary and inhibit its execution. In some respects, the network of cameras and voice recording devices are incidental, for all the bodies watching and listening in, are doing so to record information related to individual tenants residing in a large Manhattan housing block. The film's very objective is determined by the architectural situation. A similarly "silent" form of surveillance is underway in *Caché* (2005) where the film's most disturbing shots take place in the Parisian street outside Georges and Anne's upper-class home. Such seemingly "passive" shots appear benign, but it is precisely their focus which is uncomfortable—perpetually gazing at the home's large glass windows. Whilst Haneke's narrative is undeniably intended to bridge the subject of surveillance with that of the 1961 Paris Massacre, the film's incessant use of *home* surveillance appears to differentiate it from mass surveillance movies made in the post 9/11 era. Indeed, as Todd Herzog argued *Caché* is "about being looked at rather than looking at something or someone" (2010, 2). Herzog's comments further imply an ambiguity concerning who (or what) is doing the looking, though this does not detract from the film's repeated insistence on home surveillance and home "invasion" through the framing of the surveillance lens.

Other site/sight specific forms of surveillance can be found in films such as *Disturbia* (2007) and *The Truman Show* (1998), where the presence of surveillance is both legitimised and purposed by the home's suburban location, whilst the horror genre has similarly attached itself to architectural structures which suggest impermanence and temporality in motels, from Hitchcock's *Psycho* (1960) to 1997s *Vacancy.* Bernice Murphy's *The Highway Horror Film* (2014) argues for the use of motels as a space where the frequency "in which innocent travellers just passing through are preyed upon", whilst the indeterminacy of motel location is testament to "the representatives of order and chaos" (2014, 3). What is perhaps most poignant of all is not the fact that all these movies take place in certain spaces, but that even when surveillance occurs in-between spaces (such as in a motel in on the highway), it is still a defined space which is *between* other defined spaces. In all four examples discussed above, the presence of surveillance is both legitimised and problematised by the building's location in a city (*The Anderson Tapes*), the suburb (*Disturbia*), and in-between (*Vacancy*). Architecture and spatial location therefore are as important as surveillance itself—one impacts upon the other in a constitutional way.

The fundamental yet "silent" nature of spatial surveillance is also evident in how we frame our perception of surveillance and watchedness. Torin Monahan's *Surveillance in the Time of Insecurity* (2010) argues for the hyper-regulation of boundaries as a response to our desire for organisation in an unstable and insecure historical moment, where surveillance contributes to "spatial exclusion by means of its integration into urban space" (81). Indeed, Monahan's thesis agrees with the editor's and contributor's arguments presented here, where "fortified spaces" "highlight the ways that built forms and social norms function politically to enforce… segregation" (82). Whilst Monahan's text considers the sociological impact of surveillance systems, the chapters contained in this volume voice the ways in which architectural surveillance is already in our midst. For Monahan, it is the gated community complete with CCTV which can surveil and keep certain bodies in and others out, and this undeniably creates a form of pernicious surveillance which has lasting social and political implications; yet what the chapters contained in *Surveillance, Architecture and Control* demonstrate is the possibility that in fact *all* spaces *already* surveil. In late 2010, the Tate Modern exhibited a special collection entitled "Exposed: Voyeurism, Surveillance and the Camera". Divided between five thematic sections (The Unseen Photography, Celebrity and the Public Gaze, Voyeurism and Desire, Witnessing Violence, and Surveillance), the exhibition aimed to question "the nature and character of invasive looking" in ways which complicated "the uneasy relationship between making and viewing images that deliberately cross lines of privacy and propriety" (www.tate.org.uk). The "Surveillance" exhibition features images from artists and photographers such as Shizuka Yokomizo, Jonathan Olley, and Thomas Demand, and range in date from 1997 to 2007. Whilst the website claims that the "photographers have taken surveillance technology as their subject, turning the camera back on itself" so as to "make visible what is usually hidden from public view" (www.tate.org.uk), it is notable that at no point do the artists, photographers, or editorial make mention of spatial or architectural surveillance. This is particularly surprising given that in every image, space (and indeed, built space) is not only implied but foregrounded as the vehicle by which to observe. In Yokomizo's *Stranger No. 1* (1998), and *Stranger No. 2* (1999) both images are framed by the window of the home—acting in a sense as the means by which to surveil the subject. Furthermore, Jonathan Olley's *RUC Police Station and British Army Patrol Base* (1998) and *British Army Firing Range, Magilligan Point, Lough Foyle, Co. Londonderry* (1998) are in themselves images of surveilling spaces; indeed, these are spaces with the very purpose of observation, yet their implicit watchedness is not made explicit. Instead, the editorial refers to these images as "invasive watchtowers". Olley's images are collections of windows, turrets and panoptic-like architectural shapes whose "silent" status is only fleetingly inferred. Thomas Demand's *Camera* (2007) furthers the issue of architecture's presence and silence from within surveillance discourses, presenting the viewer with an image of a CCTV camera from the corner of an unknown building. Whilst the viewer will more than likely appreciate the irony (camera taking photographs of the camera taking photographs), again, the built structure housing the camera remains implicit and also seemingly irrelevant. Such omnipresence of technological gadgetry clearly impacts upon our understanding of space, and CCTV is certainly one such element which is increasingly becoming part of our spatial fabric.

In March 2018, a New Orleans' public safety plan was the subject of an American Civil Liberties Union debate, which condemned the plans as "surveillance on steroids" (Ross Zelen, April, 2018). Reported in *Planetizen,* the proposed plan would capture more data and implement more technology in the urban areas of Southern California in order to "make lives and resource consumption more sustainable and efficient" (Zelen); whilst the adverse effect would impact individual liberty, privacy, and the trust of government agencies. The interview conducted between Peter Marx (former Los Angeles Chief Technology Officer) and Allan Alexander Opine (former Beverly Hills Mayor) for *The Planning Report* further reveals an initial rejection of CCTV cameras in residential areas in Los Angeles, specifically in Beverly Hills; yet "most residents… came to the conclusion that the security benefits of the cameras in the business area outweighed their concern with privacy" (Opine 2018). Marx responds to Opine's comments, conceding "we are not going to go back to a world where we wilfully don't know what's happening… when you're in a public place, you don't have an expectation of privacy. If you feel that you do, then maybe that's not the right place for you to be". The sentiment expressed by both interviewees ratifies the current climate of hypersurveillance in urban areas, but interestingly, expresses not only the acceptance of such gaze but also the expectation of it, and a desire for it. Whilst urban surveillance is clearly commonplace and accepted (Opine refers to over

"600 cameras" throughout LA's commercial district), it is its silent creep forward which is most alarming. As Alex Pasternack argues, "the architecture of surveillance is everywhere and nowhere" (Pasternack 2016).

In all the instances above, architecture remains the unspoken condition by which these systems of surveillance successfully operate. In the case of the films discussed, *Caché, The Anderson Tapes,* and *Disturbia* are all subjected to surveillance systems precisely as the protagonists and antagonists already reside within spaces for looking (the home, the apartment block, and the suburban home). Similarly, the collection of photographs in the Tate Modern exhibition all frame their subjects with architectural structures—the window, the turret, the fence—which actively facilitate the surveillance implied by the photographer's camera. In both the films and the photographs, the watching camera is only able to watch as the space already lends itself to be viewed. This is further compounded by the readiness of urban planners to incorporate surveillance technology in ways which are treated as security and safety conscious preventative measures. The irony being, of course, that such features are only able to provide security and safety if you are willing to allow yourself to be viewed at all times and in all spaces, whether it be the home, the park, the car, or at work. Implicit in the build environment then is the potential to watch, for all structures bear down on pedestrians and inhabitants in the same way as Bentham's Panopticon facilitated the gaze of the guards, and Foucault's panopticism acknowledged the machine already at work from within. In short, before now, and even now, we are watched.

* * *

The chapters within this collection demonstrate an attempt to grabble with the constancy of "silent" spatial surveillance. Part I considers the impact of surveillance systems from within urban landscapes, where designing commodities and privatising public spaces blur the lines between public and private, where subject and architectural arrangement can create "psychogeographical" effects on the city's power, and where the window is a tool for surveillance lending bodies to perform as public spectacle. Part II considers the role of home in predisposing the domestic environment to a space of watchedness, where architecture informs identity and performativity, where Hitchcock's *Psycho* motel and home surveil each other, where the home can eradicate identity in *American Horror Story* and resurrect the family unit as "undead", and where data mining is parodied in

Charlie Brooker's *Black Mirror*. Part III examines the nature of international spaces, investigating Vancouver's public spaces; Ireland's Magdalene Laundries and South Africa's courtrooms through the lens of gendered, subjective, and Othered bodily creation. Finally, Part IV considers the role of technology through discussion of drones, 4D cinema, bio-political structures in literature, and Lucier's hardware devices. All 15 chapters address socio-cultural issues implicit in our daily lives and sometimes outlined in filmic, technological, and artistic renditions—the fundamental manner in which our structural systems of cities and suburbia; in the home and at work; in fantasy and in reality, can scrutinise, study, and monitor our very presence, essence, and being. Whilst the topics covered in this collection are broad, they are not exhaustive, though they are representative of new and otherwise inimitable research into the nature of the built space. We are acutely aware of the limitations of such a project, and note that some of the many areas not covered by this collection such as the impact of architectural surveillance on disabled and alternative bodies, the performativity of race from within architectural settings, and the role of the physical positioning of surveillance technologies are further sites worthy of future consideration.

Concluding this collection, we hope to engender consideration and debate, offering our readers a series of intersectional lenses with which they may consider the limitations of personal freedom and spaces. We aim to bring individuals closer to challenging the manner in which surveillance can be imposed upon such liberties and some new perspectives on socio-cultural and historic instances of power and control.

Bibliography

Herzog, T. (2010). The Banality of Surveillance: Michael Haneke's *Caché* and Life After the End of Privacy. *Modern Austrian Literature, 43*, 25.

Monahan, T. (2010). *Surveillance in the Time of Insecurity*. New Brunswick: Rutgers University Press.

Murphy, B. (2014). *The Highway Horror Film*. London: Palgrave Macmillan.

Opine. (2018, March). *Surveillance in Cities: Peter Marx and Allan Alexander Opine*. Planning Report. https://www.planningreport.com/2018/03/26/surveillance-cities-peter-marx-allan-alexander-opine. Accessed 28 July 2018.

Pasternack, A. (2016, November 29). *Laura Poitras Films The Architecture of Surveillance – And Projects Films on It Too*. https://www.fastcompany.com/3066080/laura-poitras-and-the-architecture-of-surveillance. Accessed 28 July 2018.

Tate Modern. https://www.tate.org.uk/whats-on/tate-modern/exhibition/exposed/exposed-voyeurism-surveillance-and-camera-exhibition-guide. Accessed 28 July 2018.

Zelen, R. (2018, April 13). *How Surveillance Cities Are Evolving*. https://www.planetizen.com/news/2018/04/98197-how-surveillance-cities-evolving. Accessed 28 July 2018.

Index

S. Flynn, A. Mackay (eds.), *Surveillance, Architecture and Control*,
https://doi.org/10.1007/978-3-030-00371-5

The manufacturer's authorised representative in the EU is Springer Nature Customer Service Centre GmbH, Europaplatz 3, 69115 Heidelberg, Germany. If you have any concerns regarding our products, please contact ProductSafety@springernature.com

Printed and bound by CPI Group (UK) Ltd, Croydon, CR0 4YY
05/10/2026
02228422-0001